AF228444

Salvation and Destiny in Islam

The Institute of Ismaili Studies
Shiʻi Heritage Series, 5

Previously published titles:
1. Daftary, Farhad. *A History of Shiʻi Islam* (2013).
2. Daftary, Farhad, and Gurdofarid Miskinzoda, eds. *The Study of Shiʻi Islam: History, Theology and Law* (2014).
3. Mir-Kasimov, Orkhan. *Words of Power: Ḥurūfī Teachings Between Shiʻism and Sufism in Medieval Islam* (2015).
4. Asatryan, Mushegh. *Controversies in Formative Shiʻi Islam: The Ghulat Muslims and their Beliefs* (2017).

Salvation and Destiny in Islam

The Shiʻi Ismaili Perspective of
Ḥamīd al-Dīn al-Kirmānī

by
Maria De Cillis

I.B.Tauris *Publishers*
LONDON • NEW YORK
in association with
The Institute of Ismaili Studies
LONDON, 2018

Published in 2018 by
I.B.Tauris & Co. Ltd
London • New York
www.ibtauris.com

in association with The Institute of Ismaili Studies
210 Euston Road, London NW1 2DA
www.iis.ac.uk

ISBN: 978 1 78831 493 0
eISBN: 978 1 78672 550 9
ePDF: 978 1 78673 550 8

A full CIP record for this book is available from the British Library
A full CIP record is available from the Library of Congress

Library of Congress Catalog Card Number: available

Typeset in Minion Tra for The Institute of Ismaili Studies

Printed and bound in Great Britain by
T.J. International, Padstow, Cornwall

The Institute of Ismaili Studies

The Institute of Ismaili Studies was established in 1977 with the object of promoting scholarship and learning on Islam, in the historical as well as contemporary contexts, and a better understanding of its relationship with other societies and faiths.

The Institute's programmes encourage a perspective which is not confined to the theological and religious heritage of Islam, but seeks to explore the relationship of religious ideas to broader dimensions of society and culture. The programmes thus encourage an interdisciplinary approach to the materials of Islamic history and thought. Particular attention is also given to issues of modernity that arise as Muslims seek to relate their heritage to the contemporary situation.

Within the Islamic tradition, the Institute's programmes promote research on those areas which have, to date, received relatively little attention from scholars. These include the intellectual and literary expressions of Shi'ism in general, and Ismailism in particular.

In the context of Islamic societies, the Institute's programmes are informed by the full range and diversity of cultures in which Islam is practised today, from the Middle East, South and Central Asia, and Africa to the industrialised societies of the West, thus taking into consideration the variety of contexts which shape the ideals, beliefs and practices of the faith.

These objectives are realised through concrete programmes and activities organised and implemented by various departments of the Institute. The Institute also collaborates periodically, on a programme-specific basis, with other institutions of learning in the United Kingdom and abroad.

The Institute's academic publications fall into a number of inter-related categories:

1. Occasional papers or essays addressing broad themes of the relationship between religion and society, with special reference to Islam.
2. Monographs exploring specific aspects of Islamic faith and culture, or the contributions of individual Muslim thinkers or writers.
3. Editions or translations of significant primary or secondary texts.
4. Translations of poetic or literary texts which illustrate the rich heritage of spiritual, devotional and symbolic expressions in Muslim history.
5. Works on Ismaili history and thought, and the relationship of the Ismailis to other traditions, communities and schools of thought in Islam.
6. Proceedings of conferences and seminars sponsored by the Institute.
7. Bibliographical works and catalogues which document manuscripts, printed texts and other source materials.

This book falls into category five listed above.

In facilitating these and other publications, the Institute's sole aim is to encourage original research and analysis of relevant issues. While every effort is made to ensure that the publications are of a high academic standard, there is naturally bound to be a diversity of views, ideas and interpretations. As such, the opinions expressed in these publications must be understood as belonging to their authors alone.

Shiʿi Heritage Series

Shiʿi Muslims, with their rich intellectual and cultural heritage, have contributed significantly to the fecundity and diversity of the Islamic traditions throughout the centuries, enabling Islam to evolve and flourish both as a major religion and also as a civilisation. In spite of this, Shiʿi Islam has received little scholarly attention in the West, either in medieval or modern times. It is only in recent decades that academic interest has focused increasingly on Shiʿi Islam within the wider study of Islam.

The principal objective of the *Shiʿi Heritage Series*, launched by The Institute of Ismaili Studies, is to enhance general knowledge of Shiʿi Islam and promote a better understanding of its history, doctrines and practices in their historical and contemporary manifestations. Addressing all Shiʿi communities, the series also aims to engage in discussions on theoretical and methodological issues, while inspiring further research in the field.

Works published in this series include monographs, collective volumes, editions and translations of primary texts, and bibliographical projects, bringing together some of the most significant themes in the study of Shiʿi Islam through an interdisciplinary approach, and making them accessible to a wide readership.

To Ina, Biagio, Vera and John

Table of Contents

List of Abbreviations

AJAS: American Journal of Arabic Studies
BSOAS: Bulletin of the School of Oriental and African Studies
EI2: Encyclopaedia of Islam, Second Edition
EI3: Encyclopaedia of Islam, Third Edition
EIr: Encyclopaedia Iranica
EIs: Encyclopaedia Islamica
EQ: Encyclopaedia of the Qur'an
IJMES: International Journal of Middle East Studies
JAOS: Journal of the American Oriental Society
JARCE: Journal of the American Research Center in Egypt
JRAS: Journal of the Royal Asiatic Society
MIDEO: Mélanges de l'institut dominicain d'études orientales

List of Tables

Note on the Text

This study is a development and elaboration of my introductory article, 'A Preliminary Study on the Significance of *Qaḍā'* and *Qadar* in the Eighth Chapter of al-Kirmānī's *Kitāb al-Riyāḍ*', published in *L'ésotérisme shi'ite: ses racines et ses prolongements/Shi'i Esotericism: Its Roots and Developments*, edited jointly by Mohammad A. Amir-Moezzi, Maria De Cillis, Daniel De Smet and Orkhan Mir-Kasimov (Turnhout, 2016), pp. 345–367. Some of the translations and considerations featuring in the foregoing paper have been slightly modified.

The reader should be aware that throughout this study, in order to highlight their hypostatic nature and according to the gender of the words in Arabic, I refer to the Universal Intellect (also indicated as the Intellect or first intellect) and the Universal Soul (also indicated as the Soul or second intellect) by the masculine and feminine pronouns respectively. This is done to preserve their Gnostic-informed character and with the intention of differentiating them from both the remaining intellects of the celestial Pleroma and the individual souls which are purposely indicated in English by the neuter.

The expressions '*qā'im bi'l-quwwa*' and '*qā'im bi'l-fiʿl*' are widespread in Arabic philosophical texts, and they generally indicate the Aristotelian distinction between 'subsisting in potentiality' and 'subsisting in actuality'. In this study, however, I suggest that, behind such an Aristotelian reading, there might be an alternative meaning for these expressions with reference to the Ismaili figures of the *qā'im in potentiality* and the *qā'im in actuality* respectively. Whilst the term *qā'im*, literally meaning 'the one who stands up', is employed par excellence to refer to the *qā'im al-qiyāma*, the final Resurrector, it might also be understood to refer to each Imam, or even each member of the Fatimid Call. Besides the suggestion that Ismaili writers might have played with the double sense of the expressions '*qā'im bi'l-quwwa*' and '*qā'im bi'l-fiʿl*', also bearing in mind al-Kirmānī's fondness for stylistic devices such as puns – a feature clearly detectable in the *Kitāb al-Riyāḍ* – my preference to provide these expressions in the original Arabic, in order to convey their potential two-fold meaning, takes into account al-Kirmānī's pro-Fatimid and anti-Qarmaṭī agenda. Indeed, the Qarmaṭī theory of heptads in which the seventh Imam of the last prophetic era, Muḥammad b. Ismāʿīl, was to return as the final *qāʾim* was replaced by the Fatimid idea – introduced by the Imam-caliph al-Muʿizz li-Dīn Allāh (d. 365/975) and elaborated doctrinally by al-Qāḍī al-Nuʿmān (d. 364/974) – that, starting with ʿAbd Allāh al-Mahdī (d. 322/934), all Fatimid Imams were to be considered manifest embodiments of 'minor' *qāʾim*s awaiting the final Resurrector. By acknowledging himself more than one heptad of Imams in the era of Islam, al-Kirmānī was thus implicitly advocating the existence of a number of Fatimid *qāʾim*s until the Parousia of the awaited final Resurrector. This position will be made more explicit in the course of this study and will be corroborated by references to the esoteric readings of pairings such as *qaḍāʾ/qadar*, *sābiq/tālī* and *nāṭiq/imām* proposed by al-Kirmānī and other prominent Ismaili *dāʿī*s.

General references to al-Kirmānī's *Kitāb al-Riyāḍ* are from the ʿĀrif Tāmir edition, indicated as *Riyāḍ* (Beirut, 1960). Extracts in Chapter Eight refer to the Arabic text in the forthcoming edition by Faquir M. Hunzai and Hermann Landolt, which is indicated as '*Riyāḍ* (HL)'. I wish to express my indebtedness and gratitude to these two scholars for having allowed me to consult their work in progress.

In the second section of this volume, and only on some occasions, I have chosen to give in footnotes, rather than in the main text, elucidations relative to some cryptic passages in the *Kitāb al-Riyāḍ*. This has been done in order to provide the reader with immediate and useful insights, whilst attempting to keep the translated text close to the original.

Unless otherwise specified, English quotations from the Qur'an are based on Yusuf ʿAli's translation.

Acknowledgements

This book is the result of a long and fascinating intellectual journey which has seen me accompanied by many fellow travellers.

My deepest gratitude goes to Dr Daftary and Dr Gurdofarid Miskinzoda for their trust in my research and for accepting this work for publication in the *Shiʿi Heritage Series*.

My sincere gratitude goes to Professor Hermann Landolt and Dr Faquir Hunzai for having allowed me access to their forthcoming edition of Ḥamīd al-Dīn al-Kirmānī's *Kitāb al-Riyāḍ*.

I am particularly thankful to Russell Harris for his indispensable help: his expertise in the Arabic language has facilitated the investigation and translation of the original text of the *Kitāb al-Riyāḍ*. His sincere editorial advice and witty comments have rendered the development of this study a thoroughly captivating experience.

My thanks go also to Kutub Kassam for his careful reading of the typescript and meticulous editorial input, and to the anonymous reviewers for their constructive criticism and detailed guidance. This research project has facilitated the consolidation of old friendships whilst igniting new ones: I am indebted to many of my colleagues, in and outside the Institute of Ismaili Studies, for their insights and suggestions: Professor Carmela Baffioni, Dr Asma Hilali, Dr David Hollenberg, Dr Toby Mayer, Dr Orkhan Mir-Kasimov, Dr Janis Esots and Dr Dagi Dagiev, to name just a few.

I wish to express my gratitude to the IIS editorial team, particularly to Tara Woolnough, Isabel Miller, Raeesah Akhtar and to the members of the Institute of Ismaili Studies library staff, Nourmamadcho Nourmamaschoev, Khadija Lalani and Alex Leach for their assistance. I am also indebted to Naushin Shariff and Julia Kolb for their emotional support.

Last but not least, my thankfulness goes to my husband, Jim, for his ever-nourishing love, to my daughter, Abigail, for her joyful tenderness, and to my family for their limitless inspiring affection.

Needless to say, any mistakes and shortcomings present in this work are entirely my responsibility.

Introduction

The debate over free will versus divine predestination – a debate
grounded in theology and politics – is a topic that has been thoroughly analysed in literature on classical Islamic thought.[1] Having

---

[1] On this topic, an extensive body of work is available. Here I indicate some pivotal
sources: Binyamin Abrahamov, "Abd al-Jabbār's Theory of Divine Assistance', *Jerusalem Studies in Arabic and Islam*, 16 (1993), pp. 41–58; Georges C. Anawati and Louis
Gardet, *Introduction à la théologie musulmane* (Paris, 1970); Majid Fakhry, 'Some Paradoxical Implications of the Muʿtazilite View of Free Will', *Muslim World*, 43 (1953),
pp. 95–109; *idem*, 'The Muʿtazilite view of Man', in *Recherches d'islamologie: recueil d'articles offert à G. Anawati et L. Gardet par leurs collègues et amis* (Leuven, 1977), pp. 107–
121; Richard M. Frank, *Early Islamic Theology: The Muʿtazilites and al-Ashʿari. Texts and
Studies on the Development and History of Kalam*, vol. II (London and New York, 2007);
*idem, Classical Islamic Theology: The Ashʿarites. Texts and Studies on the Development
and History of Kalam*, vol. III (London and New York, 2007); *idem*, 'Bodies and Atoms:
the Ashʿarite Analysis', in *Islamic Theology and Philosophy*, ed. Michael E. Marmura
(Albany, NY, 1984), pp. 39–53; *idem*, 'Several Fundamental Assumptions of the Baṣra
School of the Muʿtazila', *Studia Islamica*, 33 (1971), pp. 5–18; *idem*, 'The Autonomy
of the Human Agent in the Teaching of ʿAbd al-Jabbār', *Le Muséon, Revue des Études
Orientales*, 95 (1983), pp. 323–355; *idem*, 'The Divine Attributes according to the Teachings of Abūʾl-Hudhayl al-Allāf', *Le Muséon, Revue des Études Orientales*, 82 (1969),
pp. 451–506; *idem*, 'The Structure of Created Causality according to al-Ashʿarī. An
Analysis of the *Kitāb al-Lumaʿ*', *Studia Islamica*, 25 (1966), pp. 13–75; *idem, The Metaphysics of Created Being according to Abūʾl-Hudhayl al-Allāf* (Istanbul, 1966); Wilferd
Madelung, 'The Late Muʿtazila and Determinsism: the Philosophers' Trap', in *Yād-nāma
in Memoria di Alessandro Bausani, Volume 1, Islamistica*, ed. Biancamaria Scarcia Amoretti
and Lucia Rostagno (Rome, 1991), pp. 245–257; Louis Gardet, 'Quelques reflexions sur
un problème de théologie et de philosophie musulmanes: toute-puissance divine et
liberté humaine', *Revue de l'Occident musulman et de la Méditerranée*, 13–14 (1973),
pp. 381–394; *idem, Dieu et la destinée de l'homme* (Paris, 1967); Daniel Gimaret, 'Théories de l'acte humain dans l'école Hanbalite', *Bulletin des Études Orientales*, 29 (1977),
pp. 157–178; *idem*, 'Un problème de théologie musulmane: Dieu veut-il les actes

investigated the subject of *qaḍāʾ* and *qadar* (often translated as decree and destiny) in the thought of Avicenna, al-Ghazālī and Ibn ʿArabī,[2] the idea of exploring the same subject from the viewpoint of an Ismaili intellectual like Ḥamīd al-Dīn al-Kirmānī (d. after 411/1021) appeared initially to be a repetitive task.[3] However, once probed, the Ismaili

---

mauvais? Thèses et arguments', *Studia Islamica*, 40 (1974), pp. 5–73 and 41 (1975), pp. 63–92; *idem, Théories de l'acte humain en théologie musulmane* (Paris, 1980).

[2] Maria De Cillis, *Free Will and Predestination in Islamic Thought: Theoretical Compromises in the Works of Avicenna, al-Ghazālī and Ibn ʿArabī* (London and New York, 2014).

[3] In line with many *dāʿīs'* (missionaries) attitude of shrouding their activities in secrecy whilst living in hostile surroundings, few details are known about the life of Ḥamīd al-Dīn Aḥmad b. ʿAbd Allāh al-Kirmānī. One of the most eminent Ismaili philosophers and, as indicated by Daftary, one of the most learned and talented Ismaili theologians and authors of the entire Fatimid period, al-Kirmānī was of Persian origin and was probably born in the region of Kirmān; his date of birth remains unknown. He was certainly active in Baghdad and Baṣra but, as suggested by his honorific title ʿḥujjat al-ʿIrāqaynʾ (the chief *dāʿī* of both Iraqs, ʿIrāq al-ʿArab and ʿIrāq al-ʿAjam), he must have also operated in the northwestern and west-central parts of Persia. His activities flourished during the reign of the Imam-caliph al-Ḥākim bi-Amr Allāh (r. 386/996–411/1021) who summoned him to Cairo – at that time home to the central headquarters of the Fatimid *daʿwa* – around 405/1014–1015 and invested him with the task of refuting the views of some Ismaili extremists, who came to be known as Druzes, who were preaching the divinity of the Imam. As the most accomplished Ismaili theologian of the time, he also intervened in the controversy, relative to fundamental doctrinal issues, which had erupted among some fellow Ismaili *dāʿīs* whose discussions and arguments are reported in al-Kirmānī's *Kitāb al-Riyāḍ* (*The Book of Meadows*). Thereafter, he apparently returned to Iraq where he completed his seminal work, *Rāḥat al-ʿaql* (*Repose of the Intellect*) in 411/1020–1021 and where he died soon afterwards. On al-Kirmānī's biography, see Farhad Daftary, ʿḤamīd-al-Dīn Kermānīʾ, *EIr*, vol. XI, pp. 639–641; *idem, The Ismāʿīlīs. Their History and Doctrines* (2nd ed., Cambridge, 2007), p. 184 and references given there, particularly, al-Ḥusayn Ḥamdānī, 'Some Unknown Ismāʿīlī Authors and their Works', *JRAS* (1933), pp. 359–378; *idem, al-Ṣulayḥiyyūn waʾl-ḥaraka al-Fāṭimiyya fiʾl-Yaman* (Cairo, 1955), pp. 258–261; the introductory comments of M. Kāmil Ḥusayn and M. Muṣṭafā Ḥilmī in their edition of al-Kirmānī's *Rāḥat al-ʿaql* (Cairo, 1953). On al-Kirmānī's metaphysical system and the nature of his writings, see Daniel De Smet, *La quiétude de l'intellect. Néoplatonisme et gnose dans l'oeuvre de Ḥamîd al-Dîn al-Kirmânî* (X^e/XIe s) (Leuven, 1995); *idem,* ʿal-Kirmānī, Ḥamīd al-Dīnʾ, *EI3*, vol. 1, pp. 131–135; Paul E. Walker, *Ḥamīd al-Dīn al-Kirmānī: Ismaili Thought in the Age of al-Ḥākim* (London and New York, 1999). On the chronology of al-Kirmānī's works see Josef van Ess, 'Bio-bibliographische

stance on the issue appeared to be too unconventional and thought provoking to be casually dismissed. Besides al-Kirmānī's position, Ismaili theological and philosophical speculations on predestination have been voiced by renowned scholars such as, *inter alia*, Abū Ḥātim Aḥmad b. Ḥamdān al-Rāzī (d. 322/934), Muḥammad b. Aḥmad al-Nasafī (d. 332/943) and Abū Yaʿqūb Isḥāq b. Aḥmad al-Sijistānī (d. ca. 361/971), and the Fatimid jurist al-Qāḍī al-Nuʿmān (d. 364/974) who endeavored to interpret the precise meanings of the two words *qaḍāʾ* and *qadar* as they appear in the Qurʾan, finding for them apt correspondences with the Ismaili celestial and terrestrial hierarchies.

Theoretical debates and meticulous disputes developed – despite some apparent degree of futility, as Ivanow has highlighted – most probably because, in the Ismaili doctrine, a question of great significance was linked with the topics of *qaḍāʾ* and *qadar*, namely, the lawfulness of renouncing the prescriptions of the Islamic law (*sharīʿa*) relative to the religious obligations and the forms of worship.[4]

Notizien zur islamischen Theologie. I. Zur Chronologie der Werke des Ḥamīdaddīn al-Kirmānī', *Die Welt des Orients*, 9 (1978), pp. 255–261; Ismail K. Poonawala, *Bio-bibliography of Ismāʿīlī Literature* (Malibu, CA, 1977), pp. 94–102; Wladimir Ivanow, *Ismaili Literature: A Bibliographical Survey* (Tehran, 1963), pp. 40–45. On the Druzes, see Farhad Daftary, *The Ismāʿīlīs: Their History and Doctrines*, 2nd ed. (Cambridge, 2007), p. 186 note 91 and references given therein. Among some of the most significant contributions to the study of the Druzes, see R. B. Betts, *The Druze* (New Haven, 1988); Kais M. Firro, *A History of the Druzes* (Leiden, 1992); David R. W. Bryer, 'The Origins of the Druze Religion', *Der Islam,* 52 (1975), pp. 47–83 and 239–262; 53 (1976), pp. 5–27; Wilferd Madelung, 'Ḥamza ibn ʿAlī', *EI2*, vol. 5, p. 154; Marshall G. S. Hodgson, 'Al-Darazī and Ḥamza in the Origin of the Druze Religion', *JAOS*, 82 (1962), pp. 5–20; *idem*, 'al-Darazī', *EI2*, vol. 2, pp. 136–137, and his 'Durūz', *EI2*, vol. 2, pp. 631–634; see also Daniel De Smet, *Les Epîtres sacrées des druzes, Rasāʾil al-ḥikma: Introduction, édition critique et traduction annotée des traités attribués à Ḥamza b. ʿAlī et Ismāʿīl at-Tamīmī*, 2 vols (Leuven, 2007).

   [4]   Wladimir A. Ivanow, 'An Early Controversy in Ismailism', in his *Studies in Early Persian Ismailism* (Bombay, 1955), p. 107. The eighth chapter of al-Kirmānī's *Kitāb al-Riyāḍ* is a testimony to these disputes. I shall observe in the course of this study that the cautious critical tone that pervades the whole *Riyāḍ* is shunned when al-Kirmānī, in the 23rd *faṣl* of the eighth *bāb*, fiercely denounces al-Sijistānī's intimation about the legitimacy of setting aside the prescriptions of the religious law. It is worth remembering that one of the reasons that brought al-Kirmānī to Cairo during the reign of al-Ḥākim was his mission to contest the accusation of antinomianism levelled against the Ismailis.

Despite being almost certainly synonyms, in the Qur'an the term *qaḍāʾ* is used to indicate a measure, a judgement and a decision. Its verbal form, *qaḍā* signifies 'to decree', 'to judge', 'to accomplish'. Islamic speculative theology, *kalām* in particular, assigns to this word the idea of predetermination and refers to it as a divine 'universal decree'. *Qaḍāʾ* is a perfect and specific divine plan which is designed by God *in aeternitate*, determining all things and events.[5] On the other hand, *qadar* generally refers to the divine decree operating in time and it is often linked to the idea of fate or destiny. In the Qur'an it appears mostly in the verbal form of *qaddara*, with the meaning of determining something according to a specific measure.[6]

As will surface in this study, the need to clarify which of *qaḍāʾ* and *qadar* came first – a question that was intensified by the demand to identify which of these two corresponded to the Ismaili cosmological figure of the Antecedent (*sābiq*) and which to that of the Follower (*tālī*), which to the enunciator-prophet (*nāṭiq*) and which to the Imam/foundation (*asās*), which one to the *qāʾim biʾl-quwwa* and which to the *qāʾim biʾl-fiʿl* – suggests that something important was at stake for all those intellectuals who engaged in laborious deliberations on the topic.

Spurred mainly by the need to shield Ismaili Islam from charges of antinomianistic indulgence and incarnationist assumptions, which had spread particularly following the rise of the Druze movement during the Fatimid period, Ismaili missionaries (*dāʿī*s) such as al-Kirmānī felt the urge to formalise which doctrinal traits were legitimate and acceptable and which were not, and to anchor the former under the aegis of the Fatimid Ismaili *daʿwa*. Erroneous identifications of *qaḍāʾ* and *qadar* might have had serious implications: so, for instance, al-Sijistānī's – according to many of his peers – incorrect intimations that there existed a correspondence between the *qaḍāʾ*, the Imam and the Antecedent on the one hand, and the *qadar*, the Follower and the *nāṭiq* on the other,[7] could have led the community to a fallacious

---

5   See ʿAbd al-Qāhir Jurjānī, *Kitāb al-Taʿrīfāt*, ed. Flügel (Leipzig, 1845), tr. Maurice Gloton as *Le Livre des Définitions* (Tehran, 1994, repr. Beirut, 2006).

6   See Louis Gardet, 'al-Ḳaḍāʾ waʾl-ḳadar', *EI2*, vol. 4, pp. 365–367.

7   See below, pp. 136–137, note 33.

belief in the precedence and superiority of the esoteric hermeneutical interpretation (*ta'wīl*) of the Scriptures, provided by the *asās*, over the impositions of the *sharī'a*, legislated by the enunciator-prophet.[8]

The analysis provided here will show how discussions on *qaḍā'* and *qadar* among Ismaili thinkers raised questions on the nature and function of the *sharī'a* itself, on its exoteric and esoteric explanations, on the identity of those who were authorised to interpret it and guide the community through it, and on whether the end of the last historical and prophetic cycle would witness the dawning of a new religiously unbounded law.[9] Queries surfaced with regard to the true meaning

---

[8] See Ivanow, 'An Early Controversy', p. 109. The problematical issue of the superiority of *walāya* over prophethood (*tafḍīl al-walī 'alā al-nabī*) was widely discussed from early times in Islamic mysticism, and in both Sunni and Shi'i circles. Generally speaking, and more particularly within Sufism, the superiority of *walāya* over *nubuwwa* is not perceived as the superiority of the *walī* over the *nabī* but as the supremacy of the saintly character of a prophet, in terms of his closeness to the knowledge of the divine, over his prophetic legislative task (see Orkhan Mir-Kasimov, *Words of Power: Ḥurūfī Teachings between Shi'ism and Sufism in Medieval Islam*, London and New York, 2015, pp. 401–405 and references given there). In Ismailism, however, the issue of the superiority and precedence of sainthood over prophethood bore a number of critical theological and doctrinal implications that will be discussed in the course of this study. On the relationship between *walāya* and *nubuwwa* in Islamic doctrines see Hermann Landolt, 'Walāyah', in *The Encyclopedia of Religion,* ed. Mircea Eliade (London and New York, 1987), vol. 15, pp. 316–323, and Gerald T. Elmore, *Islamic Sainthood in the Fullness of Time: Ibn al-'Arabī's Book of the Fabulous Gryphon* (Leiden, Boston and Cologne, 1999), pp. 131–162.

[9] In general, early Ismailis of the pre-Fatimid period believed that the hierohistory of humankind develops within seven cycles or eras (*dawr*s) each one inaugurated by a speaking-prophet or enunciator-prophet (*nāṭiq*) of a revealed message which is manifest in its exoteric or literal aspect (*ẓāhir*) in a religious law (*sharī'a*). In the first six eras of human history, the enunciator-prophets were Adam, Noah, Abraham, Moses, Jesus and Muḥammad. Each *nāṭiq* was succeeded by a legatee or executor (*waṣī*), also named a foundation (*asās*) or silent one (*ṣāmit*), who revealed to an elite the esoteric truths (*ḥaqā'iq*) contained in the inner (*bāṭin*) aspect of his era's revealed message. The legatees in the first six eras were Seth, Shem, Ishmael, Aaron or Joshua, Simon Peter and 'Alī. In turn, each legatee was followed by seven Imams (or *atimmā'*, completers) responsible for guarding the real meaning of the revelation and the law in both their exoteric and esoteric dimensions. The seventh Imam of each prophetic era would rise to the rank of the *nāṭiq* of the following cycle, abrogating the *sharī'a* of the previous enunciator-prophet and promulgating a new one. This cyclical arrangement

and distinctiveness of the term *qāʾim* generally identified with the ultimate 'Regulator', the 'Riser' or 'Resurrector', who was believed either to liberate the whole of humankind from redundantly restrictive religious impositions or destined to redeem the devout community through a triumphant, omni-comprehensive and unprecedented type of *sharīʿa*.[10]

It is significant to remember that, within Ismaili hierohistory, it is acknowledged that prior to the advent of the final Resurrector, within a single prophetic cycle, such as that of Muḥammad, there are also 'minor' *qāʾim*s – approximately every seventh Imam is the *imām-qāʾim* of that cycle – bringing about a minor *qiyāma*, namely, new esoteric teachings, to the community of believers.[11] Examples of such *imām-qāʾim*s during the cycle of the Prophet were believed to be Muḥammad b. Ismāʿīl, al-Muʿizz li-Dīn Allāh and al-Ḥākim bi-Amr Allāh. All of these minor *qāʾim*s were considered to serve as harbingers of

---

would be modified with the seventh and final era. The seventh Imam of the sixth era, Muḥammad b. Ismāʿīl, after having retreated into concealment (*satr*), would then manifest himself as the final *nāṭiq*, more specifically as the *qāʾim* or *mahdī*. This is an eschatological figure responsible for revealing to the whole of humanity all the esoteric truths contained in the preceding messages which were conveyed only partially and hence imperfectly. In his messianic era, no distinction will exist between the *ẓāhir* and the *bāṭin*, the literality of the law and its inherent spiritual core. He would be the *qāʾim al-qiyāma*, the Imam of Resurrection, sealing the end of human history and time. See Daftary, *The Ismāʿīlīs*, pp. 131–132; on the Ismaili cyclical view of time and history see Henry Corbin, *Cyclical Time and Ismaili Gnosis*, tr. Ralph Manheim and James W. Morris (London, 1983).

[10] As briefly mentioned in the notes to the text, the word *qāʾim* literally means 'the one who stands up'. Although the term is employed par excellence to refer to *qāʾim al-qiyāma*, the last Resurrector, each Imam, or even each member of the Ismaili Call is a *qāʾim* in potentiality. See Ivanow, *Ismaili Tradition concerning the the Rise of the Fatimids* (London, etc., 1942), pp. 242–243 (pp. 54–55 of the Arabic text). See also Henry Corbin, *Temple and Contemplation,* tr. Philip Sherrard and Liadain Sherrard (London and New York, 1986), p. 159 note 91 and p. 162.

[11] Generally speaking, it is understood that the *nuṭāqāʾ* are the lords of the major cycles (*adwār*, sg. *dawr*), which are also referred to as the greater days. These days are divided into seven days which are indicated as the minor cycles (*zamana*), i.e. the cycles of the Imams. See Corbin, *Cyclical Time and Ismaili Gnosis*, pp. 184–185; Nāṣir-i Khusraw, *Wajh-i dīn*, ed. Gholam-Reza Aavani (Tehran, 1977), pp. 13, 127.

the final *qāʾim* with minor *qiyāma*s foreshadowing the great Resurrection.[12] Even though the exact identification of such figures goes beyond the scope of this work, it will be pointed out – particularly in Part II – how veiled under the discussions on *qaḍāʾ* and *qadar* were suggestions aimed at identifying the nature, roles and ranks of such *qāʾim*s, particularly in relation to the final Riser.

Within Sunni Islam, the issue of decree and destiny, also discussed in terms of predestination versus free will, received great attention from a very early stage. This inaugurated theoretical debates between the schools of thought espousing the predestinarian view – initially identified with the Jabriyya (from *jabr*, compulsion) for whom all is pre-ordained by God's will, and their opponents – designated by their challengers as Qadariyya (*qadar*, destiny), who sponsored the idea that human beings act according to their will and are consequentially responsible for their deeds. From the 4th/10th century, some among the speculative theologians of Islam, the Muʿtazilites, who were predominantly concerned with defending the ethical nature of God's justice, maintained that humans are capable of distinguishing good from evil, with or without divine revelation, and are capable of choosing freely which way to act, thus becoming responsible for their actions. Hence, in their view, in the hereafter, humans are rewarded or punished accordingly by God.[13]

In contrast, the Ashʿarites – whose theological stances prevailed between the 4th and 5th/10th and 11th centuries – mainly propounded a predestinarian view. Their arguments, which were eventually followed by the majority of Sunni traditionalists, stressed God's omnipotence: God creates both good and evil acts as He is not bound by any compulsion or any duty towards humankind. What He commands is necessarily right, and what He condemns is necessarily wrong. Therefore, since what God creates is intrinsically and necessarily just, He cannot be accused of unjustly punishing humans for actions He created for them.

As illustrated by Farhad Daftary and Faquir Muhammad Hunzai, the classical Ismaili views in this theological debate date back to the

---

12 Corbin, *Temple and Contemplation,* p. 162 and references in note 57, p. 148.
13 For an overview, see De Cillis, *Free Will and Predestination*, pp. 5–16.

4th/10th century, the early Fatimid period of Ismaili history.[14] In early Imami texts, a preference for an intermediate position between pure necessitarianism (*jabr*) and empowerment (*qadar*) emerges. This is attested to by a *ḥadīth* reported by Imam Jaʿfar-al-Ṣādiq (d. 148/765) who, speaking of free will *versus* predestination, stated: '*lā jabr wa-lā tafwīḍ wa-lākin amr bayn amrayn*' (there is neither [complete] necessitarianism nor [complete] delegation but something in between).[15] Similar 'midway' views, rejecting both *jabr* and *qadar*, were expounded by al-Qāḍī al-Nuʿmān and the *dāʿī* Ḥamīd al-Dīn al-Kirmānī, culminating in the writings of Nāṣir-i Khusraw (d. after 465/1072).[16]

Al-Kirmānī's initial contribution to the debate drew on his earlier Imami Shiʿi heritage, which was centred on the doctrine of the imamate and its emphasis on the need that humankind has of guidance with regards to spiritual matters.[17] Needless to say, for an Ismaili author such as al-Kirmānī it was important to accommodate a contentious topic like divine predestination within the framework of Fatimid Ismaili theological doctrines. The Ismaili distinction between the external or literal (*ẓāhir*) and the hidden or esoteric (*bāṭin*) dimensions of religion, and the belief that no ordinary man can access the religious truths (*ḥaqāʾiq*, sg. *ḥaqīqa*) concealed in the *bāṭin* to which the secret of divine predestination (*sirr al-qadar*) pertains, makes it necessary for the believer to have faith in the infallible (*maʿṣūm*) authorities and their exclusive ability to understand the real meaning of the Qurʾan. It is thanks to their divinely inspired guidance, exercised through *taʾwīl* or esoteric exegesis of the divine Word, that humankind can identify

---

[14] Farhad Daftary and Faquir Muhammad Hunzai, 'Free Will in Ismaʿili Shiʿism', *EIr*, vol. X, pp. 202–205.

[15] Muḥammad b. Yaʿqūb al-Kulaynī, *al-Uṣūl min al-kāfī*, ed. ʿAlī A. Ghaffārī (Tehran, 1375/1955; repr. Beirut, 1405/1985), vol. 1 p. 160, *ḥadīth* no. 13; Martin J. McDermott, *The Theology of al-Shaikh al-Mufīd* (Beirut, 1978); al-Shaykh al-Ṣadūq Ibn Bābūya, *Risālat al-iʿtiqādāt al-imāmiyya* (Tehran, 1370/1992), tr. Asaf A. A. Fyzee as *A Shīʿite Creed* (Oxford, 1942), pp. 32–33; Wilferd Madelung, 'Imamism and Muʿtazilite Theology', in *Le Shīʿisme imāmite*, ed. Toufic Fahd (Paris, 1970), p. 18 note 1.

[16] See Daftary and Hunzai, 'Free Will', p. 203 and references given there. See also Nāṣir-i Khusraw, *Gushāyish wa rahāyish*, ed. and tr. Faquir M. Hunzai as *Knowledge and Liberation: A Treatise on Philosophical Theology* (London and New York, 1998), pp. 113–114 (English text), pp. 74–75 (Persian text).

[17] Daftary and Hunzai, 'Free Will', p. 203.

the real meaning of the revelation and the *sharīʿa* with its precepts and *dicta*.[18]

Generally speaking, al-Kirmānī's position on divine decree and destiny reflects that of the majority of Ismaili authors of the Fatimid era in their belief that if, on the one hand, humans have the freedom to choose between good and evil deeds, on the other hand, they lack understanding of the Qurʾanic truth which makes such freedom insufficient to guarantee their salvation. In order to attain deliverance and reward in the next life, man's knowledge – which is inadequate for him to be able to make the right choice and elevate him along the spiritual ladder of redemption – needs to be honed by the guidance of a divinely appointed hierarchy of authoritative teachers: the prophet, his legatee (*waṣī*), the rightful Imam of the time and the whole chain of dignitaries including the *ḥujjas* and the *dāʿīs*. Despite the great emphasis placed on the philosophical quest, Ismaili doctrine such as al-Kirmānī's 'remained essentially revelational rather than rational',[19] and this meant that no rational enquiry could ever indicate the right path on its own and that, by extension, no pure rational approach could ever be addressed to the issue of divine predestination.

In the course of this study, it will be examined how the concept of Revelation – intended as *tanzīl* and *sharīʿa* – brought about by the enunciator-prophet and interpreted by his Imam, shapes the core of al-Kirmānī's notion of the imamate. On the one hand, his attitude to the discussions on predestination aims to 'canonise' the irrevocability of both the imamate – in particular the Fatimid view of the Imam-caliph's role – and the religious law, in both its esoteric and exoteric facets, thus harmonising some discordant positions held by a number of his fellow theologians. And on the other hand, it intends to moderate potentially extremist views, curbing these according to al-Ḥākim's Fatimid Ismaili doctrine. Indeed, the historical backdrop against which al-Kirmānī operates – the theological, philosophical and legal debates that had originated and developed within Ismailism

---

[18]   Ḥamīd al-Dīn al-Kirmānī, *Tanbīh al-hādī waʾl-mustahdī*, MS 1230, The Zahid Ali Collection, London, Ismaili Special Collections Unit at The Institute of Ismaili Studies, fols. 134, 144–145.

[19]   See Daftary and Hunzai, 'Free Will', p. 204.

up to the reign of al-Ḥākim – provides the reader with the theoretical frame with which al-Kirmānī's discourse of *qaḍāʾ* and *qadar* must be approached.[20]

Following the reform of ʿAbd Allāh al-Mahdī (d. 322/934) in 286/899 and his claim to the imamate as Jaʿfar al-Ṣādiq's descendant, the Ismaili cyclical scheme of religious history underwent significant changes. The idea of continuity of the imamate, allowed by the newly proposed belief in the subsistence of more than one heptad in the era of Islam, consequently withdrew any eschatological flavour from the seventh era – until that time perceived as the spiritual age of the Mahdī. In contrast to the Fatimid Ismailis, the non-conforming Qarmaṭīs, after the schism of 286/899, continued to believe that with the first appearance of Muḥammad b. Ismāʿīl the final, seventh era of history had already begun. In particular, they emphasised that Muḥammad b. Ismāʿīl's mahdiship would bring to a conclusion the era of Islam.[21] The exoteric aspect of Muḥammad's law was to be lifted and, consequently, rituals and religious obligations of Islam would be revoked. Ideas on such a messianic figure started to be detailed in many sources, such as al-Nasafī's *Kitāb al-Maḥṣūl* (Book of the Result), where the cycle marking the end of the sacred history of humanity is portrayed as an age in which the religious law could be dispensed with.[22]

---

[20] On the nature of al-Ḥākim's reign and the impact of his personal undertaking within the Fatimid Ismaili *daʿwa*, see Paul E. Walker, 'The Ismaili *Daʿwa* in the Reign of the Fatimid Caliph al-Ḥākim', *JARCE*, 30 (1993), pp. 161–182.

[21] Wilferd Madelung, 'Das Imamat in der frühen ismailitischen Lehre', *Der Islam*, 37 (2009), pp. 46–47.

[22] According to Abū Ḥātim al-Rāzī, al-Nasafī propounded that the cycle of the last *qāʾim* would not enforce any religious work (*ʿamal*), regulated in the sacred laws of preceeding *nuṭaqāʾ*. See Abū Ḥātim al-Rāzī, *Kitāb al-Iṣlāḥ*, ed. Ḥasan Mīnūchehr and Mehdī Moḥaghegh (Tehran, 2004), pp. 64–66; Daftary, *The Ismāʿīlīs*, pp. 133, 226. According to Daftary (ibid., p. 154), prior to the episode that saw the 'Persian Mahdī' declared an imposter and then killed per order of Abū Ṭāhir al-Jannābī (d. 332/944), the *Kitāb al-Maḥṣūl* played an important role in providing eastern Qarmaṭīs with a unified understanding of their beliefs. Al-Nasafī affirmed the imamate of Muḥammad b. Ismāʿīl, whose return as the Mahdī he awaited. In his view, the seventh, lawless *dawr* had already begun with no Imams being there but only the twelve *lawāḥiq* (sg. *lāḥiq*, adjunct) assuming command with one acting as the deputy (*khalīfa*) of the absent Imam. This position led some to regard al-Nasafī's views as being entrenched in

Given that with 'Abd Allāh al-Mahdī's reform, the advent of the Lord of the Resurrection (*qā'im al-qiyāma*) had been indeterminately deferred, questions on the identity, role and modes of manifestation of the final *qā'im* began to surface. It was probably al-Qāḍī al-Nuʿmān who first provided somewhat acceptable 'Fatimid' answers to justify (i) the denial of Muḥammad b. Ismāʿīl's corporeal return as the ultimate *qā'im* and (ii) the idea of him being exempted from inaugurating a new *sharīʿa*.[23] By expounding the idea that the *qā'im* had various degrees of manifestation at different levels – that of the corporeal world, that of Resurrection in the spiritual world and that of reckoning upon Judgement Day – al-Qāḍī al-Nuʿmān was to introduce an innovative element in the *qā'im*'s dual-corporeal grade of appearance, firstly as a *nāṭiq* and secondly as the *nāṭiq*'s rightly guided deputies (*al-khulafāʾ al-rāshidūn*). Because in his first corporeal manifestation as the seventh enunciator-prophet Muḥammad b. Ismāʿīl was in a state of concealment (*satr*), his esoteric hermeneutical interpretation would have remained concealed too, were it not to be revealed through his second corporeal degree of manifestation, that is, his deputies, the Fatimid Imams, who thus fulfilled the *qā'im*'s prophesised deeds.[24]

Al-Qāḍī al-Nuʿmān's views became more and more consolidated in Fatimid Ismailism: in the analysis of al-Kirmānī's *Riyāḍ*, we shall find al-Sijistānī being persuaded to similar concepts whose main traits, permeated by a Neoplatonised Ismaili cosmology, were reiterated in the works of al-Muʿizz li-Dīn Allāh (d. 365/975) and the

---

antinomian tendencies. As Madelung points out, it is probable that it was also with the intention of censoring such antinomian issues embedded in the *Maḥṣūl* that al-Rāzī wrote the *Kitāb al-Iṣlāḥ*. See Wilferd Madelung, 'Karmaṭī', *EI2*, vol. 4, p. 622; *idem*, 'Das Imamat', p. 103; Patricia Crone and Luke Treadwell, 'A New Text on Ismailism at the Samanid Court', in *Texts, Documents and Artefacts: Ismaili Studies in Honour of D. S. Richards*, ed. Chase F. Robinson (Leiden and Boston, 2003), p. 65.

[23] Walker has highlighted how the writings of al-Qāḍī al-Nuʿmān 'deliberately sought to create a constitutional base for Fatimid rule'. See his 'The Ismaili *Daʿwa* in the Reign of the Fatimid Caliph al-Ḥākim', p. 166.

[24] Attributed to al-Qāḍī al-Nuʿmān, *al-Risāla al-Mudhhiba*, in *Khams Rasāʾil Ismāʿīliyya*, ed. ʿĀrif Tāmir (Salamiyya, 1956), pp. 55ff. It should be noted that al-Qāḍī al-Nuʿmān's authorship of the *Risāla* is contested by scholars such as Poonawala.

dāʿī Jaʿfar b. Manṣūr al-Yaman (d. 10th century).[25] It is well known that al-Sijistānī – despite his defense of al-Nasafī's pronouncements in the *Nuṣra* – in his late 'career' was encouraged to embrace al-Muʿizz's policies and accept the legitimacy of the Fatimid caliphs.[26] In particular, al-Muʿizz's strategy implemented important shifts in the Fatimid doctrine. Refuting ʿAbd Allāh al-Mahdī's claim that Muḥammad b. Ismāʿīl had been a cover name for all the legitimate Imams after ʿAbd Allāh b. Jaʿfar (d. 149/766) as well as for himself as the awaited *qāʾim*, al-Muʿizz held that Muḥammad b. Ismāʿīl himself would not return as the Mahdī and that his descendants, the Fatimids, would discharge his duties. After having manifested briefly as a corporeal *ḥadd* (limit, rank) during 'the period of the hidden Imams' (*dawr al-satr*) and after having returned as ʿAbd Allāh al-Mahdī at the beginning of 'the period of disclosure' (*dawr al-kashf*), he was currently in his spiritual limit (*al-ḥadd al-rūḥānī*),[27] being represented by the Fatimid Imams before his final, purely spiritual reappearance.[28]

Indeed, due to the success of the Qarmaṭī propaganda (which had also won over, to a certain extent, the *dāʿī* al-Rāzī) in the eastern regions such as Iraq, Persia and Transoxiana, the political-doctrinal preoccupations of al-Muʿizz needed the allegiance of an influential

---

[25] On al-Muʿizz's and Jaʿfar's works see Daftary, *The Ismāʿīlīs*, p. 165 notes 46, 47, 48 and references given therein.

[26] It is well known that al-Sijistānī, at some point, recognised the Fatimids as *khulafāʾ* of Muḥammad b. Ismāʿīl (as the final *qāʾim*), namely, as those responsible for gradually discharging his mission. Al-Sijistānī, *Kitāb Ithbāt al-nubuwwāt*, ed. ʿĀrif Tāmir (Beirut, 1966), p. 186; *idem, Kitāb al-Yanābīʿ*, ed. Muṣṭafā Ghālib (Beirut, 1965), tr. Paul E. Walker as *The Wellsprings of Wisdom* (Salt Lake City, UT, 1994), pp. 30, 131, 144; *idem, 'Risālat Tuḥfat al-mustajībīn'*, in *Khams Rasāʾil Ismāʿīliyya*, ed. ʿĀrif Tāmir p. 153; see also Paul E. Walker, *Early Philosophical Shiism. The Ismaili Neoplatonism of Abū Yaʿqūb al-Sijistānī* (Cambridge, 1993), pp. 21–24; Crone and Treadwell, 'A New Text on Ismailism', p. 65; and David Hollenberg, *Beyond the Qurʾān: Early Ismāʿīlī Taʾwīl and the Secrets of the Prophets* (Columbia, SC, 2016), p. 23. I am very grateful to Dr Hollenberg for having shared the material of his book before its publication.

[27] It will be shown later in this study how al-Sijistānī, in discussing the identity of *qaḍāʾ* and *qadar*, insists on their spiritual limits, thus hinting at Muḥammad b. Ismāʿīl's potential nature as both the Imam in *satr* and as the final Resurrector. On *ḥudūd*, see note 58 below.

[28] Madelung, 'Das Imamat', pp. 87–101; Crone and Treadwell, 'A New Text on Ismailism', p. 65; Hollenberg, *Beyond the Qurʾān*, p. 30.

dāʿī such as al-Sijistānī – mainly active in Makrān, Khurāsān and Sīstān – in order to win over followers of the Imam-caliphs in the East, beyond the recently established Fatimid capital city of Cairo.[29] Nonetheless, in my analysis of the *Kitāb al-Riyāḍ*, al-Sijistānī's perceptions of *qaḍāʾ* and *qadar* will bare a Qarmaṭī character, in particular with regard to his oblique identifications of the Antecedent (*sābiq*) with the *qāʾim bi'l-quwwa* (i.e. Muḥammad b. Ismāʿīl as the *qāʾim* in *satr*), and the Follower (*tālī*) with the *qāʾim bi'l-fiʿl* (i.e. Muḥammad b. Ismāʿīl returning as the final Resurrector).

On his part, al-Kirmānī, in his function as a 'mediator' between ostensibly contrasting views (which he reviews in his *Riyāḍ*), will draw from al-Qāḍī al-Nuʿmān's stance on the 'perpetrated presence' of the *qāʾim* even during *satr*, which is carried out through his *ḥujjas* and *dāʿīs*. Although it is with the Nizārī Ḥasan II *ʿalā dhikrihi al-salām* – during the proclamation of *qiyāma* at Alamūt (559/1164) – that the status of the Imam's *khalīfa* (or deputy) with full authority undergoes a drastic shift,[30] the idea that the Imam's 'presence' is rendered actual *also* via his *ḥudūd* is already detectable in the thought of al-Kirmānī.[31] In particular, as this investigation will attempt to show, in dealing with issues intertwined with the idea of decree and destiny, al-Kirmānī

---

[29] Farhad Daftary, *Ismaili Literature: A Bibliography of Sources and Studies* (London, 2004), pp. 27–28; Madelung, 'Das Imamat', pp. 87–101.

[30] In his proclamation at Alamūt, Daftary explains, Ḥasan II had declared himself not simply as the Imam's *ḥujja* and *dāʿī*, as done already by his predecessors, but also as the Imam's sole vice-regent and deputy (*qāʾim maqām va nāʾib-i munfarid*). By doing so, he had implicitly 'shifted' his status as the Imam's *khalīfa* to that of God's *khalīfa*. In other words, from being the deputy of the Imam in *satr*, he was, through the *khuṭba* he delivered, equating himself to God's deputy, namely, the Imam himself and, in particular, the *imām-qāʾim*. See Daftary, *The Ismāʿīlīs*, pp. 358–361. On the doctrine of the *qiyāma*, refer to Madelung, 'Das Imamat'; on the meaning of the *qiyāma* following Ḥasan II's declaration, see Ḥasan-i Maḥmūd-i Kātib, *Haft bāb*, ed. and tr. by S. Jalal Badakhchani as *Spiritual Resurrection in Shiʿi Islam: An Early Ismaili Treatise on the Doctrine of Qiyāmat* (London, 2017).

[31] In Ismailism, the term *ḥudūd* – seemingly inspired by Q 65:1 ('*wa tilka ḥudūd 'llāhi*', 'there are limits set by Allāh') – is used to indicate a series of intermediaries (*wasāʾiṭ*) appointed by God between Him and His creatures. For a definition of this word see al-Sijistānī, '*Risālat Tuḥfat al-mustajībīn*', p. 149. On the different ranks of *ḥudūd* see note 52 below.

endeavours to emphasise the status of actuality of *qaḍāʾ* and *qadar*, of the Imams and the religious dignitaries of the Ismaili *daʿwa*, even justifying in what terms the awaited *qāʾim* can be proclaimed to be *qāʾim biʾl-quwwa*. Al-Kirmānī's stance, refuting tenets that had been at the core of Fatimid Ismailism in the previous forty years or so, pushes a less allegorised form of Islam which does not allow any exemption of the *sharīʿa*, which depicts Adam as the father of humankind who brought the first law, and which looks at the Fatimid Imams neither as divine beings nor as a series of final saviours.[32]

Al-Kirmānī's discussions on *qaḍāʾ* and *qadar* – scattered and often implicitly addressed throughout a number of his works whilst being more deliberately tackled in the *Riyāḍ* – encompass this and earlier ideas on the *qāʾim*, whether he was to announce a new *sharīʿa* or simply reveal the *bāṭinī* meanings of the preceding laws. But I would posit that it also purports a distinctive reading of the notion of *qiyāma*, hinting at elaborating in what terms *qāʾim*s are personifications of individual souls who have undergone spiritual resurrection whilst still in their bodies.

In addition, al-Kirmānī's considerations strongly resonate with his task of having to counter provocative and often highly controversial doctrinal divergences voiced either by his esteemed predecessors (al-Nasafī, al-Rāzī and al-Sijistānī, on themes such as the nature and function of the pairs *amr/kalima*, *ʿaql/nafs*, *sābiq/tālī*), or articulated by the so-called exaggerationists (*ghulāt*) such as the Druzes who believed in al-Ḥākim's divinity (*ulūhiyya*), the redundancy of *sharīʿa* and its antinominalist consequences.[33]

Drawing from the Qurʾanic predestinarian connotations given to *qaḍāʾ* and *qadar*, al-Kirmānī's Fatimid Ismaili conveyance of these terms is conditioned by his understanding of issues such as the imamate (particularly the legitimacy of the Fatimid imamate's succession and its necessity), the obligation for Fatimid Ismaili believers to submit to the injunctions of the religious law, and the need to reassess

---

[32] Madelung, 'Das Imamat', pp. 118–119; Hollenberg, *Beyond the Qurʾān*, p. 32.

[33] On the *ghulāt*, see M. G. S. Hodgson, 'Ghulāt', *EI2*, vol. 2, pp. 1119–1121, and Mushegh Asatryan, *Controversies in Formative Shiʿi Islam: The Ghulat Muslims and Their Beliefs* (London, 2017), particularly chapter 2, pp. 43–78.

earlier, as well as contemporary, allegedly Ismaili-related tendencies concerning incarnationistic/transmigrationist postulations.

Significantly, it will be noted that al-Kirmānī does not portray *qaḍāʾ* and *qadar* as, respectively, the Qurʾanic eternal or temporal facet of a decree predetermined by a 'withdrawn' God, but rather as 'means' that are actualised in creation. Primarily, they are subtly presented as forms personified in the members of the religious *daʿwa* (i.e. in the *qāʾim* who is not intended solely as the last Resurrector but as each *nāṭiq*, each Imam and each member of the Ismaili Call who is also potentially a 'lord of the Resurrection'),[34] in whom, through intellectual intermediaries, divine providentiality finds its recipients and its soteriological instruments. Secondly, on several occasions, as will beccome clear throughout this analysis, al-Kirmānī stresses that *qaḍāʾ* and *qadar*, although originating from the primordial world of *ibdāʿ*, pertain to the corporeal realm and not the realm of the intellects. Veiled under this idea, I believe, is not only al-Kirmānī's understanding of *qiyāma* but also his condemnation of the supporters of al-Ḥākim's *ulūhiyya*: al-Ḥākim is a divinely appointed Imam, not a divinity himself.[35] This parallelism is not as speculative as it might

---

[34] Corbin, *Temple and Contemplation*, p. 162.

[35] In his *Mabāsim al-bishārāt biʾl-imām al-Ḥākim bi-Amr Allāh*, a *risāla* written in 405–406/1014–1015 to explain the nature of the imamate and the role of al-Ḥākim as the legitimate divinely appointed Imam of the time, al-Kirmānī rejects al-Ḥākim's divinity and condemns it as as a *ghuluww* belief (al-Kirmānī, *Risālat Mabāsim al-bishārāt biʾl-imān al-Ḥākim bi-Amr Allāh*, in *Majmūʿat rasāʾil al-Kirmānī*, ed. Muṣṭafā Ghālib (Beirut, 1969), pp. 113–133; Joseph Van Ess, 'Bio-bibliographische Notizen zur Islamischen Theologie', pp. 256–257; Daftary, *The Ismāʿīlīs*, p. 188). Al-Kirmānī wrote another major work, probably around 408/1017, entitled *al-Risāla al-Wāʿiẓa fī nafy daʿwa ulūhiyyāt al-Ḥākim bi-Amr Allāh* condemning the dissenters supporting the divinity of the Imam-caliph. See al-Kirmānī, *al-Risāla al-wāʿiẓa*, ed. M. Kāmil Ḥusayn, *Bulletin of the Faculty of Arts, Fouad I University*, 14, part 1 (1952), pp. 1–29, also in al-Kirmānī, *Majmūʿat rasāʾil*, pp. 113–133. References to this work are in Mehdi Aminrazavi, 'Ḥamīd al-Dīn al-Kirmānī', in *An Anthology of Philosophy in Persia, vol. II: Ismaili Thought in the Classical Age*, ed. Seyyed Hossein Nasr and Mehdi Aminrazavi (London, 2008), p. 179. On the problems related to the assumed divinity of al-Ḥākim, see Daniel De Smet, 'Le *Kitāb rāḥat al-ʿaql* de Ḥamīd al-Dīn al-Kirmānī et la cosmologie ismaélienne à lʾépoque fatimide', *Acta Orientalia Belgica*, 7 (1992), p. 86, n. 24; and Faquir Muhammad Hunzai, 'The Concept of *Tawḥīd* in the Thought of Ḥamīd al-Dīn al-Kirmānī', PhD thesis, McGill University (Montreal, 1986), pp. 92–96.

first appear; in the arguments aimed at proving the ranks and roles of *qaḍāʾ* and *qadar*, al-Kirmānī explains how the ideals of divine blessings and salvation are to be envisaged as commandments to know what the universe really is in all of its parts – celestial and terrestrial – and demands the understanding of the roles and limits (*ḥudūd*) of humans in the whole system.[36] The acknowledgment of the guiding roles played by all the Fatimid Imams and all the ranks (*ḥudūd*) of the *daʿwa* – each of which is but a 'transitional' *qāʾim* in potentiality[37] – together with the realisation of one's own limitations and the recognition of one's own task in the cosmic and terrestrial hierarchy, is very significant apropos the issue of predestination. In fact, this becomes vital for identifying the spiritual/intellectual value of the Resurrection as well as the absolute non-divinity of anything other than God. A concept such as this, is what for al-Kirmānī entails the true meaning of divine unity (*tawḥīd*).[38]

A clear message that emerges from al-Kirmānī is that God, through His '*qāʾims*', fulfils His decree by way of bestowing intellectual emanations upon all souls and that acknowledgment of ontic non-divinity must not be read as a concession to a condescending God, but as a grateful recognition of how divine providence really operates. In al-Kirmānī's view, God's providential decree runs across different levels, and these are investigated here: on a cosmogonic plane, as will be expounded in the *kūnī-qadar* myth, later examined in detail; on a cosmological level, detectable in the nature of the Intellect and the Soul, the 'relationship' they have with the Godhead, each other and the rest of the cosmic elements (i.e. the remaining intellects, the celestial

---

[36] Walker, *Ḥamīd al-Dīn al-Kirmānī*, p. 115. Generally speaking, the aim of the Ismaili *daʿwa* to instruct and steer people towards a right and complete understanding of the Qurʾan and the religious law becomes an obligation to teach and guide the individuals who worship God through what al-Kirmānī identifies as 'the double worship' by knowledge and action. Ibid., pp. 107–117. On the theory of 'double worship', see al-Kirmānī, *al-Maṣābīḥ fī ithbāt al-imāma*, ed. and tr. Walker, *Master of the Age*, Arabic text pp. 21–22 and p. 24, English text pp. 56–57, 59; Walker, *Ḥamīd al-Dīn al-Kirmānī*, pp. 107–117; De Smet, *La quiétude de l'intellect*, pp. 21–22, 312, 354, 357–358, 361, 397.

[37] On this argument, see Corbin, *Temple and Contemplation*, p. 162.

[38] On al-Kirmānī's understanding of *tawḥīd*, see more below, p. 54 and note 8 therein.

spheres and their bodies etc.); and in a religious/corporeal dimension, where divine providence manifests in all associates of the Ismaili *da'wa* and their salvific missionary tools (i.e. the *nāṭiq*'s legislation of the *sharī'a*; the Fatimid Imam-caliphs' esoteric interpretations of the law and the consolidation of their teachings whose continuity is ensured by designated deputies such as the *ḥujjas* and the *dā'īs*).

In a sense, the salient impression emerging from al-Kirmānī's works is that the very structure of the imamate, the very idea of the advent of a series of 'potential *qā'ims*' symbolising 'the end of one order, the judgement, and the beginning of another order, different but not discontinuous',[39] and the very concept of *tawḥīd* delineate for him a profoundly Fatimid Ismaili understanding of the divine decree.

In particular, if on a spiritual/religious level appreciation of God's sole divinity must translate for the Fatimid believer into full obedience to divine arrangements, including the divinely appointed representatives and a divinely established *sharī'a*, on a political level, such acknowledgement becomes a weapon (*silāḥ*) – a specific term that in the twenty-third *faṣl* of chapter eight in the *Riyāḍ* our *dā'ī* appears to indicate the insight of those Ismailis who engaged in the analysis of incorrect beliefs – to condemn extremist views propounding the divinity of any prophet or Imam. Such postulations are covertly expounded in the section of the *Riyāḍ* under investigation, and particularly in the accounts relative to Moses' attainment of *nāṭiq*-ship under the religious guidance of Shu'ayb.[40]

It is unquestionable that in all his works linked to the notions of divine decree and destiny as well as human freedom, al-Kirmānī stresses that any personal striving to attain religious knowledge (including understanding the real meaning of *tawḥīd*) necessitates a remission to the spiritual guidance of the Imams and their epistemological mission. In his view, the way towards divine grace and eternal redemption should be paved not merely with obedience to the authoritative teachers but also, in clear opposition to the Qarmaṭī views, with the observation of the ritual acts and the performance of good deeds. Thus, the training

---

[39] Boustan Hirji, 'A Study of *al-Risālah al-bāhirah*', PhD thesis, McGill University (Montreal, 1994), p. 155.

[40] See below, pp. 231, 238 notes 5 and 6, 239 note 28, 240–241, and 243 note 43.

of the human soul encouraged by the *sharīʿa* becomes an imperative by virtue of which the soul detaches itself from earthly desires, choosing moral principles over enslaving material desires. Only by doing so can the soul aspire to attain an understanding of its origins in the universe in its endless effort to get closer to the world of the intellects.

Undoubtedly, for Fatimid Ismailism, permeated with philosophy and Greek sciences, epistemological methods differed from those of the *falāsifa*, the *mutakallimūn* and even the Sufis.[41] The Ismailis were convinced that there exists a perfect harmony (*muṭābaqa*), a correspondence (*munāsaba*) and a strict equilibrium (*muwāzana*) among all levels of being. So, Abū Yaʿqūb al-Sijistānī – who, as already mentioned, was to become at a later stage of his career one of the most prominent Fatimid *dāʿīs* – speaks of two hierarchies through and by which the whole cosmic system is created and maintained: the spiritual realm, to which belong the Intellect and the Soul – this teaching being derived from a pre-Fārābian-type of Neoplatonism – and the religious realm, to which belong the *nāṭiq* and the *asās*.[42] By partially adapting al-Sijistānī's view, al-Kirmānī distinguishes between the spiritual realm, also referred to as the realm of the Intellect (*ʿālam al-ʿaql*) or the realm of unity (*ʿālam al-waḥda*), encompassing the Pleroma of ten separate intellects, and the world of nature (*ʿālam al-ṭabīʿa*) including the spheres, the celestial bodies and the sublunar realm.

All these elements are clearly reminiscent of the Fārābian emanative schema. Al-Fārābī (d. 339/950) describes a Pleroma of separate intellects, each of which enjoys a two-fold kind of contemplation: by thinking of the Principle, the Intellect emanates another intellect,

---

[41] Wilferd Madelung stresses that whilst the core of Ismaili teaching exemplifies general Islamic and Shiʿi tenets, it also incorporated some aspects of the Hellenistic theoretical heritage which was mostly condemned or shunned by more conservative Sunni scholars. Madelung emphasises, however, that Ismaili doctrine did not borrow unsystematically but rather 'selected what it found congenial to its basic convictions and amalgamated it into a coherent synthesis of its own'. Wilferd Madelung, 'Aspects of Ismaili Theology: The Prophetic Chain and the God beyond Being', in *Ismāʿīlī Contributions to Islamic Culture*, ed. S. H. Nasr (Tehran, 1977), p. 54.

[42] Paul E. Walker, 'Cosmic Hierarchies in Early Ismaili Thought', *Muslim World*, 66 (1976), pp. 14–28; see also Ismail K. Poonawala in his Introduction to al-Sijistānī's *Kitāb al-Maqālīd al-malakūtiyya* (Tunis, 2011), p. 53. Henceforth, Introduction.

whilst by thinking of himself, he emanates a celestial sphere. This process continues down to the last Intellect of *Dator Formarum* (*wāhib al-ṣuwar*) which is considered the demiurge of the material realm due to its capacity to bestow 'forms' upon the matter of this world.[43]

Al-Kirmānī took over al-Fārābī's cosmological system and modified it substantially:[44] to the nine intellects which, in al-Fārābī's cosmology, descend from the outermost Sphere (or starless Sphere) to the sphere of the Moon, al-Kirmānī adds a tenth intellect which, positioned between God and the rest of the intelligible Pleroma, stands above all other intellects and is not linked to the uppermost sphere. In truth, it appears that all intellects but the tenth are prevented any relationship with matter to the extent that they appear to be dissociated from their spheres that are reminiscent of the Ptolemaic astronomical celestial bodies.[45] In contrast to what is believed to occur in the Fārābian schema described above, according to al-Kirmānī the formation of the spheres is enacted through the lowest, tenth intellect which receives

---

[43] On al-Fārābī's adaptation of both Neoplatonic emanation and Ptolemic astronomy to the Islamic paradigms, see Abū Naṣr al-Fārābī, *Mabādi' ārā' ahl al-madīna al-fāḍila* (Beirut, 1982), pp. 100–104, 122. On al-Fārābī's theory of ten intellects and its sources, see Damien Janos, *Method, Structure and Development in al-Fārābī's Cosmology* (Leiden and Boston, 2012); on Avicenna's reading of al-Fārābī's emanative scheme, see Avicenna's *Kitāb al-Najāt* (Cairo, 1923); see also Herbert A. Davidson, *Alfarabi, Avicenna and Averroes on Intellect* (New York and Oxford, 1992), pp. 44–48; Ian R. Netton, *Allāh Transcendent: Studies in the Structure and Semiotics of Islamic Philosophy, Theology and Cosmology* (London and New York, 1989), pp. 114–117. The majority of scholars agree that the theory of ten separate intellects in the emanative schema was firstly elaborated by al-Fārābī. See, for instance, David C. Reisman, 'Al-Fārābī and the Philosophical Curriculum', in *The Cambridge Companion to Arabic Philosophy*, ed. Peter Adamson and Richard C. Taylor (Cambridge, 2005), pp. 52–71; Davidson, *Alfarabi, Avicenna and Averroes on Intellect*, pp. 45–47.

[44] On similarities and differences between al-Fārābī's and al-Kirmānī's conceptions of God and the intellects, see Carmela Baffioni, 'Contrariety and Similarity in God according to al-Farabi and al-Kirmani: A Comparison', in *Classical Arabic Philosophy: Sources and Reception*, ed. Peter Adamson (London and Turin, 2007), pp. 1–20.

[45] De Smet, *La quiétude de l'intellect*, p. 283. On al-Kirmānī's indebtness to al-Fārābī see, *idem*, 'Al-Fārābī's Influence on Ḥamīd al-Dīn al-Kirmānī's Theory of Intellect and Soul', in *In the Age of al-Fārābī: Arabic Philosophy in the Fourth/Tenth Century*, ed. Peter Adamson (London, 2008), pp. 131–150.

from the preceding intellects all the necessary forms, thus acting as the demiurge of the terrestrial domain.[46]

Moreover, differently from al-Fārābī's cosmological features, al-Kirmānī adds the world of religion (*'ālam al-dīn*), which refers to the levels of the Ismaili *da'wa* – namely, the cycles of the prophets and Imams, together with what al-Sijistānī too considered the realm of the religious law (*'ālam al-waḍ'*),[47] encompassing the prescriptions of the *sharī'a*, and the microcosm (*'ālam al-ṣaghīr*), referring to humans. The member of each realm perfectly corresponds to the entity that occupies the same rank in the hierarchy of existence pertaining to a different realm.[48] The understanding that all degrees of existence are connected and mutually symbolised led al-Kirmānī to the awareness that there exist also balance and unity in knowledge.[49] In order to

---

[46]   De Smet, *La quiétude de l'intellect*, p. 274.

[47]   Before al-Kirmānī, it was al-Sijistānī who detailed the diversity of those realms and provided a philosophical and doctrinal framework to the Ismaili hierarchical organisation of the *da'wa* with its dignitaries (*ḥudūd*) becoming constituent parts of the *'ālam al-waḍ'*, the world of normative order (lit. the world of entrusting). By mentioning the concept of *'ālam al-waḍ'* as a third realm above the world of Nature (*'ālam al-ṭabī'a*) and the world of the Soul (*'ālam al-nafs*), al-Sijistānī intended to stress the 'mediative' function of the Ismaili *da'wa*'s members. This idea is further emphasised because, in al-Sijistānī's system, the *'ālam al-waḍ'* is identical to the *'ālam al-dīn*. As Walker clarifies, such an identification is due to the fact that the earthly dignitaries carry the responsibility of implementing and safeguarding religious faith as well as humankind's devotion to it (see Walker, *Early Philosophical Shiism*, pp. 110–111). Indeed, contrary to al-Kirmānī's view, for which the earthly *ḥudūd* represent only members of the world of religion, in al-Sijistānī's *'ālam al-waḍ'* the hierarchy of hypostatical spiritual *ḥudūd* are placed alongside the dignitaries of the *'alam al-dīn*. The spiritual entities of the Intellect, the Soul and the three angels/faculties of *al-jadd*, *al-fatḥ* and *al-khayāl* (on these see more below), are assimilated to the highest physical members of the Ismaili *da'wa*: the law-giving prophets (*nuṭaqā'*), the founders (sg. *asās*), the Imams (or completers, *atimmā'*, sg. *mutimm*), the adjuncts (*lawāḥiq*) and the wings (*ajniḥa*, sg. *janāḥ*). See al-Sijistānī, *Kitāb al-Yanābī'*, ed. and tr. Walker, *The Wellsprings of Wisdom*, p. 118; Simonetta Calderini, "'Ālam al-dīn in Ismā'īlism: World of Obedience or World of Immobility?', *BSOAS*, 56 (1993), pp. 459–469, at 461–462.

[48]   See, in particular, al-Kirmānī, *Rāḥat al-'aql, ed.* Muṣṭafā Ghālib (Beirut, 1967) pp. 184–185, 279.

[49]   On the symbolism of the different degrees of existents in Ismaili thought, see Henry Corbin, *Étude préliminaire pour le 'Livre réunissant les deux sagesses' de Nāṣir-e Khosraw* (Tehran and Paris, 1953), pp. 74–91.

reveal the harmony among all expressions of existence and understanding, al-Kirmānī adopts the method of the balance of religion (*mīzān al-diyāna*), whose methodology aims at establishing an equilibrium between the comprehension of the sensible and intelligible realities acquired through 'foreign sciences' such as Neoplatonic, Fārābian-type metaphysics and Aristotelian physics, and the religious realities disclosed in the Islamic revelation.[50] In the course of this study, it will be observed that al-Kirmānī violated neither his Ismaili beliefs nor his understanding of Aristotelian and Fārābian metaphysics by applying the *mīzān al-diyāna* methodology to his cosmological system. In it, the ten intellects of the *'ālam al-'aql,* which have their correspondent spheres in the world of Nature, are reflected in the ten dignitaries of the Ismaili mission pertaining to the *'ālam al-dīn*.[51] Their role as intermediaries between God and His creation testifies to al-Kirmānī's intention of promoting the programme of the *da'wa* by emphasising the intermediaries' positions as teachers of the knowledge necessary

---

[50] Daniel De Smet, '*Mīzān al-diyāna* ou l'équilibre entre science et religion dans la pensée ismaélienne', *Acta Orientalia Belgica*, 8 (1993), pp. 247–254, at 249–250.

[51] Broadly speaking, for the majority of Ismaili thinkers, there are five higher *ḥudūd* (*al-ḥudūd al-'āliyya*) or spiritual *ḥudūd* (*al-ḥudūd al-rūḥāniyya*) and five lower (*al-ḥudūd al-dāniyya*) or physical *ḥudūd* (*al-ḥudūd al-jismāniyya*). The spiritual *ḥudūd* are given philosophical names, such as Universal Intellect (*al-'aql al-kullī*), Universal Soul (*al-nafs al-kullī*), *al-jadd* (Fortune-Majesty), *al-fatḥ* (Opening-Unveiling) and *al-khayāl* (Vision-Imagination), but they are also often referred to respectively as the Pen (*qalam*), the Tablet (*lawḥ*) and the three archangels Gabriel, Michael and Serafiel. On the origin and meaning of these names, see Nāṣir-i Khusraw, *Khwān al-Ikhwān*, ed. Yaḥyā al-Khashshāb (Cairo, 1359/1940), pp. 170–176; al-Sijistānī, '*Risālat Tuḥfat al-mustajībīn*', pp. 146–155; Corbin, *Étude préliminaire*, pp. 91–112; Hunzai, 'The Concept of *Tawḥīd*', pp. 72–74; Netton, *Allāh Transcendent*, pp. 203–208. Their earthly counterparts are the law-giving prophet (*nāṭiq*), the founder or executor (*asās*), the guide (*imām*), the gate (*bāb*) and the proof (*ḥujja*). Al-Kirmānī, probably driven by the need to find correspondences for the ten intellects of his cosmological schema, slightly strays from this general position and propounds that in the hierarchy of the earthly dimension there exist ten *ḥudūd* which are, however, divided into five ranks: the law-giving prophet, the founder or executor, the Imam, the *ḥujja* and the *dā'ī*. Their specific functions are well explained: 'a lawgiver must legislate laws, a founder must explain and expound them, an Imam must preserve them, a *ḥujja* must teach them, a *dā'ī* must appeal to and create a desire for them'. See al-Kirmānī, *Rāḥat al-'aql*, p. 297, cited in Walker, *Ḥamīd al-Dīn al-Kirmānī*, p. 113.

to serve God. These members, as al-Kirmānī's works testify, not only play a fundamental role in instructing the community on the best way to worship the deity and how to obey His message, thus attaining salvation, but – according to some of the views purported by al-Sijistānī and al-Rāzī, which are critically reviewed by al-Kirmānī – as earthly correspondences to the respective celestial intellects and, in unfurling their mission, they fulfil and actualise the worldly signifiers of *qaḍāʾ* and *qadar*.[52]

The distinction between the visible and invisible realms indicated above, which is alluded to in the Qur'anic distinction between the *ʿālam al-ghayb* and the *ʿālam al-shahāda*,[53] was certainly not new to al-Kirmānī or the Ismailis: Sunni theologians, too, differentiated these dominions, obviously offering for them different interpretations. This was the case for the champion of Sunni Islam, the 'Proof of Islam' (*ḥujjat al-islām*) Abū Ḥāmid al-Ghazālī (d. 505/1111) who speaks of the *jabarūt* realm as a midway kingdom between that of *mulk*, the material world (also called the *ʿālam al-khalq*), and that of *malakūt*, the world of mystery and sovereignty (also called *ʿālam al-amr* or the reign of command). Al-Ghazālī identifies the latter as the world of the preserved Tablet (*al-lawḥ al-maḥfūẓ*) on which divine predestination is recorded. Due to its intermediary status, al-Ghazālī believed the world of *jabarūt* to be conjoined to the world of *malakūt* by the eternal power of God.[54] Although al-Ghazālī never stressed that there occurs a rigid correlation between the things in the world of creation and the realm of command as al-Kirmānī does, he emphasised that being aware of the nature of *jabarūt* allowed humankind to realise that all existents and events of this earthly world are merely symbols (*amthāl*) of the world of *malakūt*.[55] For 'the Proof of Islam', the crossing of the *jabarūt* realm by the wayfarer on the path of knowledge meant discovering the real sense

---

[52]   Al-Kirmānī, *Riyāḍ* (HL), pp. 126–129.

[53]   See, for instance, Q 39:46.

[54]   Kojiro Nakamura, 'Imam Ghazālī's Cosmology Reconsidered with Special Reference to the Concept of "*Jabarūt*"', *Studia Islamica*, 80 (1994), pp. 29–46, at 32–38. On the notion of *khalq* and *amr* in al-Ghazālī, see Duncan B. Macdonald, 'The Development of the Idea of Spirit in Islam', *Acta Orientalia*, 9 (1931), pp. 307–351.

[55]   Al-Ghazālī, *Jawāhir al-Qurʾān wa-duraruh*, cited in Nakamura, 'Imam Ghazālī's Cosmology Reconsidered', p. 33.

of *tawḥīd,* with the human being attaining realisation of God as the ulti-mate disposer of causes and the principle of predestination.[56] In similar terms, it will be observed, al-Kirmānī speaks of the *ʿālam al-dīn* as the point of contact between the world of the Intellect – or world of origina-tion – and the physical world.[57] As an intermediate realm, access to this linking dominion, he clarifies, requires all Ismaili believers to embark on a process of perfection,[58] aiming at developing a deeper understand-ing of their soul, thus necessitating for the latter the acquisition of its full intellectual nature. This is reachable by attaining to the real sense of *tawḥīd* – namely, acknowledgment of all existents' non-divinity – and comprehension of the functions of the *ḥudūd* in the Ismaili hierarchy through whose mediation perfection becomes possible. In order to rec-ognise the dignitaries' status, the believer must obey them as a whole.[59] Consequently, obedience to the dignitaries corresponds to obedience to the highest living dignitary, the Imam of the time, and indirectly, obedience to God.[60] Such a stance will surface in al-Kirmānī's treat-ment of the notions of Resurrection and transmigrationism.

For al-Kirmānī's Ismaili noetics, it is the teaching of the prophets and the Imams – often referred to as the human manifestations of the Agent, or Active, Intellect[61] – that is the instrument through which

---

[56] Al-Ghazālī understood the acquired wayfarer's awareness as the result of a knowledge that is bestowed from a celestial source in terms similar to the Avicennan idea for which the passage from *intellectus possibilis* to *intellectus in actu* is made pos-sible only through the knowledge dispensed by the Agent Intellect. On this argument, see De Cillis, *Free Will and Predestination,* pp. 138–141 and references therein.

[57] Al-Kirmānī, *Riyāḍ,* ed. Ārif Tāmir (Beirut, 1960), pp. 194–195.

[58] Ibid.

[59] The Imam Jaʿfar al-Ṣādiq is reported to have said: 'Through us God is wor-shipped and through us He is obeyed. Thus he who has obeyed us has indeed obeyed God, and he who has disobeyed us has indeed disobeyed God.' See al-Qāḍī al-Nuʿmān, *Daʿāʾm al-Islām,* ed. Asaf A. A. Fyzee (Cairo, 1951–1960), vol. I, p. 57; al-Kirmānī, *Riyāḍ,* p. 146.

[60] Calderini has observed the political implications of al-Kirmānī's doctrine of the dignitaries: obedience to the *ḥudūd* meant obedience to the highest living dig-nitary, the Imam of the time, al-Ḥākim whom al-Kirmānī is called to protect against certain *ghulāt* propositions that saw him as an embodied God. Calderini, *"ʿĀlam al-Dīn* in Ismāʿīlism',* p. 463.

[61] Al-Kirmānī, *Rāḥat al-ʿaql,* pp. 160–161, 165.

the human soul can actualise its potential intellective/rational nature, becoming truly 'human' and thus able to open the door to salvation.[62] The latter, it will be elucidated, Ḥamīd al-Dīn perceived as the result of humans' choosing to obey the guidance of their guides, the Imams. And it is with this perspective in mind that, throughout this study, the *'ālam al-dīn* will disclose itself to be the dominion in which the notion of a merciless predestination is relativised: by bringing forward a religious law and by providing instructions on its injunctions in both their exoteric and esoteric aspects, the members of this realm allow the believer to understand and experience that the way to recompense and reward transcends any ruthless predestinarian perspective.

Now, should the question of predestination from a Fatimid Ismaili angle be shifted onto the level of the Intellect's realm given that God is beyond any direct relationship with the created world? Is it then the Intellect who takes on the 'duties' of the Qur'anic God and His role as Predeterminer? Or are the prophets and the Imams, as human manifestations of the Intellect and the Soul respectively, responsible for predestination? Is there any predestination given that human agents are free to choose between good and evil after having been guided by their authoritative teachers?

The present investigation will attempt to tackle these and further questions. It is divided into two main parts: the first, rather than being merely an introduction to the second part, provides an overview of al-Kirmānī's central ideas, investigating the influence exercised on his thought and works by, *inter alia*, the writings of Plotinus and Proclus, the Neoplatonic-inspired al-Fārābī, and al-Kirmānī's fellow *dā'īs* al-Nasafī, al-Sijistānī and al-Rāzī. By analysing primary and secondary sources, the first section aims to familiarise the reader with al-Kirmānī's theories on God, cosmogony, cosmology, the notion of the imamate, the eschatological roles of prophets and Imams, and so forth. In addition, it attempts to provide links between the foregoing concepts and the notions of *qaḍā'* and *qadar*.

---

[62] De Smet argues that this teaching becomes the necessary condition for all kinds of human rational thought. Without such teaching, philosophy, the natural sciences as well as the interpretation of the Qur'an and of the *sharī'a* would be impossible. The harmony between all these sciences finds its basis within the Imams' teaching. De Smet, '*Mīzān al-diyāna*', p. 253.

The second part focuses more specifically on the issue of pre-destination by looking in particular at the concepts of *qaḍāʾ* and *qadar* as these are presented in the eighth chapter of al-Kirmānī's *Riyāḍ*. To this end, this work offers a translation and a thorough analysis of that eighth chapter, providing extracts in translation from several of al-Sijistānī's works (in an endeavour to corroborate the views he held in the no longer extant *Kitāb al-Nuṣra*) as well as al-Rāzī's *Kitāb al-Iṣlāḥ*, whose shortcomings were denounced in al-Kirmānī's *Riyāḍ*.

One of the main aims of this study is to clarify why al-Kirmānī links the notion of actuality to the problematic task of identifying which entity corresponded to the figure of the Antecedent (*sābiq*). As will emerge from the analysis of the eighth chapter of the *Riyāḍ*, whereas al-Kirmānī's fellow *dāʿī*s, al-Nasafī, al-Sijistānī and al-Rāzī, made such an entity correspond either to the *qaḍāʾ* or the *qadar*, al-Kirmānī's rejection of some of his fellow Ismailis' ideas and the emphasis placed on the identification of the Antecedent with the first originated being – (*al-mubdaʿ al-awwal*), that is, the Intellect – was intended to avoid connecting the *sābiq* with the eternal divine *amr/kalima* (Command) which was thought by such pivotal Ismaili thinkers to precede even the first intellect, thus entailing an elusive form of *shirk* (polytheism) to be in place.

It will be further observed why al-Kirmānī charges the notion of actuality of the *qāʾim* in particular, and the imamate in general, with high importance in order to prove, besides their necessary character, the mistaken nature of al-Sijistānī's and al-Rāzī's outlooks. Further, the necessity of the imamate comes to be associated with the task of demonstrating – in the discourse on predestination – which of *qaḍāʾ* and *qadar* corresponds to the *nāṭiq* and which to the Imam of the time. For al-Kirmānī, establishing the precedence of the prophet over the Imam as the manifested/actualised forms of the Antecedent and the Follower brought in also the delicate discourse of having to institute the precedence (and indispensability) of the prophetic *sharīʿa* (including all its precepts and injunctions) over its solely esoteric explanation which, carried out by the Imam, was perceived as the major tool triggering the passage from the potentiality embedded in the religious law – locked into its exoteric facet – to its fully actualised character.

Other significant issues will be touched upon in the discussion on the divine decree: particularly, it will be analysed why al-Sijistānī's belief – apparently explicitly stated in *al-Nuṣra* – that the Soul could be identified with the actualised *qadar* urged al-Kirmānī to challenge the difficult question of the Soul's fall into Nature and its lurking underpinnings of transmigration (*tanāsukh*).[63]

Overall, this study will reveal in what terms al-Kirmānī's discourse on *qaḍāʾ* and *qadar* served as the grounds on which to consolidate fundamental doctrinal points whose Fatimid Ismaili nature needed to become definitive.

---

[63] If it is admitted that everything is already predetermined, given that all things in existence are already encompassed as forms in the unicity of the Intellect, one might ask whether individual souls can be perceived as pre-existing their bodies and, if so, why metempsychosis should be inconceivable. Daniel Gimaret individuates two forms of transmigration used in heresiographical sources, particularly the 'transmigration of spirits' (*tanāsukh al-arwāḥ*) or metempsychosis/metensomatosis and the transmigration of a divine element from one Imam to another. See Gimaret, '*Tanāsukh*', *EI2*, vol. 10, pp. 181–183. On the various forms of *tanāsukh*, see also Hermann Landolt, 'Ismāʿīlī and Ṣūfī Attitudes to Transmigration', in *International Congress of Human Sciences in Asia and North Africa. Proceedings of ICHSANA*, vol. I, ed. Y. Tatsuro (Tokyo, 1984), pp. 293–294 [abstract of paper]; Wilferd Madelung, 'Abū Yaʿqūb al-Sijistānī and Metempsychosis', in *Iranica Varia: Papers in Honor of Professor Ehsan Yarshater*, ed. D. Amin, M. Kasheff and A. Sh. Shahbazi (Leiden, 1990), pp. 131–143; Paul E. Walker, 'The Doctrine of Metempsychosis in Islam', in *Islamic Studies Presented to Charles J. Adams*, ed. Wael B. Hallaq and Donald P. Little (Leiden, 1991), pp. 219–238.

PART ONE

DELINEATING AL-KIRMĀNĪ'S THEORETICAL SYSTEM

1

The Plotinian Legacy and al-Sijistānī's Influence: A Preliminary Approach to al-Kirmānī's Understanding of the Intellect

In order to establish whether and to what extent the *ʿālam al-dīn* and its components, rather than the *ʿālam al-ʿaql*, can be linked to the Qurʾanic notions of *qaḍāʾ* and *qadar*, it is essential to investigate al-Kirmānī's views of the Intellect, his origin, his relationship with God and with the other intellects in the celestial Pleroma. Even prior to that, it might be helpful to outline by what means and through which sources of inspiration al-Kirmānī's thought was sculpted. We can do this by looking in particular at Plotinus, al-Fārābī and al-Sijistānī.

Al-Kirmānī is by and large credited with having introduced into Ismaili cosmology al-Fārābī's hierarchical emanatory schema of ten separate intellects which, new to Ismailism, will also be adopted by the majority of *falāsifa* such as Ibn Sīnā (Avicenna, d. 428/1037) who considered themselves to be peripatetics.[1] On the one hand, al-Kirmānī's understanding of God or, rather, his way of stressing the impossibility of knowing Him or of addressing Him in terms of 'being', testifies that al-Kirmānī followed Plotinus (d. 270 CE) – who regarded 'being' as belonging to the category of creation and therefore incapable of designating God. On the other hand, al-Kirmānī, following earlier Ismaili philosophers like al-Sijistānī, permeated his cosmology with monotheistic and creationistic adaptations derived from the *Neoplatonica Arabica*,[2] insisting on the uniqueness of the divine act of *ibdāʿ*

---

[1]   Netton, *Allāh Transcendent*, p. 223.

[2]   In this corpus, the One, delineated by Plotinus, is identified with the Aristotelian First Principle as this is described in the Book *Lambda* of Aristotle's *Metaphysics*. See Peter Adamson, *The Arabic Plotinus: A Philosophical Study of the 'Theology of Aristotle'* (London, 2002), pp. 111–137.

(origination) and its irreconcilability with the original ideas on emanation expressed by Plotinus and Proclus.[3]

Our first task, which is to understand whether and to what extent al-Kirmānī borrows and adapts from Plotinus, requires a review of the latter's main metaphysical positions. For Plotinus, the domain of being begins at the level of the first intellect (*Nous*) and, accordingly, the first intellect enjoys merely a relative independence because his existence actually depends on the One. The latter, which represents the most mystifying concept in Plotinus' philosophy, as Armstrong suggests, can be approached from a positive and a negative perspective. According to the first perspective, It is called a pure will,[4] absolute energy (ἐνέργεια),[5] love, love of Itself, cause of Itself and of all that proceeds from It. From this standpoint, the One is not simply an ineffable 'ground of being' standing outside any possible definition or perception, but it is rather an entity that has the predicable, identifiable aspects of a first cause, such as that of having a will that openly wills

---

[3]   Al-Kirmānī clearly propounds that the first intellect does not owe his existence to himself. Rather, his existence is due to the originating act of God (*ibdāʿ*), with which he is partially identified and through which all creatures are generated 'at once' (*dafʿat*^{an} *wāḥidat*^{an}). The Intellect in effect already possesses in himself all the other entities in the hierarchy of existence, as in Plotinus. See his *Enneads*, V. 5.9. In all probability, al-Nasafī was the first to speak of the Intellect in terms of *ibdāʿ* as an extra-temporal instantiation. Originated 'at once' by the Creator, the Intellect contains in himself all the forms of the two worlds (the spiritual and the material worlds). On this topic, see the references to al-Nasafī's *Kitāb al-Maḥṣūl* quoted in al-Kirmānī's *Riyāḍ* (Beirut, 1960), p. 220. Al-Sijistānī reiterates al-Nasafī's concept by saying that the Intellect contains in himself the seed of both worlds (*tukhm-i dū jahān*). See al-Sijistānī, *Kashf al-maḥjūb*, partial English trans. Hermann Landolt as *Unveiling of the Hidden*, in *An Anthology of Philosophy in Persia, vol. II*, ed. Nasr and Aminrazavi, p. 93, pp. 96–97; French trans. Henry Corbin as *Le dévoilement des choses cachées* (Lagrasse, 1988), pp. 55–57. This idea is reiterated in al-Sijistānī's *Kitāb al-Yanābīʿ*, 124; *The Wellsprings of Wisdom*, pp. 79–80. On *ibdāʿ* see also Carmela Baffioni, 'Ibdaʿ, Divine Imperative and Prophecy in the *Rasāʾil Ikhwān al-Ṣafāʾ*', in *Fortresses of the Intellect: Ismaili and other Islamic Studies in Honour of Farhad Daftary*, ed. Omar Ali-de-Unzaga (London-New York, 2011), pp. 213–226.

[4]   Plotinus, *Enneads*, VI. 8.13, 21. Arthur H. Armstrong, *The Architecture of the Intelligible Universe in the Philosophy of Plotinus* (Cambridge, 1940, repr. Cambridge, 2013), p. 3.

[5]   Plotinus, *Enneads*, V. 6.6.

Itself and all that comes from It.[6] The positive side of the One makes It a substance (ousia, οὐσία), or rather a One-Many, namely, a being to which predicates can be applied just like the Aristotelian Theos (θεός).[7] By contrast, Plotinus advances another view from which to address the One: a 'negative' way, regarding It as an inextricable oneness, impossible to divide even in thought. The One becomes, in this sense, a primal unity standing outside any intellectual or intuitive perception.[8] As the result of the Pythagorean tendency to read Platonism as a philosophy of numbers, the One – seen from this angle – becomes a principle of measure or limit that is beyond what Itself measures or limits; It is the mathematical One, the source of all numbers whose nature, being beyond boundaries, could be better conveyed if compared to the symbol of zero,[9] or to John Scotus Eriugena's concept of nothing.[10]

---

[6] Armstrong, *The Architecture of the Intelligible Universe*, pp. 3–4.

[7] The One of Plotinus – in Its positive aspect – as a self-directed, self-loving God whose Being is Acts directed towards Its own perfection, transcends the Aristotelian concept of God as a self-thinking Mind. Particularly, as it is described in the *Enneads*, the One, with Its inevitable duality between subject and object, does not merely think Itself, but wills and loves Itself too. This, Armstrong explains, might be due to the fact that the *Enneads* was primarily concerned with the question of free will and that, in addition, Plotinus must have been aware that the unity of a self-willing and self-loving entity had less of the duality implied in the idea of a subject of knowledge which becomes the object of its own thinking activity. Ibid., pp. 12–13.

[8] Plotinus must have realised that in order to free the One from any ascription or determination, the latter must be beyond intellect. Any thinking activity would have inferred a duality derived from the One becoming limited as the subject-object of Its own thinking.

[9] William R. Inge, *The Philosophy of Plotinus* (London and New York, 1948; repr. London, 1954), vol. II, pp. 107–108.

[10] Plotinus speaks of the Pythagoreans, who symbolically called the One 'Apollo' (Ἀπόλλων from ἀ-πολύς, non-plurality) – a name which is the very negation of multiplicity. See Plotinus, *Enneads*, V. 5.6; see also Armstrong, *The Architecture of the Intelligible Universe*, pp. 26–28; *idem, The Cambridge History of Later Greek and Early Medieval Philosophy* (Cambridge, 1980), pp. 236ff; Hunzai, 'The Concept of *Tawḥīd*', p. 67. According to al-Kirmānī though, the essence of the Intellect bridges unicity and multiplicity (*yakūn jāmiʿ liʾl-wāḥida waʾl-kathīra*). As highlighted by Peterson, this is a peculiar kind of unity which can be better understood as a form of unification; see Daniel C. Peterson, 'Cosmogony in the *Rāḥat al-ʿaql* of Ḥamīd al-Dīn al-Kirmānī', PhD thesis (Los Angeles, 1990), p. 421. The unity of the Intellect is a participative

When Plotinus investigates the question of how the One generates Intellect, the answer that he provides is somewhat ambiguous as he does not state anywhere that the One performs any 'activity'. Conversely, Nous is the first stage in the emanation of the universe from the One. Nous is described as a spontaneous and necessary efflux of life (or power) from the One, which leaves his source untouched. The relationship occurring between the One and the Intellect is defined in metaphorical terms like that between the sun and its light,[11] a clarification that Plotinus himself regarded as rather unsatisfactory.[12] On some occasions, however, Plotinus describes the Intellect as being almost capable of self-generation, such as when he states that 'by his [Intellect's] return to It [the One], he sees: and this seeing (ὅρασις) is Intellect.'[13] The Intellect's action of gazing upon the One grants the Intellect his share in being because '[the Intellect] halts and turns

---

unity and even when the Intellect is seen as life, namely as the most *primal* expression of self-sufficient 'essentiality' (logically prior and independent of the other attributes), he still preserves, in his nature as the *ibdāʿ*, the multiplicity of all further attributes that are already entailed in the very first divine creative act of origination. This implies that the Intellect's nature, as a merely *relative* unity, is decreed through God's choice of originating the Intellect via *ibdāʿ*. Absolute unity cannot be associated with the Intellect but must transcend and precede the Intellect. One would expect that ultimate oneness or unity must pertain to the essence of the Plotinian One, however, al-Kirmānī believes that the Ultimate Reality transcends all numbers including the number one. Al-Kirmānī, *Rāḥat al-ʿaql*, pp. 178–179, pp. 240–241; *idem, al-Risāla al-Durriyya fī maʿnā al-tawḥīd*, in *Majmūʿat rasāʾil al-Kirmānī*, ed. Muṣṭafā Ghālib (Beirut, 1969), pp. 21–23. This treatise has been translated into English by Faquir M. Hunzai as '*al-Risālat al-durriyah*', in *An Anthology of Philosophy in Persia, vol. II*, ed. Nasr and Aminrazavi, pp. 200–207.

[11] Plotinus, *Enneads*, I. 7.1, V. 1.7, V. 3.12, VI. 8.18, VI. 9.9. In Plotinus' system, light is given a very special status on the border between the physical, material realm and the spiritual dimension. It is no longer, as in Stoic or Aristotelian materialism, merely a physical occurrence but, thanks to the strict parallelism drawn between life and light, rather 'a manifestation of the spiritual principle of reality or activity in the luminary, its λόγος or εἶδος'. Armstrong, *The Architecture of the Intelligible Universe*, p. 54.

[12] Plotinus, *Enneads*, VII. 6.4. Armstrong suggests that the concept of emanation does not have any precise philosophical meaning; it rather belongs to the domain of metaphors, like in the classical image of the sun and the rays that emanated from the luminous source. Arthur H. Armstrong, 'Emanation in Plotinus', *Mind*, 46 (1937), pp. 61–62.

[13] Plotinus, *Enneads*, V. 1.7, tr. Armstrong (Cambridge, MA, 1966–1988).

toward the One that he may see, [and] he becomes at once Intellect and being'.[14] What this means is that it is absolutely necessary for the One to be existent, so that the Intellect may turn towards It and make It the object of his 'seeing'. The One is, from this perspective, the source or the ultimate principle on which the Intellect depends for his existence. The identification between, on the one hand, the Intellect's intrinsic intellectual activity which pertains to his essence as an intellect (permanently in actuality and therefore a true existent) and, on the other hand, his quiddity, which is given by the immediate intuition of the object of his intellection, makes the Intellect a unity.[15] Significantly, Plotinus hastens to specify that, in contrast to any other intellect in which the objects of intellectual action and the essence as intelligible are coupled, the first intellect 'thinks not by seeking but by having [knowledge]'.[16] This explains that the Intellect's knowledge is 'locked' within his essence, or rather that his knowledge is his essence. The Intellect is what he thinks/knows. Consequently, the Intellect's contemplative activity is actually directed towards himself and this allows the Intellect to remain fundamentally a simplex.[17]

Despite this, the Intellect's 'halting' and his simultaneous 'turning' towards the One/Source so that it may 'see' It, indicate that a kind of duality and connected activity, involving plurality and movement, are present.[18] Yet, it is his inherent duality in unity that makes the Intellect

---

[14] Émile Bréhier, *The Philosophy of Plotinus*, tr. Joseph Thomas (Chicago, 1958), p. 189.

[15] 'In the Nous, contemplation is intellectual knowledge. The Nous possesses, or rather, *is* truth because there is in [him] the *identity* of knower, knowing, and thing known, of contemplator, contemplation and object of contemplation.' See John N. Deck, *Nature, Contemplation and the One: A Study in the Philosophy of Plotinus* (Toronto, 1967), p. 25 cited in Peterson, *Cosmogony in the Rāḥat al-ʿaql*, p. 398. My emphasis.

[16] Plotinus, *Enneads*, V. 1.4

[17] Ibid., V. 3. 5–6. Plotinus stresses that 'contemplation ascends from Nature to Soul, and Soul to Intellect, and the contemplations become always more intimate and united to the contemplators [...] the objects known tend to become identical with the knowing subject [...] In Intellect, thinking and being are the same.' He adds: 'this is living contemplation, not an object of contemplation like that in something else'. See his *Enneads*, III. 8.8.

[18] Inge, *The Philosophy of Plotinus*, vol. II, p. 64. The same paradoxical combination of stillness and movement in the Intellect is reported in the Pseudo-Aristotle's

resemble the One in Its positive aspect as the οὐσία/One-Many. Nous almost becomes the One as the ultimate principle and highest point of unity. In some instances, one might even sense Plotinus' intention to invalidate any real distinction between the One and Nous. This impression is offered in some passages of the *Enneads* in which the whole idea of emanation is undermined because no real distinction is implied between the source of emanation and the emanant.[19] Intellect's multiplicity in unity is implicit even more when Plotinus states that the Intellect 'is the real beings' (literally, 'what they actually are' Ὁ νοῦς ἄρα τὰ ὄντα ὄντως'),[20] and that the 'Intellect is [embraces] the totality of things'.[21] Implicitly, it is suggested that the Intellect already 'contains' in himself all the other hypostases: 'since the [Intellect] has real existence, he knows and posits reality [… Intellect] is all that really exists'.[22] But Plotinus also recalls that 'all things are in the One',[23] that is, organically connected to the One.[24] As this is the case, one might wonder what has happened to the gulf between the Nous and the One which is so characteristic of Plotinus' thought?

According to Armstrong, a real 'otherness' between the two levels appears when a religious, or theological, sense is conveyed onto the One. This occurs when the One is considered as God, as 'the transcendent, worshipful "being-above-being"'.[25] Given that the basic element in worship is the distinction between the object and the subject of worship, it follows that the otherness between the One-God and the Nous comes to be emphasised. The transcendence and separateness between the two is stressed any time the intellectual activity of Nous is accentuated. In these instances, the One becomes the primary object of the second hypostasis' contemplation which,

---

Theology of Aristotle, p. 137, quoted in Peterson, *Cosmogony in the Rāḥat al-ʿaql*, p. 404.

[19] See the passages cited by Armstrong, *The Architecture of the Intelligible Universe*, pp. 59–60.

[20] Plotinus, *Enneads*, V. 9.5.

[21] Ibid., V. 1.4; VI. 7.8 cited in Peterson, *Cosmogony in the Rāḥat al-ʿaql*, p. 399.

[22] Inge, *The Philosophy of Plotinus*, p. 63.

[23] Plotinus, *Enneads*, V. 5.9.

[24] Ibid., V. 3.12; V. 2.1.

[25] Armstrong, *The Architecture of the Intelligible Universe*, p. 31.

by its act of contemplation, generates the multiplicity of Ideas. The generation of multiplicity from the absolute unity of the One is a factor Plotinus insists upon. This is explained as the result of the inadequacy of the contemplating intellect to reproduce the absolute unity in himself. The activity of contemplation unfurls itself in two stages: in the first stage, Nous (as a 'sight no longer seeing') attempts to apprehend the One in Its simplicity; unsuccessful, in the second stage, it comes out holding that which he himself has multiplied.[26]

In al-Kirmānī's cosmogonic-cosmological schema, the insistence on the remoteness and absolute transcendence of God and the endeavour to identify a relationship between the ineffable deity and His first originated being are discussed with similar prominence. The positive aspect that Plotinus ascribes to the One is shifted by al-Kirmānī onto the Intellect that becomes, in effect, the Plotinian One-Many, leaving the deity shrouded in His unknowability. For al-Kirmānī, no created being, including the Intellect, is necessary per se as all things in existence depend upon the divinely willed act of origination (*ibdā'*): any 'being' (*ays*) can be nothing else but a 'being put-into-being' (*mu'ayyas*).[27] Consequently, al-Kirmānī denounces the futility (*buṭlān*) of attributing God with *ays*,[28] espousing Plotinus' idea that the One is 'beyond being'.[29]

---

[26] Ibid., p. 69.

[27] De Smet, *La quiétude de l'intellect*, pp. 42–44.

[28] Al-Kirmānī, *Rāḥat al-'aql*, pp. 131–134. On the etymology and technical significance of *ays* and its contrary *lays*, see Muḥammad b. Mūsā Khwārizmī, *Mafātiḥ al-'ulūm*, ed. G. Van Vloten (Tehran, 1968), p. 23; William Wright, *A Grammar of the Arabic Language*, 3rd ed., vol. I (Cambridge, 1981), p. 96. On al-Kirmānī's use of the terms, see De Smet, *La quiétude de l'intellect*, pp. 41–44 and 83–84.

[29] Plotinus, *Enneads*, V. 5.6. In truth, according to Plotinus the One can be approached, in one way, as an absolute unity whose ground of 'being' is beyond any other ground, a substance to which 'being' cannot be attributed in terms similar to any other substance. *Enneads*, V. 5.13. See MacKenna's translation: '[The only way not to alter Its nature as Absolute Good is ...] to permit only the "*It is*", in which we pretend no affirmation of non-existent attribute' (my emphasis). On the other hand, the One can be also perceived as participating in the cosmos, thus becoming connected to Its 'ground of being', in harmony with what Plotinus' emanationist system necessitates.

However, al-Kirmānī takes a different stand on the emanatory schema of Plotinus and stresses its being at odds with the divine act of *ibdāʿ* described in the Qurʾan. In so doing, he follows his predecessor al-Sijistānī, for whom the divine act of origination, which is accomplished through the divine Command (*amr*) – also referred to as the Word (*kalima*) – is perfect and there is no need to modify or add to it in any way.[30] This means that the successive procession of the nine following intellects from the first *ʿaql* which characterises the Neoplatonic emanative cosmological schema would have been redundant for al-Sijistānī. For al-Sijistānī, the creation of all beings is encompassed within the original act of *ibdāʿ* and God does not need to issue a second command of origination or to trigger a series of emanations, since His creation is already perfect and complete.

Al-Sijistānī sets the command outside any temporal framework and proposes that the *amr* is a *laysa* ('not') (*nafy al-aysiyya wa'l-laysiyya* – neither 'being' nor 'non-being'), thus implicitly inferring its un-manifestedness (that is, its un-actualised aspect).[31] This represented a problem for intellectuals such as al-Kirmānī who detected in this thought a clear form of *shirk*.[32] As will become evident in the

---

[30]   Al-Sijistānī speaks of the Intellect by referring to terms such as *kamāl* (perfection) and *ghunya* (self-subsistence). In addition, the Intellect is also addressed with references to the notions of *dahr* (eternity), *ḥaqq* (truth) and *ḥayāt* (life) among others. See al-Sijistānī, *Kitāb al-Yanābīʿ*, pp. 115–117; *The Wellsprings of Wisdom*, pp. 68–70. See also Walker, *Early Philosophical Shiism*, pp. 90–91; *idem*, 'Cosmic Hierarchies in Early Ismaili Thought', p. 19 note 32. It will be observed that the notion of the Intellect as 'the Living' is of primary importance in al-Kirmānī's understanding of the nature of the first originated being. See pp. 96–97 below.

[31]   Al-Sijistānī, *Kitāb al-Yanābīʿ*, p. 39. See also al-Kirmānī, 'al-Risāla al-muḍīʾa fī al-amr wa'l-āmir wa'l-maʾmūr', ed. Muṣṭafā Ghālib, in *Majmūʿat rasāʾil al-Kirmānī* (Beirut, 1969), pp. 49–53; Hamid Haji, *A Distinguished Dāʿī under the Shade of the Fatimids: Ḥamīd al-Dīn al-Kirmānī and His Epistles* (London, 1998), p. 31.

[32]   Abū Ḥātim al-Rāzī was the object of gentler criticism probably because he identified the *amr* with *ibdāʿ* and clarified that the act of origination, as the command (and as prime matter, *al-hayūlā al-ūlā*), is 'conceptual' or 'imaginal' (*wahmī*) in that its essence (*dhāt*) is actualised only through the Intellect, that is, the first originated thing (*al-mubdaʿ al-awwal*). See al-Rāzī, *Kitāb al-Iṣlāḥ*, p. 39. This implicitly denies any separate hypostatic manifestation of the *amr*. The *ibdāʿ/amr* and the Intellect are considered one being (*ays wāḥid*) in manifestation, which is a position clearly shared by al-Kirmānī and many other Ismaili Neoplatonists. See al-Rāzī, ibid., pp. 24–27, 32,

following study on *qaḍāʾ* and *qadar*, particularly subject to his criticism was al-Sijistānī's identification of the *amr/kalima* with the Antecedent (*sābiq*), which suggested not only that the Command/Word as a non-existentiated entity (*lā muʾayyas*) was co-existent with God, but also that it preceeded the *ʿaql* which was commonly understood to be the first originated being (*al-mubdaʿ al-awwal*).[33] In contrast to this position, al-Kirmānī, attempting to break away from a purely Plotinian emanative outlook, explicitly denounces the impossibility for any true Ismaili believer to affirm that the Intellect is originated through the *amr/kalima* – thus denying that the Intellect is preceded by it – and argues that the Intellect is rather the essence of the *amr/kalima*, which are also synonyms of *ibdāʿ*.[34] In his view, the process of emanation and its source cannot strictly speaking be differentiated because, though not identical, they are linked together in existence (like the sun and the light emanating from it).[35] God instantiates the first intellect via

---

35–39, 48–49; al-Kirmānī, *Riyāḍ* (Beirut, 1960), pp. 58, pp. 101–102, 119, 139; Heinz Halm, *Kosmologie und heilslehre der frühen Ismāʿīlīya: Eine studie zur Islamischen gnosis* (Wiesbaden, 1978), pp. 128–131, 224. Further references in Michael Ebstein, *Mysticism and Philosphy in al-Andalus: Ibn Masarra, Ibn al-ʿArabī and the Ismāʿīlī Tradition* (Leiden and Boston, 2014), p. 44 note 43. However, al-Kirmānī rejects al-Rāzī's definition of the *amr* as the first cause (*al-ʿilla al-ūlā*) because this inferred its role as the intermediary by which God instantiated the Intellect. Al-Kirmānī specifies that just as prime matter is conceptual (*wahmī*), so is the first originated being, which is not a body and, therefore, can be predicated neither through motion nor rest. His argument is constructed to reply to al-Rāzī's analogy of motion and rest as spirit to matter and form, and reject the opposite views held by al-Nasafī and al-Sijistānī who identified motion and quiescence as the body (*jism*) for both matter and form. Al-Kirmānī, *Riyāḍ* (Beirut, 1960), pp. 135–142. Similar discussions are to be found in Poonawala's Introduction, p. 40.

[33]   On the identification between the *kalima* and the Antecedent/Intellect see al-Sijistānī, *Kitāb al-Yanābīʿ*, p. 72; trans. Walker, *The Wellsprings of Wisdom*, p. 50; Walker, *Early Philosophical Shiʿism*, pp. 82–83; *idem*, 'Cosmic Hierarchies in Early Ismaili Thought', p. 19. It is upon manifestation that the *amr/kalima* is united with the Intellect and, because of this conjunction, the first originated being becomes the source of multiplicity, namely, the Plotinian οὐσία. On the topic of al-Sijistānī's concept of *wāḥid* and its relation with the divine command, see Hunzai, 'The Concept of *Tawḥīd*', p. 88.

[34]   Al-Kirmānī, *Riyāḍ*, Ch. 4. See also discussions in Poonawala's Introduction, p. 39.

[35]   Azim Nanji, 'Ismaili Philosophy', in *History of Islamic Philosophy*, ed. Oliver Leaman and Seyyed Hossein Nasr (London, 2008), vol. I, p. 150.

*ibdā*ʿ which is an absolute innovative act, different from the action of *khalq* which is said to occur from a thing (*min shay*ʾ).[36]

Despite his criticism of al-Sijistānī, the problematic question of what constitutes the nature of the *ibdā*ʿ prior to its joining with the Intellect is only hinted at by al-Kirmānī too. He explains that in its 'self-disclosure', *ibdā*ʿ is identical with the first originated being which is instantiated through it.[37] Therefore, at the level of the originated entities, *ibdā*ʿ becomes nothing else but the first intellect. More precisely, the essence of *ibdā*ʿ becomes the object of the Intellect's thought with which the Intellect identifies himself. So *ibdā*ʿ (the act of origination)

---

[36]   Henry Corbin defines *ibdā*ʿ as a timeless existentiation, an 'instauration créatrice primordiale'. See Henry Corbin, 'Étude préliminaire', in Nāṣir-i Khusraw, *Jāmiʿ al-ḥikmatayn*, ed. Henry Corbin and M. Muʿīn (Tehran and Paris, 1953), p. 114. Walker has stressed that the term *ibdā*ʿ corresponds to the act of bringing about something not from something (*lā min shay*ʾ). He has pointed out that it is not accurate to see this act as the bringing about of something out of nothing since the term 'nothing' (or 'nothingness') does not indicate a prior situation – namely, a situation that precedes in time the presence of something. This is because no-thing is simply the negation of some-thing, not a prior condition (Walker, *Ismaili Thought in the Age of al-Ḥākim*, p. 92). In addition, Walker stresses that *ibdā*ʿ marks the 'radical coming-to-be of being from what is not-being […] is an innovation rather than a beginning, for beginning implies an ending'. See his 'The Ismaili Vocabulary of Creation', p. 82. The latter view resembles Ibn Sīnā's stance on the issue: '*ibdā*ʿ is the becoming of existence of a thing from another thing, which depends only on it without the intermediary of any matter, instrument or time'. Ibn Sīnā, *al-Ishārāt waʾl-tanbīhāt* cited in Hunzai, 'The Concept of Tawḥīd''', p. 79. On De Smet's views of *ibdā*ʿ, see his *La quiétude de l'intellect*, pp. 41–44, 87–89, 101–102.

[37]   It should be noted that al-Sijistānī also speaks of the command as becoming manifest with Intellect. He goes so far as to explain how the Intellect becomes one with the *amr* when the latter is expressed as Oneness, Word, Knowledge, and the Command itself. Notwithstanding this idea, al-Sijistānī continued to profess a sort of precedence of the Command over the Intellect. Such precedence, which is not temporal, is emphasised in al-Sijistānī's identification of the Command with the act of 'making-to-be' or Origination, and of Intellect with the first 'made-to-be' or Originated being. Moreover, Intellect's awareness of his own existence is said to occur only after the passage from the stage of Origination (*gāh-i ibdā*ʿ) to the stage of generation (*gāh-i tawlīd*) has occurred, thus hinting at *amr*'s precedence. Al-Sijistānī, *Kashf al-maḥjūb*, tr. Landolt, *Unveiling of the Hidden*, pp. 91–96. Against *amr*'s antecedence, see al-Kirmānī, *Riyāḍ* (Beirut, 1960), p. 66; Habib Feki, *Les idées religieuses et philosophiques de l'is-maélisme fatimide* (Tunis, 1978), p. 104.

and *mubdaʿ* (the object of the act of origination) are conceived as two different faces, referring to the same essence of the Intellect, which are capable of expressing two different aspects or qualities of the Intellect without implying any plurality within it. To validate this point, al-Kirmānī states that the Intellect is one in essence and multiple with regard to his ascriptions (*wāḥid bi'l-dhāt kathīr bi'l-iḍāfāt*), thus resembling Plotinus' One-Many.[38]

One might be tempted to think that *ibdāʿ*, occurring between the domain of non-being (as the act originated by the Principle) and being (once it enters existence it is one with the first originated being), is the first (and only) entity that humans can correlate with God and His 'actions'. This, however, from an Ismaili perspective is not admissible: even if in Ismaili metaphysics the Godhead is believed to 'originate' through the act of *ibdāʿ*, there cannot be any relations ascribed to God. God cannot ever be known, since only what participates in being can be understood,[39] and what participates in being is necessarily a 'thing'.

---

[38] Al-Kirmānī, *Rāḥat al-ʿaql*, p. 177; De Smet, *La quiétude de l'intellect*, pp. 148–149. Elsewhere, De Smet has explained that in al-Kirmānī's view, *ibdāʿ* can be perceived as the name of the Intellect seen from the view of his 'instauration' in conjunction with the Principle on which his self-instauration depends. In turn, *mubdaʿ* must be understood as the name of the Intellect in his quality as an instantiated being, and as the product of his self-instauration which is perceived in relation to his essence. The divine imperative, *amr/kalima*, which for al-Sijistānī is the cause of the Intellect, is for al-Kirmānī simply another name for the Intellect's essence. De Smet, *La quiétude de l'intellect*, pp. 122–123.

[39] Al-Kirmānī mentions that the canonical 'five ways' to attain understanding of God – definition (*ḥadd*), analysis (*taḥlīl*), division (*qisma*), composition (*tarkīb*) and demonstration (*burhān*) – are in fact inadequate for this task (al-Kirmānī, *Rāḥat al-ʿaql*, p. 137). Whilst for al-Fārābī, the weakness (*ḍaʿf*) and the imperfect nature (*naqṣ*) of the human intellect make perception of God simply difficult, for al-Kirmānī the latter is utterly impossible. The Ultimate Reality remains always concealed because of the incapacity (*ʿajz*) of both celestial and human intellects to transcend their essences by thinking or apprehending what is neither intellect nor intelligible (De Smet, 'Al-Fārābī's Influence', p. 137). God is so well concealed from His creatures also because they lack, in their essences, the necessary strength (*quwwa*) to address God with any attribute that may potentially truly pertain to Him. Significantly, al-Kirmānī refers to a dazzling power (*al-qudra al-bāhira*) which makes humans incapable of perceiving what God can be equated to. See al-Kirmānī, *Rāḥat al-ʿaql*, p. 135.

As al-Kirmānī explains, the act of *ibdāʿ* can only be associated with that 'thing' which is at the summit of creation:

> [It] came into existence through *ibdāʿ* and *ikhtirāʿ*, not from a thing (*lā min shayʾ*), not related to a thing (*lā ʿalā shayʾ*), not in a thing (*lā fī shayʾ*), not through a thing (*lā bi-shayʾ*), not for a thing (*lā li-shayʾ*), and not with a thing (*lā maʿa shayʾ*): it is the first thing (*al-shayʾ al-āwwal*).[40]

These views beg the question: how can the action of origination be associated with a God who remains unknown and unknowable, placed beyond any form of speculative and even intuitive activity? The answer to this is that *ibdāʿ* does not constitute an action as such but it is rather a term alluding to the relationship occurring between God and the first originated thing which pertains to the level of being and which can be consequently grasped or understood by humans. The first intellect is conscious of the fact that his existence is due to his having been brought into being via *ibdāʿ* and he is therefore, at once, the act that causes the first intellect's self-knowledge (as Intellect's cognition of his essence having been originated through *ibdāʿ*), and also himself knowledge, insofar as he can be known. In simpler terms, under the 'guise' of *ibdāʿ*, the Intellect is an object of knowledge for humans as they understand him to be the closest and most direct product of divine origination that can ever be speculated about.[41] As an intelligence capable of thinking and as the object of his self-intellection – *intellegere* derives from Latin *intus* (within) and *legere* (to read), meaning 'to read within oneself' – the first originated entity assumes practically the traits of the Aristotelian 'Thought–Thinking–Thought' (*Nous–Noesis–Noeseos*) corresponding to the Arabic, *ʿaql–ʿāqil–maʿqūl*.

---

[40] Ibid., p. 156.

[41] Walker, *Ismaili Thought in the Age of al-Ḥakim*, pp. 92–93. In similar terms, when Armstrong deals with aspects of the One that make it most 'Nous-like', he describes the Intellect as being 'always the universal correlative to our highest mental state; [the Intellect] is the realm of νόησις, a realm well within our own human sphere'. Armstrong, *The Architecture of the Intelligible Universe*, p. 4.

Notwithstanding the nature of the Intellect as a Thought–Thinking–Thought, al-Kirmānī explains that the Intellect is 'limited' by his nature as a perfect entity deprived of any need of what is outside himself. This means that the Intellect does not need to think of anything outside himself in order to acquire perfection, as he is already perfect.[42] Even more specifically, he *cannot* acquire any other perfection through his intellective activity. Therefore, the latter is exercised exclusively on his own essence.[43]

---

[42] This concept is not unique to al-Kirmānī: for al-Sijistānī, too, Intellect knows only his absolute uniqueness, and this ensures his state of repose. See al-Sijistānī, *Kitāb al-Yanābīʿ*, pp. 86–87; *The Wellsprings of Wisdom*, pp. 58–59.

[43] Al-Kirmānī, *Rāḥat al-ʿaql*, pp. 184–185; *idem*, *Riyāḍ* (Beirut, 1960), pp. 176–212. The identification of the First created being with *ʿaql* recalls a famous Tradition attributed to the sixth Imam, Jaʿfar al-Ṣādiq known as 'the tradition of the armies of *ʿaql*'. In this Tradition, the *ʿaql*, proceeding from God's light, is described as the first of God's creations and is characterised by its submission and its will to be near to God. See al-Kulaynī, *al-Uṣūl min al-kāfī*, quoted in Mohammad A. Amir-Moezzi, *The Divine Guide in Early Shiʿism*, tr. David Streight (Albany, NY, 1994), p. 8. The activity of thinking about something outside one's own essence is delegated to the second intellect. It is well known that al-Kirmānī transfers many characteristics attributed to the First Being by Muslim philosophers such as al-Fārābī and Avicenna to the Intellect. The shifting of characteristics from the Creator to the first intellect is typical of Ismaili philosophy. On this topic, see Daniel Peterson, 'Al-Kirmānī on the Divine *Tawḥīd*', in *Proceedings of the Third European Conference of Iranian Studies, II: Mediaeval and Modern Persian Studies*, ed. Charles Melville (Wiesbaden, 1999), pp. 179–194.

2

Al-Kirmānī's Views on the Agent and the Nature of the Intellect

One of the key issues debated by Muʿtazilites and Ashʿarites in relation to the topic of free will versus predestination was the identity of the agent (*fāʿil*). The Muʿtazilites, focusing on the concept of *qudra* or power of efficient causality, regarded the human being as a real *fāʿil* (doer), an *ʿālim* (knower), a *qāṣid* (a being able to act consciously) and a *murīd* (a willing being). Accordingly, the individual was perceived as a real agent capable of choosing which act to carry out following his free will. Conversely, the Ashʿarites generally spoke of a divinely created power in humans (a generated power, *quwwa/qudra muḥdatha*) through which they became agents or 'proximate causes' of an act. However, they stressed that it was only simultaneously with the realisation of the act that God created in the human agent such 'generated power of causality'. The latter, as a temporally created power, was thought to belong to man, thus making him a *qādir*.[1] The human being was a *muktasib* of the act, that is, a person who actually realises the act by performing it through a *qudra* created by God on behalf of all human beings. On different grounds, the peripatetic philosophers attributed a different meaning to the word 'agent': for Aristotle it meant an 'efficient mover', defining the actual

---

[1] Abū al-Ḥasan al-Ashʿarī, *Kitāb al-Lumaʿ*, tr. Richard J. McCarthy as *The Theology of al-Ashʿarī: the Arabic texts of al-Ashʿarī's Kitāb al-Lumaʿ and Risālat Istiḥsān al-khawḍ fī ʿilm al-kalām* (Beirut, 1953), pp. 77–78. The *qudra*, created by God with the act and for the act, becomes the proof that humans are *qādir*s exclusively by way of being the locus (*maḥall*) for the divinely created power-to-act. On this issue, see Muḥammad b. al-Ḥasan b. Fūrak, *Mujarrad Maqālāt al-Shaykh Abī al-Ḥasan al-Ashʿarī*, ed. Daniel Gimaret as *Mujarrad Maqālāt al-shaykh Abī al-Ḥasan al-Ashʿarī. Exposé de la doctrine d'al-Ašʿarī* (Beirut, 1987), p. 92.

status of things; for Ibn Sīnā it referred to an 'efficient cause' (either animate or inanimate).[2] For a Sunni theologian such as al-Ghazālī, an agent could only refer to a 'voluntary agent', namely, a person who has a will, acts freely, has knowledge of what is willed and awareness of its consequences.[3]

In line with classical arguments, al-Kirmānī acknowledges the necessity for an action to occur in the presence of an agent and of a substratum to act upon.[4] He clarifies that at the end of what Aristotle would have considered a causal chain – consisting of the three elements agent (*fāʿil*), act (*fiʿl*), acted-upon-object (*mafʿūl*) – in order to avoid an infinite number of agents, there must be an ultimate link which cannot be identified as an agent. Since any agent depends on another agent who precedes it, the first agent in the chain must be the product of an entity that does not have the quality of an agent. God, who is beyond existence and has no need for either matter or a substratum upon which potentially to act, must be identified with such an ultimate principle. Taking into account al-Kirmānī's adoption of the creationistic theory of *ibdāʿ*, one would expect to see him supporting the theological position for which God is the only real Agent intervening occasionistically in the world of created beings. Paradoxically, instead al-Kirmānī arrives at the same conclusion as Ibn Sīnā who could not address the Necessary Existent (*wājib al-wujūd*) as an agent.[5] Similarly, al-Kirmānī proves that it is impossible for God to be

---

[2] De Cillis, *Free Will and Predestination*, pp. 113–114.

[3] Abū Ḥāmid al-Ghazālī, *Tahāfut al-falāsifa*, tr. Michael E. Marmura as *The Incoherence of the Philosophers* (Provo, UT, 1997), pp. 167–169.

[4] Al-Kirmānī, *Risālat al-rawḍa*, ed. Muṣṭafā Ghālib, in *Majmūʿat rasāʾil al-Kirmānī* (Beirut, 1969), p. 85. Proclus believed that 'activity' requires both a substance and a potentiality. In his view, the triad of *energeia* (activity)/*ousia* (substance)/*dynamis* (potentiality) was irreconcilable with the notion of the One because this threatened the One's unity. The One is the cause of all beings without being able to perform any action. It is an 'effecter' simply by being one. See Carlos Steel, ed., *Proclus. Commentaire sur le Parménide de Platon: Traduction de Guillaume de Moerbeke. Tome II: Livres V à VII et Notes marginales de Nicolas de Cues* (Leuven, 1985), pp. 1167–1168, cited in De Smet, *La quiétude de l'intellect*, pp. 133–134.

[5] In Ibn Sīnā's view, the absence of pure intentionality in God's will and the absence of free choice in His creation make God 'exempted' from acting. See Ibn Sīnā, *al-Risāla al-aḍhawiya fī'l-maʿād*, tr. Francesca Lucchetta as *Avicenna, Epistola sulla Vita Futura: Testo Arabo, Traduzione, Introduzione e Note* (Padova, 1969), pp 68–74;

credited with the character of agency (*fāʿiliyya*); should God have the quality of an agent, He would depend on the entity to which He would have conferred the act.[6] Thus, al-Kirmānī is ready to preserve the utter divine transcendence over the Qurʾanic quality of God as a *fāʿil*. It has to be borne in mind that an eventual adoption of *kalāmic* occasionalism would have meant acknowledging the possibility for God to enter the domain of existent creatures by way of acting either directly or through secondary causes at any given time. Voicing Ismaili metaphysics, al-Kirmānī believes that activity pertains to the world of creation rather than to the realm of the divine.

Once these considerations are taken into account, it is easy to detect why al-Kirmānī identifies the first agent with the first intellect. Given that the Intellect proceeds from God and that God does not act as such, it follows that the first intellect can only be the act in his own essence, the producer of an act (i.e. an agent) in his own essence and the recipient of his own action. That is to say, the Intellect is an act in his essence, acts on his essence and is the subject of his own action in his essence (*fiʿl fī dhātihi, fāʿil fī dhātihi, mafʿūl biʾl-dhātihi*).[7] Since, as an act, the first intellect is *ibdāʿ*, *a fortiori*, as an agent, the first intellect must be responsible for some kind of 'creationistic' activity and might be for this reason identified with the Qurʾanic Originator. Nevertheless, even if the first intellect is identical with the act of origination at the level of existence, he cannot be assumed to be a self-existentiated being because his existence is not guaranteed by his essence.[8] In truth,

---

idem, Kitāb al-Najāt, ed. Ṣabrī al-Kurdī (Cairo, 1938), p. 274; see also Amelie M. Goichon, *La Distinction de l'Essence et de l'Existence d'après Ibn Sīnā (Avicenne)* (Paris, 1937), pp. 216–218.

[6] Because it is established that any agent requires the presence of a substratum to act on and given that this substratum is absent in the case of the deity, God could do nothing but act on Himself, thus introducing a plurality in His essence by becoming simultaneously the subject and the object of His act. This is obviously inconceivable. It is therefore due to the dependency on another element and the potentiality of adding a plurality to the deity that God cannot be identified as an agent. On other arguments relative to the impossibility for God to be an agent, see De Smet, *La quiétude de l'intellect*, pp. 126–127.

[7] Al-Kirmānī, *Rāḥat al-ʿaql*, p. 160; De Smet, *La quiétude de l'intellect*, p. 126.

[8] The Intellect is considered simultaneously as the effect of God's act of origination (the Intellect does not come about through his essence but via *ibdāʿ*), and as the

as a being-put-into-being (*mu'ayyas*), the Intellect's existence depends on the ultimate principle whose ipseity (He-ness, *huwiyya*) cannot be denied and whose nature remains beyond comprehension.[9] Al-Kirmānī adopts the method of double negation which, first devised by Damascius in his *Dubitationes et solutiones de primis principiis* and in Ismaili circles already used by al-Sijistānī,[10] denounces the insufficiency of the *via negationis* (*ṭarīq al-nafī*). The latter method was used by many theologians, in particular the Muʿtazilites, and aimed at preserving God from becoming the object of any comparison to created beings. For al-Kirmānī, as well as al-Sijistānī, to deny that God is similar to any creatures implies that He can be compared to spiritual beings, thus showing that one form of negation is not sufficient to safeguard divine transcendence.[11] Al-Kirmānī explains that the *via negativa* represents only the first step of a process which must progress by adding another negation to the first one. With the first stage, the *via negationis* presents God as the *lā mawṣūf*, namely as the bearer of no attributes. However, even such an expression implies a sort of qualification, since God can be said to be characterised by the attribute of not being the bearer of any attribute. A solution to this is given by adding another negation to the first one – thus referring to God as to *'huwa lā mawṣūf wa lā huwa lā mawṣūf'*, namely, as He who is the bearer of no

---

first cause on which the existence of all other beings depends. However, as a cause/agent, the Intellect does not act upon matter that is other than himself. Al-Kirmānī, *Rāḥat al-ʿaql*, p. 158.

[9] Al-Kirmānī dedicates two chapters of his *Rāḥat al-ʿaql* to prove that neither 'being' (*ays*) nor 'non-being' (*lays*) can be attributed to God. Al-Kirmānī, *Rāḥat al-ʿaql*, pp. 129–134.

[10] See Leendert G. Westerink, Joseph Combès, ed. and tr., *Damascius, Traité des premiers principes*, 3 vols (Paris, 1986–1991) in index; see also Stephen Gersh, ed., *Interpreting Proclus: From Antiquity to the Renaissance* (Cambridge, 2014) p. 128; *idem, Being Different: More Neoplatonism after Derrida. Ancient Mediterranean and Medieval Texts and Contexts. Studies in Platonism, Neoplatonism, and the Platonic Tradition, 16* (Leiden and Boston, 2014), pp. 121, 138, 146.

[11] See al-Sijistānī, *Kashf al-maḥjūb*, tr. Landolt, *Unveiling of the Hidden*, pp. 88–90; Corbin, *Cyclical Time and Ismaili Gnosis*, p. 85; Paul E. Walker, 'An Ismāʿīlī Answer to the Problem of Worshipping the Unknowable, Neoplatonic God', *AJAS*, 2 (1972), pp. 12–22.

attributes and also as He who is not *not* the bearer of any attribute.[12] The negation of the negation leads to a form of affirmation (*ījāb*) of a non-absolute, which is indicated by the expression *ghayr mujarrad*.[13]

Following Proclus' views on the Nous, al-Kirmānī believes that the Intellect is self-subsistent in his essence and yet he is still dependent on something external for his being put into existence. In this light, it is clear that even if one takes *ibdāʿ* as a constitutive aspect of the first intellect's essence, one must also acknowledge that the Intellect is the *ibdāʿ* as well as the *mubdaʿ*, the first originated being.

These notions may instinctively recall the Avicennan metaphysical concept of the *wājib bi'l-ghayr*, the possible entity in itself which is made necessary by something other than itself.[14] According to Ibn Sīnā, any being is simultaneously a possible existent in itself and a necessary existent through another. For al-Kirmānī, the Intellect – despite being an originated entity – is rendered a necessarily existent beyond time. Intellect is always in actuality, and in this sense a passage from his status of potential intellect to actual intellect is never fully contemplated. It follows that he is fully self-contained: the Intellect comes into existence as a perfect being (*kāmil^{an}*) and, outside time, as a sempiternal existent (*azaliyy^{an}*).[15] It should be borne in mind that no temporality as such is contemplated by al-Kirmānī with regard to the act of divine origination, existentiating the Intellect, and that no

---

[12] See al-Kirmānī, *Rāḥat al-ʿaql*, pp. 148–149.

[13] De Smet suggests that this notion makes God 'He who is even beyond what He has been stripped of: He is stripped of His own being stripped of.' De Smet, *La quiétude de l'intellect*, p. 80.

[14] The concept of the *wājib bi'l-ghayr* is closely linked to Ibn Sīnā's understanding of determinism; for the philosopher, determination is conceived as 'the existence of causes and occasions and their harmonisation according to their arrangement (*tartīb*) and order (*niẓām*), leading to the effects and caused beings', the latter constituting 'what is made necessary by the Decree and what follows from it'. This means that determinism occurs through causes whose nature as causes is necessarily arranged by God and whose order only ultimately subordinates them to the divine decree. Their destinies, i.e. the determinations of their future characters, lay exactly in their nature as being necessary existents by virtue of something other than themselves. De Cillis, *Free Will and Predestination*, p. 37; Catarina Belo, *Chance and Determinism in Avicenna and Averroes* (Leiden and Boston, 2007), p. 122.

[15] Al-Kirmānī, *Rāḥat al-ʿaql*, p. 163.

passage from a status of potentiality into that of actuality is ever truly admitted with regards to the first originated thing. The impossibility of the Intellect undergoing a passage from potentiality into actuality is a topos al-Kirmānī insists on throughout chapter eight of his *Riyāḍ*. This is done in order to identify the eternality of the Intellect, which is made to correspond to the Antecedent (*sābiq*), and in order to highlight the different character of the third intellect, which is described as '*al-muta'akhkhir fi'l-wujūd*'.[16]

Paradoxically, despite the fact that the Intellect is the cause/effect of his own action/essence, he is still not capable of self-existentiation. The gap between Ibn Sīnā's Necessary Existent and the first intellect, instantiated in the emanative scheme, is not as unbridgeable as the chasm between the unknowable God of al-Kirmānī and his idea of the Intellect. In the first instance, according to Ibn Sīnā, God is Existence in His own essence and He also participates in 'being'; He is the ultimate Cause of existence of any *wājib bi'l-ghayr* (the necessary existent being through something other than itself). Ibn Sīnā clearly follows al-Fārābī, for whom God – who is identified with the First Existent (*al-mawjūd al-awwal*) – has 'the most elevated rank of perfect existence' (*kamāl al-wujūd fī arfaʿ al-marātib*).[17] In al-Kirmānī's instance, however, God – set beyond 'being' – is not a cause that necessitates beings.[18] The existence of the first intellect, which is identified with the Fārābian *al-mawjūd al-awwal*,[19] is not by virtue of his essence

---

[16] On this expression, see pp. 55, 176 and 179. It should be noted that the eternity (*azaliyya*), which al-Fārābī attributes to the Ultimate Reality/God, is shifted by al-Kirmānī onto the Intellect. See al-Kirmānī, *Rāḥat al-ʿaql*, pp. 162–163; 186–187; *idem, Risālat al-rawḍa*, in *Majmūʿat rasāʾil al-Kirmānī*, pp. 86–87; cf., Haji, *A Distinguished Dāʿī*, pp. 39–40; De Smet, *La quiétude de l'intellect*, pp. 68, 76; *idem*, 'Al-Fārābī's Influence on Ḥamīd al-Dīn al-Kirmānī', p. 135.

[17] Al-Fārābī, *Mabādiʾ ārāʾ ahl al-madīna al-fāḍila* (Beirut, 1982), p. 56; De Smet, 'Al-Fārābī's Influence on Ḥamīd al-Dīn al-Kirmānī', p. 135.

[18] God is the creator (*mubdiʿ*) of the Intellect but not his cause. The first cause is the Intellect (al-Kirmānī, *Rāḥat al-ʿaql*, pp. 157–158). It will be observed why al-Kirmānī is adamant at denying the hypostatic nature of the divine *amr/kalima* as the first cause.

[19] Al-Kirmānī, *Rāḥat al-ʿaql*, p. 157.

(*wujūduhu lā bi-dhātihi*) as the Intellect derives his existence from God's act of origination (*bi-ibdāʿ al-mutaʿālī*).[20]

In al-Kirmānī's metaphysics, the Intellect is said to come into existence by *ibdāʿ* and *ikhtirāʿ* (invention). This meaning that his self-subsistence, which does not suffice his existence, is given to him by his nature as the 'manifested' aspect of divine *ibdāʿ*, rather than as the act of origination itself. Put differently, *ibdāʿ* as *ibdāʿ* is nothing other than an instrument offered by God to the Intellect through which he comes into existence according to God's *ikhtirāʿ*. From this perspective, *ibdāʿ* can effortlessly be identified with 'a principle of relationship' rather than a real action.[21] However, even this definition of *ibdāʿ* is not completely satisfactory: de facto, the relationship occurring between God and the Intellect, via *ibdāʿ*, is neither a relationship of activity nor a relationship of causality. Its nature remains indescribable and, actually, it is not even correct to regard it as a real relationship. This impossibility is simply due to the fact that there is neither continuity nor a real link between the Creator and His creatures, and therefore there cannot be any form of relationship between them.

Al-Kirmānī was probably aware of Proclus' idea that the One does not entertain any connection of efficient causality with anything other than Itself and that for this reason it is impossible to define *ibdāʿ* as a proper 'relationship'. However, contrary to al-Kirmānī, Proclus believes that the One does exercise causality without being Itself a cause, Its causality being superior to and different from all others.[22] Spurred by the intention of delineating with greater precision the relationship and distinction occurring between Plotinus' One and the Intellect, Proclus speaks of a triad – Being, Life and Intellect – which are made to correspond ontologically to the intelligible Being (*noêton* – the object of intellectual intuition), the intermediary level of the *noêton-noeron* (what is being intelligised and intelligising) and the intellective (*noeron* – what is intelligising). As a mediator, Life represents 'thinking' as such and is conceived

---

[20] Ibid., p. 158.

[21] Walker, 'The Ismaili Vocabulary of Creation', p. 83.

[22] See *Proclus: Théologie platonicienne*, ed. and tr. H. D. Saffrey and L. G. Westerink, 6 vols., vol. 5 (Paris, 1987), p. 58.

as a flowing energy, linking the thinking subject to the object of thought, thus rendering theirs a dynamic relationship.[23] In this way, Proclus suggests that indeed an intimate relationship exists among the three elements, a relation of immanence, procession and reversion (*monê-prohodos-epistrophê*) which, as an underlying principle of all triadic structures, allows us to explain – through the other triad of the Unparticipated-Participated-Participating (*amethekton-metechomenon-metechon*) – the Neoplatonic metaphysical question of how multiplicity proceeds from the One.[24]

The discourse of the self-thinking activity of the Intellect brings forward further considerations; in the second part of this study, which centres on the chapter dedicated to the topic of decree and destiny in the *Riyāḍ*, the nature of the relationship of the first, second and third intellect with the recipients of their blessings in the persons of the prophets, founders and Imams will come under scrutiny. In particular, we shall observe that the identification of the Intellect with the Antecedent (*sābiq*) reveals how the oneness of the Intellect providentially levies limits on the Intellect himself, fulfilling the divine decree. It will be pointed out that the Intellect's oneness precludes humans a direct approach to the first originated being, whose guidance unfolds, rather, through intermediary spiritual faculties.

---

[23]   Radek Chlup, *Proclus: An Introduction* (Cambridge, 2012), p. 94.

[24]   Proclus, *The Elements of Theology*, tr. Eric R. Dodds (Oxford, 1963), § 35 cited in Christoph Helmig and Carlos Steel, 'Proclus', *The Stanford Encyclopedia of Philosophy* (2015), ed. Edward N. Zalta, at http://plato.stanford.edu/archives/sum2015/entries/proclus/, last accessed on 24 May 2018.

3

Meritorious Determination: Outlining al-Kirmānī's Cosmological Scheme

It has been shown previously how al-Kirmānī explains in distinct terms why God cannot be regarded as an agent. Conversely, al-Kirmānī remains rather reticent on the reason why God cannot be seen as the cause of the Intellect's existence.[1] He merely identifies the first cause with the Intellect, thus depriving God of such an 'identity'.[2]

---

[1] Al-Kirmānī's position is strikingly similar to Ibn 'Arabī's concern about God's transcendence. The Shaykh al-Akbar believed that any identification of God with the 'Cause' of existence would suggest that God is in a necessary relation with His own creation, thus contradicting His Essence as 'the Independent of the Worlds'. See Ibn 'Arabī, *al-Futūḥāt al-Makkiyya* (Cairo, 1329/1911), reprinted by Dār al-Ṣādir (Beirut, 1968), p. 90; William C. Chittick, *The Self-Disclosure of God: Principles of Ibn al-'Arabī's Cosmology* (Albany, NY, 1988), p. 17. On Ibn 'Arabī's criticism of the philosophers and theologians' understanding of causes, see *Futūḥāt*, III, p. 355; *Futūḥāt*, IV, p. 378. It is worth remembering that al-Ghazālī too levelled against the philosophers a strong criticism, as he pointed out that, notwithstanding their identification of God with the first cause, they also paradoxically believed that God's actions are not voluntary and that creatures are the products of a necessary emanative overflowing. See al-Ghazālī, *Tahāfut al-falāsifa*, Discussion 3.

[2] The Intellect must exist because he is the first cause (*al-'illa al-ūlā*) upon which the existence of all other things depends. As such, he has the characteristic of the first thing (*al-shay' al-awwal*) whose precedence over all other things guarantees their existence (a second and a third thing could not possibly exist without a first thing). The mere existence of the universe in which things act as causes (*'ilal*) 'proves' the actual presence of a 'first principle' (*al-mubda' al-awwal*), or a first thing, which is identified with the first intellect (*al-'aql al-awwal*) or the first existent (*al-mawjūd al-awwal*). Should this principle be absent, we would witness an infinite chain of causes, which is absurd. See al-Kirmānī, *Rāḥat al-'aql*, pp. 157–158. The first cause, al-Kirmānī explains, is the product 'of Him of whom it is not appropriate to say that He is an agent'. See Peterson, *Cosmogony in the Rāḥat al-'aql*, p. 412.

51

This is certainly an important move, which allows the accentuation of the Godhead's transcendence. Given that God does not have an effusing nature, which is instead assigned to Him by the Neoplatonic philosophers, how can al-Kirmānī's cosmological system, which develops also through *inbiʿāth*,[3] be accountable for the predestination of the future status of the creatures present in it? This question is closely connected with the issue of prophecy: for those philosophers who adopted a creationistic vocabulary, emanation is often conceived in metaphorical and gnoseological terms and described as the proceeding of a luminous outpouring from God down to the creatures. The flux of emanation is mediated through the intelligences and the prophets; the latter, in contrast to the majority of humans, have an instantaneous access to the knowledge of the intellects, which is communicated to them by the Agent Intellect. Emanation gives the prophets and philosophers a positive knowledge of the Principle and offers the hope of attaining some understanding of the transcendent Neoplatonic One.[4] On the contrary, the Ismaili doctrine, denying any accessibility to God, needs necessarily to find an alternative to the Sunni concept of prophecy and its soteriological nature. If, according to al-Kirmānī, the mystery of the divine nature remains hidden, then the role of the prophet as the mediator who guides humankind towards salvation and as the instrument which allows the divine decree to unfold has to be re-elaborated. A prophet does not achieve any direct knowledge of God because his ultimate knowledge reaches the threshold of the first intellect without attainment of the Supreme Unattainable.

---

[3] *Inbiʿāth* (procession) differs from *fayḍ* (emanation): the former is more suitable to convey the idea of the image of the sun being reflected in a pool of water; such a reflection is certainly not the sun itself but a mere representation of it. Given its nature as a process of manifestation rather than of emanation, the product of any *inbiʿāthī* activity clearly discloses itself as having its origin from something; in other terms, by being figurative, such an entity allows one to retrace its original source, a possibility that is inconceivable for the product of the action of origination. See Nanji, 'Ismaili Philosophy', p. 151.

[4] In other terms, emanation allows speaking of the possibility of a return of all being to their Origin precisely because all members of the emanative hierarchy, as well as the objects of their influences in the sublunar world, have awareness of at least some aspects of their original Principle.

Taking these positions into account, a series of questions come instinctively to mind: how can an unknowable God be worshipped and served in an appropriate way as to allow His creatures to merit reward rather than punishment? If the act of origination by *ibdāʿ* hinders any possibility of continuity between God and the world, how can the prophet – who cannot attain knowledge of God – fulfil his role as a *nāṭiq* (enunciator-prophet)? How can he assure the unfolding of the divine decree and destiny?

In an earlier study, I have shown that for Fārābian/Avicennean-type cosmologies, emanation becomes indicative of a determinism for which the current order and the future developments of all entities are determined by their own nature, which drives them to act as causes and effects according to a providential divine decree.[5] Given the similar character of al-Kirmānī's cosmology, one might conclude that also in his theoretical arrangement a theistic-orientated causal determination should prevail. However, this is not the case. Heralding Ṭayyibī hermeneutics and their mythical 'drama in heaven',[6] al-Kirmānī infers

---

[5] On the link between emanation and determinism, see De Cillis, *Free Will and Predestination*, pp. 30–40.

[6] Introduced in Ṭayyibī Ismaili cosmology by Ibrāhīm al-Ḥāmidī (d. 596/1199) in his *Kitāb Kanz al-walad* (ed. Muṣṭafā Ghālib, Wiesbaden, 1971; reprinted Beirut, 1979, see especially pp. 66–69, 78–79, 132, 258, 296–297), the 'drame dans le ciel', so named by Henry Corbin (in his *Trilogie ismaélienne* [Tehran and Paris, 1961], pp. 135–136), sees the two primordial beings immediately following the first intellect (i.e. the second and third intellect) competing for the second position in the celestial hierarchy. It is the first emanation (i.e. al-Kirmānī's second intellect) that, between the two, attains the second rank due to its superior effort and faster response to the call (*daʿwa*) launched by the Intellect, through which the second intellect acknowledges the precedence of both the Originator and the first intellect. The third intellect, on its part, fallen into a state of stupor (*sahw*) and a refusal to assign pre-eminence to its preceding intellects, precipitates from the third rank to the tenth position in the Pleroma, thus engendering the world of Nature (De Smet, *La quiétude de l'intellect*, p. 249). Awakened, it discovers itself to have been downgraded seven ranks by the other seven intellects which, in the meantime, have responded to the Intellect's invitation. The third intellect's hesitation – due to its initial insubordination – gives way to a temporal delay (*takhalluf*) in the Pleroma which, as a 'retarded-eternity' (Corbin, *Cyclical Time and Ismaili Gnosis*, pp. 30, 39–41), may be considered, Daftary explains, as the prototype of cyclical time based on the number seven typical of Ṭayyibī hierohistory (Daftary, *The Ismāʿīlīs*, p. 270). On the Ṭayyibīs' cosmological views and their

that the rank of any being that is part of his cosmology is not merely due to its inherent make-up but also to a meritorial scheme which makes each entity deserve its position by means of its own chosen conduct. So, the prominence and precedence of the first originated being is accorded not just in line with his ontic antecedence – linked to his uttermost simplicity, which renders the Intellect the closest to God given that the being that is the closer (*aqrab*) to the One (*wāḥid*) is the simpler (*absaṭ*)[7] – but also according to the Intellect's capacity for carrying out the most complete form of *tawḥīd*,[8] by which *al-mubdaʿ al-awwal* is the foremost to acknowledge his Originator (*al-mubdiʿ*) and, consequently, his own non-divinity.[9]

Following the Intellect, the first two emanations from it – the second and third intellect – are less and less perfect, not only in their cognitive character but also in their demeanours: the first *inbiʿāthī*

---

link to Valentinian Gnosis, see Corbin, *Cyclical Time and Ismaili Gnosis*, p. 178, 180; De Smet, *La quiétude de l'intellect*, p. 249; Ibn al-Walīd, *al-Risāla al-Mufīda*, ed. and tr. Wilferd Madelung and Toby Mayer as *Avicenna's Allegory on the Soul: An Ismaili Interpretation* (London, 2016), pp. 83–86.

   [7]   Al-Kirmānī, *Rāḥat al-ʿaql*, p. 261.

   [8]   Al-Sijistānī himself explained that the Intellect's apprehension is different from all other apprehensions. Whenever the Intellect is about to differentiate among quiddity, quality and other categories, God prevents him from doing so, thus making it incumbent for the Intellect to confirm His transcendent oneness: 'By looking at himself from the point of view of Oneness, he [the Intellect] sees things not as multiple or diverse; no, he sees pure Origination (*ibdāʿ-i maḥḍ*) and nothing but the sheer act of making-to-be (*hast kardan-i mujarrad*), without any difference.' Al-Sijistānī, *Kashf al-maḥjūb*, tr. Landolt, *Unveiling of the Hidden*, p. 92 (translation slightly modified).

   [9]   This corroborates al-Kirmānī's claim that the Intellect is perfect both in essence and in action. Hunzai has highlighted that, according to al-Kirmānī, *tawḥīd* cannot be a description of God but only of His existents. *Wāḥid* (one), as the object of *tawḥīd*, by being contingent in both its composition and essence cannot be applied to God. The only one worthy of this most noble attribute is the Intellect. *Tawḥīd*, Hunzai explains, is applicaple to the first originated being in two senses: in the sense of the act of God, i.e. *ibdāʿ*, and in the sense of the act of the believer (*mu'min*), which is to divest the *wāḥid*, i.e. the Intellect from divinity. By realising his contingent nature as being composed of two entities – *waḥda* (oneness), and its recipient – the Intellect divests himself of any divine claim and becomes the ultimate *mu'min*. Through such sanctification (*taqdīs*), the Intellect establishes that divinity belongs to God alone. See Hunzai, 'The Concept of *Tawḥīd*', p. 178.

being, or first emanation (*al-munbaʿith al-awwal*), is said to be perfect in its essence, as it proceeds from the perfect Intellect, but defective with respect to its preceder, in its action. This would seem to suggest that its attestation of *tawḥīd* is slightly flawed as it acknowledges two entities preceding itself: the Originator and the first originated being. Al-Kirmānī identifies the third intellect with the entity that comes into existence later (*al-mutaʾakhkhir*) and with the intellect that is raised (*al-ʿaql al-murtaqī*) from the world of Nature through acquisition by means of knowledge and action,[10] thus seemingly suggesting that its rank in the celestial hierarchy is not merely linked to its defective nature but also gained through its own epistemological effort.[11]

I have previously mentioned that in al-Fārābī's *Mabādiʾ ārāʾ ahl al-madīna al-fāḍila*, the whole process of emanation is caused by the double objects each intellect contemplates: as a result of thinking about the First, an intellect gives rise to a new intellect, whilst by thinking about its own essence, it emanates a heavenly sphere.[12] This emanation system, which proceeds in a vertical line up to the tenth intellect, is re-elaborated by Ibn Sīnā. In his *Ilāhiyyāt* of the *Shifāʾ*, which contains some of the most detailed accounts of his view

---

[10] Al-Kirmānī, *Riyāḍ* (HL), pp. 129–130.

[11] It is sensible to argue that the rank of the third intellect is accorded due to its hylomorphic nature since the presence of matter contributes to the deterioration of its degree of perfection which is already considered inferior, being the result of the Intellect's passive, rather than active, self-cogitation. Moreover, the presence of matter certainly explains the receptive disposition which the third intellect 'inherits' from the relationship the Intellect entertains with himself as a *ʿaql maʿqūl* (intelligised intellect). (On al-Kirmānī's adaptation of the Aristotelian and Plotinian concept of the hylomorphic sensible world, see De Smet, *La quiétude de l'intellect*, pp. 221–223). The potentiality embedded in the third intellect is necessary to explain why it is only at this level that real plurality occurs. In fact, multiplicity – whose different forms are still not differentiated within the Intellect although already present in him – is manifested exclusively with the occurrence of the third intellect, which is endowed with the material substratum capable of receiving various forms – at this level identifiable as the archetypes of the sensible world – responsible for diversity and plurality (De Smet, *La quiétude de l'intellect*, p. 224). This explains why for al-Kirmānī this world, to which the third intellect is linked due to its hylomorphism, is not the world of remembrance or recompense but rather the world of acquisition (*al-dunyā dār al-iktisāb*). On this topic, see more below, pp. 88–89.

[12] Al-Fārābī, *Mabādiʾ ārāʾ ahl al-madīna al-fāḍila*, particularly Chapters 5–6.

on the Neoplatonic system of ten intellects, as the greatest disciple of al-Fārābī, he describes the whole system of emanation as being triggered by the movements of celestial spheres whose initiation is granted by the intellects' capacity to think of themselves, of their immediate principles and, ultimately, of the First Cause.[13] Their thinking is perpetually active as the intellects strive to imitate their source. In their attempts to 'perfect' their natures, they implicitly contribute to shaping the whole creation's destiny.[14]

In al-Kirmānī's thought, the Intellect, who is limited by his own perfection and self-intellection, is denied the possibility to attain the Principle. As Corbin explains, the Intellect – which initiates *tawḥīd* by recognising the Unifier of his essence as being beyond all categories and all predicates – by denying divinity for himself, becomes the Veil, the horizon and the limit (*ḥadd*) by which the Godhead appears to the following intelligence: 'Thus, from level to level, from each limit to that which it limits (its *maḥdūd*), and which is in turn the limit or horizon for the one following it, this *tawḥīd* maintains the entire Pleroma in an ascending movement', with each intellect addressing its preceding 'Veil/limit' as its Lord.[15]

Fascinated by the ineffable mystery of the divine nature, the Intellect, with his self-awareness of being merely an intellect rather than the ultimate source, is 'trapped' in his own incapacity to know the last Principle.[16] Nonetheless, following al-Fārābī's belief – also found in

---

[13]   Ibn Sīnā, *Kitāb al-Shifāʾ: al-ilāhiyyāt*, tr. Michael E. Marmura, *The Metaphysics of the Healing* (Provo, UT, 2005), pp. 330–334; *idem, Kitāb al-Najāt*, p. 277.

[14]   De Cillis, *Free Will and Predestination*, pp. 30–40.

[15]   Corbin, *Cyclical Time and Ismaili Gnosis*, p. 177.

[16]   This realisation precipitates the Intellect in a state of confusion (*ḥayra*) as he realises that, in order to gain understanding of anything other than himself, he must renounce (literally, exit himself from – *khurūjihu min*) his own intellective essence (*kūnat ʿaql*^{an}), turning himself into ignorance (*jahlihi*) (al-Kirmānī, *Rāḥat al-ʿaql*, pp. 174, 194; De Smet, *La quiétude de l'intellect*, pp. 176–177). The awareness that the goal of his pursuit lies beyond his capacities fills the Intellect with sadness (*ḥāsir*) (ibid., pp. 193–194). The striving towards the object of love which in the Fārābian philosophers is identified in the ultimate divine Goodness/Perfection is interrupted by al-Kirmānī at the level of the Intellect. The Neoplatonic concept of *rujūʿ*, signalling the return of all beings to their Origin, is interdicted: even though the Ismaili originates the Intellect via *ibdāʿ*, God cannot be the point of return for the Intellect.

Ibn Sīnā – that all members of creation hasten to imitate their immediate preceding beings up to the First being, al-Kirmānī propounds that the dynamism of the whole of creation is triggered by a form of desire for perfection which compels intellects as well as other entities to know their sources. More specifically, in al-Kirmānī's view, two kinds of perfection pertain to any being: the first perfection (*al-kamāl al-awwal*) which, as De Smet puts it, signifies the existence of the essence of the entity and functions as the bearer of its attributes (*mawṣūfa*), and the second perfection (*al-kamāl al-thānī*) which relates to the nobility (*sharaf*) of this essence and acts as the attribute (*ṣifa*) thereof.[17]

Al-Kirmānī regards perfection (*kamāl*) as the highest (*ajall*) of attributes for existing things. It implies permanence in the status of what things consist (*baqā' 'alā ḥāl mā 'alayhi wujūd al-shay'*).[18] Perfection does not admit change (from one state to another) because this would entail a lack of permanence. Changes are possible only through a kind of 'acquisition' (*iktisāb*), considered to be an addition to a form that is 'lacking' something. Therefore, the Intellect, by being perfect and in need of nothing whatsoever, cannot ever change. Al-Sijistānī had already advanced similar concepts: he stated that unlike the acquisition in natural beings (*al-ṭabī'iyyāt*), which move from a state of potentiality (*quwwa*) to that of actuality (*fi'l*), the Intellect is perpetually in actuality and does not acquire (*ghayr muktasaba*) his power (*quwwatahu*) and nobility (*sharafahu*) from something other than himself (*min shay' ākhar*). Were it otherwise, it could be said of the Intellect that he existed in potentiality and that, through the acquisition of what he is lacking, he is admitted into actuality. Such fluctuation from potentiality into actuality is precluded because the Intellect is perfect. It is only the Intellect's manifestations (*ẓuhūruhu*) (i.e. the forms encompassed within the Intellect) that have potentiality and actuality at once (*bi'l-quwwa wa bi'l-fi'l ma^{'an}*).[19] Al-Sijistānī's

---

The emphasis that al-Kirmānī puts on the impossibility for the Intellect to attain God under any circumstance is an implicit condemnation of the principle of emanation and the continuity it entails between the Emanator and the product of His emanation.

[17] De Smet, *La quiétude de l'intellect*, p. 151 citing al-Kirmānī, *Rāḥat al-'aql*, p. 177.

[18] De Smet, *La quiétude de l'intellect*, p. 181.

[19] Al-Sijistānī, *Kitāb al-Yanābī'*, p. 89; tr. Walker, *The Wellsprings of Wisdom*, pp. 59–60.

views on the modality by which the Intellect perceives all the forms of existents are hinted at in his disussions on *qaḍā'* and *qadar*, which are analysed in the second part of this volume.

Al-Kirmānī, on his side, states clearly that the first perfection concerns the actualisation of a thing, namely, the 'entering into existence' of a thing, whilst the second perfection relates to the multitude of attributes or actions that follow from such an actualisation. Because the first intellect is the instantaneous 'product' of *ibdāʿ* and because he encompasses in himself all aspects – and modalities – of his essence by being simultaneously agent/act/acted upon, cause/causation/ effect and so on, he is 'by default' also perfect. Particularly, the Intellect is perfect by way of being in actuality.[20] Because he is one in his essence and multiple with respect to his attributes, the Intellect's first perfection is identical with his second perfection.[21] From this, it follows that the second perfection lies inherently within the first Intellect in an essential manner (*bi-jawharihi*). This makes the Intellect free from any need of development or improvement.[22] Furthermore,

---

[20]   On the perfection of the Intellect and its immutability, see al-Kirmānī, *Rāḥat al-ʿaql*, pp. 181–183 and 187.

[21]   Such a unity in the Intellect's essence is due to the fact that the Intellect is the first originated being. If one postulates that the *ibdāʿ* instantiates simultaneously a substratum and an attribute in the Intellect as two different things, this would imply (i) that there is the simultaneous instauration of more than one thing, which is impossible, and (ii) that the *ibdāʿ* must be preceded by another being. See De Smet, *La quiétude de l'intellect*, pp. 152–153.

[22]   The Intellect, being necessarily perfect in himself, is stripped of any need or potentiality: he cannot lose or gain anything from outside his essence. He stays perpetually in the same state in which he was instantiated, with no change or development ever occurring. Such immobility implies a complete repose (*rāḥa*) of the Intellect, which makes him indifferent or insensible to anything other than himself (al-Kirmānī, *Rāḥat al-ʿaql*, p. 170). How can we then explain the providential function the Intellect exercises on humans? Is his providentiality merely the gift of actualisation, i.e. putting creation into existence? This would explain (i) al-Kirmānī's identification of the Intellect with the existantiating command; (ii) the reason why the blessings coming from the Intellect do not reach humans directly. Is it the case that these blessings never truly leave the first originated being and that what reaches out to humans are simply the blessings of the second and third intellect? I shall attempt to answer these questions in the second part of this study.

as a principle unendingly *in actu*, the Intellect is the source of all actualisations.[23]

His perfection becomes, however, a sort of limitation: given that the Intellect does not think about anything but himself, he is precluded from thinking about the Principle. This restriction cannot be regarded as a real flaw if one considers that the Principle is, in any case, attainable neither via intellect nor via vision or mystical ecstatic experience. As previously mentioned, for the Intellect, any form of return to the Source is necessarily excluded.[24]

As far as the rest of the intellects are concerned, al-Kirmānī borrows from the Fārābian-type Neoplatonic tradition of emanation and, as noted above, explains that the Intellect's self-intellection produces other intellectual beings by way of a process (*inbiʿāth*). This, however, is not perceived as an action (*fiʿl*) but rather as a passive action, a 'passion' (*infiʿāl*) or a by-product of the Intellect's restricted activity, which – given the Intellect's absolute perfection – cannot be anything

---

[23] This is true despite the fact that the Intellect does not pertain to the world of generation and corruption. This is self-evident given that the Intellect is perfect and permanent and, as such, in stark contrast to the world of coming-to-be and ceasing-to-be (*ʿālam al-kawn waʾl-fasād*). Al-Kirmānī, *Rāḥat al-ʿaql*, p. 183.

[24] Ibid., pp. 194–195. The impossibility of a return to the Originator which extends to the whole creation, De Smet explains, testifies the anti-mystical character of the Ismaili doctrine. See Daniel De Smet, 'Le *Kitāb rāḥat al-ʿaql* de Ḥamīd al-Dīn al-Kirmānī et la cosmologie ismaélienne à l'époque fatimide', p. 88; *idem*, '"Le Mystère des Mystères est inaccessible à l'engagement du cœur et à la perception de l'intellect". Néoplatonisme et (anti)mysticisme dans la pensée ismaélienne', in *Mystique at philosophie dans les trois monothéismes*, ed. Danielle Cohen-Levinas, Géraldine Roux and Meryem Sebti (Paris, 2015), pp. 67–87. However, in a sense, a form of 'shifted' mystical return can be contemplated if one considers that the Qurʾanic God, the Originator who in Ismailism remains absolutely inaccessible and ineffable as *Theos agnostos* or *Deus absconditus*, is 'replaced' by the Intellect in his alluring role as *Deus revelatus*. Therefore, in his unadulterated perfection and by acting as the first cause of all things in existence, the Intellect becomes the object of contemplation and love of all beings emanated from him, all of which yearn to attain the Intellect's essence and completeness. And it is exactly in this manner that the rest of the intellects reach for their second perfection: in their desire to resemble the Intellect's completeness, they increase their self-knowledge, the knowledge of the intelligence immediately preceding them and, ultimately, the knowledge of the first intellect.

but self-intellection. Al-Kirmānī speaks of *inbi'āth* as the necessary product of the Intellect's self-intellective modus operandi: it is not the product of a primary intention (*lā 'an qaṣd awwal*),[25] he states, but the secondary product of the Intellect's self-cogitation, which necessarily has a passive character. It is evident that because the Intellect acts as an absolute and perfect self-sufficient being, the by-product, which we call procession, is simply the upshot of a kind of determinism: the Intellect is what he is and acts in the way he acts because of his divinely given nature, which makes the Intellect the result of an act of origination. Intellect's thought, namely his *tawḥīd* (as acknowledgment of his Originator and his own being originated), is indeed the Intellect's act, which generates the second and third intellect 'accidentally'. In this perspective, it is not sensible to speak of a divinely ordained plan; al-Kirmānī is far from the Qur'anic creationistic theory and its proposition that God acts according to His will, but he is capable of rescuing God from the accusation, levelled against the Neoplatonic *falāsifa*, of creating without intention. Such an 'équivocité théologique' is superseded because the procession proceeds necessarily and naturally from the first Intellect rather than from God Himself.[26]

Despite his efforts, al-Kirmānī only manages to explain the passage from the unity and unicity (*al-wāḥidiyya wa'l-aḥadiyya*) of the Intellect to the plurality of the remaining nine intellects in his cosmology in a convoluted way.[27] The Intellect is said to be the purest knowable creature worthy of being instantiated through *ibdā'*. Nevertheless, his nature as the first cause implies a plurality in himself. The novelty of al-Kirmānī's thought comes to light when he acknowledges that the procession starting from the first intellect generates not a unity but a plurality, or rather, a pair (*zawj*) which constitutes the first degree of multiplicity.[28] This pair is what follows immediately after the simplicity

---

[25] Al-Kirmānī, *Rāḥat al-'aql*, p. 207.

[26] De Smet, *La quiétude de l'intellect*, p. 202.

[27] Unity and unicity are identified as 'qualities' which are intrinsic to the Intellect's essence due to the Intellect's ultimate perfection. Al-Kirmānī, *Rāḥat al-'aql*, pp. 231 and 233.

[28] Interestingly, according to Madelung, in *Kawn al-'ālam* – whose authorship is still disputed – al-Nasafī had already emphasised that the first created matter came to be two because it was caused (*ma'lūl*) as well as being a cause (*'illa*). Al-Nasafī

of the Intellect and is the result of the relation (*nisba*) which his essence retains with himself via his ascriptions (*bi'l-iḍāfāt*) rather than via his unity.[29] In other words, the Intellect, which is simple (*fard*), unique (*aḥad*) and one (*wāḥid*) in his essence, is also simultaneously multiple through his ascriptions.[30] These, in turn, are responsible for instilling in the Intellect a duality.[31] The Intellect's simplicity is granted by his active self-cogitation as an intelligising intellect (*'aql 'āqil*); the passive aspect of his cogitation – which occurs when he perceives himself as an intelligised intellect (*'aql ma'qūl*) – generates a duality which is due to the distinction occurring between the subject and object of intellection.[32]

Through the intellection of himself as a thinking intellect, the first originated being generates the second intellect (the Soul) which is simple and in actuality.[33] By way of recognising himself as the object of his own intellective action, the Intellect generates the third intellect which is in potency and therefore less noble and less perfect, being also multiple in its essence which is made of matter and form.[34]

---

thus suggests that creation should be called a pair (*zawj*) because it is 'made' (*maf'ūl*), hence it is a made thing which requires a maker. See Wilferd Madelung, '*Kawn al-'ālam*: The Cosmogony of the Ismā'īlī *dā'ī* Muḥammad b. Aḥmad al-Nasafī', in *Ismaili and Fatimid Studies in Honor of Paul E. Walker*, ed. Bruce D. Craig (Chicago, 2010), p. 25. I am grateful to Toby Mayer for having brought this work to my attention.

[29] Al-Kirmānī, *Rāḥat al-'aql*, p. 232.

[30] 'Indeed *ibdā'* is single (*fard*) in one aspect and a pair (*zawj*) in another. Therefore, from the existence of pairedness (*izdiwāj*), which is the sign of origination (*āyat al-ikhtirā'*) in existence, the proof may be established that *ibdā'* is not *a parte ante* eternal (*azaliyya al-awwal*), rather but comes to an end towards its *mubdi'* i.e. the Originator; and, by the existence of singleness (*fardāniyya*) in it, the proof may become evident that it is the first of origination (*awwal al-ikhtirā'*)'. Al-Kirmānī, *Rāḥat al-'aql*, tr. Hunzai, 'The Concept of *Tawḥīd*', pp. 81–82.

[31] De Smet, *La quiétude de l'intellect*, p. 216.

[32] Ibid., p. 216; *idem, Le Kitāb rāḥat al-'aql de Ḥamīd al-Dīn al-Kirmānī*, p. 90.

[33] Al-Kirmānī, *Rāḥat al-'aql*, pp. 212–214; al-Kirmānī dedicates the first three chapters of his *Riyāḍ* to clarifying al-Nasafī's, al-Rāzī's and al-Sijistānī's divergences on the true nature of the Intellect (as the first originated being), the Soul (as the first emanated being) and whether there are similarities between the two. Al-Kirmānī believes that the Soul, by merely being in actuality, is in a certain aspect perfect in her essence. More details on the three *dā'īs'* views of Soul and rational human souls will follow.

[34] Al-Kirmānī, *Rāḥat al-'aql*, p. 213.

By contemplating his absolute perfection, the Intellect feels an overwhelming joy which overflows his essence, naturally provoking the procession of the second intellect. The natural (and necessary) activity that the Intellect performs whilst thinking of his essence as that of a single, simple and perfect being automatically produces the emanation of the second intellect. The result is an intellect which is itself simple (*fard*) and yet specific (*mukhaṣṣ*): a separate form (*al-ṣūra al-mujarrada*).[35]

Whilst with the origination via *ibdāʿ* the Intellect does not entertain a relationship with the Principle, the procession via *inbiʿāth* rests exactly on the necessary relation between cause and effect. More specifically, self-contemplation does not guarantee the second intellect permanence in actuality and, as a consequence, it is compelled to think constantly of its cause because it is exclusively this object of cognisance that gives the second intellect its (first) perfection (i.e. actuality/existence).[36]

It should be remembered that al-Kirmānī speaks of the second intellect as a perfect intelligence in act; however, given the dual object of its intellection – itself and the Intellect through which it receives the form (*ṣūra*) of its cause – the second intellect would more appropriately be described as an intellect *in potentia* (as in the case of the third intellect). This idea is convincing if it is taken into account that the perfection of the second intellect resides in its being aware mainly of the Intellect rather than of itself or of the relationship that it entertains with its immediate cause. Al-Kirmānī states that ʿperfection of what follows [the Intellect] in existence consists of the knowledge it has of what is anterior to it, rather than consisting of the knowledge it has

---

[35] Ibid. I have already pointed out that the rank of the second intellect is due to its perfection being inferior in degree to the perfection of the Intellect. This diverse scale of excellence is generally explained with reference to the intellects' respective way of professing *tawḥīd* by way of reflecting on their own objects of intellection; so, whilst the Intellect's action is revolved only on himself (his cognisance occurring always inwardly despite being differentiated in the Intellect's self-perception of his relations with his essence as *ʿaql ʿāqil* and *ʿaql maʿqūl*), the second intellect thinks of itself and of the Intellect as its cause, and these increasing objects of intellection affect the purity of the second intellect's thought.

[36] De Smet, *La quiétude de l'intellect*, pp. 227–229 citing references to al-Kirmānī, *Rāḥat al-ʿaql*, pp. 212–220.

established with the latter'.[37] Nonetheless, it is fairly clear that al-Kirmānī is willing to emphasise the perfect nature of the second intellect. Conversely, according to al-Nasafī and al-Sijistānī, the Soul is the second being and is incomplete and imperfect in relation to the Intellect. She needs to seek and acquire perfection from something outside herself.[38] For al-Kirmāni, the Soul is deficient only when it comes to her rank, for hers is an inferior degree of excellence only in relation to the Intellect's. The Soul occupies the ultimate level of perfection within the realm of the emanated (*inbiʿāthī*) beings in the same way as the Intellect represents the absolute liminal perfection in the world of origination.[39] In contrast to the third intellect, the second intellect is deprived of any hylomorphic character and this probably explains why al-Kirmānī never speaks of it as being in potentiality.

Since the modality (*kayfiyya*) of the relationship occurring between God and the first intellect through *ibdāʿ* remains beyond definition or comprehension, the nature of God's *qaḍāʾ* (which must reflect a volitional nature considering al-Kirmānī's rejection of the Neoplatonic perspective of the godhead that is deprived of willingness) in respect to the Intellect eludes the classical Sunni position.

Ibn Sīnā, probably following al-Fārābī, speaks of God's *qaḍāʾ* as His first and unique command (*ḥukm*) from which all things derive, and identifies the *qadar* with the destiny which all beings have embedded in their given nature,[40] whereas, as we shall see in the course of this study, al-Kirmānī acknowledges a new 'identity' for the divine decree. The prophetic injunction against humans discussing the issue of predestination is slightly modified by al-Kirmānī,[41] who stresses Muḥammad's insistence on the possibility for humankind to talk about what is created (*makhlūq*)

---

[37]   Ibid., p. 216.

[38]   Al-Kirmānī's *Riyāḍ* (Beirut, 1960), pp. 58, 62 and 65. See also Paul E. Walker, 'The Universal Soul and the Particular Soul in Ismāʿīlī Neoplatonism', in *Neoplatonism and Islamic Thought*, ed. Parviz Morewedge (New York, 1992), pp. 156–157.

[39]   Al-Kirmānī, *Rāḥat al-ʿaql*, p. 212.

[40]   Ibn Sīnā, *Risāla fiʾl-qaḍāʾ*, in *Lettre au Vizier Abū Saʿad*, ed. Y. Michot (Beirut, 2000), pp. 103–105. See also De Cillis, *Free Will and Predestination*, pp. 36–37.

[41]   A *ḥadīth* reports the Prophet saying: 'Do not talk about the *qadar* because it is the secret of God. Do not dare to explain the secret of God.' ʿAlī al-Muttaqī al-Hindī, *Kanz al-ʿummāl fī sunan al-aqwāl waʾl afʿāl* (Beirut, 1971).

but to avoid discussions about the Creator (*al-khāliq*).[42] Particularly in his magnum opus, the *Rāḥat al-ʿaql*, al-Kirmānī quotes the Prophet's words: '*Takallamū fiʾl-makhlūq wa lā tatakallamū fiʾl-khāliq* (Speak of the creation and do not speak of the Creator)'. This is significant because in his *Riyāḍ*, *qadar* is actually identified with *makhlūq* (what is created/creation).[43] So, in a sense, for al-Kirmānī it is conceivable to speculate on the nature of the decree and other issues that are conventionally consigned to theology because these, in effect, are not directly linked to the Godhead. We shall see that throughout chapter eight of the *Riyāḍ*, al-Kirmānī endeavours to elucidate that *qaḍāʾ* and *qadar* are manifestations that are not linked to the world of the intellects.

Conversely, the impossibility of discussing the inexpressible nature of the Creator is something divinely sanctioned, something which even the perfect nature of the first intellect is deterministically compelled to observe. It is exactly the acknowledgment of his own limitation, namely the impossibility for the Intellect's self-intelligising nature to grasp anything different from himself, that confirms the Intellect's value as the first and most perfect among the created beings.[44] Despite his desire to know God, the Intellect is resigned to his own destiny of 'ignorance'. He accepts the role 'willed' for him by a God who decrees to remain unknowable by choosing to originate the Intellect through *ibdāʿ* rather than through *inbiʿāth*.

Paradoxically, in clear contrast to the position of both philosophers and mystics who regarded God's desire to be known as the goal of creation, the Ismaili doctrine of origination and the emphasis it puts on the supreme divine mystery overtly opposes the concept that the divine *qaḍāʾ* is predetermined to be unfolded through a kind of knowledge that is not comprehension of God, but rather awareness of the guidance offered by divinely inspired legitimate leaders who, cosmologically speaking, are none other than terrestrial manifestations of their intellectual counterparts. Indeed, the continued presence of

---

[42] Al-Kirmānī, *Rāḥat al-ʿaql*, p. 195. On the origins of such a tradition, see De Smet, *La quiétude de l'intellect*, p. 181 note 180.

[43] 'The *qadar* of God […] is the creation (*khalq*) […] from the superior [beings] (*āfāq*) and the souls and their functional movements (*al-ḥarakāt al-dāla*) as He has decreed them to be'. Al-Kirmānī, *Riyāḍ* (HL), p. 138.

[44] Al-Kirmānī, *Rāḥat al-ʿaql*, pp. 173, 175.

a 'personified' intellect on earth is the necessary condition for human salvation because, through the precepts of the law, the prophets and Imams indicate to humankind the way to serve God by worshipping Him through action (*al-ʿibāda al-ʿamaliyya*) whilst, with their teaching of *taʾwīl*, they guide humans towards the worship of God through knowledge (*al-ʿibāda al-ʿilmiyya*).[45]

---

45 De Smet, *La quiétude de l'intellect*, p. 312.

4

The Human Soul and Providence

In his *al-Maqṣad al-asnā fī sharḥ maʿānī asmāʾ Allāh al-ḥusnā*, al-Ghazālī engages in the exegesis of Qurʾan 59:24 (*'huwa Allāh al-khāliq al-bāriʾ al-muṣawwir lahu al-asmāʾ al-ḥusnā'*; 'He is the Creator, the Evolver, the Bestower of Forms. To Him belong the most beautiful names') and presents God's nature and His relation to His acts according to three principal epithets: (i) God as the Creator (*al-khāliq*) in a general sense; (ii) God as the Evolver (*al-bāriʾ*) by causing the existence of things; (iii) God as the Bestower of Forms (*al-muṣawwir*) through His ordering the forms of created beings.[1] He acknowledges that whilst the first two names signify God in His quality as the creator *ex nihilo*, the third name is usually employed by exegetes to indicate God's action by which He appoints each thing with its appropriate form (*taṣwīr*).[2]

Al-Kirmānī formulates an audacious exegesis of the same Qurʾanic verse and describes the three divine names as those of the first three intellects, assigning them all with demiurgic functions.[3] An important outcome of his interpretation is that the most beautiful among the divine names, *Allāh*, is not attributed to God but rather to the first originated being – also identified with the name *al-muṣawwir* – whose task is that of generating all the forms (*takwīn al-ṣuwar*) which are, in turn, considered essences of the principles in existence (*āʿyān al-mabādiʾ fiʾl-wujūd*).[4] The second intellect is identified with the

---

[1] Abū Ḥāmid al-Ghazālī, *al-Maqṣad al-asnā fī sharḥ maʿānī asmāʾ Allāh al-ḥusnā*, ed. Fadlou Shedadi (Beirut, 1986, repr. Beirut, 1982), pp. 79–80; tr. David B. Burrel and Nazih Daher as *The Ninety-nine Beautiful Names of God* (Cambridge, 1992), p. 68.

[2] Daniel Gimaret, *Les noms divins en Islam: exégèse lexicographique et théologique* (Paris, 1988), pp. 286–288.

[3] Al-Kirmānī, *Rāḥat al-ʿaql*, p. 254.

[4] Al-Kirmānī, ibid analysed in De Smet, *La quiétude de l'intellect*, pp. 264–265.

name *al-bāri'*, who invests the forms in existence with what suits them the most in accordance to the requirements of the order of wisdom (*naẓm al-ḥikma*).[5] The third intellect corresponds to the name *al-khāliq*, as it is responsible for composition and organisation (*tarkīb*).[6] As De Smet has highlighted, al-Kirmānī's exegesis sets the creative function of the first three intellects at the level of the forms: the Intellect produces them; the second intellect distributes them according to the divine wisdom, also making sure that each being receives the form which is most suitable for it; and the third intellect is in charge of the composition and organisation of beings, a task Neoplatonic followers previously assigned to the tenth intellect.

The world of the intellects is set beyond space and time as we know them, with time being generated through the movements of the celestial bodies.[7] Al-Kirmānī refutes Abū Ḥātim al-Rāzī's idea that time is the same as Intellect and proceeds from Intellect simultaneously with Soul. Basically, according to al-Rāzī, Intellect, Time as well as the act of origination are one and the same thing (*ays wāḥīd*). God originates all existents in one extra-temporal action, including the Intellect who encompasses all things. The second existent which proceeds from the first and is complete in its essence like it, exists side-by-side with time and therefore acts in a temporal dimension.[8] In the section of the *Riyāḍ* that will be investigated, the third intellect is presented as the intellect that is delayed and whose attainment of the first and second

---

[5] Ibid.

[6] Ibid. Significantly, throughout the *Riyāḍ*, al-Kirmānī delineates correspondences among the third intellect as Nature (*ṭabīʿa*), creation (*khalq*) and the *sharīʿa*. The third intellect governs the realm of Nature, whose created arrangement reflects the character of a composition (*tarkīb*) which resembles the redaction (*taʾlīf*) of the religious legislation. Contrary to al-Kirmānī, it is the Soul which, for al-Sijistānī, is charged with the responsibility of *tarkīb*. Through this function, the Soul creates Nature. That is, the Soul, by receiving intellectual benefits from the Intellect, triggers the *tarkīb* of the sensible world. Similarly, the mission that each enunciator-prophet fulfils following the bestowal of intellectual benefits is nothing but the 'composition' of a *sharīʿa* that regulates human life. Al-Sijistānī, *Kitāb al-Yanābīʿ*, pp. 63–64; tr. Walker, *The Wellsprings of Wisdom*, p. 45, pp. 119–120.

[7] Al-Kirmānī, *Rāḥat al-ʿaql*, pp. 257–260; *idem, Riyāḍ* (Beirut, 1960), p. 59.

[8] See Walker, 'The Universal Soul', p. 153. On al-Sijistānī's concept of time, see more below.

perfections is not a simultaneous acquisition. In truth, the passage from potentiality into actuality is a way to emphasise that the first and second perfections are not essentially embedded in the third intellect but are the result of the external intervention from the other intellects.[9] De Smet has convincingly explained the ambiguity residing in al-Kirmānī's understanding of the nature of the third intellect and why it has the same characteristics as the tenth intellect: the third intellect is surely considered inferior to the other intellects given its potential nature, which is transmitted through its hylomorphism. More specifically, the third intellect's status of potentiality is due to the fact that it receives the activity of other intellects: it is a *muʾaththar*.[10] By way of being a receptacle for actions, the third intellect is identified with the *hayūlā*;[11] it is characterised by an essential imperfection due to its intrinsic composite nature, being made of matter and form.[12] The third intellect's first perfection does not necessitate its second perfection, which can be attained only by the intervention of other intellects. For the third intellect, the passage from the rank of possibility (*rutbat al-imkān*) to the rank of necessity (*rutbat al-wujūb*), namely the passage from the first to the second perfection, is perceived by al-Kirmānī as a providential work offered by the intellects in actuality to their less perfect kin which, despite being an intellect itself, belongs to a different genre due to its hylomorphism. Once in the status of actuality, the third intellect can function as the cause of the sublunar world. It thus becomes the philosophers' Agent Intellect (*al-ʿaql al-faʿʿāl*), the actual demiurge of the natural world.

---

[9] Al-Kirmānī, *Riyāḍ* (HL), pp. 129–131. De Smet, *La quiétude de l'intellect*, pp. 240–243. Al-Kirmānī's thought thus appears to have absorbed within his system the Gnostic theme of the fall of the third intellect which is recounted by al-Ḥamīdī in his *Kitāb Kanz al-walad* (See *Kanz al-walad*, pp. 66–69 and 296–297). Al-Ḥamīdī regarded the error committed by one of the intellects as transformed into its 'fall' – or its rank's degradation – in the emanative hierarchy followed by its final rescue through the assistance of all the other intellects. Al-Kirmānī, De Smet argues, gives these theories a philosophical legitimisation by placing them within the Neoplatonic theoretical construct. See De Smet, *La quiétude de l'intellect*, pp. 248–251.

[10] Al-Kirmānī, *Rāḥat al-ʿaql*, p. 219.

[11] Ibid., p. 223.

[12] Ibid., pp. 222, 228.

The full actualisation of the third intellect is a 'change' that occurs in a temporal dimension that is, however, not as we usually conceive it.[13] The remaining seven intellects, whose nature is said to be that of pure forms and intellects in actuality, follow from the second intellect rather than the third. In effect, they all contribute towards the third intellect's perfection which, '*after*' their intervention, is raised from the tenth position in the hierarchy of the intelligences – the farthest from the Intellect and, as such, the least perfect – closest to the world of Nature, to a level that is parallel (*muwāzī*) to that of the second intellect.[14] This explains why the tenth intellect is identifiable with the third intellect, which has stepped out of its potentiality and has been invested with the role of the demiurge of the sublunar dominion.

In al-Kirmānī's system, the sublunar world is composed of material beings. Each one is endowed in its own corporeality with an active principle which is alternately called 'life' (*ḥayāt*), 'form' (*ṣūra*), 'soul' (*nafs*) or nature (*ṭabī'a*). Emanated from the realm of the separate intelligences, this principle is an active force which makes all bodies achieve their goals by developing in accordance to their natural dispositions. All corporeal bodies except humans are able to have access to their second perfection both through the inner force of their 'soul' and through the external influx (*fayḍ*) of the celestial bodies.[15] For humans, however, the attainment of the second perfection and the accomplishment of their return to the world of the intellects depends on the aid provided to their souls by the Intellect, which manifests himself in the forms of the prophets and the Imams. Indeed, the very notion of a second perfection for human souls displays al-Kirmānī's Ismaili concept of the imamate. Human souls attain to their second perfection exclusively through the guidance and instruction (*ta'līm*)

---

[13]   The instantaneous passage from the state of potentiality to that of actuality is something observable also in Ibn Sīnā's system. In particular, the potential nature of anything other than God is traceable at the very moment beings enter existence, that is, the very moment the passage from the status of possibility to that of necessity is actualised. See Jules Jannsens, 'Creation and Emanation in Ibn Sīnā', *Documenti e Studi sulla Tradizione Filosofica Medievale*, 8 (1997), p. 473.

[14]   Al-Kirmānī, *Riyāḍ* (HL), pp. 129–131.

[15]   On this topic see more at pp. 74–76.

of those who receive spiritual assistance from heaven, 'the spiritually supported ones' (*al-mu'ayyadūn min al-samā'*).[16]

All human beings are endowed with a soul which enters the domain of existence only through and with the natural body. As a substance found only in bodies, the human soul attains the first perfection through its own body but, between the individual body and the soul, it is to the soul that it is more correct to ascribe any action.[17] As in al-Kirmānī's words, God has made the substance of the soul (*jawhar al-nafs*) a life (*ḥayāt*), a being capable (*qādir*) of doing both good and evil (*fa'il al-khayr wa'l-sharr*) and of choosing between obedience and disobedience (*al-ṭā'a wa'l-ma'ṣiya*).[18] It is evident that the human soul might pursue the path towards damnation and punishment rather than choosing salvation and reward (*jazā'*). The latter functions as a distinctive element (*fāṣila firqān^{an}*) which, as al-Kirmānī explains, allows the nobility of the creating power (*sharaf al-khāliqiyya*) and the splendour of Lordship (*majd al-rubūbiyya*) to be manifest.[19] This occurs because the recompense allows one, as al-Kirmānī puts it, to differentiate the commander from the commanded (*al-amr min al-mā'mūr*) in their manifested forms,[20] the bestower of blessings from those on whom they are bestowed (*al-mun'im min al-mun'am 'alayhi*), the preceder from the one who is preceded (*al-sābiq min al-masbūq*), the lord from the servant (*al-rabb min al-marbūb*) and the worshipper from the one who is worshipped (*al-'abd min al-ma'būd*).[21] By doing so, the recompense acts as a governing principle (*siyāsa qā'ima*), being itself the form (*ṣūra*) of a divine principle (*siyāsa rabbāniyya*) which, providentially and justly, proves that there is a distinction between

---

[16]   Al-Kirmānī, *Rāḥat al-'aql*, p. 447.

[17]   Al-Kirmānī, *al-Maṣābīḥ fī ithbāt al-imāma*, Arabic text, p. 19; English text, p. 54.

[18]   Ibid., Arabic text, p. 18; English text, p. 53.

[19]   Ibid., Arabic text, pp. 18–19, English text, pp. 53–54.

[20]   The philosopher Naṣīr al-Dīn al-Ṭūsī explained to his co-religionists that it is not simply to the command (*farmān*) that the believers should be attached to but also the one who issues the command (*farmān-dih*), i.e. the Prophet and the Imams. See his *Sayr wa-sulūk*, ed. and tr. S. Jalal Badakhchani as *Contemplation and Action: The Spiritual Autobiography of a Muslim Scholar* (London, 1998), pp. 50–51.

[21]   Al-Kirmānī, *al-Maṣābīḥ fī ithbāt al-imāma*, Arabic text, pp. 18-19, English text, pp. 53–54.

the good obedient soul (*al-nafs al-khayr al-ṭā'i'*) and the disobedient wicked soul (*al-nafs al-sharīr al-'aṣiyya*).

It is because these differentiations are in place that reward and punishment exist. Put in more simple terms, al-Kirmānī believes that the soul has the power-to-act (*qudra*), the knowledge (*'ilm*) to distinguish between good and evil and the capacity-of-choosing (*ikhtiyār*) between obedience and disobedience so that it is rewarded or punished accordingly.[22] Thus, al-Kirmānī specifies, the human species (*naw' al-bashariyya*) has been made legally capable (*mukallafīn*)[23] through command and prohibition (*taḥt al-amr wa'l-nahy*). That is, the human being is morally responsible under the law because the latter clearly delineates what is commendable and what is not. Because God has provided humans with the power of discernment (*tamyīz*) by means of which they distinguish themselves from other species, it is necessary for any human soul, who has chosen to pursue the imitation of the spiritual intelligences, to be rewarded and, conversely, for any soul who has pursued the pleasures of worldly sensations to be punished.[24] If, on the one hand, thanks to its innate intellectual potentialities, the human soul is hypothetically capable of making decisions and carrying out choices, on the other hand, it is also true that the human soul fully actualises its rational 'faculty', as a proper capacity of discrimination and knowledge, only when it reaches a sufficient degree of closeness with the Intellect that, ultimately, operates as the soul's true rational faculty (*al-quwwa al-nāṭiqa*).

The human soul is endowed with four main faculties: (i) the nutritive faculty (*al-quwwa al-ghādhiyya*); (ii) the sensitive faculty (*al-quwwa al-ḥāss*); (iii) the representative faculty (*al-quwwa al-mutakhayyila*); and (iv) the rational faculty.[25] The fourth faculty is split between a practical aspect (*'amaliyya*) and a theoretical aspect (*naẓariyya*). The practical aspect allows humans to distinguish between good and evil and, by following the prescription of the religious law, to worship God

---

22   Ibid., Arabic text, p. 19, English text, p. 54.

23   Significantly, the term '*mukallaf*' also bears the meaning of 'being obliged to observe (the precepts of religion)'. Al-Kirmānī, *al-Maṣābīḥ fī ithbāt al-imāma*, Arabic text, p. 19, English text, p. 54. The English translation has been slightly modified.

24   Ibid., Arabic text, p. 19, English text, pp. 54–55; *idem, Rāḥat al-'aql*, p. 506.

25   Ibid., p. 480.

through action (*al-ʿibāda al-ʿamaliyya*).[26] With the theoretical aspect, the human intellect contemplates the intelligible forms and worships God through knowledge (*al-ʿibāda al-ʿilmiyya*).[27] Once actualised in existence, that is, once its first perfection is achieved, the human soul can aspire to attain its second perfection and a purely intellectual existence[28] by entering into a closer relationship with the Intellect.[29] Significantly, the rising up to the second perfection is achieved through the human soul's acquisition (*iktisāb*) of a fuller kind of knowledge, which remains inaccessible without the specific teaching (*taʿlīm*) by the divinely chosen prophets, Imams and dignitaries of the Ismaili *daʿwa*.[30] As a living substance the human soul has the capacity 'of enduring beyond the dissolution of the material body, on the basis of what it acquires in the way of knowledge and good deeds.'[31]

---

[26]   This means that through this aspect, the human being becomes subject to morality. Ibid., p. 462.

[27]   Ibid., pp. 456, 462, 465, 467, 471, 476, 497.

[28]   Daniel De Smet, '"Perfectio prima" – "perfectio secunda", ou les vicissitudes d'une notion', *Recherches de Théologie et Philosophie Mediévales*, 66/2 (1999), pp. 254–288. In contrast to all inferior souls, the human soul can set itself free from earthly desires, thus attaining a perfection which will allow it to subsist even after its detachment from the body. See al-Kirmānī, *Rāḥat al-ʿaql*, p. 446.

[29]   Walker, *Ḥamīd al-Dīn al-Kirmānī*, pp. 99–100.

[30]   Al-Kirmānī, *Rāḥat al-ʿaql*, pp. 160–161, 190, 447, 467, 470, 491. The teaching of the prophets and the Imams becomes the necessary condition for humankind to exercise any form of rational activity because without such teachings all kinds of rational speculation employed in sciences such as metaphysics, physics, Qurʾanic exegesis and so on, which are equally valid according to the principle of the unity of knowledge established through the balance of religion, would be impossible (see De Smet, '*Mīzān al-diyāna*', p. 253). This implies that any attempt at compromise or harmonisation among all avenues of knowledge finds its justification within the concept of *taʿlīm*, the teachings of the Imams. De Smet has observed that 'Il n'existe dès lors aucune opposition entre les différentes disciplines (les distinctions entre philosophie, science ou *taʾwīl* étant purement formelles), mais uniquement entre une connaissance vraie et exacte (acquise par l'initié qui, ayant accepté l'einsegnement de l'Imam, a su actualiser sa faculté rationelle et est devenu un 'sage', un *ḥakīm*), at une pseudo-connaissance, qui ne permet qu'une approche erronée et trompeuse de la réalité'. See De Smet, ibid., p. 253.

[31]   Al-Kirmānī, *al-Maṣābīḥ fī ithbāt al-imāma*, tr. Walker, *Ḥamīd al-Dīn al-Kirmānī*, p. 100. This does not imply that soul pre-exists its manifestation in body. It simply suggests that each soul survives its departure from its *jism*.

This means that the body becomes superfluous once the soul reaches the final stage of its development, namely the second procession (*al-munba'ith al-thānī*). After the actualisation of the rational faculty's practical aspect, which is realised by embracing the teaching of the *sharī'a* – as this has been revealed by the prophets, preserved and explained by the Imams who are also responsible for implementing its precepts[32] – the actualisation of the theoretical faculty becomes incumbent. This is achieved by attaining knowledge of the esoteric significance of the revelation and the law, uncovered through the *ta'wīl* carried out by the *waṣi*s and the Imams, as al-Kirmānī' explains in his masterpiece, the *Rāḥat al-'aql*.[33]

I have explained that for al-Kirmānī the ability to acquire true knowledge pertains to the soul only potentially: to lead the soul away from its essential status of imperfection there are intelligent powers acting providentially. God, in fact, created the world of the Intellect and the Soul and made it an abode (*dār*) from which emanate the blessings of His word (*barakāt kalimat Allāh*).[34] The Pleroma of the intellects fulfils its providential function in different ways: besides creating corporeal and material beings, it ensures that these develop and attain to the ultimate goal of their existence, that is, their second perfection, by endowing them with souls. The latter, in turn, act as inherent principles of movement, spurring their respective bodies towards their governing intellects. The intellects broaden their providentiality by determining the course of events in this world and they do so through the 'brokerage' of the celestial bodies.[35] Just as each intellect bestows upon its own sphere and its corresponding planet a specific power or blessing (*baraka*), so does the planet which pours the same

---

[32] Al-Kirmānī, *Rāḥat al-'aql*, pp. 164–165, 273–274, 464, 470; De Smet, *La quiétude de l'intellect*, p. 357.

[33] Al-Kirmānī, *Rāḥat al-'aql*, p. 358.

[34] Al-Kirmānī, *al-Maṣābīḥ fī ithbāt al-imāma*, Arabic text, p. 20, English text, p. 55.

[35] Celestial bodies have specific functions: so, for example, the moon presides over the generation of bodies, whilst the sun is responsible for the emanation of souls. Besides their demiurgic tasks, they function as tools that allow the intellects to exercise their actions towards our world. Al-Kirmānī, *Rāḥat al-'aql*, pp. 224, 280–281, 306–307, 315–317, 322–323, 333, 390; De Smet, *La quiétude de l'intellect*, pp. 343–344.

blessings upon sublunar beings.[36] This pouring is the perpetual emanation of an influx (*fayḍ*) which enables entities to remain in existence and attain to their ultimate end, namely the profession of *tawḥīd* and their return to their principle (the Intellect).[37] The bestowal of this

---

[36] Al-Kirmānī, *Rāḥat al-ʿaql*, pp. 277–278; De Smet, *La quiétude de l'intellect*, p. 346. Al-Kirmānī suggests that intellects do not have direct access to the domain of matter, with the exclusion of the tenth intellect (De Smet, ibid., p. 283). The nine celestial spheres and each celestial body belong to a different species for which they are the only representatives; they are directly emanated by the tenth intellect without any intermediary (*wāsiṭa*) and they are considered perfect in their essence. Despite having a hylomorphic nature, they are not subjected to any change in their form since their matter has been provided with the most suitable form from the very instant they became actualised. They are characterised by immutability and permanence, although being subject to movement. This, however, is a perfect movement in itself which does not imply any form of change: it is an eternal, constant and circular movement which departs from a perfect status and goes back to it without entailing any passage from potentiality to actuality (al-Kirmānī, *Rāḥat al-ʿaql*, pp. 306, 308 and 346). The celestial bodies' movements and perfect essences make them the causes of the existence of the sublunar beings (ibid., p. 306). In this sense, they become instruments (*ālāt*) of the tenth intellect. The latter, however, is considered to be able to employ the celestial bodies' activity on condition that there is a material substratum capable of receiving (*mādda qābila*) their influences. It is with the intent of utilising the influx of the celestial bodies that the demiurge emanates from celestial matter a 'new' matter that is completely devoid of any characterisation and is, therefore, pure receptivity: prime matter (*al-mādda al-ūlā*) (ibid., pp. 322–323 and 325). Having attained all the necessary tools, the tenth intellect gives the first qualification to prime matter through which it attains the three dimensions, thus being transformed into an extended body. Such an absolute body (*al-jism al-muṭlaq*), is the subject of the celestial bodies' movements which, in turn, become the cause of heat on that matter which comes into contact with them: the part of matter that is closer to the heat is associated with the element of fire; the farther from the heat, the colder the matter, till we reach the element earth. The latter, due to its supreme degree of obscurity, coldness and intensity, is associated with evil. More specifically, al-Kirmānī associates earth with dissension and error (*al-ikhtilāf wa'l-ḍalāl*) occurring among the members of the rebellious community (*al-umma al-ʿāṣiya*) that refuses the teaching of the Imam. See De Smet, *La quiétude de l'intellect*, pp. 313–318.

[37] Al-Sijistānī propounded similar views by stating that all beings pertaining to the world of natural generation (*mawālīd*) are under the active influence of the celestial bodies which, together with the elements, provide such beings with their attributes. Interestingly, al-Sijistānī establishes a well-defined hierarchy which places the creative Word (*kalima*) before the Intellect: 'the elements and the [celestial]

external influx and the mediation of the celestial bodies are elements that enable the intellects to carry out their providential assignment of protecting and maintaining creation within a fixed order. Undeniably, divine providence (*al-ʿināya al-ilāhiyya*) manifests itself at different levels across the whole creation: it surfaces in the constitution of the intellects, in assigning to each of them with their place and role in the cosmic hierarchy, in making each intellect correspond to its sphere,[38] in determining the position and function of celestial bodies,[39] and in granting each entity a specific place and role in the universe. Providence is described as what

> provides (*taʿāla*) for all existent beings (*al-mawjūdāt*) the preservation of their totality (*al-ḥāfiẓa li-jamīʿihā*) according to an immutable order (*niẓām thābit*) so that no things can escape it (*lā yaghriba ʿanhā*); [providence] is that on which the existence of all things depends; it is what establishes (*yataʿallaq*) everything through everything (*al-kull bi'l-kull*) in the guise of assistance (*ʿawnan*) either through one intermediary or through multiple ones so as to convey the whole existence towards its purpose (*ghāyatuhu*), its perfection (*kamāluhu*) and its limit (*nihāyatuhu*).[40]

This means that divine providence acts as an all-encompassing principle of order in a double way: (i) in a more static fashion, it regulates the preservation in existence (and rank) of all entities, and (ii) in a rather dynamic sense, through intermediaries, it spurs all existents towards

---

bodies receive their attributes from Nature; Nature from Soul; Soul from Intellect; and Intellect from the [creative] Word'. See al-Sijistānī, *Kashf al-maḥjūb*, tr. Landolt, *Unveiling of the Hidden*, p. 86.

[38] Al-Kirmānī, *Rāḥat al-ʿaql*, pp. 249, 261; De Smet, *La quiétude de l'intellect*, pp. 247–248, 347.

[39] Al-Kirmānī, *Rāḥat al-ʿaql*, pp. 223, 321; De Smet, *La quiétude de l'intellect*, p. 347.

[40] Al-Kirmānī, *Rāḥat al-ʿaql*, p. 417. Because providence operates through intermediaries, it cannot be placed at the level of the *mubdiʿ* directly, as this would imply a continuity between the unreachable Originator and the product of His origination. Consequently, it is linked to the ultimate knowable limit, the Intellect, from which it spreads penetrating all the levels of existence. Cf. De Smet, *La quiétude de l'intellect*, p. 348.

their ultimate actualisation (i.e. the realisation of their potentialities, as well as of their completeness and roles in the cosmic hierarchy). It is obvious that it is not exclusively at the level of the celestial bodies that providence penetrates: it is, in fact, from the world of the Soul or the world of Holiness (*'ālam al-quds*), which is in the larger cosmic sense the Spirit of Holiness (*rūḥ al-quds*),[41] that the emanation of the individual souls proceeds. Because it is also through the inherent motor-soul in individuals that existents can aspire to realise their two perfections – (i) existence and (ii) intellectual actualisation and the profession of *tawḥīd* in an optimum way[42] – it is clear that the world of the Soul has its share in the principle of providence.

It is the world of the Soul which conveys to sublunar souls the magnanimities of the oneness of God (*karamāt waḥdāniyyat Allāh*) as a gratuitous favour (*daf'ʿan*).[43] According to al-Kirmānī, this occurs because the human souls resemble, even if in an imperfect way, the souls and the intellects of the celestial realm, individual souls being traces (*āthār*) of the Universal Soul.[44] More specifically, the substances of the souls (*jawāhir al-anfus*) are believed to be of the same kind as the world of the Intellect and the Soul (*'ālam al-'aql wa'l-nafs*) and this makes them fit to receive the foregoing divine gift. It is the potential intellectual nature of the human soul – preserved in its *ibdā'ī* and *inbi'āthī* qualities – that prompts the celestial beings to 'retain a providential responsibility for human beings.'[45]

The same providential intervention is manifested by the whole Pleroma of intellects upon the third intellect which aspires to attain

---

[41] Al-Kirmānī, *al-Maṣābīḥ fī ithbāt al-imāma*, Arabic text, p. 26, English text, p. 61; Walker, *Ḥamīd al-Dīn al-Kirmānī*, p. 101.

[42] Al-Kirmānī, *Rāḥat al-'aql*, pp. 224–225, 287–288, 370–371, 418; De Smet, *La quiétude de l'intellect*, p. 347.

[43] Al-Kirmānī, *al-Maṣābīḥ fī ithbāt al-imāma*, Arabic text, p. 20, English text, p. 55. Divine providence comes from above (*min fawqin*) and it is in all existing beings (*fī kull shay' min al-mawjūdāt*); it radiates from the intelligences and penetrates the realm of Nature. See al-Kirmānī, *Rāḥat al-'aql*, pp. 224–225.

[44] Al-Rāzī was of the same opinion. See his *Iṣlāḥ*, pp. 33–34. On Proclus' influence on al-Rāzī's doctrine of the soul see Walker, *Early Philosophical Shiism*, pp. 55, 99–100; *idem*, 'The Universal Soul and the Particular Soul in Ismā'īlī Neoplatonism', in *Neoplatonism and Islamic Thought*, ed. Parviz Morewedge, pp. 149–166.

[45] Walker, *Ḥamīd al-Dīn al-Kirmānī*, p. 101.

its true actuality, namely, its second perfection. In similar terms, al-Sijistānī speaks of a sentiment of pity (mercy, *raḥma*) which the Intellect pours upon the Soul because of her attachment to corporeal beings. Despite this legacy, the Intellect still entertains a lower form of communication (*al-khiṭāb al-suflī*) with the Soul through which the living form (*al-ṣūra al-mutanaffisa*) – which is the outcome (*maḥṣūl*) of the natural world (*al-ʿālam al-ṭabīʿī*) – realises the fulfilment (*tamāmiyya*) of what has been decreed by wisdom (*ḥikma*). The communication of the Intellect to the Soul surfaces in the make-up of composite beings (i.e. Nature): the Intellect's innate disposition (*gharīza*) makes composite entities free from necessitating what does not pertain to them. In addition, it also instructs the Soul on how (*kayfa*) – upon the actualisation of the material compound given by the coming to be of matter (*hayūla*) and form (*ṣūra*) – the Soul should arrange things in order to manifest the nobility of wisdom (*sharaf al-ḥikma*).[46]

I have mentioned above that, according to al-Kirmānī, celestial responsibility – in the guise of providence – extends also to all creatures other than humans; these are subjected to comprehensive predestination, unfurling through the activity of the intelligential Pleroma upon the world of Nature. However, this is not a capricious and deterministic imposition but rather a supervising, providential, harmonic force which simultaneously (i) allows each being, by merely following its inner natural dispositions and naturally complying to the laws of external forces, to live and develop in the best possible way,[47] and (ii) directs each existent towards its principle and towards

---

[46]   Al-Sijistānī, *Kitāb al-Yanābīʿ*, p. 93; tr. Walker, *The Wellsprings of Wisdom*, p. 62. This form of providential wisdom coming from the Intellect recalls al-Fārābī's and Ibn Sīnā's reading of the Agent Intellect as the Aristotelian *Dator Formarum*: the 'supervising' cause that enables the receptive nature of matter to be joined to a suitable form, thus producing a material compound (see De Cillis, *Free Will and Predestination*, pp. 44–46). It is significant that for both al-Kirmānī and al-Sijistānī, the notion of nobility (*sharaf*) appears to be associated with some form of creating power, perfection and self-subsistence, that is, with concepts echoing the idea of actualisation. Even more specifically, nobility is subtly linked with the fulfilment of the passage from potentiality into actuality, which means compliance with what the ultimate wisdom (i.e. the Intellect's wisdom and rationality) decrees.

[47]   Al-Sijistānī associates this natural way of being with the influences that the celestial bodies and constellations exercise on species by preserving and subtracting

the implementation of *tawḥīd*. Nonetheless, distinct from minerals, plants and animals, the human being subtracts themselves from this cosmic determinism because they are ultimately free. What providential determinism provides for all other existents does not suffice for humans to attain their ultimate perfection: a life led 'selon la nature', as De Smet explains, will not permit them to upgrade themselves from the animal level to that of a rational human being.[48] Compliance with providential determinism must come through a wilful submission, through a conscious desire to reach complete actualisation, which for a human soul means to accomplish a passage from its innate status of intellect *in potentia* (*bi'l-quwwa*) to the acquired status of intellect in actuality (*bi'l-fiʿl*) (i.e. the fullest actualisation of both the practical and theoretical rational faculties). This passage occurs, as I have already elucidated, when the human soul chooses to follow the redeeming teaching of an appointed guide. The latter is 'selected' by the last intellect in the heavenly hierarchy, the tenth intellect, which the whole system of separate intellects invests with the responsibility of generating its intellectual representative on earth.[49] This representative must be a human individual possessing a fully and perfectly accomplished intellectual nature, 'a wise man to whom the mark of ignorance is

---

them from evolution or extinction (al-Sijistānī, *Kashf al-maḥjūb*, tr. Landolt, *Unveiling of the Hidden*, pp. 109–110; Corbin, *Le dévoilement des choses cachées*, pp. 89–102). The inadmissibility for species to mix after separation from their bodies is a delicate issue as it is directly linked to the condemned doctrine of transmigration (*tanāsukh*). This issue and al-Sijistānī's personal understanding of it emerge, in my opinion, in the discourse of *qaḍāʾ* and *qadar* in al-Kirmānī's *Riyāḍ*. See below.

[48] De Smet, *La quiétude de l'intellect*, pp. 350–351. Al-Sijistānī also distinguished between a natural existence (*al-kawn al-ṭabīʿī*) and a soul-like existence (*al-kawn al-nafsānī*). The former comes from the influences of the celestial bodies and encompasses all entified beings; the latter is due to the emanations of the Intellect and the Soul and encompasses the individual soul's reception of spiritual support (*qabūl al-taʾyīd*) and of teaching and spiritual exercise (*qabūl al-taʿlīm wa'l-riyāḍa*). Al-Sijistānī, 'al-Risāla al-Bāhira', ed. Boustan Hirji, in *Taḥqīqāt-i Islāmī*, 7 (1992), Ch. 5.

[49] Upon such a representative is exercised the emanation of all the higher intellects. See Walker, *Ḥamīd al-Dīn al-Kirmānī*, p. 102, quoting al-Kirmānī, *al-Risāla al-Waḍīʾa fī maʿālim al-dīn*, MS. Fyzee Collection, Bombay University Library, 14a–16b; al-Kirmānī, *Riyāḍ* (Beirut, 1960), p. 222.

foreign'.[50] Such humans, as already mentioned, are all the prophets and the founders of religions (the *aṣḥāb al-adwār,* or masters of the cycles) and, more specifically, the future Resurrector (*qā'im*) who will be the perfect enactment of the human intellectual make-up.[51]

It should be kept in mind that the repositories of the teaching coming from the world of the Soul or the world of Holiness are the recipients of an emanation that is bequeathed in the form of regulations (*rusūm*) and utterances (*aqwāl*) which, in turn, are brought forward by the messengers (*rusul*) as laws (*sharā'i'*) and Scriptures (*kutub*).[52] Therefore, al-Kirmānī states, laws are necessary and cannot be obliterated since they are the objectified facet of that wisdom (*ḥikma*) and knowledge (*ma'rifa*) – that is, the flux coming from the world of Holiness – that is converted into attainable forms of sensation such as letters (*ḥurūf*) and written precepts (*waḍā'i'*).[53]

It is significant at this point to recall that, according to the principle of the balance of religion, the member of each world perfectly corresponds to the being that occupies the same rank in the hierarchy of a different realm. Hence, for al-Kirmānī, the members of the world of religion (*'ālam al-dīn*) who, contrary to what al-Sijistānī believed, correspond exclusively to the corporeal *ḥudūd,*[54] are ten in number – in keeping with his quasi-Fārābian cosmological system.[55] The ten

---

[50] Al-Kirmānī, *al-Maṣābīḥ fī ithbāt al-imāma,* Arabic text p. 29, English text (modified) p. 63.

[51] Walker, *Ḥamīd al-Dīn al-Kirmānī,* p. 102.

[52] Al-Kirmānī, *al-Maṣābīḥ fī ithbāt al-imāma,* Arabic text p. 26, English text (slightly modified) p. 61.

[53] Ibid., Arabic text p. 26, English text (modified) p. 61.

[54] This position might be read as yet another veiled attempt to dismiss any identification between al-Ḥākim as the Imam and al-Ḥākim as the divinity.

[55] The ten dignitaries of the world of religion are as follows: the *nāṭiq,* the *waṣī, imām, bāb* (gate), *ḥujja* (proof), *dā'ī al-balāgh* (missionary of the message), *al-dā'ī al-muṭlaq* (general missionary), *al-dā'ī al-maḥṣūr* or *al-maḥdūd* (limited missionary), *al-ma'dhūn al-muṭlaq* (general legatee) and *al-ma'dhūn al-maḥṣūr* or *al-mukāsir* (limited legatee); al-Kirmānī, *Rāḥat al-'aql,* pp. 253–256, 272–273; Calderini '"*Ālam al-Dīn*" in Ismā'īlism', p. 462 note 35. On the decadic structure of al-Kirmānī's world of religion and the specific role of its components, see Abbas Ḥamdani, 'Evolution of the Organizational Structure of the Fāṭimī *Da'wah', Arabian Studies,* 3 (1976), pp. 92–94; and Feki, *Les idées religieuses,* pp. 160, 166–171. De Smet has argued that

ranks of the *ʿālam al-dīn* are presented according to a synchronic and diachronic perspective: according to the former, the dignitaries are the ranks of the Ismaili *daʿwa* from the *nāṭiq* (enunciator-prophet) to the *mukāsir* (limited legatee). Diachronically, the *ḥudūd* are the ranks of a prophetic cycle initiated by the Prophet and encompassing the *waṣī*, the seven Imams and the final *qaʾim*.[56]

These viewpoints are important if one takes into account that the Intellect of the *ʿālam al-ʿaql* corresponds to the enunciator-prophet of the *ʿālam al-dīn*,[57] and that the tenth intellect is not merely charged with the responsibility of producing its intellectual representative on earth but itself corresponds to this representative.[58] It should also be remembered that the tenth intellect corresponds to the third intellect – the intellect in potentiality – 'prior' to its being 'upgraded', whereby it is raised up and made to be the second *inbiʿāthī* being. Similarly, the *qāʾim* as the final Resurrector is the one who raises up and returns, in his allotted time, to his appointed soteriological role. Just as the tenth intellect's knowledge is the repository of all the intellectual blessings coming from the preceding intellects in act – the tenth intellect operating as the demiurge of the corporeal world – likewise, the final *qāʾim*'s knowledge will enable him to disclose the ultimate significance of the revelation and the religious law in their most complete forms through a totalising *taʾwīl*, and will achieve the completion of the world of religion, thereby realising the second creation.[59]

It is in the final *qāʾim*, as we shall see, that all limits converge: the Intellect's identity as the first limit (*al-nihāya al-ūlā*), which is applied to the Intellect as the first originated being, is mirrored in the identity

---

the above structure must have been purely theoretical, finding no actual correspondence in the real organisation of the *daʿwa*. See De Smet, *La quiétude de l'intellect*, p. 365; see also Heinz Halm, 'Methoden und Formen der frühesten ismailitischen daʿwa', in *Studien zur Geschichte und Kultur des Vorderen Orients. Festschrift für B. Spuler zum siebzigsten Geburtstag*, ed. Hans R. Römer and Alberecht Noth (Leiden, 1981), pp. 135–136.

[56] Calderini "'Ālam al-Dīn" in Ismāʿīlism', p. 462.

[57] Al-Kirmānī, *Rāḥat al-ʿaql*, p. 213, 234.

[58] Ibid., pp. 244 (table), 254; al-Kirmānī, *Riyāḍ* (Beirut, 1960), pp. 197–198, 201–202.

[59] Cf. De Smet, *La quiétude de l'intellect*, p. 363.

of the last *qā'im* as the most authentic, ultimate second limit (*al-nihāya al-thāniyya*),[60] that is, as the master of the seventh cycle (*ṣāḥib al-dawr al-sābiʿ*). The ultimate *qā'im* concludes the last cycle of human history and, as the most perfectly human actualised intellect, he becomes the final point of all cosmic dynamics through which all existents return to their original intellectual source.[61] Even if al-Kirmānī does not indicate this through evidence, it is probable that the *qā'im* represents the most complete manifestation of that 'unique form' which is mentioned when al-Kirmānī depicts the correspondence entertained between the first limit (the Intellect) and the second limit (the perfectly actualised human).[62]

It should also not be forgotten that all affiliates of the Ismaili hierarchy play fundamental roles in the same way as all members of the world of origination are charged with specific and indispensable tasks. From both a theological and a metaphysical angle, this means that the true knowledge which allows human souls to attain their perfection – consisting in understanding and applying *tawḥīd* and the divine rule (*siyāsa ilāhiyya*)[63] – is, above all, acknowledgment of the authority of all members of the earthly hierarchy down to the lowest associate. Such acknowledgment, as Simonetta Calderini aptly suggests, is ultimately represented 'in general by obedience to the *ḥudūd* as a whole, which is equivalent to obedience to God, and in particular by obedience to the hierarchical rank superior to one's own.'[64]

---

[60] This is the case of a human being whose intellect has reached perfect actualisation, thus representing the second limit and the final point of the cosmic process (De Smet, ibid., pp. 369–370). The notion of one own's limits has a fundamental impact on al-Kirmānī's discussion of *qaḍā'* and *qadar* in the *Riyāḍ*. See below.

[61] Al-Kirmānī, *Rāḥat al-ʿaql*, pp. 262–265.

[62] This might be also an allusion to al-Sijistānī's 'human form' (*al-ṣūra al-insāniyya*), which is often related to the figures of the *qā'im*, the Lord of the *qiyāma*, the *nafs zakiyya* and the Prophet. On the 'Human Form' in al-Sijistānī's thought, see Hirji, 'A Study of *al-Risālah al-bāhirah*', pp. 86–87.

[63] Al-Kirmānī, *Rāḥat al-ʿaql*, pp. 107–108, 475–477; *idem*, *Riyāḍ* (HL), pp. 145–148.

[64] Calderini '"ʿĀlam al-Dīn" in Ismāʿīlism', p. 463, referring to al-Kirmānī, *Rāḥat al-ʿaql* (Leiden, 1953), p. 106.

The topic of obedience to God as obedience to the dignitaries emerges also, as will be shown, in al-Kirmānī's *Riyāḍ*, *faṣl* 23, chapter eight. From a political point of view, al-Kirmānī's elaboration of the *ʿālam al-dīn* in the foregoing terms served to validate both the legal veridicity of the Imam of the time, al-Ḥākim bi-Amr Allāh, and to establish his non-divinity.

5

Human Actions in the Realm of Acquisition

In *al-Maṣābīḥ fī ithbāt al-imāma*, devoted to attesting the indispensability of the imamate, having proved the existence of the divine reward in the afterlife,[1] al-Kirmānī moves on to demonstrate the importance and necessity of good deeds. He resorts again to the idea of God's justice (*ʿadl*) and, in a very Muʿtazilite approach, claims that this requires a confirmation of the existence of the reward, as discussed above, as well as the idea that deserving a reward (*istiḥqāq al-jazāʾ*) is linked to believing that humans are the source of those good actions (*aʿyān al-aʿmāl*) that are suitable for the worship of God.[2]

The human soul, our author explains, is prone by nature (*bi'l-ṭabʿ*) to acquire ill dispositions, and the continuation (*istimrār*) of this practice (*ʿāda*) causes it to produce vileness (*radhāla*). However, through acts of devotion (*ʿibādāt*) any soul will gain those virtues (*faḍāʾil*) or moral traits that can be found in the human species. Such acts of devotion, which are nothing but good deeds, as al-Kirmānī words it, are necessary for the training (*riyāḍa*) of those souls who pursue the nobility of perfection (*sharaf al-kamāl*).[3] Al-Kirmānī states that in order to attain to his second perfection, also indicated as the second emanation (*al-inbiʿāth al-thānī*), the human being needs a second kind of knowledge, imparted by prophets and Imams, which pertains to him only potentially and which, differently from a primary form of knowledge that concerns the mere preservation of bodies,[4] instructs on how to attain happiness and final salvation. The passage of such second knowledge from potentiality

---

[1] Al-Kirmānī, *al-Maṣābīḥ fī ithbāt al-imāma*, Arabic text pp. 18–24, English text pp. 53–58.

[2] Ibid., Arabic text pp. 21–22 and 24, English text pp. 56–57 and 59.

[3] Ibid., Arabic text pp. 24–25, English text pp. 59–61.

[4] Al-Kirmānī, *Rāḥat al-ʿaql*, p. 286.

85

into actuality requires training or exercise (*riyāḍa*), suffering (*'anā'*), acquisition (*iktisāb*) and following the example (*iqtidā'*) of the 'the spiritually supported ones' (*mu'ayyadūn min al-samā'*).[5]

Good deeds, it is pointed out, are nothing but the laws (*sharā'i'*) with their regulations (*aḥkām*) and norms (*sunan*).[6] In this last instance, in a rather metonymic way, al-Kirmānī identifies good deeds with the laws, hinting at the necessary character underpinning them both, an aspect that is elucidated further in the *Maṣābīḥ*.

In the same treatise, it is clarified that the making of the hereafter (*'imārat al-ākhira*) pertains to the souls of those humans who apply (*tatawaffar*) themselves to worship (*'ibāda*); this means that the afterlife is nothing but the result of individual devotional struggles and that the survival of the human species and the perpetuation of good actions depend on the existence of laws and the implementation of their regulations and edicts.[7] Given that human souls are potentially capable of performing good deeds, a good deed is to be intended as the actualisation (*al-fi'l huwa al-'amal*) of a potentiality. However, embedded in this potentiality is a kind of necessitation: this is so because what is in potentiality does not achieve nobility except by proceeding into actuality through what is already actual.[8] Because the All-wise (*al-ḥakīm*) in His providence/wisdom causes such potentiality to

---

[5]   Ibid., p. 447.

[6]   Al-Kirmānī, *al-Maṣābīḥ fī ithbāt al-imāma*, Arabic text pp. 24–25, English text p. 59. Cf. al-Kirmānī, *al-Risāla al-Kāfiya*, ed. Muṣṭafā Ghālib, in *Majmū'at rasā'il al-Kirmānī* (Beirut, 1969), p. 152.

[7]   Al-Kirmānī, *al-Maṣābīḥ fī ithbāt al-imāma*, Arabic text, p. 25, English text p. 60. Similar arguments are propounded by al-Sijistānī in *Kashf al-maḥjūb*, particularly in Issue Seven titled 'That noble action is of greatest benefit in view of the Call to Arise'. See Landolt's translation, *Unveiling of the Hidden*, pp. 127–128.

[8]   Al-Kirmānī's argument is that the passage of a thing from the condition of potentiality to that of actuality occurs only because of what is already actual. This concept is already found in the Arabic Plotinus (see *Risāla fi'l-'ilm al-Ilāhī*, in *Plotinus apud Arabes*, ed. Abdu Rahman Badawī [Cairo, 1955], p. 168, and Aristotle's *De Anima*, 3.5.430a, 10–15). Anything that in the sublunar world passes from potentiality into actuality does so only through a cause which is actual. Such a cause is identified by philosophers like Ibn Sīnā with the Agent Intellect; see Ibn Sīnā, *Kitāb al-Najāt*, pp. 192–193; Davidson, *Alfarabi, Avicenna & Averroes on Intellect*, pp. 86–87; Fazlur Rahman, *Avicenna's Psychology: An English Translation of Kitāb al-Najāt, Book II*,

convert necessarily into actuality, it follows that the progress of good deeds (*a'māl*) from potentiality into the state of actuality is something inescapable. This establishes that good deeds, which are the sanctioned rules of the prophets (*sunan al-anbiyā'*) and the trainings of the soul (*riyāḍat al-anfus*), are in turn also necessary.[9]

Again, in *al-Maṣābīḥ fī ithbāt al-imāma*, al-Kirmānī indulges in a series of demonstrations in order to prove that this world, the world of Nature, is not the domain of reward. If, on the one hand, al-Kirmānī's need to clarify this might have been a reaction to some of his fellow philosophers' belief in a 'naturalised' version of rewards and punishments,[10] on the other hand, this endeavour was probably dictated by the necessity to counter Druze statements purporting the imminent

---

Chapter VI, with Historico-Philosophical Notes and Textual Improvements on the Cairo Edition (Oxford, 1952), pp. 68–69. It is worth remembering that for al-Kirmānī the tenth intellect is embodied in an already perfect intellectually actualised human representative (the Imam). It is through the latter and his guidance, in regard to revelation and law, that human souls can transit from their state of intellectual potentiality to a state of intellectual actuality.

[9] Al-Kirmānī, *al-Maṣābīḥ fī ithbāt al-imāma*, Arabic text p. 27 English text, p. 62.

[10] Ibid., Arabic text pp. 21–23, English text pp. 56–58. The same concept is repeated, including a reference to his book *al-Maṣābīḥ*, in the *Rāḥat al-'aql*, pp. 505–506. Ibn Sīnā, probably following al-Fārābī, was among the thinkers who propounded that the concepts of recompense and punishment in the hereafter should be only taken respectively, as stimuli (*targhīb*) and deterrents (*tarhīb*). Ibn Sīnā, in particular, denies the corporeal resurrection which is described in the Qur'an and replaces it with a spiritual resurrection. He explains that the 'images' of corporeal recompense and punishments awaiting humans in the afterlife, as they appear in the Book, solely have the function of making believers aware that the condition of the human soul in the next life will be the natural prolongation of the soul's life on earth. This means that the more the soul is dependent on material appetites, the more it will suffer once deprived of its link with corporeality. Therefore, the soul's 'punishment' in the hereafter is but the result of its own inadequacy to fulfil its intellectual potentiality remaining bridled to material dictates. Similarly to al-Kirmānī, Ibn Sīnā highlights the guiding function of the revealed law which facilitates believers on the best course to take to avoid suffering: the law, in fact, with its impositions *trains* the soul and, if its precepts are met, prepares the soul for its future state of bliss (see Ibn Sīnā, *al-Risālat al-aḍhawiyya fī'l-ma'ād*, pp. 42–46, 60, 74; Michael E. Marmura, 'Divine Omniscience and Future Contingents in Alfarabi and Avicenna', in *Divine Omniscience and Omnipotence in Medieval Philosophy: Islamic, Jewish and Christian Perspectives*, ed. Tamar Rudavsky [Dordrecht, 1985], p. 92). Interestingly, al-Kirmānī seems to partially share Ibn Sīnā's

advent of the *qāʾim*.[11] To ensure this, he takes into account humans' authorship of actions: 'human beings are responsible for actions (*kāna al-bashar fi'l-dunyā rahīn al-ʿamal*)', al-Kirmānī holds, and for this reason it can be proven that this world is the abode of deeds (*al-dunyā dār al-ʿamal*) rather than the abode of recompense. More specifically, this realm is the abode of acquisition (*al-dunyā dār al-iktisāb*): this is so because the recompense is the result of good actions – hence actions are prior to the recompense – and divine justice requires that the recompense must be deserved (*istiḥqāq al-jazāʾ*).[12] Our author specifies that the recompense is granted only in relation to a previous acquisition (*lā yakūn illā bi-sābiq al-iktisāb*), which is the outcome of deeds or thoughts. Because there is no other way (*lā sabīl*) for the soul to acquire action if not through the individual's bodily manifestation, or to acquire thoughts and beliefs if not through instructions (*taʿālīm*) and postulates (*mawḍūʿāt*), which are all in this world, it becomes clear that our world is indeed the abode of acquisition.[13] Awareness of this reality should spur humans towards such acquisition which

---

views and elucidates that in his preachings, Muḥammad described Paradise and Hell as abodes of vision and corporeal sensations because it was incumbent upon him to follow the rule of metaphors in order to form similies (*majrā al-amthāl fī al-tashbīhi*). Basically, the Prophet's *façon de parler* was necessary to convey, through sensed representations, a reality that senses cannot attain. This is the reason why there is a need to interpret what the Prophet brought in terms of revelation and law. Interpretation is consequently necessary (*taʾwīl wājib*). On the necessity of interpretation, see al-Kirmānī, *al-Maṣābīḥ fī ithbāt al-imāma*, Arabic text pp. 21 and 28–32, English text pp. 57 and 63–67. Cf. Al-Rāzī, *Aʿlām al-nubuwwa*, ed and tr. Tarif Khalidi as *The Proofs of Prophecy* (Provo, UT, 2011), p. 80. The concept of the necessity of interpretation is intertwined with the concept of the necessity of the imamate because the individuals qualified to teach the right interpretation are the Imams. On the necessity of the imamate, see al-Kirmānī, *al-Maṣābīḥ fī ithbāt al-imāma*, particularly Arabic text pp. 32–46, English text pp. 71–79.

[11] Al-Kirmānī intended to clarify that the time of recompense had not yet started: he 'prophesied' that the *qiyāma*, as the Day of Reckoning, would take place after the appearance of 49 Imams. See Calderini, '"*Ālam al-dīn*" in Ismāʿīlism', p. 467.

[12] Al-Kirmānī, *al-Maṣābīḥ fī ithbāt al-imāma*, Arabic text, p. 32, English text, pp. 66–67.

[13] Ibid., Arabic text, p. 22, English text, p. 57. The English translation has been slightly modified.

is, ultimately, the attainment of the celestial blessings bestowed from above, providentially fulfilling humanity's second perfection.

When al-Kirmānī discusses the connection occurring between moral virtues (such as generosity) and the specific good actions through which these virtues become manifest (such as the donation of money), his way of reasoning is multi-layered. In order to provide a clear picture of his analysis, I quote, in my translation, a significant passage from al-Kirmānī's *Tanbīh al-hādī wa'l-mustahdī*:

A man is not a man if not through knowledge (*'ilm*) and the fulfilment of actions (*a'māl*) and he reaches the degree of perfection (*darajat al-kamāl*) […] by pairing (*yaqrin*) knowledge and action so that the soul becomes complete (*tamām*) and all existence [becomes] the setting (*muḥīṭa*) for the blessing (*faḍīla*). And this is for [the individual] who knows that generosity (*sakhā'*) is the medium between dissipation (*tabdhīr*) and saving (*taqṣīr*), and [that it is which] establishes [whether] a thing is opportune (*mawḍi'hu*) [with regard] to those merits (*istiḥqāq*) [which are] in conformity with what [is] the command of God. […] Generosity is real but the soul achieves the acquisition (*iktisāb*) of that blessing which is generosity by knowing it and acting [through it] together. […] [So] the perseverance (*muwāẓaba*) in knowledge and action becomes incumbent, with which the soul becomes actualised through the performance of prayer (*iqāmat al-ṣalāt*) and the profession of faith (*shahāda*) in the realisation of close faithfulness (*ṣādiqa qarība*) to God through fasting (*ṣawm*), abstinence from food and forbidden things (*al-imsāk 'an al-ṭa'ām wa'l-muḥārram*), sins (*mu'āṣ*) and misdeeds (*āthār*). Chastity (*'iffa*) and the offering of money (*aṭā' al-māl*) in the *zakāt*, [as well as] generosity and observance [of faith] (*mushāhada*) are the abodes of worships (*buyūt al-'ibādāt*) [leading] towards [reward in] the hereafter; the yearning [towards intellectual actualisation], steadfastness (*ṣabr*) in what is the command of God, bravery (*shajā'a*) and humility (*tawāḍu'*) to God, [lead to] close friendship (*awliyā' qarība*) with God; [as for the individual] who does not perform [these actions] but settles those blessings outside [himself] it is possible that the substance (*jawhar*) of his soul is falsehood (*kidhb*) and remoteness (*bu'd*) from God, profligacy (*tahattuk*) and disobedience (*'iṣyān*), avarice (*bukhl*) and cruelty (*qasāwa*). [Consequently] anguish appears […] This is

> because the human being (*insān*) knows that through the essence (*māhiyya*) of generosity (*sakhā'*) and bravery (*shajā'a*) he does not make [them respectively as] generosity and bravery but he needs the combination of his knowledge and action in order to actualise truly what is acquired [*muktasab^{an}*] via the blessing.[14]

In the foregoing, al-Kirmānī suggests, firstly, that it is mandatory for humans to understand that the moral character of a virtue such as generosity is not given by the essence of generosity; it is rather the human being who actualises its nature as a moral virtue by knowing it and acting through it. This means, secondly, that it is obligatory for an individual to identify something like the act of generosity as a commandment from God, as exemplified in the revelation, thus coating the existential character of a virtue in a moral 'veneer' through the law. Thirdly, a human is called to combine knowledge of the virtue with action (i.e. acting generously) by following the indications contained in the *sharī'a*. Finally, it is only through both knowledge and action that humans can fulfil the acquisition of those blessings which emanate from the world of the intellects as an uninterrupted flux. This occurs because only through the combination of knowledge (in both its esoteric and exoteric aspect) and action does a human being come to realise that those blessings are not simply means to the full actualisation of a moral virtue but are themselves moral virtues, entified as words in the Islamic legislation.

---

[14] Al-Kirmānī, *Tanbīh al-hādī wa'l-mustahdī*, MS 1230, The Zahid Ali Collection, Special collections Unit at The Institute of Ismaili Studies Library, fols. 149–151.

6

The Intellect's Knowledge of Particulars

It is well known that Ibn Sīnā faced much criticism from his opponents regarding his understanding of divine knowledge. According to the Shaykh al-Ra'īs, God knows particulars in a universal way only (*'alā naḥw kullī*).[1] This means essentially that the Avicennan *wājib al-wujūd* (Necessary Existent) is aware that He is the cause of existence and has knowledge exclusively of the predictable mechanisms governing His creation. The Necessary Existent is understood to know eternally by a conceptual knowledge so that the objects of His knowledge are the universals.[2] In similar terms, al-Kirmānī acknowledges that for the Intellect there exists a peculiar form of knowledge and admits that for the Intellect it is not necessary to know existents in detail:

> It is not necessary for him [the Intellect] to know more than the knowledge he has of his essence (*akthar min 'ilmihi bi-dhātihi*); it does suffice him to know that he is a created being (*mubda'*), that his existence is not from his essence but from something else (*wujūduhu lā min dhātihi bal min ghayrihi*), [...] and that

---

[1]   Ibn Sīnā, *Kitāb al-Shifā': al-ilāhiyyāt*, p. 280.

[2]   Ibn Sīnā, *Kitāb al-Hidāya li-Ibn Sīnā*, ed. Muḥammad 'Abduh, (Cairo, 1974), pp. 266–267. On this topic, see Michael E. Marmura, 'Some Aspects of Avicenna's Theory of God's Knowledge of Particulars', *JAOS*, 82 (1962), pp. 299–312; *idem*, 'Divine Omniscience and Future Contingents in Alfarabi and Avicenna', pp. 88–91; Rahim Acar, 'Reconsidering Avicenna's Position on God's Knowledge of Particulars', in *Interpreting Avicenna: Science and Philosophy in Medieval Islam*, ed. John McGinnis and David C. Reisman (London, 2004), pp. 142–156; Peter Adamson, 'On Knowledge of Particulars', *Proceedings of the Aristotelian Society*, 105 (2005), pp. 273–294. Abū Ḥamid al-Ghazālī condemned Ibn Sīnā's denial of God's knowledge of particulars as a position of unbelief (*kufr*), together with the philosopher's negation of bodily resurrection and the idea of the eternity of the world. See the 17th Discussion in al-Ghazālī's *Tahāfut al-falāsifa*.

he is the cause of existence for that which is inferior to him (*'illa li-wujūd mā dūnihi*).[3]

Al-Kirmānī compares the Intellect's limited knowledge of details to the knowledge of the Imam: in the same way as the Intellect 'knows' to be the cause of existence for the beings that are inferior to him and knows that he acts as an intermediary (*wāsiṭ*) between the Principle who precedes him and the entities that follow him, likewise the Imam is aware of being the cause of salvation (*khalāṣ*) for humankind but, despite this, it is not necessary for him to know all his followers individually because this knowledge would not improve the nature of his mission.[4]

As in Ibn Sīnā's theoretical construct, al-Kirmānī's Intellect is aware that he is an entity necessitated by something external to his essence, and he simultaneously perceives himself as the cause for those beings that are placed below him in the hierarchy of existence. However, in contrast to the fully conscious activities of Ibn Sīnā's celestial intellects, which enjoy a multiple contemplation,[5] The Intellect's knowledge is, for al-Kirmānī, rather a form of intuition. The reason for this is that (i) the Intellect's cognitive action is necessarily orientated exclusively towards himself, and (ii) his essential perfection would clearly not benefit from a supplementary knowledge. The Intellect 'knows' that other existents depend on him without knowing them as particulars or in a detailed fashion. As in the case of God for Ibn Sīnā, perfection and self-intellection become the 'limits' which make knowledge of particulars superfluous.

Apropos the concept of divine knowledge, in Ismaili belief God is not an intellect and, consequently, the question of divine knowledge cannot be considered with reference to the issue of self-intellection. The denial

---

[3]   Al-Kirmānī, *Riyāḍ* (Beirut, 1960), p. 220.

[4]   Ibid.

[5]   Avicenna inherits al-Fārābī's emanatory schema but adjusts it to his theological and metaphysical needs. Each intellect in his system thinks about (i) the superordinate intellect as the reason of its existence, this leading to the production of another intellect; (ii) itself as a necessary existent, this leading to the production of the soul of one of the heavens; (iii) itself as a possible existent, this leading to the production of matter or the sphere of the corresponding heaven. See Ibn Sīnā, *al-Najāt* (1938), p. 277; *idem, al-Ishārāt wa'l-tanbīhāt*, ed. J. Forget (Leiden, 1892), p. 174.

that God has an intellectual nature dates back to Plotinus and the emphasis he put on the essential divine perfection.[6] As a perfect being, God is so absolutely simple that to regard Him as an intellect would mean to undermine His very simplicity, for intelligence entails the logical duality of essence and act, of subject and object.[7] Nevertheless, Plotinus never states that the Godhead is 'unconscious' or 'unaware'; rather, he highlights that He exists by an immediate self-consciousness whose nature is different from the thinking of the Intellect.[8]

The question of how al-Kirmānī regards the Intellect's knowledge has its root in the identification of the Intellect with the Nous of the Neoplatonic philosophers, and it is linked to the polemics that discuss the capacity for the Intellect to embrace in his essence all the forms of the world. These are, according to such Ismaili philosophers as al-Nasafī and al-Sijistānī, potentially present in the Intellect and so make the Intellect's essence simultaneously actual and potential.[9] This position is rejected by al-Kirmānī, whose stance on the subject of the forms within the Intellect remains fuzzy nonetheless.[10] It makes sense

---

[6] Inge, *The Philosophy of Plotinus*, p. 113.

[7] Peterson, *Cosmogony in the Rāḥat al-'aql*, pp. 437–438.

[8] This difference is significant because the One does not even need to be the object of Its self-knowing. Should such a need occur, the One would lose all the characteristics of the 'One', thereby becoming dangerously close to the sphere of the Neoplatonic Nous. Plotinus claims that the apparent contradiction emerging from the idea that the One is self-conscious without depending on Its self-knowledge – thus obviating the duality issuing from the separation between the subject and the object of knowledge – is resolved if one considers that, in contrast to the Intellect, the One is not 'Thought directed towards Itself' but It is simply and utterly 'Thought'. See Bréhier, *Plotinus*, p. 189.

[9] According to al-Nasafī, 'The Intellect's knowledge embraces (all forms) and they are known by him; even though the Intellect precedes them in actuality, he is both in actuality and in potentiality, and the forms exist simultaneously [in him]'. Al-Nasafī's *Maḥsūl* quoted in al-Kirmānī, *Riyāḍ* (Beirut, 1960). See also De Smet, *La quiétude de l'intellect*, p. 185 note 188. On this topic, see my analysis and interpretation of the eighth *faṣl* of the *Riyāḍ*. Al-Nasafī's view heralded what al-Sijistānī said with regard to the nature of un-actualised forms being present in the *qaḍā'* which he identifies with the Antecedent/Intellect. See below.

[10] In the *Riyāḍ*, the author clearly states that the *'aql*, which is most fit to be regarded as the compendium of the forms of the two worlds, is the third intellect rather than the first one. Ibid., pp. 146–148.

to argue, as De Smet does, that al-Kirmānī would have adopted the position exemplified in the *Plotiniana Arabica* for which the Intellect, by intelligising only his essence, thinks of the forms within himself as something not distinct from himself.[11] Thus intended, the action of self-intellection would not entail any passage from potentiality into actuality for such forms.[12]

The legitimacy of this stance is also confirmed by the fact that, as previously observed, the Intellect does not need to know the beings that are inferior to him. This is because the Intellect is himself all those entities *in actu* at the highest ever possible degree of perfection. By his self-intellection, the Intellect knows all beings entirely or, rather, to the extent that he 'needs' to know them.[13] At this point, one cannot but wonder what kind of impact a restricted knowledge might have on the Intellect; because the latter does not need to know individuals as individuals, it cannot be held responsible for intimately intervening and shaping their destinies according to some Islamic theistic ideas. Al-Kirmānī, as will be observed in Part II, inclines to regard the Intellect as the Antecedent whose actions reach created existents through the intermediacy of spiritual faculties. Al-Sijistānī, on

---

[11] Al-Kirmānī's understanding of the forms that are present in the Intellect recalls Ibn 'Arabī's perception of the divine Names and Attributes. According to Ibn 'Arabī, a Divine Name is but a 'limited' form of the Divine Essence prior to its manifestation. And an Attribute of God is but a Divine Name manifested in the world. Moreover, every Name indicates the Essence and the particular concept which it conveys and which it requires. See Ibn 'Arabī, *Fuṣūṣ al-ḥikam*, ed. and tr. R. W. J. Austin, as *The Bezels of Wisdom* (Mahwah, NJ, 1980), pp. 79–80. Likewise, for al-Kirmānī the forms are encompassed within the omni-comprehensiveness of the first intellect; they are expressions that detail the Intellect's undifferentiated essence and are in themselves simply conceptual relations (*nisab*) to the Intellect's oneness. In their manifested aspect, however, forms pertain to the third intellect rather than the first. It is the multiplicity embedded in the third intellect which allows forms' entification through matter, thus sparing the Intellect from any link with materiality and potentiality.

[12] This position is inferred when al-Kirmānī, in the section of the *Riyāḍ* under investigation, denounces al-Sijistānī's intimation that both the entified forms of the *qaḍāʾ* and the *qadar* – despite belonging to the same category as spiritual things – are, nonetheless, simultaneously potential and actual, just as the *qāʾim* in concealment is potential and yet actual through his *daʿwa*'s representatives.

[13] De Smet, *La quiétude de l'intellect*, p. 186.

his part, spurred on by the need to accommodate his cosmology within the Ismaili tradition inherited from al-Nasafī, identifies the Intellect with the *qaḍāʾ* and conveys onto the Intellect faculties such as eternity, perfection and self-sufficiency which are also found in the Kirmānian first originated being. In addition, al-Sijistānī describes the Intellect as the Qurʾanic Pen (*qalam*),[14] with al-Kirmānī himself referring to the Pen as the first intellect.[15] More specifically, al-Kirmānī identifies the Intellect with the Qurʾanic 'angel brought near' (*al-malik al-muqarrab*) which, he specifies, according to the divine *Sunna* and the prophetic legislation (*al-sunna al-ilāhiyya waʾl-sharīʿa al-nabawiyya*) is called the *qalam*.[16] The Intellect is also indicated by the noun *kalima* (word),[17] and al-Kirmānī highlights that the above denomination also occurs in accordance with the use of the Arabic language and the divine *Sunna*. Clearly, his intention is to show that there exists a correspondence between the metaphysical realities that belong to his cosmological

---

[14]   He consequently identifies the Soul as the Qurʾanic Tablet (*lawḥ maḥfūz*). See al-Sijistānī, *Kitāb al-Iftikhār*, ed. Ismail K. Poonawala (Beirut, 2000), pp. 110–115; *idem, Risālat tuḥfat al-mustajībīn*, pp. 148–149; al-Kirmānī, *Riyāḍ* (HL), Chapter 8, tenth *faṣl*, pp. 132–133; Walker, 'Cosmic Hierarchies in Early Ismaili Thought', p. 19. References to the Pen and the Tablet can be found in Q 3:7, 13:39, 43:4, 68:1, 85:22. On the meaning of the Pen and Tablet in Muslim theology, see Arent J. Wensink, *The Muslim Creed* (Cambridge, 1932), index, s. v. 'Pen', 'Table'.

[15]   Generally speaking, in al-Kirmānī's thought, the first intellect corresponds to the Pen and the second intellect to the Tablet as in al-Kirmānī's *Waḍīʿa*, 33a. The same ideas can be found throughout his *Rāḥat al-ʿaql*. More often, however, in the *Repose of the Intellect*, al-Kirmānī identifies the second intellect as the Pen and the third intellect as the Tablet. See *Rāḥat al-ʿaql*, pp. 212–220, 221–229.

[16]   Ibid., p. 219. The Shiʿi Imams often have referred to the Pen and Tablet as angels. See Muḥammad Bāqir Majlisī, *Biḥār al-anwār al-jāmiʿa li-durar akhbār al-aʾimma al-aṭhār* (Beirut, 1983), pp. 369–370. See also Ibn Bābūya, *Risālat al-Iʿtiqādāt al-imāmiyyah*, ed and tr. A. A. Fyzee, *A Shīʿite Creed*, p. 44.

[17]   As mentioned in his *al-Risāla al-Muḍīʿa* (particularly, pp. 49–50), al-Kirmānī, citing extensively from the chapter of al-Sijistānī's *Kitāb al-Maqālīd*, criticises the latter's stance on *amr* (command). He then exhibits his own understanding of the command as a word (*kalima*) rather than as a spiritual form of willingness. He explains that there cannot be any intermediary substance between the word and the one who utters the word. Between the Creator and the *kalima* no emanation occurs because the word does not contain any part of the speaker. See Haji, *A Distinguished Dāʿī*, p. 31.

schema and the entities that are described in the Prophet's *Sunna* and in the canonical language of the Qur'anic revelation.

Among other characteristics of the Intellect, al-Kirmānī lists a series of terms such as the living (*ḥayy*), the intelligising (*ʿāqil*), the powerful (*qādir*) and the agent/doer (*fāʿil*). These are all thought to be concomitant, with the last one, *fāʿil*, being indirectly derivable from the first attribute, *ḥayy*.[18] Al-Kirmānī's reasoning seems to be built on Proclus' understanding of 'life' as one aspect of the Intellect. In Plato's *Sophist* (248e–249a), life is considered as one of the attributes of Being; drawing from Plato, Plotinus makes life an aspect of the Intellect. However, it was Proclus the first of the Neoplatonists who hyspostasised 'Life', making it the potency (*dynamis*) or the unlimited stream of energy from the Intellect which is inseparably linked with the latter and the other hypostasy, Being.[19]

Al-Kirmānī emphasises quite extensively that should the attribute of life be removed, all the other attributes would no longer be in a state of permanence (namely, they would cease to exist). Therefore, their existence must depend first and foremost on the attribute of life.[20] Yet, life is never openly classified as the 'cause' for the existence of its dependant attributes.[21] 'Life' is rather given a form of 'priority' over all other attributes, like the Aristotelian essential priority of the cause to its effect or the Avicennan substantial priority of the form to

---

[18]   Al-Kirmānī, *Rāḥat al-ʿaql*, pp. 187–188. Al-Kirmānī confers on the Intellect several attributes ('the Knower', 'the Truth', 'the Living', 'the One', 'the Powerful', 'the Eternal' and 'the First'). These are among the so-called Most Beautiful Names of God (*al-asmāʾ al-ḥusna*) that Sunni Islam generally associates with Allāh. On the identification of the Imams as the vehichles of the divine names and attributes, see Mohammad A. Amir-Moezzi, 'Notes on Imami *Walāya*', in his *The Spirituality of Shiʿi Islam* (London, 2011), pp. 449, 254.

[19]   See Chlup, *Proclus: An Introduction*, pp. 94–95; De Smet, *La quiétude de l'intellect*, 'ḥayāt' in index.

[20]   Plotinus speaks of life as the act of the Good and of the Intellect as the life that has received a limit (see *Enneads*, VI. 7, 17.25). Al-Kirmānī reiterates the same concepts, and adds that the Intellect is living as he acts through an act which is limited, carrying within himself his own limit. See De Smet's analysis, *La quiétude de l'intellect*, pp. 166–167.

[21]   This position differs from Proclus' idea for which, in the first term of any tryad, the other two are embraced as in their cause. See Chlup, *Proclus: An Introduction*, p. 95.

the matter.[22] This is so because 'life' operates as a receptive substance (*al-jawhar al-qābil*) in the Intellect to which many other attributes add themselves as predicates.[23] Significantly, al-Kirmānī also defines life as the Intellect's 'first perfection' (*al-kamāl al-awwal*) and as the substrate (lit. supporter/carrier, *ḥāmil*) for all the remaining superadded attributes which constitute its 'second perfection' (*al-kamāl al-thānī*).[24] 'Life' then must be identified with, or pertain to, the essence of the Intellect which functions as the bearer of all the other attributes.

The differentiation occurring between the preceding attribute of life and the dependant attributes within the Intellect does not jeopardise the Intellect's unity: his essence, let us not forget, is through his wholeness (*bi-jumlatiha*), his being living, powerful, knowing, eternal (*azalī* or extra-temporal), all-encompassing (*muḥīṭ*), perfect, one, first existent, truth and originated. This means that the collective superadded attributes are permanent (constant/immutable, *thābita*) within the essence of the Intellect and that they are all encompassed by it. The Intellect is inextricably and simultaneously the truth (*ḥaqq*) and the reality (*ḥaqīqa*), the first existent (*al-mawjūd al-awwal*) and the first existence (*al-wujūd al-awwal*), oneness (*al-waḥda*) and the one (*al-wāḥid*), sempiternity (*al-azal*) and sempiternal (*al-azalī*), the first intellect (*al-ʿaql al-awwal*) and first intellected thing (*al-maʿqūl al-awwal*), knowledge (*ʿilm*) and the first knower (*al-ʿālim al-awwal*), power (*qudra*) and the first powerful thing (*al-qādir al-awwal*), life (*ḥayāt*) and the first living [thing] (al-ḥayy al-awwal).[25]

Despite these differentiations, which hint at an inherent plurality in the essence of the Intellect, al-Kirmānī demonstrates that the latter

---

[22] In the Avicennan construct, form has a *status* superior to the one enjoyed by matter with regard to their nature as substances. The reason for this lies in the fact that form is among the substances subsistent in themselves, whereas matter is recognised among those receiving their substantiality only in potentiality. For a classification of causes in Aristotle and Ibn Sīnā, see Jean Jolivet, 'La repartition des causes chez Aristote et Avicenne: le sens d'un déplacement', in *Lectionum Varietates: Hommage à Paul Vignaux*, ed. Jean Jolivet, Zénon Kaluza and Alain de Libera (1904–1987) (Paris, 1991), pp. 49–65. See also Michael Marmura, 'Avicenna on Causal Priority', in *Islamic Philosophy and Mysticism*, ed. Parviz Morewedge, pp. 67–68.

[23] Peterson, *Cosmogony in the Rāḥat al-ʿaql*, p. 418.

[24] Al-Kirmānī, *Rāḥat al-ʿaql*, p. 188.

[25] Ibid., p. 189.

remains one and unchanged. The Intellect is like fire: it might burn, dissolve or congeal depending on the receiving material substrata upon which it acts, and yet its essence remains unaffected.[26] The differences of the effects produced by the fire are differences of ascription (*iḍāfa*), al-Kirmānī explains, due not to the nature of fire but to the nature of the diverse receptive substrata which respond to the action of fire.[27]

---

[26] On al-Sijistānī idea of fire as the Antecedent, see more below.

[27] Al-Kirmānī, *Rāḥat al-ʿaql*, p. 189.

7

Drawing Correspondences between the *ʿālam al-waḥda* and the *ʿālam al-dīn*

In the *Rāḥat al-ʿaql*, we find two tables relating to the composition of the realm of unity (*ʿālam al-waḥda*) and the realm of religion (*ʿālam al-dīn*), which are reproduced below.[1] At the top of the first world (Table 1) is the first intellect (*al-ʿaql al-awwal*) followed, on a corresponding level, by (i) the second intellect (*al-ʿaql al-thānī*) which al-Kirmānī defines as being *qāʾim biʾl-fiʿl*, and (ii) by another intellect which he defines as being *qāʾim biʾl-quwwa*. He does not specify the rank of this last *ʿaql*. It is not named as the third intellect, which is however something implicit given its collocation in the schema: its nature is described as being made of matter and form (*huwa al-hayūla waʾl-ṣūra*). Following the second intellect in the composition of the realm of unity are angels who are assigned to the world of Nature; these are multiple in number and the existence of each of them derives from one prior to it (a hint at the emanationist cascade of intellects).[2] On the other hand, following the hylomorphic intellect in the table, there is the world of Nature with its stars and planets and what is in them, which encompasses multiplicity.

---

[1] The tables (in Arabic) are found in the *Rāḥat al-ʿaql*, pp. 168–170. They are reproduced in English in their entirety by Daniel C. Peterson, 'Repose of the Intellect', in *An Anthology of Philosophy in Persia, vol. II*, ed. Nasr and Aminrazavi, pp. 189–190. Peterson's translation differs from mine. The tables are reproduced in translation here only with regard to parts that are relevant to this investigation.

[2] Such angels, it should be recalled, are also intellects *in actu*, with the exception of the third which is *in potentia* due to its lesser perfection bound to the multiplicity of its ascriptions. I am grateful to Carmela Baffioni for having pointed this out.

99

**_Table 1. The World of Unity from the Aspect
of its Composition_**

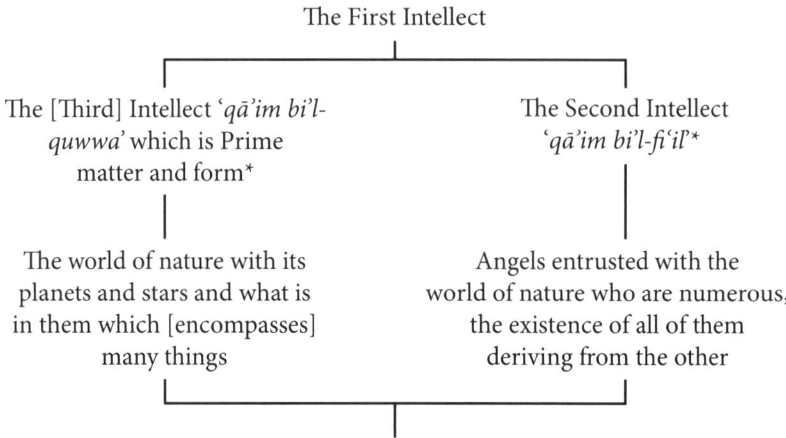

At the top of the realm of religion (Table 2) is the *nāṭiq* (enunciator-prophet); below him – and in correspondence with the second intellect – we find the Imam who is defined as being *qā'im bi'l-fi'l*, that is, an actual, living, subsisting *qā'im*, and as the Foundation (*asās*). The reference here is to the Imam of the age who is present in the world of religion as a living Imam and who, through his task of interpreting the Scriptures, acts as the 'current' 'resurrector' of human souls. Following the *imām qā'im bi'l-fi'l* are the numerous Imams who, as subsisting (*qā'imūn*) Imams, are upholders of the religious law, being responsible for the preservation (*ḥifẓ*) of the *sharī'a*.

In direct correspondence to the position occupied by the hylomorphic third intellect in the world of unity is the Imam (*qā'im bi'l-quwwa*), identified with the Book (*kitāb*). Is al-Kirmānī cryptically suggesting that the figure of the Imam in potentiality is that of a *qā'im in potential* who will return as the final Resurrector to unveil

Table 2. The World of Religion from the Aspect of its Composition

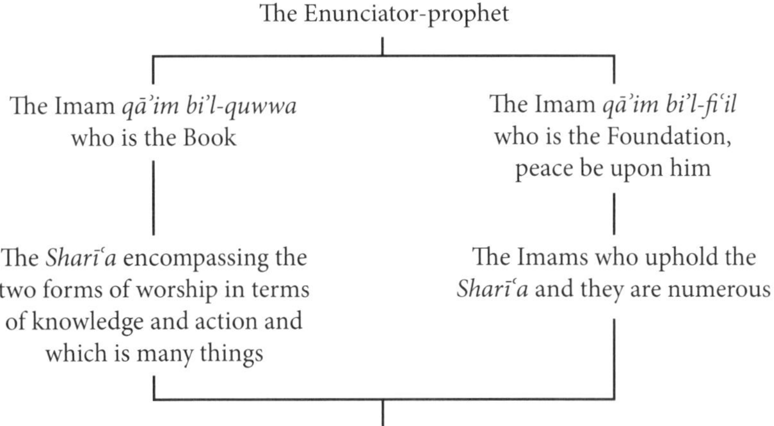

all the *ḥaqāʾiq*, including the esoteric meaning of the Book? Following the *imām qāʾim biʾl-quwwa* is the *sharīʿa* with the two 'forms of worship' – knowledge and action. In the schema, one finds the human being (*insān*) who is said to become truly human through the perfection of his soul (*bi-kamāl nafsihi*).[3]

The actual passages that describe these tables in the *Rāḥat al-ʿaql* explain that the perfection of the human soul revolves around many things which are brought together essentially by two elements: (i) the law and (ii) the Imam. The law includes the regulations governing the two forms of worship (*marāsim al-ʿibādatayn*) by knowledge and action. In one form of worship is the shaping of the soul (*taṣwīr al-nafs*) and in the other is its rectification (*taqwīmuhā*) which enables the human soul, through its perfection, to become the channel (*majran*) of the macrocosm (*al-ʿālam al-kabīr*). The latter includes the

---

3   Al-Kirmānī, *Rāḥat al-ʿaql*, pp. 168–170.

celestial spheres and stars as well as the natural powers. These things are said to correspond to the prophetic work (*al-ṣanʿa al-nabuwiyya*). As for the second element in the soul's perfection, the Imam, he is acknowledged as the one who unites the dignitaries of the religion's hierarchy that preserves the religious law, unfurls (*basara*) its characteristic traits (*maʿālimuhā*), and calls to knowledge and action according to it. These *ḥudūd*, by means of their place (*bi-makānihum*) (in the hierarchy of the world of religion) and their teachings (*bi-taʿlīmihim*), make the human being truly human (*insān*).[4]

Some aspects of these descriptions require a careful analysis: the emphasis laid on the *sharīʿa*, which is communicated by the *nabī* as a prophetic work, is not accidental. As I shall observe throughout the study of the eighth chapter of the *Riyāḍ*, al-Kirmānī endeavours to establish the essentiality of the law and its principles, together with the necessary mandate of the Imams and the other dignitaries of the *daʿwa* as promulgators and preservers of the esoteric meaning of the *sharīʿa*. The identification of the religious law and the Imam as the two elements around which the perfection of the human soul revolves establishes a mandatory nature for both. Furthermore, in the same section of the *Rāḥat al-ʿaql*, the roles of the Imams and the *ḥudūd* – who through their teachings and guidance (*hidāya*) bring the human soul to the degree of perfection (*darajat al-kamāl*) pertaining to the position of the intellects (*manzilat al-ʿuqūl*) – are made to correspond to the tasks of the angels (*al-malāʾika*) who are entrusted with the world. These angels, who, it is specified, are actual with respect to the world (*qāʾimīn biʾl-fiʿl min al-ʿālam*), exercise an influence (*taʾthīr*) upon the world's bodies and natural powers in order to extract (*ikhrāj*) 'what is meant to be' in terms of animals, plants and minerals. Just as the natural elements of the world and their powers are not able to extract their offspring (*mawālīd*) except with the intervention of something which acts upon them, similarly the sciences of the law and its principles (*ʿulūm al-sharīʿa wa arkānuhā*) are not unfurled except by the dignitaries who are entrusted with the spreading of their sciences and the disclosing of what is hidden in them.[5] By drawing such a comparison,

---

4   Ibid., p. 164.

5   Ibid.

al-Kirmānī is once again underlining the necessary nature of the imamate and of all the members of the religious hierarchy.

Moreover, there is another subtlety that emerges: just as the Imams are meant to be actual (in every age, the world necessitates an Imam who discloses the hidden meaning of the revelation and the law), likewise the angels are actual for they are tasked with exercising everlastingly their providential influence upon all the existents of this world. In fact, as has already been mentioned, al-Kirmānī assigns the intellects/angelic beings a creative function which is essentially linked to the generation of forms, the constitution of the celestial spheres and bodies, and eventually the formation of the sublunar world. Besides these responsibilities, it is imperative also to recall two additional functions: a 'providential' role, related to the organisation and the maintenance of the terrestrial realm, and a soteriological function which is exercised through the prophets and the Imams aiming at actualising the human intellect.[6] In particular, as part of his duties towards humans, the first intellect serves as the God that humankind can know and understand because, as pointed out by Hunzai, it is only by divesting the first intellect of divinity that humankind can reach the One. This explains why the Prophet said: '*Al-muʾmin muwaḥḥid wa-allāh muwaḥḥid* (The believer is the *muwaḥḥid* and God is the *muwaḥḥid*)'.[7] If God is a *muwaḥḥid* (unifier) in that He originated the first intellect as the symbol of the One, the believer is a *muwaḥḥid* by way of his/her capacity to understand that the first intellect is not actually God but rather an *ishāra*, an allusion or a pointer towards the Godhead.

Significantly in the above tables, al-Kirmānī, by identifying the manifestation of the Intellect with the enunciator-prophet (*nāṭiq*), alludes most probably to the character of guidance provided by such Intellect. It is well known that, within Islam, the Qurʾan is the guidance par excellence so one might expect the first intellect to be identified

---

[6]   De Smet, *La quiétude de l'intellect*, p. 264.

[7]   Al-Kirmānī, '*al-Risāla al-durriyya*', p. 205; Hunzai, 'The Concept of *Tawḥīd*', pp. 167–168; Nanji, 'Ismaili Philosophy', p. 152; see also Haji's comments to al-Kirmānī's '*al-Risāla al-durriyya fī maʿnā al-tawḥīd, wa'l-muwaḥḥid wa'l-muwaḥḥad*', in his *A Distinguished Dāʿī*, pp. 22–24.

also with the Qur'an.[8] Al-Kirmānī, instead, identifies all of the intellects but the third as the Pen (*qalam*). They act on the Tablet (*lawḥ*), namely the third intellect which functions as the *hayūlā*,[9] or as the recipient of the intellects' active element.[10] Clearly, the Tablet is a reference to the 'preserved tablet' (*al-lawḥ al-maḥfūẓ*), the celestial

---

[8]   Al-Kirmānī acknowledges the religious understanding of the Intellect as the 'word' (*kalima*), but he also specifies that this is so according to the religious practice (*al-sunna al-ilāhiyya*). See *Rāḥat al-ʿaql*, pp. 185, 239.

[9]   In the *Riyāḍ* (Beirut, 1960, pp. 68–69), al-Kirmānī specifies that the *hayūlā* is not an emanation from the Soul (*min al-nafs*) but an emanation that occurs *with* the Soul (*maʿa al-nafs*). From the latter come the celestial spheres and all other things that are in existence in the physical world. The *hayūlā* is therefore identified with the third intellect, namely with the *ʿaql* which is the result of the first intellect's relationship (*nisbat*) with himself as a *maʿlūl*.

[10]   Specifically, the intellect in potentiality is regarded as the Tablet which, due to its receptive character, receives all the forms from the intellects in the same way as any tablet receives the forms of writings from any pen. Al-Kirmānī states that what the philosophers call *hayūlā* is the *lawḥ* according to *al-sunna al-ilāhiyya* (ibid., p. 222). For the peripatetic philosophers, the noblest category of matter is that of celestial/spiritual matter which constitutes the celestial spheres. It emanates directly from the intellects; it is pure and incorruptible and defies any change by being perpetually joined to the same form (see al-Fārābī, *Mabādiʾ ārāʾ ahl al-madīna al-fāḍila*, VIII, 1, p. 134; English translation, pp. 373–375). The other category of matter is 'the absolute prime matter' (*al-hayūlā al-ūlā al-muṭlaqa*), which is classified as pure receptivity. This is deprived of any determination and is the substratum for the world of generation and corruption (al-Fārābī, ibid., VI, 1, p. 112; Ibn Sīnā, *al-Najāt* [1938], p. 300; *idem, Kitāb al-Ḥudūd*, pp. 17–18). It is important to remember that for these philosophers the only entities deprived of matter are the separate intellects (al-Fārābī, ibid., III, pp. 1–10, English translation, pp. 100–104). According to Ibn Sīnā, all intellects are immaterial and incorporeal substances (see his *al-Najāt* [1938], p. 338). For the members of the Ikhwān al-Ṣafāʾ, prime matter is a spiritual form (*ṣūra rūḥāniyya*) which pertains to the spiritual and divine entities together with the Agent Intellect (*al-ʿaql al-faʿʿāl*) and the Universal Soul (*al-nafs al-kulliyya*). They are all created at once by the divine imperative (see Ikhwān al-Ṣafāʾ, *Rasāʾil Ikhwān al-Ṣafāʾ wa khullān al-wafāʾ*, ed. Buṭrus al-Bustānī [Beirut, 1957], III, pp. 184, 187, 197, 238). In particular, prime matter is the product of the emanation by the Universal Soul and represents the inferior limit of the intelligible world (*Rasāʾil Ikhwān al-Ṣafāʾ*, II, p. 7; III, pp. 236–237). Due to its position as the farthest from God among the intelligible beings, prime matter depends on the Universal Soul to attain its missing perfection. Like al-Kirmānī, the Ikhwān al-Ṣafāʾ made the *hayūlā* the last hypostasis of the intelligible realm which is preceded by the Intellect and the Soul; it receives its forms (which allow its perfection)

prototype of the holy Qurʾan.[11] It appears evident that al-Kirmānī plays with traditional cosmological correspondences: so in his writings, the soul of the supreme sphere is identified with the Throne (*kursī*) whilst the sphere in its materiality (i.e. the body of the sphere) is associated with the Footstool (*ʿarsh*). By doing so, al-Kirmānī dismisses contemporary interpretations that used to subordinate the *kursī* to the *ʿarsh*.[12] As pointed out by De Smet, al-Kirmānī also abandons the Neoplatonic tendency to associate *qalam* exclusively with the Intellect, the *lawḥ* with the Soul, and both *kursī* and *ʿarsh* with the action of Nature, and keeps introducing Neoplatonic concepts within the Ismaili context.[13] Thus, he links the intellects of his scheme to the angels that are responsible for supervising the affairs of the world,[14] and associates the seven intellects proceeding from the second intellect with the seven higher letters of the Qurʾan (*al-ḥurūf al-ʿulwiyya*).[15]

Last but not least, among the parallels drawn between all elements of the two tables, it is striking to find references to two expressions containing the word *qāʾim*: following the Intellect/enunciator-prophet (*nāṭiq*), are (i) the second intellect/Foundation (*asās*), which is

---

through the other intellects and, once actualised, it engenders the sensible world. On these topics, see De Smet, *La quiétude de l'intellect*, pp. 255–259.

[11] It is worth highlighting that Aristotle had already assigned the role of a tablet to the receptive nature of the human intellect in his *De Anima*, drawing parallels between the 'passive' character of the intellect in potentiality and the nature of a tablet, which is ready to receive the writing finalising its potential perfection. See Aristotle, *De Anima*, III, 4, 429a10–24, 429b30–31.

[12] Al-Kirmānī, *Rāḥat al-ʿaql*, p. 285, pp. 295–296.

[13] For references see De Smet, *La quiétude de l'intellect*, p. 384 note 16.

[14] Al-Kirmānī, *Rāḥat al-ʿaql*, pp. 159–160, 165, 168, 185, 211, 216, 257, 295, 297. De Smet has noticed that the theme of the angels is a typical product of the Christian Neoplatonism, which can easily be found in all the peripatetic *falāsifa*. See De Smet, *La quiétude de l'intellect*, p. 385.

[15] The reference to the letters, Halm believes, is linked to cabbalistic cosmogony, being an element present in early Ismaili doctrine (Halm, *Kosmologie*, p. 44). For a general overview of the science of letters in Islam, see Denis Gril's introduction in Ibn ʿArabī, *Les illuminations de la Mecque*, pp. 385–438. On the diverse reading of the science of letters, see Michael Ebstein and Sara Sviri, 'The So-called *risālat al-ḥurūf* (*Epistle on Letters*) ascribed to Sahl al-Tustarī and Letter Mysticism in al-Andalus', *Journal Asiatique* 299, 1 (2011), pp. 213–270. On the significance of these letters see also below.

referred to as *qāʾim biʾl-fiʿil*, and (ii) the (third) intellect/Book, referred to as *qāʾim biʾl-quwwa*. Whilst the first locution, *qāʾim biʾl-fiʿil*, might simply be translated in the Aristotelian sense (as 'subsisting in actuality'), it might also be a subtle reference to the figure of the *qāʾim* who is actual because present among the community as the Foundation. The second expression, *qāʾim biʾl-quwwa*, again translatable in the Aristotelian sense (as 'subsisting in potentiality'), might also refer to the potential *qāʾim* – corresponding to the intellect which, having acquired its perfection, is elevated to the rank parallel to the second intellect. Such a figure is *in potentia* just as the seventh Imam of each cycle who becomes the *imām-qāʾim* of that *dawr*, a human being (composed of matter and form) whose hermeneutical mission links his nature to the very essence of the Book. Obviously, indirectly such a *qāʾim* can also be linked to the figure of the final Resurrector who is perfected by the knowledge and the laws (potentially embedded in the Book) of all preceding Imams.

The second part of this study will show in more details the nature of the above described figures, relying on the translation and analytical investigation of chapter eight from al-Kirmānī's *Riyaḍ*.

PART TWO

A TRANSLATION WITH ANALYTICAL COMMENTARY OF CHAPTER EIGHT OF AL-KIRMĀNĪ'S *KITĀB AL-RIYĀḌ*

Overview of the *qaḍāʾ waʾl-qadar*
Debate in the *Riyāḍ*

During the reign of the Fatimid Imam-caliph al-Ḥākim bi-Amr Allāh, al-Kirmānī arrived in Cairo, where he was summoned, among other affairs, to eradicate the proto-Druze movement and its incarnationistic assumptions that looked at the Imam as an embodied God.[1] As one of the most influential *dāʿī*s during the reign of al-Ḥākim, al-Kirmānī found himself compelled also to solve an even earlier controversy concerning major doctrinal issues that had erupted within the so-called Iranian school of Ismaili thought. At the heart of this debate were the three major representatives of this school: al-Nasafī, Abū Ḥātim al-Rāzī and al-Sijistānī. The controversy is believed to have originated with the circulation of al-Nasafī's *Kitāb al-Maḥṣūl*, particularly among Ismaili *dāʿī*s in Khurāsān.[2] Although no longer extant, this

---

[1] Walker suggests that al-Kirmānī left Iraq and arrived in Egypt probably in the period 405–407/1015–1017, when al-Ḥākim had already ordained the closure of the *majlis al-ḥikma* and had appointed Khatkīn al-Ḍayf as the new Ismaili chief *dāʿī* (*dāʿī al-duʿāt*). Once in Cairo, al-Kirmānī, by his own admission, finds the local *daʿwa* in a perplexed and powerless state, ascribing this in part to the 'relentless inconsistency' of al-Ḥākim's leadership which had driven his followers either to abandon their religious position or to embrace extremism. Walker, 'The Ismaili *Daʿwa* in the reign of the Fatimid Caliph al-Ḥākim', *JARCE*, 30 (1993), p. 178; al-Kirmānī, *al-Maṣābīḥ fī ithbāt al-imāma*, ed. and tr. Walker, *Master of the Age*, p. 10. On the role of al-Ḥākim sourced in Fatimid documents, see Paul E. Walker, 'The Role of the Imam-Caliph as Depicted in Official Treatises and Documents Issued by the Fatimids', in *The Study of Shiʿi Islam*, ed. Farhad Daftary and Gurdofarid Miskinzoda (London and New York, 2013), pp. 411–432.

[2] Al-Nasafī's *Kitāb al-Maḥṣūl* was probably written around 300/912 and it is no longer extant. Passages of this work survive in al-Rāzī's *Iṣlāḥ*, in al-Kirmānī's *Riyāḍ* and the *Kitāb al-Shajara* attributed to Abū Tammām. On the latter, see Paul E. Walker, 'Abū Tammām and his *Kitāb al-Shajara*: A New Ismaili Treatise from Tenth-century

work appears to have been a *summa* of early Ismaili doctrines which imported into Ismaili cosmology a pre-Fārābian version of Neoplatonism.[3] In the *Kitāb al-Maḥṣūl*, al-Nasafī introduces and expounds the three Plotinian hypostases (the One, the Intellect and the Soul) and speaks of creation as a gradual issuing forth of the cosmos from the One. Unsurprisingly, al-Nasafī's Qarmaṭī attempt to interpret and adapt Neoplatonic cosmology to Islamic monotheistic dogmas and to Ismaili teachings provoked discussion, if not disapproval and objection, from other intellectuals within the Ismaili *daʿwa*.

The first to voice his dissent was al-Rāzī. In his *Kitāb al-Iṣlāḥ* (*Book of the Correction*), he denounced al-Nasafī's shortcomings, provoking a reaction from al-Sijistānī, who in his now lost *Kitāb al-Nuṣra* (the *'Support'*) penned a defence of his teacher al-Nasafī. Al-Nasafī's errors were pointed out by al-Rāzī, and Ismail K. Poonawala has articulated al-Sijistānī's defensive arguments thoroughly in his introduction to al-Sijistānī's *Kitāb al-Maqālīd al-malakūtiyya*.[4] It is worth highlighting, however, that al-Kirmānī composed the *Riyāḍ* in an attempt to reconcile the debate 'from a vantage point of post-Fārābian philosophy';[5] his intent was certainly not that of rebuking the teachings of his fellow *dāʿī*s en masse but rather that of 'updating' them according to what he believed to be the latest 'scientific' findings. The full title of his book explains its contents and the author's purpose of resolving a long-standing dispute by correcting the doctrinal divergences that had emerged among his highly esteemed colleagues within the

---

Khurasan', *JAOS*, 114 (1994), pp. 343–352; see also *idem*, *Early Philosophical Shiism*, pp. 57–55; Daftary, *The Ismāʿīlīs*, pp. 223–234, and his *Ismaili Literature: A Bibliography of Sources and Studies* (London, 2004), pp. 13, 29, 125.

[3] See my 'A Preliminary Study on the Significance of *Qaḍāʾ* and *Qadar* in the Eighth Chapter of al-Kirmānī's *Kitāb al-Riyāḍ*, in *L'Ésotérisme shiʿite: ses racines et ses prolongements/Shiʿi Esotericism: Its Roots and Developments*, ed. Mohammad A. Amir-Moezzi, Maria De Cillis, Daniel De Smet and Orkhan Mir-Kasimov (Turnhout, 2016), pp. 347–348.

[4] See Poonawala's views in his Introduction, pp. 30–47. Ivanow has analysed and explained the nature of the debate in his 'An Early Controversy in Ismailism', in his *Studies in Early Persian Ismailism* (Bombay, 1955), pp. 87–122. In addition, Walker has provided a summary of the dispute focusing mainly on al-Kirmānī's perspective. See his *Ḥamīd al-Dīn al-Kirmānī*, pp. 44–45.

[5] Ismail K. Poonawala, 'An Early Doctrinal Controversy in the Iranian School of Ismaili Thought and its Implications', *Journal of Persianate Studies* 5 (2012), pp. 17–34.

daʿwa: Kitāb al-Riyāḍ fiʾl-ḥukm bayn al-ṣadayn: ṣāḥib al-iṣlāḥ wa-ṣāḥib al-nuṣra (The Book of the Meadows in Judgement between [the authors of the books with] the Two Letters *ṣād*: the Author of *al-Iṣlāḥ* and the Author of *al-Nuṣra*).[6]

Throughout this work, al-Kirmānī endeavours to point out that the starting positions of al-Nasafī, al-Rāzī and al-Sijistānī concerned fundamental principles about which no disagreements should have been raised. He suggests that Abū Ḥātim aptly intended to amend what he considered to be unsound in the doctrine propounded in the *Maḥṣūl*; however, instead of focusing his attention on major issues such as those relative to *tawḥīd* and the nature of the Intellect – which occupies a great deal of al-Nasafī's work – in his *Iṣlāḥ*, al-Rāzī concentrates on discussions pertaining to secondary rules (*furūʿ*), thereby neglecting fundamental principles (*uṣūl*) and thus potentially creating, al-Kirmānī suggests, harmful discord among the members of the Ismaili community.[7] For his part, al-Sijistānī supported his master, testifying to the soundness of al-Nasafī's positions, the majority of which, however, al-Kirmānī considered outdated and not accurate. Al-Kirmānī then cites the authors' statements with the intention of correcting and complementing the *Iṣlāḥ*, whilst mostly refuting the *Nuṣra*. In his pedagogic intent, he does not reproach his predecessors' teachings but aims at complementing them with the latest views.[8]

---

[6]   According to Edward W. Lane *Arabic–English Lexicon* (London, 1863), *riyāḍ* (root: *r-y-ḍ*) can generally be translated as 'meadows'. In particular, when linked to certain prophetic sayings, the word is understood to refer to the meadows of Paradise. The second form verb, *rayyiḍ*, on the other hand, conveys the meaning of physical or mental training or exercising (I am grateful to Russell Harris for having pointed out this multiplicity of meanings). It is arguable that al-Kirmānī used *riyāḍ* in the title of his work as a wordplay to emphasise the mental dialectics applied in judging the respective positions of al-Nasafī, al-Rāzī and al-Sijistānī.

[7]   Al-Kirmānī, *Riyāḍ* (Beirut, 1960), pp. 59–60.

[8]   Ibid., p. 214. This attitude is made explicit in a passage used as an introduction to the last chapter of his book. Therein, al-Kirmānī provides a justification for the theoretical shortcomings of his colleagues by stressing that the sciences of religion are too numerous to be comprehended by any single individual other than the Imam: 'Religion is in them like a single individual who is composed of its parts, and they are to him like the senses by means of which things are perceived. Should an item escape one of them, another will perceive it without the perception by the second

The *Riyāḍ* is divided into ten chapters (*abwāb*, sg. *bāb*) each of which is further subdivided into several sections (*fuṣūl*, sg. *faṣl*). The book focuses on issues relative to the nature of the Soul, the first intellect and prime matter, and whether human souls are a part or a trace of the Universal Soul,[9] on what basis it can be stated that the human being is a fruit of this world, the relationship of movement and rest to matter and form, the constitution of this world, discussions on divine decree and destiny, the nature of Adam's prophethood and, finally, a chapter on rectifying the major doctrinal issues on divine unity and on the originated being (i.e. the first Intellect), a subject overlooked by al-Rāzī. The choice of these topics and the order in which they are dealt with is quite obvious: they reflect the way al-Rāzī and, subsequently al-Sijistānī, decided to treat the *Maḥṣūl*'s stances on these issues. Nevertheless, it is significant that al-Kirmānī relegates primary concerns to the tenth and last chapter of the *Riyāḍ*: his intention was certainly that of reconciling the inconsistencies among the three authors and to ensure their ideas' acceptance within the Fatimid Ismaili community.[10]

The eighth chapter of the *Riyāḍ* focuses on the topic of *qaḍā' wa'l-qadar* and contains the longest extracts from the *Iṣlāḥ* and the *Nuṣra*. In effect, al-Kirmānī authors, in line with a trend of the time, an adjudication-commentary (*muḥākama*) in which he compares, criticises and supplements with his own opinions al-Sijistānī's and al-Rāzī's postures on the issue of divine decree and destiny. These positions are presented as dialogues with frequent interventions by al-Kirmānī who points out their virtues and limitations.

Al-Kirmānī's review commences by examining al-Rāzī's critique of an early Ismaili tradition adopted by al-Nasafī. This tradition identifies the *qaḍā'* with the Antecedent and the *qadar* with the Follower. This identification appears to be rooted in early Ismaili cosmological

---

implying any fault in the first who failed to perceive it or in any other of the senses'. Al-Kirmānī, *Riyāḍ*, pp. 213–214, tr. by Walker in his *Ḥamīd al-Dīn al-Kirmānī*, pp. 60–61. Poonawala has provided the edited Arabic passage in Appendix no. 2 of his study on al-Sijistānī's *Kitāb al-Maqālīd*.

[9] On this topic, see De Smet, 'L'âme humaine: une 'partie' ou une 'empreinte' de l'Âme universelle', in De Smet, *La Philosophie Ismaélienne: un ésotérisme chiite entre néoplatonisme et gnose* (Paris, 2012), pp. 113–125.

[10] See Poonawala's perspective in his Introduction, p. 43.

accounts which had not yet been affected by the revisited Neoplatonic ideas introduced onto the Islamic scene by al-Fārābī.

In his translation of the *Kitāb al-Yanābiʿ*, Walker points out that the terms *sābiq* and *tālī*, which were how both al-Nasafī and al-Sijistānī referred to the Universal Intellect and the Universal Soul respectively, are terms that did not occur in the Arabic Neoplatonic texts translated from Greek or Syriac.[11] These were indicated merely with terms like *ʿaql* (corresponding to the Greek *Nous*) and *nafs* (corresponding to the Greek *Psyche*).[12] The names 'Antecedent' and 'Follower' seem to have appeared in connection with the question of creation and determination in a treatise discovered by Samuel M. Stern, authored by Abū ʿĪsā al-Murshid, a Fatimid *dāʿī* who was active during the reign of the Fatimid Imam-caliph al-Muʿizz (r. 341/953–365/975).[13] Different themes in this text mirror some of the motifs that can also be found in the works of tenth-century Ismaili Neoplatonists and in anti-Ismaili polemical Zaydī texts.[14] Many topics already present in al-Murshid's treatise will surface in the above-mentioned works by al-Sijistānī and al-Rāzī, and for this reason I shall refer here in some detail to some of the doctrinal issues contained therein.

The treatise speaks about the cosmogonic myth in which God once conceived a will and wish (*fa lammā arāda irādat^{an} wa-shāʾa mashīʾat^{an}*), created a light (*fa-khalaqa nūr^{an}*) and created by it a creature (*wa-khalaqa min dhālika al-nūr khalq^{an}*). This light remained for a portion of time (*burha min dahrihi*) not knowing (*lā yadrī*) whether it was a creator (*khāliq*) or a created being (*makhlūq*). Then

---

[11]   Walker, *The Wellsprings of Wisdom*, pp. 115–116.

[12]   The terms 'Antecedent' and 'Follower' were preferred by al-Sijistānī for they conveyed the idea of position and rank in the hierarchical order of the cosmos.

[13]   The *Risāla* by Abū ʿĪsā al-Murshid has been edited and translated by Samuel M. Stern, 'The Earliest Cosmological Doctrines of Ismāʿīlism', in *Studies in Early Ismāʿīlism* (Jerusalem and Leiden, 1983), pp. 3–29. For a full discussion on the pre-Sijistānī origin of this theory and its gnostic roots, see Halm, *Kosmologie*, pp. 53–74, 89–90, 98–99, 115–127, 133–135.

[14]   These sources corroborate the theory that the myth contained in this treatise was already known by the Qarmaṭīs, among other Ismaili groups, between the end of the ninth and the first half of the tenth centuries CE. See Stern, 'The Earliest Cosmological Doctrines', pp. 3–6, 17; Halm, *Kosmologie*, pp. 79–80; Daftary, *The Ismāʿīlīs*, pp. 133–136; Ebstein, *Mysticism and Philosophy in al-Andalus*, p. 41.

God breathed into it a spirit (*rūḥ*) and directed to it a command: 'Be!' (*kun!*) So it came to be with God's permission. Through the two letters, *kāf* and *nūn* [forming the imperative *kun*] God brought all things into being.[15] Then through the letters *wāw* and *yā'*, the name acquired its feminine form (*kūnī*).[16] In the spiritual world, *kūnī*, as the female

---

[15]   At this point, the text reads: '[There is] bringing-into-being (*takawwun*), one who brings-into-being (*mukawwin*), and a thing which is brought-into being (*kā'in*). Then there is Allāh.' Ebstein suggests that 'then there is Allāh' might be a reference to *kūnī* (see Ebstein, *Mysticism and Philosophy in al-Andalus*, p. 42 note 35 and p. 87). It is also possible to speculate that, rather than in Allāh, *kūnī* is signified in the correspondence of *takawwun*, *mukawwin* and *kā'in* which heralds al-Kirmānī's identification of the Intellect with both the *ibdā'* and the *mubda'*, the origination and the orginated. Separate from these beings, which are one in manifestation, is God who stands apart and above all aspects of 'being' and 'non-being'. The elevation of God above any pairing is a fundamental and constitutive dogma in Ismailism. On this topic, see Wilferd Madelung and Paul E. Walker, 'The *Kitāb al-Rusūm wa'l-izdiwāj wa'l-tartīb* attributed to 'Abdān (d. 286/899): Edition of the Arabic Text and Translation', in *Fortresses of the Intellect: Ismaili and Other Islamic Studies in Honour of Farhad Daftary*, ed. Omar Ali-de-Unzaga (London, 2011), pp. 103–165.

[16]   Halm has suggested that the transformation of the masculine imperative *kun* into the feminine form of the Arabic imperative *kūnī* has a special meaning. It bears witness to the fact that the cosmology of Abū 'Īsā al-Murshid's treatise preserves, among other gnostic characteristics, the idea that the first of God's creatures, whose 'fall' becomes the cause of the emergence of the cosmos, is usually of the female sex (see the notion of *Sophia*). Heinz Halm, 'The Cosmology of the pre-Fatimid Ismā'īliyya', in *Mediaeval Ismai'li History and Thought*, ed. Farhad Daftary (Cambridge, 1996), p. 81; see also Daftary, *The Ismā'īlīs*, pp. 230–231; Corbin, *Cyclical Time and Ismaili Gnosis*, pp. 184–185; Hirji, 'A Study of *al-Risālah al-bāhirah*', p. 84 note 97. Al-Murshid's text specifies that *kūnī* became a name for 'what is above it (*fawqaha*)' (see Stern, 'The Earliest Cosmological Doctrines', Arabic text, p. 8). Halm, followed by Ebstein, suggests that 'what is above it' means 'that which is above *Qadar*', *Qadar* being the hypostatised entity below *kūnī* (see Halm, *Kosmologie*, p. 75 note 5; and Ebstein, *Mysticism and Philosophy in al-Andalus*, p. 42 note 35). However, it can also be contemplated that *kūnī* becomes the name for the *amr*, the divine command through which *kūnī* is instantiated, and which is therefore above *kūnī*, preceding it in a sort of 'causative' way. This would corroborate the idea that the first originated entity is identical to the command once it is existentiated. *kūnī* 'becomes' (*ṣāra*) another name for the entity which is above it (*amr/kalima*) only when it 'attains' its manifested aspect. It is certainly not accidental that the specification of this naming occurs only after, in al-Murshid's text, it is clarified that there exists a correspondence among *takawwun*, *mukawwin* and *kā'in* and that, separated from these and shrouded in His unreachability, there is God, the One who voices the command.

hypostasis of the creative imperative, creates seven cherubs (*karūbiyya*).[17] *kūnī*, arrogantly believing herself to be the only existent thing, causes the immediate emanation of six dignitaries (*ḥudūd*) through God's power. Aware that such emanation occurred neither through her own power nor her own will, *kūnī* relinquishes her pride and acknowledges the existence of an indiscernible Originator.[18] Then the Command of God (*amr*) ordered *kūnī* to create for herself and out of her light a male assistant named *qadar*. The latter, following *kūnī*'s order, creates twelve spiritual ranks (*al-ḥudūd al-rūḥāniyya*).[19] *kūnī* and *qadar* are therefore the first two principles (two Roots, *aslān*, sg. *asl*) of creation. From the higher letters (*al-ḥurūf al-ʿulwiyya*), namely the seven letters forming the pair *kūnī-qadar* – also identified

---

[17] Their names are: *ʿazama* (might), *ʿizza* (glory), *hudā* (right guidance), *bahā᾽* (splendour), *ra᾽fa* (mercy), *amr* (command), *mu᾽tamar* (counsel). See Stern, 'The Earliest Cosmological Doctrines of Ismāʿīlism', Arabic text, p. 9, English text, p. 20.

[18] It will be observed in this second chapter that a form of 'self-over-estimation' is exhibited in the Qur᾽anic account of Moses who believed it possible to be admitted to a direct contemplation of God's face (Q 7:143). Like *kūnī*, who acknowledges the presence of an Originator, thus realising that she is merely a 'limited' originated being, Moses becomes aware of his own limits and repents. Just as in the *kūnī-qadar* myth the emanation of six dignitaries has the redemptive task of leading *kūnī* onto the path of monotheism, so in the story of Moses, it will be observed, the warning about the impossibility of a direct vision of the divine 'face' plays the redeeming function of setting Moses within his hierarchical and gnoseological limits, prior to the attainment of his full *nāṭiq*-ship. In addition, it can be detected that the emphasis on the impossibility of perceiving the invisible Originator which features in both al-Murshid's text and in the Qur᾽anic account of Moses is also present in al-Sijistānī's *Kitāb al-Yanābīʿ*. Therewith, when the pure identity of the Originator is analysed, it is stated: 'not that an identity is *there* that actually exists or does not exist (*lā an hunāk huwiyya mawjūda wa-lā huwiyya maʿdūma*). It is merely something that appears to the Antecedent from its own existentiality (*min aysiyyatihi*)'. See *Kitāb al-Yanābīʿ*, p. 71; *The Wellsprings of Wisdom*, p. 49 (my emphasis).

[19] Of the six dignitaries (*ḥudūd*) emanated by *kūnī*, three are above her and three below; among the former, one finds *tawahhum* (imagination), *irāda* (will) and *mashī᾽a* (wish). Among the latter was Iblīs, who refused *kūnī*'s order to submit to *qadar*, the heavenly Adam, and thus became the chief devil. *Kūnī* and *qadar* also formed a pentad together with three spiritual forces, *al-jadd*, *al-fatḥ* and *al-khāyal*, mediating between the spiritual world and the religious hierarchy in the corporeal realm. See Stern, 'Earliest Cosmological Doctrines', pp. 12–13, 14–15; Ebstein, *Mysticism and Philosophy in al-Andalus*, pp. 42–43.

as the archetypes of the seven *nāṭiq*s and their messages – emerged all other letters, the names that these formed as well as all named beings.[20] It was through *kūnī* that God brought all entities into being (*kawwana*), including spiritual and physical entities, and through *qadar* He determined (*qaddara*) them.[21]

What surfaces in this text is the fundamental role of the divine command (*amr*) which is held responsible for the creation of the world and its control over it.[22] Whilst the hypostatic female imperative *kūnī*! – the result of God's will manifested in His existentiating order – is the means through which the divine command brings all things into being, *qadar*, which emerges from *kūnī*'s light as she obeys a further divine command, acts as the tool through which God appoints to all created entities their measured shares.[23]

It is interesting to note that in the text there are explicit references to distinct commands: the first is the existentiating imperative *kun*, through which *kūnī* enters existence; the second is the divine order (*amr*) imposed on *kūnī* to create for herself the helper, *qadar*. The distinction between these two commands is significant if we draw a correspondence (i) between *kūnī* and the concept of the Antecedent, and (ii) between *qadar* and the concept of the Follower. Indeed, in al-Murshid's treatise, a number of Qur'anic verses (Q 3:52; 16:42; 23:18; 54:49; 77:23; 87:1–4; 97:1) are quoted to reinforce exactly the idea that *kūnī* – accountable for the creation of the physical world[24] – is to be identified with the *sābiq*, and that *qadar* – the hypostasis of measure and governance – is to be identified with the

---

[20]	Daftary, *Ismaili Literature*, p. 20.

[21]	Stern, 'The Earliest Cosmological Doctrines', p. 18. On the soteriological purpose of this early cosmology featuring in this text, see Daftary, *Ismaili Literature*, p. 20; De Cillis, 'A Preliminary Study on the Significance of *Qaḍā'* and *Qadar*', pp. 348–349.

[22]	Ebstein, *Mysticism and Philosphy in al-Andalus*, pp. 42–43.

[23]	The term *qadar* is usually associated with the concept of 'measuring' and 'decreeing'. See Halm, *Kosmologie*, p. 57, 65; al-Sijistānī, 'Risālat tuḥfat al-mustajībīn', p. 149.

[24]	Moreover, it is reported in the text that the limit of the First (i.e. the limit of the Antecedent/*kūnī*) (*ḥadd al-awwal*) is the limit of the totality (*majmuʿ*) of the subtle beings (*al-laṭā'if*) and spirits (*arwāḥ*) which return to it. Conversely, to the limit of the Follower (*ḥadd al-tālī*) pertain bodies (*ajsād*) and all dense entities (*kullu kathīf*). Stern, 'The Earliest Cosmological Doctrines of Ismāʿīlism', Arabic text, p. 9, English text, p. 23.

tālī who is entrusted by God with the world of dense, composite and decayable substances.[25] It is natural to draw also a further comparison between the Antecedent/*kūnī* and the Intellect who, in Ismaili metaphysics, is effectively identified with the first being – mentioned in the text[26] – which is originated by the divine *ibdā'*, the latter being no different from the *kalima/amr*, that is, the first of the two mentioned commands. From the Intellect, the Soul is brought forth (hence the Soul's possible identification with the Follower/*qadar*) and so are all the other existents. What is unusual to find in the text is the emphasis laid on the Soul/Follower/*Qadar* being the recipient of a second command issued by the Intellect/Antecedent/*kūnī*. To this command a third order is added when *kūnī* compels *qadar* to create out of his light those spiritual beings who act as intermediaries between *kūnī*, *qadar*, the enunciator-prophets (*nuṭaqā'*) and their friends (*awliyā'*).[27] However, the series of instantiations resulting from these

---

[25] Ibid., Arabic text, p. 9, English text, p. 23. The doctrine on the primordial couple *kūnī-qadar* – corresponding to the primal set of Antecedent-Follower – has been traced back to the third/ninth century when it appears to have become synonymous with the doctrine of Ismailism. (On the profound Gnostic character of the themes of the *Risāla* and the different forms in which they appeared in the earliest texts of Ismaili literature, see Paul E. Walker, *Abu Ya'qub al-Sijistānī: Intellectual Missionary* [London and New York, 1996], pp. 35–37; and Halm, *Kosmologie*, particularly pp. 53–66; *idem*, 'The Cosmology of the pre-Fatimid Ismā'īliyya', pp. 76–77.) Al-Sijistānī seems to have drawn from these themes and have adapted them to his cosmological system. In particular, he interprets the letters forming the words *kūnī* and *qadar* (k, u, n, y, q, d, r) as the 'seven higher letters' (*al-ḥurūf al-'ulwiyya al-sab'a*) (see al-Sijistānī, *Kitāb al-Yanābī'*, pp. 67–70, and Walker's comments in *The Wellsprings of Wisdom*, pp. 123–125). Furthermore, in his *Kitāb al-Iftikhār*, al-Sijistānī, following al-Nasafī, identifies the first six letters with six enunciator-prophets, respectively: Adam, Noah, Abraham, Moses, Jesus and Muḥammad. Six *nuṭaqā'* have come, each one bringing a letter. One more *nāṭiq* is necessary to complete the metahistorical order of *kūnī-qadar*. Muḥammad, as the sixth prophet is the last through which divine governance is exercised through a religious law. He will be followed by the last *qā'im* who will not bring a new *sharī'a*. The seventh letter, *rā'*, is identified with such a *qā'im*. See al-Sijistānī, *Kitāb al-Iftikhār*, ed. Poonawala, pp. 123–137; Halm, *Kosmologie*, pp. 55–58; Walker, *Intellectual Missionary*, pp. 76–77.

[26] Stern, 'The Earliest Cosmological Doctrines of Ismā'īlism', Arabic text, p. 9, English text, p. 23.

[27] *Qadar* names these spiritual beings as: *al-jadd, al-fatḥ, al-khayāl, al-naṣr, riḍwān, malik, malakūt, munkar, nakīr, jabarūt* and *kibriyā'*. Stern, 'The Earliest

commands (i.e. the creation of *kūnī*, that of the six dignitaries and the divine order addressed to *kūnī* to create *qadar*) do not occur in time, coming about simultaneously;[28] the insistence on a number of commands is probably employed by the author of the treatise to stress more and more the aspect of willingness which is firstly manifested in the divine inception of all existence through *ibdāʿ* and which is retained in all the 'successive' commands.[29] It should be kept in mind that even when *kūnī* exhibits, in her command to the Follower, a form of willingness, the Follower is but a channel through which the one and only *amr* acts. The Qurʾanic verse, 'Our command is but one [act], like the twinkling of an eye' (54:50), is introduced in the text, thus underlining that, in truth, there is only one command, which occurs outside time.[30]

Interestingly, the same Qurʾanic verse is mentioned by al-Kirmānī who, in *al-Risāla al-Muḍīʾa*, differentiates among three types of *amr*. The first type precedes the existent (*mawjūd*), that is, creation, which is due *ʿalā al-zamān*, meaning that it is *outside* time. This type is explained as a kind of command that transcends the realm of nature (*khārij min ʿālam al-ṭabīʿa*) and relates to the Almighty as in Q 54:50. With the second type of *amr*, acting on the world of Nature, creation enters existence simultaneously *with* time (*amr yūjadu al-mawjūd bihi maʿa al-zamān*); the third type of command is the *amr* through which creation occurs *in* time (*amr yūjadu bihi al-mawjūd biʾl-zamān*). The latter results in creation and in time, being linked to natural phenomena such as storms and earthquakes.[31]

Eventually, in al-Murshid's treatise, it is God who brings into being, through *kūnī*, and who determines existents, through *Qadar*, by

---

Cosmological Doctrines of Ismāʿīlism', Arabic text, p. 9, English text, p. 21.

[28]　Ibid., Arabic text, p. 13, English text, p. 25.

[29]　The emphasis on willingness is kept at the level of the *ibdāʿ* but is rarefied in the cosmological systems of al-Nasafī, al-Sijistānī, al-Rāzī and al-Kirmānī, which contemplate the production of the Soul/Follower and of entities below her as a phenomenon of natural procession (*inbiʿāth*).

[30]　Stern, 'The Earliest Cosmological Doctrines of Ismāʿīlism', Arabic text, p. 9, English text, p. 25.

[31]　Al-Kirmānī, *al-Risāla al-Muḍīʾa*, pp. 55–57; Haji, *A Distinguished Dāʿī*, pp. 32–33.

means of *one* atemporal command.[32] Another possible explanation for the differentiation of these commands might be the necessity of providing the Antecedent with a form of 'eminence' with respect to the Follower: given that such prominence could not be conveyed through a temporal precedence, *kūnī* could be identified with the Antecedent only with regards to her superior rank which allows the imposition of a command upon her Follower, *qadar*.

These elements, with some refined modifications, can be easily traced in the discussions on *qaḍāʾ* and *qadar* that feature in the eighth chapter of the *Riyāḍ*, wherein a difference occurs in the substitution of the term *kūnī* with the word *qaḍāʾ*. It is probable that the replacement of *kūnī* with the religious nomenclature of *qaḍāʾ* might have seemed a safer and more suitable option, apt for identifying it with the Intellect/Pen, which are – in Arabic – of the male gender.[33] This replacement

---

[32] This concept is corroborated also in another passage of the same treatise, that even the twelve spiritual beings proceeding from *Qadar*'s light are a creation of God (*khalq Allāh*). Stern, 'The Earliest Cosmological Doctrines of Ismāʿīlism', Arabic text, p. 15, English text, p. 21.

[33] It will be observed that al-Sijistānī, following his master's stand, identifies the Antecedent with the Pen (*qalam*) and the Decree (*qaḍāʾ*) (al-Kirmānī, *Riyāḍ*, p. 140; Walker, *Intellectual Missionary*, p. 36). On the male/female relationship relative to the pairs Pen/Tablet and Intellect/Soul, see Sachico Murata, *The Tao of Islam: A Sourcebook on Gender Relationships in Islamic Thought* (Albany, NY, 1992), pp. 153–158. Needless to say, the identification of the Intellect with the Pen, and the Soul with the Tablet, is a recurrent topos. So, according to the members of the Ikhwān al-Ṣafāʾ, the cosmic Pen signifies the Universal Intellect with his active character, whilst the cosmic Tablet signifies the Universal Soul whose character is passive. The Qurʾanic Throne (*ʿarsh*) and Footstool (*kursī*) are signifiers for the Intellect and the Soul too. In addition to these pairs, the Ikhwān al-Ṣafāʾ offer a series of sets of names they considered to be synonymous with the pairs Intellect and Soul, Pen and Tablet, respectively. Among these there are light and darkness, spiritual and corporeal, existence and non-existence, time and space, cause and effect, origin and return, manifest and non-manifest (see Ikhwān al-Ṣafāʾ, *Jāmiʿat al-jāmiʿa*, ed. ʿĀrif Tāmir [Beirut, 1970], pp. 67–69). Ibn ʿArabī speaks of the Pen and the Tablet as the spiritual Adam and the spiritual Eve, i.e. the principles of created duality needed by the cosmos in the same way as the human world needed Adam and Eve. Moreover, Ibn ʿArabī in a typical Ismaili formulation, identifies the Pen as the Intellect with the first teacher (*ustādh*) bestowing his gnoseological gifts upon the Tablet, as the Soul, which is the first student (*mutaʿallim*), namely the 'locus', receiving the activity of the Intellect. See Muḥyi al-Dīn Muḥammad b. ʿAlī b. ʿArabī, *al-Futūḥāt al-Makkiyya* (Cairo, 1911),

might have occurred also in view of the attempts, clearly detectable in the eighth chapter of the *Riyāḍ*, carried out by Ismaili scholars such as al-Sijistānī, to draw correspondences between, on the one hand, the immutability of the Intellect and *qaḍāʾ* and, on the other hand, the mutability of *qadar* which, like the Soul – more directly connected to the variability of matter and form – is subject to change.

The application of the opposites, immutability/mutability, to the pairing of *qaḍāʾ/qadar* respectively did not originate within Ismailism. The triumphant Ashʿarism of Sunni Islam in the 5th/11th and 6th/12th centuries affected the collective perception of these notions. *Qaḍāʾ* had become, for the Ashʿarites, a term for divine creation which includes what is right and wrong in accordance with their concept of God as the Creator of evil as well as good acts. *Qaḍāʾ* represented, for the Ashʿarites, a pre-eternal divine decree which incorporates all existents and their immutable status within the divine knowledge. *Qadar*, conversely, was perceived as the aspect of the divine decree which realises the passage from potentiality into actuality according to God's will, and it was therefore thought of as something susceptible to change. It was generally considered to be directed towards a specific act or thing, so that through *qadar* God grants all creatures with their measures and limitations. Whereas *qaḍāʾ* came to be connected to the pre-eternal will of God and was classified as an attribute of existence, co-existing in its immutability with God, *qadar* was linked to the temporal aspect of the divine will, identified with His wish and regarded as a contingent being prone to fluctuations.[34]

Al-Sijistānī's emphasis on the immutability of *qaḍāʾ* and the mutability of *qadar* heralds al-Shahrastānī's theory of the two rulings. Such theory – it will be shown, also hinted at by al-Rāzī – distinguishes between the sphere of the *mafrūgh* (accomplished) in which an eternal divine decree has already been elaborated and conclusively actualised

---

repr. Dār Ṣādir (Beirut, 1968), vol. III, p. 399. On these and other sources reproducing similar correspondences see again, Murata, *The Tao of Islam*, pp. 153–169; Ebstein, *Mysticism and Philosophy in al-Andalus*, pp. 50–57.

[34]   On the Ashʿarites' view of *qaḍāʾ* as creation see Abū al-Ḥasan al-Ashʿarī, *Kitāb al-Lumaʿ*, tr. Richard J. McCarthy as *The Theology of al-Ashʿarī: the Arabic texts of al-Ashʿarī's Kitāb al-Lumaʿ and Risālat Istiḥsān al-khawḍ fī ʿilm al-kalām* (Beirut, 1953), pp. 45–46, 65–67.

by God, and the sphere of the *musta'naf* (inchoative), namely a realm of impending decree still in the process of becoming.[35]

Al-Kirmānī's analysis of *Faṣl* One opens with a restatement of al-Rāzī's position which reminds his readers that *qaḍā'* and *qadar* are expressions that feature in *kalām*: according to *kalām*, *qadar* is an evaluation/measuring (*taqdīr*), whilst *qaḍā'* signifies a final decision/judgement (*tafṣīl*). Al-Rāzī expounds on these meanings and attempts to dismiss al-Nasafī's views.

---

[35]   On this, see pp. 128–129.

Faṣl One

The author of the *Iṣlāḥ* [al-Rāzī] said: 'As for [al-Nasafī's] saying that "the *qaḍāʾ* signifies the Antecedent (*sābiq*) and that the *qadar* signifies the Follower (*tālī*)", it is an error (*khaṭaʾ*) because the *qadar* is before the *qaḍāʾ* just as the Antecedent is before the Follower. It is not permissible to apply the *qaḍāʾ* which is after the *qadar* to the Antecedent, which is what comes before the Follower. *Qadar* and *qaḍāʾ* are two expressions whose meaning is well known from speculative theology (*kalām*).

[Thus] *qadar* means the estimation/measuring (*taqdīr*) whilst *qaḍāʾ* means the decision (*tafṣīl*).[1] There is no decision except after estimation, [just as] the first comes before the second and not after it.[2] Corroborations of this matter in the Book of God are: 'The matter about which you both enquire has been decided (*quḍiyā*)' [Q. 12:41]. That is, [the matter] has been decided and finished. He [also] said: 'Then, when the prayer has been decreed (*quḍiyat*)' [Q. 62:10], that is, it has been finished.[3] [Thus] the *qadar* is like the cloth which the tailor (*khayyāṭ*) estimates. That is, before he decides [on its size], he estimates it, increasing or decreasing it [i.e. its size], broadening or narrowing it; once he has decided

---

[1]　Ivanow has translated *taqdīr* as 'making something possible' and *tafṣīl* as 'separation, cutting off'. See Ivanow, 'An Early Controversy', p. 108.

[2]　This is might be an allusion to the first and the second intellects.

[3]　Cf. al-Rāzī, *Iṣlāḥ*, pp. 45–46. In the same work, al-Rāzī quotes other Qurʾanic verses to corroborate the above ideas: 'and then Satan will say when the matter is decreed (*lammā quḍiya al-amr*)' (Q 14:22). This is used to explain that everything has been decreed (*kullu shayʾin quḍiyā*) and separated (*faragha*) through this decision, just as the people of Paradise are separated from the People of Fire. Another verse is: 'We decreed (*qaḍaynā*) to the Children of Israel' (Q 17:4). In it, al-Rāzī explains, the term *qaḍaynā* refers to something that has been sealed (*khutima*) and decided upon (*umḍiya*). Ibid., p. 46.

[on its size], he has determined it and he is done with it. There can neither be increase nor decrease [in its size]. This is an analogy (*mathal*) of the *qaḍā'* and the *qadar*.[4]

The gist of his [al-Rāzī's] statement: the *qaḍā'* cannot be said of the Antecedent for it is after the *qadar*, and the *qadar* cannot be said of the Follower for it is before the *qaḍā'*. The *qadar* is the estimation/measuring (*taqdīr*) and the *qaḍā'* is the decision (*tafṣīl*); as long as it [the cloth] is in the state of estimation it is possible to increase or decrease [its size], to broaden or narrow [its size], but once he [the tailor] has estimated (*faṣṣala*) and decreed it (*qaḍḍaya*), it is not possible to increase or decrease it [i.e. its size].[5]

The author of the *Nuṣra* [al-Sijistānī] said: 'The *qaḍā'* is not the *tafṣīl*, because the state of the *tafṣīl* itself in the *qaḍā'* is no less than that of the state of the object-of-decision (*munfaṣil*); because the subsistence (*thabāt*) of the *munfaṣil* on its shape/form (*hay'a*) depends on a *qaḍā'* which necessitates that, as the *munfaṣil* also subsists on what is decided (*quḍiya*) for it. As for the *qadar*, it is *taqdīr*, according to what he [al-Rāzī] mentioned, but *taqdīr* can only come about by a *qaḍā'* which necessitates that *taqdīr*. As for the corroborations that he cites from the Book of God Almighty that the *qaḍā'* is finishing (*farāgh*), they are irrefutable (*ghayr madfūʿ*). [That is] because the sages have said: "When God Almighty originated the Intellect He finished (*faragha*) [originating] the two worlds." This is because [the Intellect] is

---

⁴ Translation slightly modified in De Cillis, 'A Preliminary Study on the Significance of *Qaḍā'* and *Qadar*', p. 350. Al-Kirmānī seems here to have changed the actual wording of the *Iṣlāḥ*, which runs as follows: 'and if any matter has been decreed (*quḍiyā*), the decision is irrevocable [lit. there is no revocation – *irtijāʿ* – for it]. A matter which has been decreed (*muqaddar*), is revocable for it is possible that the estimation (*taqdīr*) which has been decided (*yunqaḍā*) with regards to that [affair] [moves] towards [another decision which] is different from it. This is because the *qadar* is the *taqdīr*. And the making [lit. the engineering, *handasa*] [...] of the cloth, is decreed (*yuqaddiruhu*) by the tailoring. The latter decrees it before finalising it (*qabla an yufaṣṣiluhu*) and makes it bigger or smaller, wide or tight and alters it (*yughayyiruhu*) [by substituting] its estimation with another estimation as long as it is *muqaddar*^{an}. For when he [the tailor] makes a [final] decision for it (*faṣṣalhu*), he decides it (*qaḍḍāhu*) and finishes it off (*atahu*) – whereby no letting out or taking in [can be applied] to it to make it larger or smaller [in size]. And this is an analogy for the *qaḍā'* and the *qadar*'. Al-Rāzī, *Iṣlāḥ*, p. 47.

⁵ Al-Kirmānī, *Riyāḍ* (HL), pp. 123–124.

the totality of the forms of the two worlds (*majmūʿ ṣuwar al-ʿālamayn*), and nothing of the forms of the two worlds escaped from the Intellect. It is a pure accomplishment (*al-farāgh al-maḥḍ*),[6] except that the author of the *Iṣlāḥ* made a serious error (*asāʾa*) in his comparison of *qaḍāʾ* and *qadar* with the cloth which the tailor estimates, in making his estimation/measuring (*taqdīr*) analogous to the *qadar* and [in making] his decision (*tafṣīl*) analogous to the *qaḍāʾ*. This comparison is not sound (*lā yastaqīm*). It was incumbent upon him [al-Rāzī] to make the form of tailoring (*ṣūrat al-khiyāṭa*), which is in the mind of the tailor, analogous to the *qaḍāʾ* because it is [something] spiritual (*rūḥānī*), and to make the estimation, which the tailor estimates according to the tailoring, analogous to the *qadar*, which is also a spiritual thing which has not yet come out to the limit (*ḥadd*) of actuality. This is what is meant by the form of the two roots (*ṣūrat al-aṣlayn*). Then, the *tafṣīl* that [the tailor] performs after the *taqdīr*, is according to the corporeal *ḥudūd* which appeared from the First and the Second [intellects].

'As the matter is according to what we [al-Sijistānī] have described, then indeed the *qaḍāʾ* is before the *qadar*, just as the tailoring is before the estimation and by that tailoring the estimation is prepared for the tailoring concerning what he [the tailor] estimates (*yaqdar*). Therefore, it is correct [to state] that the *qaḍāʾ* signifies the Antecedent and the *qadar* the Follower'.[7]

The gist of his [al-Sijistānī's] statement is: the *qaḍāʾ* precedes the *qadar* for there is no *taqdīr* except by a *qaḍāʾ* and that the *qaḍāʾ* signifies the Antecedent and *qadar* the Follower.

We [al-Kirmānī] say that the *taʾwīl* which both the authors [al-Rāzī and al-Sijistānī] have propounded and argued, in view of the meaning of the expressions *qaḍāʾ* and *qadar* being as we have explained, is an impossible *taʾwīl* in whatever respect the *qaḍāʾ* and the *qadar* may be connected to the Antecedent and the

---

[6] The root *f-r-gh*, in *faragha* and *farāgh*, is used with a double meaning in this context: (i) it conveys the idea of completeness and it can indicate that through the act of origination via *ibdāʿ* the two worlds and the Intellect are created at once; (ii) it can also indicate that the Intellect is complete (hence perfect and pure) and in some way disengaged from the two worlds, in the sense that it cannot be affected by them.

[7] The translation has been slightly modified from De Cillis, 'A Preliminary Study on the Significance of *Qaḍāʾ* and *Qadar*', pp. 353–354.

Follower. That is because the author of the *Iṣlāḥ* – by his saying that 'the *qadar* is the *taqdīr* and that the *qaḍā'* is the *tafṣīl*' and by the analogy he has written concerning the matter of the cloth and the form of the tailoring – makes it necessary for the *qadar* to be a *qā'im bi'l-quwwa* and possible to come into existence, and for the *qaḍā'* to be a *qā'im bi'l-fiʿl* that has come out of the limit of possibility, that is, from potentiality to actuality.[8] And if the meaning of *qadar* and *qaḍā'* is thus, then it cannot be said at all that they [the *qadar* and the *qaḍā'*] signify the Antecedent and the Follower. For neither the one nor the other was ever potential then came out into actuality according to the proofs [given] above.[9]

Analysis and interpretation: Al-Kirmānī opens this chapter by reporting al-Rāzī's quotations from his *Iṣlāḥ*, in which he condemns al-Nasafī's idea (supposedly expressed in his *Maḥṣūl*) that the *qaḍā'* signifies the Antecedent whilst the *qadar* signifies the Follower. Al-Rāzī initially simply explains that the *qadar* comes before the *qaḍā'* just as the Antecedent comes before the Follower; however, he never explicitly identifies the *qadar* as the Antecedent-*qua*-Antecedent or the *qaḍā'* as the Follower-*qua*-Follower. He is merely outlining their respective positions, which see the *qaḍā'* coming after the *qadar*, just as the Follower comes after the Antecedent. His argument deepens as he compares the *qaḍā'* to a cloth which the tailor produces by making a garment according to a preceding estimation. It should be noticed that al-Rāzī exhibits a clear pedagogical commitment in the use of this analogy. He was probably set to adapt such a difficult topic and make it more comprensible for a wider audience. Examples of such an attitude were common for members of the Ismaili *daʿwa*, as testified in texts dating from the earliest period of the Fatimid caliphate. It is recounted that one of the teaching methods adopted by the supreme *dāʿī* Aflaḥ b. Ḥarūn al-Malūsī (d. before 923 CE) was that to adapt his language to different audiences: 'To the artisan he spoke about his respective trade; to the tailor, for instance, about needle and thread, and eyelet

---

[8] As specified in the 'Notes to the Text', I have chosen to leave the expressions *qā'im bi'l-quwwa* and *qā'im bi'l-fiʿl* untranslated in order to convey their possible double meaning as 'subsisting in potentiality' and 'subsisting in actuality', and as the *qā'im in potentiality* and the *qā'im in actuality* respectively.

[9] Al-Kirmānī, *Riyāḍ* (HL), pp. 124–125.

and scissors; to the shepherd about his staff and wrap, and the flock and the shepherd's pouch.'[10]

According to al-Rāzī, it is the mental action of estimating that allows the tailor to judge to what extent changes can be made to a cloth, which is compared to the *qadar*. Should the tailor make a final decision concerning the cloth and cut it to size without having estimated it beforehand, this would result in the garment being either too loose or too tight. Al-Rāzī believes that the *qadar* precedes the *qaḍāʾ* because only after estimation/measuring (*taqdīr*) is it feasible to take a final decision (*tafṣīl*) and thus produce a fitted cloth. Basically, continuing with the analogy proposed in the text, the mental exercise of estimation happens before the action of cutting out the cloth, which renders it a made-to-measure garment; once the tailor has cut the cloth he has determined its final fit.[11]

A reader might wonder why al-Rāzī ventures into such detailed discussion about the possibility of bringing changes to a not-yet actualised garment. A possible explanation is to read these and following arguments on changes – including the passage from a state of potentiality into that of actuality, which is often mentioned in the following passages by all of the three *dāʿīs* – not merely in connection with the concepts of the Intellect and the Soul, but also in the light of the concept of a minor *qiyāma* being the 'end of the world', namely the end of one prophetic cycle which *changes* into another.[12] If one takes into

---

[10] See Halm, ed., 'Biography of the Imam al-Mahdī' (*Sīrat al-Imām al-Mahdī*), quoted in Heinz Halm, *The Fatimids and their Traditions of Learning* (London, 1997), p. 27.

[11] It is worth noting that al-Rāzī employs a series of wordplays in the analogy of the cloth: the term he uses to explain the actual meaning of *qadar* is *taqdīr*, which is a second form verbal noun derived from the same root as *qadar q-d-r*. Whilst the noun *qadar* generally conveys the idea of evaluating/measuring, *taqdīr* is used here to indicate the specific action of the tailor in taking measurements. As for the *qaḍāʾ* which is commonly associated with the idea of a final decision/judgement, it is explained through the term *tafṣīl*, whose meaning is again derived from the sartorial domain and refers to the cutting out of a garment.

[12] 'Amongst these [worlds] is the revolution that takes place when one cycle changes into another, when one prophetic tradition (*sunnat*) and custom (*āʾin*) changes to another, and one religion (*millat*) changes to another. Each one of these is a world [...] and when each changes, one may say that such and such a cycle, a

account the understanding of *qiyāma* as an ongoing spiritual resurrection which is repeated at regular intervals with the periodical advent of several minor *qāʾim*s who are the foreshadowers of the final *qāʾim al-qiyāma*, then al-Rāzī's, al-Sijistānī's and al-Kirmānī's stances on the issue of *qaḍāʾ* and *qadar* will appear much more comprehensible and somewhat more coherent.

Al-Rāzī's line of reasoning appears to foreshow Muḥammad b. ʿAbd al-Karīm al-Shahrastānī's (d. 548/1153) argument of the two principles of the accomplished (*mafrūgh*) and the inchoative (*mustaʾnaf*). Applied by the Prophet to enlighten ʿUmar and Abū Bakr on the middle path existing between *jabr* (necessitarianism) and *tafwīḍ* (delegation), al-Shahrastānī draws from the prophetic tradition of the angel that God had created half of fire and half of ice, and propounds the complementarity of a dimension in which actions and events have already been accomplished and actualised (*mafrūgh*) – alluded to by the angel's fire – and a realm in which things are still in becoming, impending (*mustaʾnaf*) – alluded to by the angel's ice.[13] Interestingly, al-Shahrastānī extends such division from the world of creation to the realm of the Command: thus, he speaks of accomplished rulings (*aḥkām mafrūgha*) – which have become perfect in words and therefore completed – and inchoative rulings (*aḥkām mustaʾnafa*) – which are on the way to perfection and completion. To the first allude verses such as Q 6:115 and traditions such as 'Your Lord has finished with (*faragha*) the matter of creation, character, livelihood and the time of death',[14] with the latter significantly resembling al-Sijistānī's citation

---

prophetic tradition and a religion, which did not exist and then came into existence, was a separate world which underwent non-existence and then existence'. Naṣīr al-Dīn al-Ṭūsī, *Paradise of Submission: A Medieval Treatise on Ismaili Thought*, ed. and tr. S. Jalal Badakhchani (London, 2005), p. 68.

[13]   See Toby Mayer, tr., *Keys to the Arcana: Shahrastānī's Esoteric Commentary to the Qurʾān. A Translation of the Commentary on Sūrat al-Fātiḥa from Muḥammad b. ʿAbd al-Karīm al-Shahrastānī's* Mafātīḥ al-asrār wa maṣābīḥ al-abrār (London, 2009), Introduction, pp. 28–30; Arabic text, pp. 55–60; English text., pp. 113–118; al-Shahrastānī's *Majlis-i maktūb-i Shahrastānī munʿaqid dar Khwārazm*, French trans. D. Steigerwald, as *Majlis: discours sur l'ordre et la création* (Quebec, 1998), Introduction, p. 27.

[14]   Hindī, *Kanz al-ʿummāl*, vol. 1, p. 187, *ḥadīth* 608, cited in Mayer, *Keys to the Arcana*, Arabic text, p. 56; English text, p. 115.

already mentioned in this study.[15] To the second refer verses of divine commandment (*taklīf*), instruction (*taʿrīf*), admonition (*indhār*) and warning (*taḥdhīr*) with verses of examination (*imtiḥān*), temptation (*aftatān*), of giving hope (*tarjīa*) and desire (*aṭmāʿ*) being predicated on it, such as in Q 74:2, 19:39, 40:18.[16]

Al-Sijistānī is quoted replying to al-Rāzī's points suggesting that the analogy of the cloth is deceptive. In particular, in his view, *qaḍāʾ* is not the actualised decision per se – probably an allusion to the final *qāʾim*, who is linked to the idea of the final decision (on Judgement Day), or more simply an allusion to the actual Imam who, within the interval of any prophetic cycle, is simultaneously a *qāʾim* in potentiality before the advent of the *qāʾim al-qiyāma* – but it is rather the decision in its state prior to actualisation. This could be a possible reference to the *qāʾim* in potentiality (i.e. Muḥammad b. Ismāʿīl in concealment), as well as a reference to each member of the *daʿwa* who is potentially a subsisting *qāʾim*. More specifically, al-Sijistānī suggests that al-Rāzī should have identified the decision in potentiality, which is nothing but the form of tailoring present in the mind of the tailor, with the *qaḍāʾ* because it is of a conceptual nature. Thus, the estimation that the tailor makes according to the tailoring corresponds to the state of the decided-upon-object (i.e. the object-of-decision, *munfaṣil*) prior

---

[15] See the fourth paragraph of *Faṣl* One where the same verb, *faragha*, is used.

[16] Mayer, *Keys to the Arcana*, Arabic text. p. 57, English text, slightly modified, p. 115. On this see also Leonard Lewisohn, 'From the "Moses of Reason" to the "Khidr of the Resurrection": The Oxymoronic Transcendent in Shahrastānī's *Majlis-i maktūb-i…dar Khwārazm*', in *Fortresses of the Intellect: Ismaili and Other Islamic Studies in Honour of Farhad Daftary*, ed. Ali-de-Unzaga, pp. 403–429. Jalal Badakhchani has observed how the terms primordial decree (*ḥukm-i mafrūgh*) and subsequent (or inchoative) decree (*ḥukm-i mustaʾnaf*) are related to the notions of primordial past (*mafrūgh*), namely the realm of predestination, and subsequent (or inchoative) future, namely the realm of free will (see his comments in Ṭūsī's *Contemplation and Action*, p. 70 note 39). He further claims that Shahrastānī's distinction between the time-bound application of the legalistic rule of the *sharīʿa* (*ḥukm-i mafrūg*) and the esoteric rule of the *qiyāma* (*ḥukm-i mustaʾnaf*) – 'occurring in a time-less realm where Resurrection has already happened by a pre-ordained decree' – is echoed in Naṣīr al-Dīn Ṭūsī's thought. See Hasan-i Maḥmūd-i Kātib, *Haft bāb*, tr. S. J. Badakhchani as *Spiritual Resurrection in Shiʿi Islam: An Early Ismaili Treatise on the Doctrine of Qiyāmat* (London and New York, 2017), pp. 21–30.

to manifestation. The permanence of its identity depends on the mental form that has been decided for it, necessarily through a *qaḍāʾ*.[17]

In simpler terms, the decision (*tafṣīl*) prior to actualisation becomes for al-Sijistānī synonymous with al-Rāzī's estimation/measuring (*taqdīr*), which is said to correspond to the object-of-decision prior to its manifestation (*munfaṣil*). These are identical by being spiritual things (or forms) which are not yet manifested in reality. As they are prior to manifestation, they are deprived of outer limits and combination. Despite this, however, they are decided and finished, that is, *decreed*.

All this can be interpreted in line with the early Ismaili idea that the *nāṭiq*, prior to the advent of the last *qāʾim*, is as much in potentiality as is the Imam prior to his attainment of a full *nāṭiq*-ship. Despite their potential character, however, these members of the Ismaili Call are integral part of the imamate's structure, whose decreed designation is incontestable. However, even more subtly, al-Sijistānī's ideas may be read through a Qarmaṭī outlook: the *qaḍāʾ*/decision might be, according to al-Sijistānī, the Antecedent itself, Muḥammad b. Ismāʿīl. The latter is as much the Imam of the time as he is the final Resurrector (i.e. the *qadar* as the Follower of the *qaḍāʾ*/Antecedent), being in a potential state both in his current *satr* and with regard to his final return. It has already been emphasised that what characterises the *qaḍāʾ* and the *qadar* is, despite their conceptual character, their determined nature. Thus, according to al-Sijistānī, *qaḍāʾ* is before the *qadar* just as the conceptual tailoring (Muḥammad b. Ismāʿīl's imamate, which is merely 'conceptual' as it is pragmatically carried out only through his *lawāḥiq* [adjuncts]) is before the estimation (Muḥammad b. Ismāʿīl's imamate, which will be actual upon his return as a purely 'spiritual' *qāʾim al-qiyāma*).[18]

---

[17] De Cillis, 'A Preliminary Study on the Significance of *Qaḍāʾ* and *Qadar*', pp. 354–356.

[18] Another possible reading would be that any member of the *daʿwa* is a potential *qāʾim* before the advent of the final decision (the Day of Resurrection). This would imply, as will be further elaborated in the following, that what makes a member of the Call a *qāʾim* is the spiritual resurrection that his/her soul undergoes within his/her body prior to the advent of the last *qiyāma*. This is in line with what al-Sijistānī claims in his *al-Risāla al-Bāhira*: 'The Resurrection to which the prophets have summoned people is a spiritual influence (*taʾthīratun nafsāniyya*) which will be manifested from a

It should be remembered that, from a cosmological perspective, the *qaḍāʾ* and the *qadar* are also identifiable respectively with the forms of the Intellect and the Soul (the two roots, *aṣlān*). In al-Sijistānī's *Kitāb al-Yanābīʿ*, the author states that the four words that are in the profession of faith (*shahāda*) are the four principles: the two Roots (*aṣlān*) and the two Foundations (*asāsān*).[19] In particular, the Antecedent is described as the key (*miftāḥ*) to the totality of existents (*jamīʿ al-aysiyyāt*) for any existent (*ays*) is an image/symbol (*mithl*) of everything the Antecedent has in its identity (*huwiyyatuhu*) through the origination (*bi-ibdāʿ*) of the Originator (*al-mubdiʿ*). The Follower, on the other hand, is said to be the key (*miftāḥ*) for the totality of things (*jamīʿ al-ashyāʾ*), possessing order (*naẓm*) and composition (*tāʾlīf*). Ordered, composite things (*al-ashyāʾ al-manẓūma al-muʾallafa*) cannot be imagined/conceived of (*lā tatawahham*) except (*illā*) in the form (*muṣawwara*) of the sublime souls (*al-anfās al-laṭīfa*) before (*qabl*) their manifestation (*ẓuhūrihā*) as ordered and composite things. This means, al-Sijistānī claims, that whilst through the Antecedent the totality of existents 'open' (*fataḥa*) themselves from (*min*) the Word (*kalima*) to their manifestation as existent beings, through the Follower all things 'open' (*fataḥa*) themselves from the Word to their manifestation as ordered and composed beings. Still faithful to the idea of a precedence of the Word to the first originated being, al-Sijistānī holds that the Antecedent is the key that 'unlocks' the existence of all entities, corporeal and spiritual, into their manifestation, and that the Follower is the key that 'unlocks' the allotting of measure, limit and order onto all of those things upon their manifestation.[20]

---

pure soul, the *qāʾim*. Al-Sijistānī, 'al-Risāla al-Bāhira', quoted in Badakhchani's introduction to *Haft bāb: Spiritual Resurrection in Shiʿi Islam*, p. 15.

[19] Al-Sijistānī speaks of the *farʿān* (branches), the *aṣlān* (roots) and the *asāsān* (foundations or bases) as corresponding to the Ismaili *daʿwa*, the spiritual world and the physical world. See Elizabeth R. Alexandrin, *Walāyah in the Fāṭimid Ismāʿīlī Tradition* (Albany, NY, 2017), p. 25. The *asāsān* are a specific reference to the *nāṭiq* and the *asās*.

[20] Al-Sijistānī, *Kitāb al-Yanābīʿ*, pp. 142–143; tr. Walker, *The Wellsprings of Wisdom*, pp. 91–92. With his references to the Antecedent and the Follower as 'keys', al-Sijistānī must have implicitly wanted to stress the importance of *walāya* to which a tradition attributed to the Imam al-Bāqir and recounted by al-Kulaynī, refers as the supreme Pillar in Islam: '"the key" to all the others'. See al-Kulaynī, *al-Uṣūl min al-kāfī*, Persian trans. J. Muṣṭafawī (Tehran, 1966), vol. 3, pp. 30–32, no. 5. On the link

An even more obscure argument can be detected in al-Sijistānī's formulations, which can be directly linked to his own stance on the officially condemned issue of transmigration (*tanāsukh*). In his *Kashf al-mahjūb*, in countering the idea that after the separation from the body species might become other species, thus allowing a transformation from, as he puts it, the soul of a man into the body of a dog,[21] al-Sijistānī uses arguments very similar to those reported in *Faṣl* One. Firstly, he explains that something that exists in potentiality and comes to exist in actuality will bring forth what was in it potentially from itself into actual existence. Then, he argues, 'we can see that the form of a dog is determined ['measured'] in the sperm of a dog, that it came from a dog and entered a dog and that everything needed for it to become capable of sense perception, movement, etc., was existent in that sperm.'[22]

---

between the *shahāda* and *walāya*, see Amir-Moezzi, *The Spirituality of Shiʿi Islam*, p. 243, particularly note 35.

[21] This kind of metamorphosis (*maskh*) would correspond to a transformation from a body into another, inferior body. See Gimaret, '*Tanāsukh*', p. 182.

[22] Al-Sijistānī, *Kashf al-mahjūb*, tr. Landolt, *Unveiling of the Hidden*, p. 109. The vocabulary employed here appears to recall the second of the eight meanings addressed to the term *qadar* which are reported in *Tāj al-ʿaqāʾid wa maʿdin al-fawāʾid* by ʿAlī b. Muḥammad b. al-Walīd – the fifth Yemeni *dāʿī* who occupied this position between 605/1209 and 612–1215. Ivanow argued that the treatise provided information about 'what can be regarded as the official religion of the masses, ruled by the Fatimids, and belonging to the "orthodox" Ismaili school'. In the above work, *qadar*, which is said to derive from *miqdār* bearing the meaning of measure, quantity and from *taqdīr*, namely arrangement or fixing a measure, is used in the following senses: (i) in its application to the uniformity and consistency of the laws of nature, which act automatically; (ii) in its application to the reproduction of species within a genus, when all the characteristic features are always repeated, invariably reappear and cannot be arbitrarily altered or cancelled; (iii) in its application to the unchangeable differences in the position and development of different classes of creatures, in accordance to which the human is the most perfect creature, because the world was created for its sake; (iv) in its application to the circumstances in which the worth of humans is tested, with all their qualities, mental and physical, depending on collaboration between reason and soul, thought and heart, and the correct distinction between true and false; (v) in its application to the law according to which every living creature has been endowed by the Creator with the power of obtaining its subsistence, and the food it consumes makes the body grow and exist; (vi) in its application to the religious law and its injunctions and prohibitions, which are final; (vii) in its application to the foresight of human genius, which humans receive from the Creator as

The form of a dog, which is already *determined* even though still *in potentia* in the dog's sperm, recalls to our attention the shape/form of the cloth that is already determined in the tailor's mind. In particular, the decision prior to manifestation and the object of estimation are tacitly suggested to belong to the same 'species' by being both spiritual beings that are already decreed. To this end, al-Sijistānī links the *qaḍāʾ rūḥānī* and the *qadar rūḥānī* – mentioned in the excerpt from the *Riyāḍ* – with the form of the Intellect and the form of the Soul respectively. Given that it is the form responsible for preserving a species in its being,[23] it is arguable that, according to al-Sijistānī, al-Rāzī was wrong in pushing the analogy of the cloth simply because this is a materialised/actualised form that cannot be associated with spiritual/potential beings. Specifically, al-Rāzī was incorrect in stating that as long as the cloth is in the state of estimation (*qadar*) it is subject to a possible increase or decrease of its size. Basically, al-Sijistānī criticises his colleague because if it is stated that *qadar* is the Intellect, even prior to its actualisation, the latter cannot be said to be liable to any changes whatsoever.[24]

Besides this hypothetical reading, it might be maintained that al-Sijistānī uses the conceptual nature of *qaḍāʾ* and *qadar* also to argue in favour of a specific kind of 'passage', particularly the 'transfer' of prophetic knowledge which, in his opinion, remains untouched in its being passed on as an inheritance from the Prophet to the 'proof' via

---

an essential ingredient of their nature; (viii) in application to the definition of things lawful and those which deserve punishment. Humans must know these, though they cannot comprehend the reason why one is good and the other bad, in accordance with the guidance of religion. Knowledge is acquired from the experience of the senses. But as these cannot perceive such reasons, humans should depend on divine revelation, which should be obeyed unreservedly. See Ivanow's translation, *A Creed of the Fatimids* (Bombay, 1936) pp. 70–71.

[23] In the *Kashf al-maḥjūb*, al-Sijistānī elucidates that each species has a share and a determined measure from its own source. Such sources are the celestial spheres which transmit their influx onto them in a way that no species can ever be separated from its source with regard to its form. It is in fact such form that preserves the species in its being. With these arguments, al-Sijistānī establishes that species do not mix, neither at the time of composition nor after composition. Al-Sijistānī, *Kashf al-maḥjūb*, tr. Landolt, *Unveiling of the Hidden*, p. 110.

[24] In truth, al-Rāzī never explicitly makes this identification. He actually avoids any reference to the Antecedent-*qua*-Antecedent and the Follower-*qua*-Follower.

the legatee and the Imam (culminating in the crowning knowledge of the last Resurrector). This idea can be inferred again from his *Kashf al-maḥjūb*, where al-Sijistānī explains that virtues are non-physical matters, which have forms acting as their recipients (i.e. the minor *qāʾims*?), and that a virtue might be likened to craftsmanship (*ṣināʿa*) with regard to the alteration of their recipients.[25] It is probably not accidental that al-Sijistānī speaks of the 'act of tailoring' (i.e. the estimation) – which al-Kirmānī names 'the craft of tailoring' (*ṣanʿat al-khiyāṭa*) in *Faṣl* Two – as a virtue that, like courage or knowledge,[26] moves from one individual to another, remaining of the same quality/ state (*ḥāl*) in one individual (such as the Imam in concealment?) as it is in the many (such as his representatives?).[27]

The notion that any craftsmanship does not increase or decrease in accord with the greater or smaller number of individuals engaged in it, is also subtly connected to the cosmological theory of souls' 'permanence' and its link to the concept of the final Resurrection. In *al-Risāla al-Bāhira*, al-Sijistānī argues that, in order to reconcile eternity/permanence with Judgement Day, bearing in mind the cyclical continuity of motion and time, it is essential to acknowledge that each generation serves as the *barzakh* (physical substantiated form of being) for the preceding ones.[28] So, rather than identifying the *barzakh* as the 'limbo state' in which souls abide after death but prior to the Day of Resurrection,[29] in al-Sijistānī's doctrine this term appears to indicate the successive 'resurrections' on earth undergone by an individual soul. Al-Sijistānī proposes that because creation is eternal and because the world has always been endowed with souls joined to their bodies, it follows that the world must always been filled with existing beings.[30] The latter, in their forms, are nothing but *barzakh*s for those beings that preceded them. Rather bluntly, according to Hirji, al-Sijistānī

---

[25]	Al-Sijistānī, *Kashf al-maḥjūb*, tr. Landolt, *Unveiling of the Hidden*, pp. 110–111.

[26]	Cf. Al-Kirmānī's discussion on the nature of moral virtues previously observed.

[27]	Al-Sijistānī, *Kashf al-maḥjūb*, tr. Landolt, *Unveiling of the Hidden*, pp. 110–111.

[28]	Al-Sijistānī, 'al-Risāla al-Bāhira', pp. 46–47.

[29]	As in Q 23:100; see B. Carra de Vaux, 'Barzakh', *EI2*, vol. 1, pp. 1071–1072. On the development of the concept of *barzakh* into the eschatological claims of medieval Islam, see George Archer, *A Place Between Two Places. The Qurʾānic Barzakh* (Piscataway, NJ, 2017).

[30]	See Walker, *Early Philosophical Shiism*, 'Barzakh', in index and note 10, pp. 187–188.

seems to claim that succeeding generations are born with decreed 'gifts', meaning that they are 'made to inherit' from the preceding generations 'their speech, their professions, their crafts and all manners of life'.[31]

Al-Sijistānī's foregoing argumentation recounted in the *Riyāḍ*, seems also to be directed at a particular passage of al-Rāzī's *Iṣlāḥ* which, however, al-Kirmānī does not include in this section of the *Riyāḍ*. The passage reads:

> The *qaḍāʾ* is the decision (*tafṣīl*) from the Follower, and the Follower is the estimation/measuring (*taqdīr*), and from it there occurs the decision. This is testified from all things, including all of the existents, through knowledge and *qadar*. And when its actualisation becomes manifest, in matter and form, this is the *qaḍāʾ* and no alteration or change are in it: it is irresistible (*lā maradda lahu*). This is because He has decreed it (*qaddarahā*) by His command (*bi-amrihi*), which is the Antecedent (*alladhī al-sābiq*), and then has set it forth (or arranged it in particular measures) (*faṣṣalahā*) through His *qadar* (*bi-qadarihi*) which is the Follower.
>
> So the estimation/measuring (*taqdīr*) is from the Antecedent and the decision (*tafṣīl*) is from the Follower. Matter and form, which are set forth (or arranged in particular measures) (*mufaṣṣalān*), are weak (*ʿājizān*). This is because these two are under the *qadar* from the Antecedent and under the *qaḍāʾ* from the Follower and there is no power there. For through the Antecedent who, as we have said, is God's *amr*, comes the

---

[31] See Hirji, 'A Study of *al-Risālah al-bāhirah*', pp. 93–94; 198–205; cf. De Smet 'La transmigration des âmes. Une notion problématique dans l'ismaélism d'époque fatimide', in *Unity in Diversity. Mysticism, Messianism and the Construction of Religious Authority in Islam*, ed. Orkhan Mir Kasimov (Leiden and Boston, 2014), p. 103. Al-Bīrūnī and Nāṣir-i Khusraw saw hidden in the above reasoning al-Sijistānī's idea of *tanāsukh*, which they openly condemned. See al-Bīrūnī, *Kitāb fī Taḥqīq mā li'l-Hind* (Delhi, 1958), p. 49; Nāṣir-i Khusraw, *Zād al-musāfirīn*, ed. M. Badhl Raḥmān (Berlin, 1923), pp. 421–422; Madelung, 'Abū Yaʿqūb al-Sijistānī and Metempsychosis', pp. 131–143; Walker, 'The Doctrine of Metempsychosis in Islam', pp. 219–238, particularly, pp. 230–236; *idem, Early Philosophical Shiism*, pp. 98–100. According to Nāṣir-i Khusraw and al-Kirmānī, al-Sijistānī at a later stage seems to have rejected any form of metempsychosis, probably having been persuaded to do so by the Imam of his time. See al-Sijistānī, *Kitāb al-Maqālīd, iqlīd* 44; al-Kirmānī, *Riyāḍ* (Beirut, 1960), pp. 91–93.

qadar and from it proceeds the power (*qudra*) which is His Word (*kalimatuhu*) which is His *amr* that He utters: 'Verily, We have created all things through the *qadar* (*innā kulla shay'in khalaqnāhu bi-qadar*)' [Q 54:49].

The *qadar* follows (*yalī*) the command because it is by the command (*bi'l-amr*). And the *qaḍā'* follows the *qadar* because it is by the *qadar* (*bi'l-qadar*). The *amr* is neither the *qadar* nor the *qaḍā'* (*al-amr laysa huwa qadar^{an} wa lā qaḍā$^{'an}$*). Rather it is through it that the *qadar* and *qaḍā'* are. It is superior (*ā'lā*) to *qadar* and to *qaḍā'*. For it is said 'God has decreed (*qaddara*) everything by the *amr*' and it is not said '[He] has commanded (*āmara*) everything by the *qadar*'. This is your proof that the *amr* is above (*fawqa*) the *qadar* and that the *qadar* is above the *qaḍā'*.[32]

Several points of importance emerge from the above passage: (i) al-Rāzī denies that either *qaḍā'* or *qadar* can be identified with the Antecedent without any correlation. They are both 'Followers', even though with regard to two different entities which precede them; on the one hand, the *qadar* is the Follower with regard to the Antecedent, which is the divine *amr*. On the other hand, *qadar* is the Antecedent but only with regard to the *qaḍā'* which follows it. The *qaḍā'*, in turn, is identified with the actualisation of the decision (*tafṣīl*) which comes from *qadar*. As an actualised decision, *qaḍā'* does not encompass any change. This is so because, as the above passage clearly states, it has been decreed by the divine *amr*.[33] From the latter comes the

---

[32] Al-Rāzī, *Iṣlāḥ*, p. 49.

[33] In the excerpt, al-Rāzī's reference to the necessitated nature of *qaḍā'* is something al-Sijistānī had also underlined. For the latter, what characterises *qaḍā'*, on which the decision (*tafṣīl*) and its object-of-decision (*munfaṣil*) depend, is in effect its finished or accomplished nature, which does not admit any change. However, whilst al-Rāzī had defined *qaḍā'* as the actualisation of the estimation which, susceptible to no alterations, *follows* the *qadar* which is brought about through God's Antecedent/*amr*, for al-Sijistānī, *qaḍā'* is itself the Antecedent (i.e. Muḥammad b. Ismā'īl as the Imam in *satr*). This is so because in the Antecedent are embedded both the mental decision and the object-of-decision which *precede* their actual objectification in manifestation (i.e. the *taqdīr/qadar*, which can be thought to refer to Muḥammad b. Ismā'īl as the final *qā'im*). Implicitly, *qaḍā'*'s fixed nature corroborates its identification with the Intellect that is complete (accomplished) in his immutable atemporal perfection; however, the above identification also suggests that *qaḍā'*, as the unmanifested *tafṣīl*

estimation/measuring (*taqdīr*), namely the *qadar* through which the divine *amr* is allotted (the action of allotting or distributing according to estimation/measures being not different from the decision); (ii) al-Rāzī specifies that from *qadar* proceeds a power (*qudra*) that he identifies with the divine word (*kalima*).[34] In addition, al-Rāzī argues that, in line with Neoplatonic arguments, matter and form are weak because they are dependent on the creative *amr*. It should be recalled in this context that in Plotinus' inspired emanative schemas, matter and form are both placed far down on the scale of existents, and that matter is metaphysically associated with privation (*'adam*) and evil (*sharr*), with the latter being generally perceived as a by-product of divine creation, or as the result of a secondary intention.[35] Hence, matter and form, it can be argued, are for al-Rāzī in themselves powerless because they are subject to the *amr*. By paraphrasing Q 54:49 (*innā kulla shay'in khalaqnāhu bi-qadar*), whose significance is examined later in detail, as well as Q 25:2 (*kulla shay'in faqaddarahu taqdīr^{an}*), al-Rāzī's concern is to place both the *qadar* and the *qaḍā'* in a position subordinate to that of the *amr*/Antecedent, whilst ranking the *qadar* above the *qaḍā'*.

---

and *munfaṣil*, includes a kind of potentiality which both al-Nasafī and al-Sijistānī address to the Intellect's capacity to encompass all the forms, thus being simultaneously *in potentia* and *in actu*. Such potentiality is also present in the *sharī'a*, which becomes fully actualised only through the esoteric hermeneutical interpretation (*ta'wīl*) provided by the Imam/foundation (*asās*). Implicitly, al-Sijistānī seems to have proposed the identification of the Antecedent/Intellect with the Imam/foundation and the signification of *qadar* with the Follower and the enunciator-prophet (*nāṭiq*). With the above identifications he was, allegedly, erroneously leading the community to believe in the precedence and superiority of the *asās* and *ta'wīl* over the *nāṭiq* and the forms of worship prescribed in the *sharī'a*.

[34] In addition, according to al-Rāzī, the *kalima* is the uttered (actualised) divine word as in Q 54:49. This appears to suggest that whilst the *amr* is prior to actualisation, the *kalima* represents its actualised facet (this is however an actualisation different from the actualisation in matter and form which pertains to the *qaḍā'*).

[35] For example, Plotinus, *Enneads*, I. 8.8; Ikhwān al-Ṣafā', *Rasā'il*, vol. 3, pp. 476–478; see further references in De Cillis, *Free Will and Predestination*, pp. 46–51; *idem*, 'Avicenna on Matter, Matter's Disobedience and Evil: Reconciling Metaphysical Stances and Qur'anic Perspectives', *Transcendent Philosophy*, 12 (2011), pp. 147–168.

Speculatively speaking, al-Rāzī's argument can also be read from a political angle and connected to his alleged critical standpoint of the Fatimid Imam al-Muʿizz's appointment of his successor. It should be remembered that Jaʿfar al-Ṣādiq, after the premature death of his son Ismāʿīl, did not appoint another successor in his son's place, at least not officially. Given the infallibility of Jaʿfar's choice, the succession, as Walker explains, 'necessarily moved thereafter beyond Ismāʿīl to his own son Muḥammad'.[36] Conversely, al-Muʿizz, rather than favouring his first son Tamīm, secretly chose his second son, ʿAbd Allāh (d. 10th century) as his successor. Although al-Muʿizz was never reticent to accord ʿAbd Allāh public favour as if he would actually succeed him, he also never publicly conferred a formal *naṣṣ* to him.[37] However, differently from Jaʿfar al-Ṣādiq, after ʿAbd Allāh's unexpected death, al-Muʿizz did appoint his third son, Nizār (d. 386/996) as the future Imam-caliph.

It is probable that al-Rāzī might not have fully accepted the role of the Fatimid caliphs as deputy-Imams of Muḥammad b. Ismāʿīl during his occultation. When al-Rāzī speaks of *qadar* as the first follower which is the estimation, and the *qaḍāʾ* as the second follower which is the decision, he is probably alluding to al-Muʿizz's controversial appointment of his successor. More specifically, he is perhaps denouncing the illegitimacy of al-Muʿizz's choice by claiming that once the caliph has decided on his successor, neither increase nor decrease (i.e. no change) should have been made to this final choice or, at least, not according to what was an unprecedented case. Just as in the *kūnī-qadar* myth, there is but one *amr* (later identified with the *nāṭiq*) truly operating, so that any final decision, following a well-measured estimation – apropos a successor – should *follow* what the one and only *amr* establishes. It is also possible that al-Rāzī's emphasis on the irrevocability of a final decision was a means to voice his rejection of the notion of *badāʾ* (change in God's will), a doctrine that was speculated upon earlier by the *ghulāt* and which was used to justify the failures of previous predictions on the Imams.[38]

---

36   Walker, 'Succession to Rule in the Shiite Caliphate', *JARCE*, 32 (1995), p. 241.

37   Ibid., p. 246.

38   On *badāʾ*, see W. Madelung, '*Badāʾ*', *EIr*, vol. III, pp. 354–355, and Daftary, *The Ismāʿīlīs*, p. 64. Interestingly, in 404/1013 the Fatimid Imam-caliph al-Ḥākim had

From a cosmological/metaphysical standpoint, it is surprising to find al-Rāzī hinting at the identification of the Antecedent-*qua*-Antecedent with the *amr*. A similar argument had been propounded by al-Sijistānī, earning him severe criticism, from al-Kirmānī. Specifically, in the twenty-fifth chapter of his *Kitāb al-Maqālīd*, al-Sijistānī speaks of the Antecedent as the *kalima*, thus suggesting that the Word precedes the *ʿaql*, which in the cosmologies of all the three *dāʿī*s is the *al-mubdaʿ al-awwal*, the first originated being. The implication of such a stance is that the Intellect is actually preceded by such *kalima* which acts as the Intellect's eternal, non-manifested cause. The latter in fact, al-Sijistānī argued, is considered as not having been brought into being (*lā muʾayyas*).[39] Despite the fact that the *kalima* cannot be classified as an entity because it is not ontologically existent in manifestation,[40] al-Kirmānī detected in al-Sijistānī's

---

nominated his cousin ʿAbd al-Raḥīm b. Iliyās as the *walī ʿahd al-muslimīn* (Heir Designate of the Muslims) during his lifetime and as the caliph after his death; he was subsequently dissatisfied with him, thus replacing ʿAbd al-Raḥīm with another cousin, the son of the Amir Ibrāhīm Abū Hāshim, al-ʿAbbās ibn Shuʿayb who was given the title *walī ʿahd al-muʾminīn*. See Walker, 'The Ismaili *Daʿwa* in the Reign of the Fatimid Caliph al-Ḥākim', p. 176, 180 and references given there; *idem*, 'Succession to Rule in the Shiite Caliphate', pp. 247–248.

[39] It is only upon entification that the *kalima* is united with the Intellect and, because of this conjunction, the first originated being becomes the source of multiplicity, namely, the Plotinian οὐσία. Plotinus, *Enneads*, V. 1.8; V. 3.13; V. 3.15; V. 4.1; Peterson, *Cosmogony in the Rāḥat al-ʿaql*, p. 396, note 9. On this topic, al-Sijistānī's concept of *wāḥid* and its relation with the divine command, see Hunzai, 'The Concept of *Tawḥīd*', p. 88. On al-Sijistānī's notion of *tawḥīd* see his *Kitāb al-Yanābīʿ*, pp. 71–72; *The Wellsprings of Wisdom*, pp. 49–50.

[40] Al-Sijistānī warns: 'Beware of seeking behind the Antecedent (*sābiq*) any identity (*huwiyya*) following the manifestation of the Antecedent (*baʿda ẓuhūr al-sābiq*). His [God's] Word (*kalima*) is its [the Antecedent's] cause (*ʿillatahu*), and since the manifestation of the Antecedent has as its cause the very first cause, upon the manifestation of the Antecedent, that cause united with it and came (*ṣārat*) to exist, like the ipseity of the Antecedent itself (*ka-huwiyyat al-sābiq*)'. Al-Sijistānī, *Kitāb al-Yanābīʿ*, p. 72; *The Wellsprings of Wisdom*, p. 50 (English translation slightly modified). On al-Sijistānī's identification between the *kalima* and the Antecedent/Intellect, see Walker, *Early Philosophical Shiism*, pp. 82–83; *idem*, 'Cosmic Hierarchies in Early Ismaili Thought', p. 19.

idea some form of *shirk*,[41] and inverted the relationship between the terms by identifying the *sābiq* with *ʿaql* and the *kalima* with the *amr*.[42] One important aspect that needs to be stressed in this context is that for al-Sijistānī the *amr* and the *kalima* are synonyms, meaning the non-entified Command/Word of God. Similarly, for al-Rāzī, the Antecedent-*qua*-Antecedent signifies the *amr* and the *kalima*, which are depicted as one originated being, joined in manifestation with the first intellect. However, differently from al-Sijistānī, al-Rāzī specifies the nature of the *amr*/*kalima* as being merely 'conceptual' (*wahmī*). In addition, the passage from the *Iṣlāḥ* reported here seems also to imply that the *kalima* is but the uttered manifestation of the *amr*.

According to al-Rāzī, the *qadar*, which is the Antecedent only with respect to *qaḍāʾ*, finds its correspondence in the enunciator-prophet (*nāṭiq*) who is the Antecedent with regards to the religious law (*sharīʿa*), for whose compilation and legislation he is responsible. The stress is laid at this point on the precedence of the *nāṭiq* with respect to the *sharīʿa* which he brings into being. Such antecedence needed to be emphasised in order to overcome the serious threat – due to the developments Shiʿi Islam underwent in certain circles – where a tendency had emerged to give predominance in rank and influence to the Imam above the enunciator-prophet and to the esoteric doctrine above the exoteric aspect of the religious law.[43]

With regard to al-Sijistānī's quoted passage in the *Riyāḍ*, Abū Yaʿqūb infers that al-Rāzī should have identified *qaḍāʾ* as the Antecedent, namely as the decision regarding the tailored cloth for this already exists (even though is not yet manifested) in the mind of the tailor, just as all *aysiyyāt* (existent beings and their forms) exist in the Antecedent/Intellect prior to their manifestation. Consequently, according to al-Sijistānī, al-Rāzī should have referred to the *qadar* as the Follower in that it is only through it that the conceptual shape that the tailor has already in his mind attains its measure as an ordered

---

[41] Namely, contemplating the existence of more than one eternal being besides God.

[42] Al-Kirmānī, *al-Risāla al-Muḍīʾa*, pp. 49–53; Hamid Haji, *A Distinguished Dāʿī*, p. 31.

[43] Ivanow, 'An Early Controversy in Ismailism', p. 109; Corbin, *Cyclical Time and Ismaili Gnosis*, pp. 184–185.

and fitted cloth prior to its material alteration.[44] Again, such arguments might shroud different readings: according to al-Rāzī, Muḥammad b. Ismāʿīl is not the Antecedent-*qua*-Antecedent – which is rather the *amr*/*nāṭiq* – but the (first) follower (i.e. the *qadar*) in the line of the Imams. Conversely, according to al-Sijistānī, *qaḍāʾ*, as the Antecedent, is but a designation for the final Riser who is the potential *qāʾim* actually personified, although in concealment, in Muḥammad b. Ismāʿīl.

It still remains to be explained how it was possible to associate the entified *amr* (as the Intellect) – which is eternal and beyond time – with the notion of the Antecedent, whose name alone seems to infer a temporal precedence before all the other existents that are actualised. As an eternal and imperishable substance, and the first cause of all existents, encompassing all beings emanated from him at once, the *amr*/Intellect would be simply perceived as the immanent 'thingness' of everything. But Intellect is much more than this: the Intellect is, as Walker suggests, also 'an angelic being standing in rank before and above all other beings. In a way, like God, the Intellect is also transcendent. As the Preceder, [he] retains a uniquely transcendent status which [he] loses by being simply Intellect and therefore immanent.'[45]

---

[44] Al-Sijistānī, *Kitāb al-Yanābīʿ*, pp. 142–143; tr. Walker, *The Wellsprings of Wisdom*, pp. 92–93 (English translation slightly modified). In the same text (*Kitāb al-Yanābīʿ*, p. 167; tr. Walker, *The Wellsprings of Wisdom*, p. 107), it is specified that the Intellect, as the most complete and sufficient perfection (*huwa al-kāfī wa'l-kamāl wa'l-tāmm*), is God's measure (*kail*) by which He metes out (*yakīl*) to creatures (*li'l-khalāʾiq*) their portion (*ḥaẓẓahum*) of His oneness (*waḥdatahu*) according to their degree (*miqdār*) and ranks (*marātibihim*). (Cf. al-Sijistānī, *Kashf al-maḥjūb*, tr. Landolt as *Unveiling of the Hidden*, p. 96 where an analogous argument is presented in a similar terminology). The task of allotting measures and limitations upon created beings is not given as the responsibility of the Follower for, in this context, it is the divine oneness that must be shared. This idea suggests that because it is the Antecedent that acts as the instrument of the oneness' allotting, probably, as for al-Kirmānī, also for al-Sijistānī it is the Intellect's awareness of being simultaneously oneness (*waḥda*) and the receptacle of oneness – by which the Intellect divests himself of any divine claim – that ultimately signifies *tawḥīd*. See al-Sijistānī, *Kitāb al-Yanābīʿ*, p. 71; *The Wellsprings of Wisdom*, p. 49.

[45] Walker, *Early Philosophical Shiism*, p. 88. For consistency, in the above quotation I have substituted the pronoun 'it' with 'he' with reference to the Intellect.

This means that as the source of all things that exist, the Intellect may be perceived as an inherent cause whilst, as the Antecedent, his superiority and disengagement form the totality of all things places him 'before' and 'outside' them.

Al-Sijistānī lays great stress on the rank and position of the Intellect in order to explain that the latter exists inside as well as outside things. The Intellect is untainted by imperfections and even if it is (and encompasses) the forms of the two worlds, in effect it transcends them. To clinch his argument, al-Sijistānī resorts to Q 28:88, stating that everything that exists will disappear except 'the face of God', and likening the latter to the Antecedent.[46] This interpretation would mean that the Intellect cannot be included within the world that is destined to perish. Consequently, the Antecedent must pertain to the Intellect only when the *sābiq* is annihilated within a specific aspect of his eternality. This idea calls for further explanations.

In the twenty-first *iqlīd* of his *Kitāb al-Maqālīd*, al-Sijistānī elaborates a complex theory of time (*zamān*) and eternity (*dahr*).[47] Just as time has three aspects (past, present and future) so does eternity, which is characterised by three states: the first is what is with God as the Originator (*mubdiʿ*), is unthinkable and indescribable and is

---

[46] Al-Sijistānī, *Kitāb al-Yanābīʿ*, p. 85; tr. Walker, *The Wellsprings of Wisdom*, p. 58. See also Walker, *Intellectual Missionary*, p. 36.

[47] His theory is formulated as a response to Abū Ḥātim al-Rāzī's exposition of his own understanding of time. In his *Aʿlām al-nubuwwa* (pp. 12–15), Abū Ḥātim al-Rāzī had criticised Abū Bakr al-Muḥammad ibn Zakariyā al-Rāzī's (d. ca. 312/925) rather vague distinction between absolute and limited time. For him, the first form of time, which is indicated by the term *mudda* and associated with duration and eternity, is said to move without interruption; the limited form of time is said to be that which exists through the movement of the celestial spheres and the course of the sun and the planets (Abū Bakr al-Rāzī, *Rasāʾil falsafiyya*, ed. P. Kraus [Cairo, 1939], p. 304). Abū Ḥātim replies to this view by propounding Aristotelian positions and declaring that time was created along with the world and the spheres. This however, Walker has noted, is in stark contrast with what Abū Ḥātim al-Rāzī suggests in his *Iṣlāḥ*, where he openly declares that the Intellect, time and the act of origination are all identical, perfect and instantiated at once. See Paul E. Walker, 'Eternal Cosmos and the Womb of History: Time in Early Ismaili Thought', *IJMES*, 3 (1978), pp. 361–362; See also Poonawala's comments in his Introduction, p. 35 and references given there to al-Rāzī's *Iṣlāḥ*, pp. 36–37.

called *azal* (Eternity Itself); the second state is what God's innovative act links to the First Being (the Intellect) and is called *azaliyya* (eternity); the third stage is what the Intellect, as the First Existent and the Antecedent, emanates upon the Soul (i.e. the Follower) in order to establish the necessary conditions for the creation of this world. This is called the *azalī*, or the eternal. Walker posits that this last aspect of time presents the Intellect as the 'overseer' of the lower world whose absence would imply annihilation.[48]

The kind of reasoning that is supported in the *Riyāḍ* seems to imply that the Intellect is the *sābiq* according to the third state of eternality because it needs its counterpart, the *tālī*, in the same way a cause is a cause only if there exists an effect. The fact that the Antecedent is linked with what proceeds from it, however, does not undermine its eternality. On the contrary, al-Sijistānī insists on the timeless aspect of eternality that pertains to the Intellect. Conversely, perceptible or quantifiable time is relegated to the realm below the Intellect. The third type of eternality obviously differs from both the eternality of God and the eternality of the Intellect in his unadulterated essence as the first originated being, which is disconnected from the Soul.

As mentioned, in the *Kitāb al-Maqālīd*, the Intellect is called the Antecedent when it is identified with 'the face of God'. Certainly, the Intellect cannot be identified with the essence of God as such, as this always remains ineffable. Rather, it relates to the face (or aspect, *wajh*) of God because the identity of God, from the perspective of the Intellect, merely corresponds to the Intellect's self-awareness that he is other than God. What the Intellect grasps of God (the face/aspect which pertains to the ipseity (*huwiyya*) of the divine) is that God cannot be known. In the same way as the Intellect corresponds to 'the face of God' – as far as his self-awareness of being other than God goes – the same Intellect can be also associated with the Antecedent or *qaḍā'*.

In the following *faṣl*, al-Kirmānī observes that the *ta'wīl* reiterated by the two Ismaili *dāʿīs* is defective in that it attempts to explain which of *qaḍā'* and *qadar* is the Antecedent. This is a misguided effort, al-Kirmānī believes, because in fact neither could be soundly associated with the *sābiq-qua-sābiq*.

---

48   Walker, 'Time in Early Ismaili Thought', pp. 361–362.

Faṣl Two

The statement by the author of the *Nuṣra* [al-Sijistānī] – 'there is no *taqdīr* (estimation/measurement) except by a *qaḍāʾ* which necessitates that *taqdīr*', and his analogy of the *qaḍāʾ* with the craft of tailoring (*ṣanʿat al-khiyāṭa*) from which the *taqdīr* comes into existence, and that it is the *qadar* that he makes to signify the Follower along with his acceptance that the meaning of the *qadar* is according to what al-Rāzī has established – necessitates that its [*qadar*'s] existence is *qāʾim bi'l-quwwa*. It is not permissible for that to be said of the Follower according to what we have said above about it being *qāʾim bi'l-fiʿl*. As this is not permissible, then *qadar* does not signify the Follower and, as *qadar* does not signify the Follower, then *qaḍāʾ* cannot possibly signify the Antecedent, for it has never been in potentiality and come into actuality so that what his [al-Sijistānī's] expression (*lafẓ*) conveys may correspond to the existent upon which the state of the Antecedent depends.

As it is also absurd that the *qaḍāʾ* and the *qadar* signi-fy the Antecedent (*sābiq*) and the Follower (*tālī*), then we [al-Kirmānī] say that their statements are correct according to the way we are going to explain, not according to what they have thought. That is, many things participate in the *qaḍāʾ* meanings and all of them are from the physical world (*ʿālam al-jism*), not from the world of origination (*ʿālam al-ibdāʿ*) and the same applies to the *qadar*.[1]

Analysis and interpretation: Al-Kirmānī emphasises that al-Sijistānī is mistaken in identifying the *qadar* with the Follower. This observa-tion, from a cosmological/metaphysical angle, might be a reference

---

[1] Al-Kirmānī, *Riyāḍ* (HL), p. 126.

to al-Kirmānī's idea that once al-Sijistānī had identified the *qadar* with the Follower, he necessarily had to identify it also with the Soul (which follows the Intellect).[2] The latter is not truly or completely in potentiality, according to al-Kirmānī, for the Soul is perfect in essential actuality, being defective – or less perfect – exclusively in relation to action. Conversely, in his *Kitāb al-Yanābī'*, al-Sijistānī hints at the Soul's imperfection. He holds that the Soul receives from the Intellect a form of perpetual longing (*al-shawq al-dā'im*) which makes the Soul yearn for her cause in order to receive the Intellect's spiritual benefits perpetually.[3] Besides such longing, the Soul is also bestowed by the Intellect with an incapacity (*'ajz*) to obtain at once all the benefits from the Intellect. This impedes the Soul to progress, as al-Sijistānī puts it, towards what is not her appointed measure (*miqdār*) and rank (*martaba*).[4] Whilst these elements are indispensable to the Soul's essence, they clearly exhibit that, in al-Sijistānī's opinion, (i) the Soul is not perfect, and that (ii) the Soul is never admitted a station above her own. It is for this reason that to Soul pertains merely the rank of the Follower.[5]

Al-Sijistānī is consequently also incorrect when he identifies the *qadā'* with the Antecedent, as the latter, made to correspond to the Intellect, has never been in potentiality. Such potentiality is something that al-Sijistānī's identification of *qadā'* with the *amr* – that is not ontologically existent and, therefore, an existent in potentiality – surely entails.

Overall, this *faṣl* tends to accentuate the impossibility of identifying the *qadar* and the *qadā'* with something merely potential. In particular,

---

[2] In his *Riyāḍ*, al-Kirmānī identifies the *tālī* with the universal *nafs* and the *hayūlā*. This is done after he has proven that the Soul is the Follower with respect to the Intellect and that the existence of the universal *nafs* is dissimilar from any other kind of existence. For this reason, the Follower is acknowledged as the first thing that is never preceded by any other of its class. Al-Kirmānī, *Riyāḍ* (Beirut, 1960), p. 69.

[3] On this topic see more infra.

[4] Al-Sijistānī, *Kitāb al-Yanābī'*, pp. 94–95; tr. Walker, *The Wellsprings of Wisdom*, pp. 62–63.

[5] Similarly, the Intellect does not supersede his limited nature as the first originated being. The Intellect is the Plotinian One-Many which can never attain the absolute, indivisible oneness of the godhead, the Intellect himself being aware of his non-divinity.

from the above excerpt it emerges that *qaḍā'* does not indicate the Antecedent, but rather signifies the existent upon which the state of the Antecedent depends. Obviously, al-Kirmānī is hinting at the Intellect and at the fact that only as the actualised entification of the *amr/kalima*, the Intellect might be accepted to signify the Antecedent without incurring any threat to divine *tawḥīd*.[6] Apart from this reading, towards the end of this passage al-Kirmānī suggests that there are many meanings that can be applied to both the *qaḍā'* and the *qadar*, all of which should be derived from the religious world rather than from the spiritual realm. So, is al-Kirmānī hinting at a different way of discerning these elements which are meant to be observed through the *qiyāma* lens? In rejecting al-Sijistānī's claim of potentiality for both *qaḍa'* and *qadar*, is al-Kirmānī also refuting their identification with Muḥammad b. Ismāʿīl, respectively as (i) the hidden Imam and (ii) the final Resurrector?

---

[6] Not to forget, in al-Kirmānī's doctrine, the Intellect corresponds also to the act of origination, *ibdāʿ*. See my comments in 'A Preliminary Study on the Significance of *Qaḍā'* and *Qadar*', p. 358.

Faṣl Three

What is *qaḍāʾ*? It firstly signifies the *nāṭiq* who was potential then came out into actuality with the support of God Almighty;[1] and it signifies [also] those who subsist in his place (*al-qāʾimīn maqāmahu*) (peace be upon them), who have reached in maturity (*bulūgh*) the position corresponding to the first procession (*al-inbiʿāth al-awwal*),[2] by dint of them all, peace upon them,

---

[1] Ibn Bābūya suggests that *qaḍāʾ* has ten meanings: (i) Knowledge as in Q 12:68; (ii) informing about someone/something as in Q 5:32; (iii) judgement as in Q 27:78; (iv) speech as in Q 40:20; (v) determining as in Q 34:14; (vi) command as in Q 17:23; (vii) creation as in Q 41:12; (viii) action as in Q 20:72; (ix) completion as in Q 28:28; (x) ending something as in Q 12:41. See Ibn Bābūya, *Kitāb al-Tawḥīd*, tr. A. Adam as *The Book of Divine Unity* (Birmingham, 2014), pp. 462–463. The renowned Shiʿi scholar al-Shaykh al-Mufīd reduces these meanings to *khalq* (creation), *amr* (command) and *iʿlām* (notification). See al-Shaykh al-Mufīd, *Taṣḥīḥuʾl-iʿtiqādāt*, in *al-Murshid*, vols I–III, cited in Ivanow, *A Shiite Creed*, p. 122, note 74.

[2] The discourse on the first procession (*al-inbiʿāth al-awwal*) and the second procession (*al-inbiʿāth al-thānī*) concerns the thorny issue of whether particular souls are parts (*ajzāʾ*) or merely traces (*āthār*) of the Universal Soul (on which see De Smet, *La Philosophie Ismaélienne*, pp. 113–125). Contrary to al-Rāzī, al-Sijistānī resorts to al-Nasafī's view that rational souls cannot be other than parts of the Universal Soul. To argue that they are only traces would mean to invalidate all the main religious tenets such as prophethood, the imamate, *wiṣāya* (trusteeship), divine revelation and the divine laws. In fact, should a particular soul be just the trace of the Universal Soul it would neither be able to perceive, understand nor derive benefits from the Soul. In addition, were the souls of the prophets merely traces of the Universal Soul, they would not have been able to grasp what was revealed to them nor to comprehend the spiritual entities that are part of the Soul. Al-Sijistānī explains that individual souls are part of the lower world and are linked to matter and its dark and corrupted nature. Despite this, they are still to be considered parts of the Soul and are connected to the luminous spiritual world because the Soul has a double dimension: a higher dimension which is orientated towards the Intellect, through which Soul receives

being actual [in executing] the command [to do good] and the prohibition [to do evil] and decreeing (*qaḍā'*) the standing mission into actuality after these [command and prohibition] had been potential, which is applicable to the meaning to which the expression *qaḍā'* alludes. And this is what the author of the *Nuṣra* intends and he is correct in that [sense] in his giving precedence to *qaḍā'* [over the *qadar*].[3]

Analysis and interpretation: Al-Kirmānī focuses on the correspondences between *qaḍā'* and the ranks of the celestial dignitaries, all of whom have their representatives within the terrestrial *da'wa*. In what al-Kirmānī suggests is al-Sijistānī's reading, the *qaḍā'* corresponds to the *nāṭiq* who was potential and subsequently became actual. The association made by al-Sijistānī remains somewhat ambiguous, as it could be read, on the one hand, as the identification of the *qaḍā'* with the *nāṭiq*-to-be, namely the seventh Imam of a prophetic era rising to the rank of the *nāṭiq* of the following cycle. This indication might find a corroboration because al-Sijistānī himself indicates that the *qaḍā'* signifies also the *nāṭiq*'s 'representatives' (literally, those who take the *nāṭiq*'s place, *qā'imūn maqāmahu*) in their state of first procession (*al-inbi'āth al-awwal*). By commanding the good, forbidding

---

the benefits (*istifāda*) of the intelligible realm, and a lower one which is directed towards the realm of Nature and through which Soul bestows benefits (*ifāda*) to the world of sensation and corruption (see al-Sijistānī, *Kitāb Ithbāt al-nubuwwāt*, ed. 'Ārif Tāmir (Beirut, 1966), p. 44; al-Kirmānī, *Riyāḍ* [Beirut, 1960], p. 66). In view of the foregoing, De Smet has pointed out that for al-Sijistānī 'l'émanation (*inbijās*) de la nature à partire de l'âme est une condition necessaire au perfectionnement de l'âme. Car, c'est dans la nature que seront générées les forms qui permettront à l'âme de recevoir les avantages de l'intellect' (De Smet, 'La doctrine avicennienne des deux faces de l'âme', *Studia Islamica*, 93 (2001), p. 81). On this basis, Madelung explains, it can be assumed that al-Nasafī too considered the rational human soul as a part of the Universal Soul in his *Maḥṣūl*, thus adopting the gnostic theme of the Soul's fall into the material world as being due to the Soul's original sin (see Madelung, '*Kawn al-'ālam*', p. 24). Al-Kirmānī responds to these views, arguing that the Soul is not a body susceptible to division, hence al-Sijistānī's argument does not stand. He elucidates that both Soul and Nature proceed ultimately from the Intellect and are subordinate to the first originated being. Al-Kirmānī, *Riyāḍ* (Beirut, 1960), pp. 111–113. See also Poonawala in his Introduction, pp. 38–39.

    [3] Al-Kirmānī, *Riyāḍ* (HL), p. 126.

the wrong and by carrying out their mission of putting into actuality what was previously in potentiality, they might well signify *qaḍāʾ* too. Concealed here is also an embryonic form of the Fatimid belief – discussed in the writings of al-Qāḍī al-Nuʿmān and developed in later works of al-Sijistānī – that the members of the *daʿwa* can be seen as the actual representatives of the Imam in *satr*. It is therefore through such agents, with whom *qaḍāʾ* is also identified, that the revelation and the law find their actualisation.

On the other hand, the issue of the transmigration of knowledge in the souls of messengers and Imams might appear to be surfacing again: the *nāṭiq*'s representatives as actual existents fulfilling their mission, are the signifiers (i.e. the actualised forms/recipients) of *qaḍāʾ* (i.e. the decision prior to manifestation/estimation/knowledge which, as previously argued, might be identified with the Imam Muḥammad b. Ismāʿīl and his spiritually conveyed imamate).[4]

It has been observed earlier that the majority of Ismaili thinkers believed there exists a perfect correspondence between, among other realms, the world of Nature (*ʿālam al-ṭabīʿa*) – in other words, the sublunar realm – the world of religion (*ʿālam al-dīn*) concerning the ranks of the Ismaili *daʿwa*, and the realm of the law (*ʿālam al-waḍʿ*) relative to the prescriptions of the *sharīʿa*. It is clear that due to such correspondences, in al-Sijistānī's opinion the first meaning of *qaḍāʾ* becomes a proof for the passage from potentiality into actuality of the commands and prohibitions which, contained in the religious law brought about by the *nāṭiq*, exit the realm of possibility only once they have undergone the esoteric interpretation of the Imam; and, even more specifically, in the case of Muḥammad b. Ismāʿīl's concealment, their actualisation occurs through the Imam's interpretative mission, which is carried out by his specific *qāʾimīn* (a possible reference to his adjuncts, the *lawāḥiq*).[5]

---

[4]   Al-Kirmānī, *Riyāḍ* (Beirut, 1960), p. 156.

[5]   As already mentioned in the introduction (see pp. 6–7 above), Muḥammad b. Ismāʿīl, together with al-Muʿizz li-Dīn Allāh and al-Ḥākim bi-Amr Allāh and others, was by many considered as an *imām-qāʾim* during the cycle of the Prophet. Such 'minor *qāʾims*' were regarded as harbingers of the final *qāʾim*. Now, in contrast to the Fatimid Ismailis, according to the Qarmaṭīs, and probably according to al-Sijistānī himself, with his first appearance, Muḥammad b. Ismāʿīl had signalled the beginning

The emphasis put on the passage from potentiality into actuality is a recurrent theme in al-Sijistānī's *Kashf al-maḥjūb*. Particularly in Discourse VI, Issue 3, which is devoted to Neoplatonism and attempts to explain why the later prophets corroborate the truthfulness of the earlier prophets, the author tacitly confirms his belief in the possibility for the same prophetic 'light' to inform different prophets.[6] He states: 'There is a common ground and likeness (*mushākilāt*) between two prophets that succeed one another. Both have truth by virtue of [*their*] *spiritual essence being one and the same* (*bi-yakī-i ḥaqīqat*), *for the rank of the preceding prophetic messenger is like the stage of potentiality, and the rank of the succeeding prophetic messenger is like the stage of actuality*' (my emphasis). If we apply this way of reasoning to what is stated in the foregoing *faṣl*, the identification suggested therein of the *qaḍā'* with both the *nāṭiq* and the *nāṭiq*'s standing representatives seems to imply the possibility that it is not merely different prophets who can be imbued with the same prophetic light, but also that such light might be shared by the *nāṭiq*'s representatives. If this reading is correct, then it becomes clear how in al-Sijistānī's thought resonates al-Qāḍī al-Nu'mān's idea of the *qā'im*'s various degrees of manifestation. By extension, it would have made sense for al-Sijistānī to speculate that the concealed Imam, Muḥammad b. Ismā'īl, might well return as the last *qā'im*.

In the fourth *faṣl*, al-Kirmānī explains the second meaning associated with *qaḍā'*.

---

of the final, seventh era of history and, with his return as the final *qā'im*, he would have fulfilled the actualisation of his interpretative mission.

   6   Landolt's translation, *Unveiling of the Hidden*, pp. 114–115.

Faṣl Four

Secondly, *qaḍāʾ* signifies what comes out by *taʾwīl* from the potentiality of the *tanzīl* and the *sharīʿa*, such as the sciences which are not explained (*laysat bi-mashrūḥa*) in both of them. They [the sciences] are in them [the *tanzīl* and the *sharīʿa*] in potentiality in [need of] explanation (*sharḥ*) and actualisation (*fiʿl*), whereby the souls exit from the limit of potentiality into the limit of actuality. This is what the author of the *Iṣlāḥ* intends in his esoteric interpretation of the expression *qaḍāʾ*.[1]

Analysis and interpretation: The second meaning of *qaḍāʾ* relates to the difference between the potential and the actual meaning of the revelation and the *sharīʿa*, which are detectable through *taʾwīl*. The character of complementarity between, on the one hand, the knowledge of the religious precepts indicated in the revelation and, on the other hand, the observance of the *dicta* made explicit in the law seems to be suggested here: it is by knowing the fullest meanings of the Scriptures that souls might attain perfection. The doctrine of 'double worship' (*ʿibādatayn*) so crucial to al-Kirmānī is intimated: to achieve proper observance of the worship of God, which is the ultimate goal for humans and their means of achieving salvation and paradise, the revelation and the *sharīʿa* must be fully comprehended in both their exoteric and esoteric meanings. As well as the acquisition of true knowledge, the performance of deeds is needed.[2] The identification of the *qaḍāʾ* with the esoteric meaning disclosed through *taʾwīl* is,

---

[1]   Al-Kirmānī, *Riyāḍ* (HL), p. 127.

[2]   These include the rites and rituals of Islam, which are meant also to be understood through the indications contained in the revelation and the law deciphered through *taʾwīl*.

al-Kirmānī states, what al-Rāzī himself held. This confirms that for the author of the *Iṣlāḥ*, *qaḍāʾ* (as the second of the two followers), that is, as the *tālī/taʾwīl* follows, in the first instance, the *amr/sābiq/nāṭiq*, and in the second instance, the *qadar*, namely the first of the two followers, that is, the *tālī/imām* (Muḥammad b. Ismāʿīl) from whom proceeds the *taqdīr*.

Al-Kirmānī then proceeds to introduce the third meaning of *qaḍāʾ* in *Faṣl* Five.

Faṣl Five

Thirdly, *qaḍāʾ* signifies the events (*aḥdāth*) and qualitative changes (*istiḥālāt*) that come out into actuality and existence (*kawn*) which have been decreed (*muqaddara*) to come into existence in the world by the movement (*bi-ḥaraka*) of the moveable [things] (*mutaḥḥarrakāt*), and the quiescence (*sukūn*) of the quiescent [things] (*sākināt*) which are irresistible (*lā maradd lahā*). Therefore, when one of those matters comes to occur and attains actuality, it is said that God's *qaḍāʾ* is irresistible. These are the things of which *qaḍāʾ* is said.[1]

Analysis and interpretation: From a third perspective, which appears to be more specifically al-Kirmānī's own understanding, given that the author has already presented his fellows' stances, the *qaḍāʾ* concerns what has already been set into actuality; *qaḍāʾ* refers particularly to the events and *qualitative* changes that have been decreed by the movement and the quiescence of moving and quiescent beings respectively. Here, cosmologically speaking, there is a reference to the forms of the heavens, in other words, the spheres which, through the mediacy of the tenth intellect, are assigned the role of governing and regulating the physical world. They observe their veneration and service to God by their perfect and unchanging circular motion which has been decreed.[2] As for quiescent beings, it is sensible to associate quiescence

---

[1]   Al-Kirmānī, *Riyāḍ* (HL), p. 127. Translation, here slightly modified, in De Cillis, 'A Preliminary Study on the Significance of *Qaḍāʾ* and *Qadar*', p. 361.

[2]   In al-Sijistānī's opinion, natural motions keep coming forth from the imaginal time (*zamān-i wahmī*) which is the lower limit of the activity of the Soul. It is through the Soul's own imaginal motion (*ḥarakat-i wahmī*), from which the Soul receives the light of the oneness of God (*nūr-i waḥdat-i īzad*), that natural time and motion subsist. Al-Sijistānī, *Kashf al-maḥjūb*, tr. Landolt, *Unveiling of the Hidden*, p. 87.

with both the first and the second intellects which are perfect and *in actu* and, therefore, still.[3] This reference might allude to al-Kirmānī's belief that intellects themselves, together with their planetary spheres and via the tenth intelligence, exercise their power in the physical world;[4] this would also confirm again the hypothesis that, according to al-Kirmānī (as well as al-Rāzī),[5] and contrary to al-Nasafī and al-Sijistānī's views, the first *inbi'athī* entity (the Soul) is perfect in her essence and defective only in her action,[6] and that the Soul can be identified with the Follower, for she follows, i.e. comes after, the first intellect only by dint of her rank and her imperfect action.[7]

Al-Kirmānī's construing also recalls the influence that celestial intellects and bodies exercise upon created beings in the form of a perpetual influx which is transmitted through celestial intermediaries.

---

[3]   Al-Sijistānī defines the differences in degrees of human virtues and vices in terms of the quantity of repose (*sukūn*) that any individual soul receives from the Intellect. The recipients of perfect repose (*al-sukūn al-tāmm*) are the *mu'ayyadūn*; these are individuals whose benefits from the Intellect and the Soul remain unchangeable and uninterrupted. See Hirji, 'A Study of *al-Risālah al-bāhirah*', p. 191.

[4]   De Smet, *La quiétude de l'intellect*, p. 274; Ibn al-Walīd, *al-Risāla al-Mufīda*, tr. Madelung and Mayer, *Avicenna's Allegory on the Soul*, p. 88.

[5]   According to al-Rāzī, stillness or repose (*sukūn*) and change or movement (*ḥaraka*) are 'two traces' united, respectively, with the first being, or Universal Intellect, and the second being or Universal Soul. Such traces (i.e. the effects of the following hypostases) remain in the Intellect in a state of potentiality. Through the procession of the Soul from the Intellect, which is with time (*ma'a al-zamān*) however, the two traces enter into actuality within the Soul. On these arguments see al-Rāzī, *Iṣlāḥ*, p. 24; al-Kirmānī, *Riyāḍ* (Beirut, 1960), pp. 101–110; Shin Nomoto, 'Early Ismā'īlī Thought on Prophecy according to the *Kitāb al-Iṣlāḥ* by Abū Ḥātim al-Rāzī', PhD thesis, McGill University (Montreal, 1999), p. 174.

[6]   Al-Rāzī, *Iṣlāḥ*, p. 24.

[7]   Conversely, al-Nasafī links the Soul mainly with motion. The Soul's restlessness, which is the result of her essential imperfection and her yearning towards the Intellects' completeness, is associated with the origin of motion and time. The corollary to this is that time is inherent in the Soul's essence whose actions occur in a temporal frame, thereby rendering the Soul imperfect. Al-Sijistānī propounded a similar idea for which the Soul herself originates in no time as a result of Intellect's self-contemplation which makes the Soul able to receive the Intellect's benefits. However, the Soul's activity, which produces imaginal motion, acts on a different level for it causes the manifestation of Nature (as matter joined with form). See al-Sijistānī, *Kitāb al-Yanābī'*, pp. 130–131; tr. Walker, *The Wellsprings of Wisdom*, pp. 85–86.

Noticeably, in the above *faṣl*, there is no mention of any form of potentiality with respect to the *qaḍāʾ* and this term is not linked to the notion of the Antecedent or the Follower directly. Is al-Kirmānī here seemingly distancing himself from al-Sijistānī's cognitive underpinnings? In particular, is the emergence of the mentioned *istiḥālāt* meant to symbolise the 'periods' or 'partial cycles' of the imamate, that is, the Imams as minor *qāʾims*,[8] whose existence and succession are decreed by the celestial beings which render them permanently in actuality? If the foregoing identification is accurate, is al-Kirmānī subtly espousing al-Rāzī's idea that the *qaḍāʾ* follows the *qadar* just like the Imam follows (and is therefore inferior in rank with respect to) the enunciator-prophet? Again, is al-Kirmānī imperceptibly denouncing the impossibility of applying the terms *sābiq* and *tālī* to al-Sijistānī's idea of the Imam in *satr* and his future manifestation as the final Resurrector?

In *Faṣl* Six, al-Kirmānī implicitly provides some answers to these questions as he continues on explaining the multiple meanings of *qadar*.

---

8   Corbin, *Cyclical Time and Ismaili Gnosis*, p. 99.

Faṣl Six

As for the *qadar*, it signifies firstly the *qā'im* (the Resurrector), who has been promised and celebrated with good news since [the time of] Adam (blessings of God upon him), and signifies his actual mission for whose preservation and elevation there are the Imams and the messengers, blessings and peace upon them, with their *dā'īs* in concealment (*satr*) and their limit (*ḥadd*) of potentiality by his [i.e. the *qā'im*] being decreed (*muqaddar^{an}*) to come out from *taqdīr* into actuality and existence (*wujūd*), and by his mission (*da'wa*) being actual (*qā'ima*) through the *ḥudūd* of the cycle (*dawr*) of the *nabī* (blessings be upon him and his family), as a *da'wa* in concealment which is *qā'im bi'l-quwwa*, not manifest which is *qā'im bi'l-fi'l*. Therefore, the *ta'wīl* of the night of *qadar* (*laylat al-qadr*) (peace be upon it) signifies the *qā'im* (blessings upon him) and who is alluded to by the shaykhs in their saying: *kūnī-qadar*.[1]

Analysis and interpretation: It is possible that the first signification of the term *qadar* reported here is an explanation of what al-Kirmānī wanted to present as al-Sijistānī's opinion. This is probable given that the next passage indicates what is described as being al-Rāzī's idea and that al-Kirmānī seems to follow the same pattern in presenting his colleagues' opinions before setting out his own. In any case, in the above extract it is stated that the term *qadar* refers to the *qā'im al-qiyāma* promised and foretold since the time of Adam, whose safeguarding and raising have been carried out by the messengers and the Imams. *Qadar* converts the passage from *taqdīr* into actuality (*fi'l*), and this

---

[1] Al-Kirmānī, *Riyāḍ* (HL), pp. 127–128. Throughout this *faṣl*, al-Kirmānī plays on the words *qadar* and *kun*, preparing the reader for his final phrase and its paronomastic effect.

means that during *satr*, the mission is carried out by the living *waṣī* of the age and his Imams who become the active force moving potentiality (what is meant to occur according to *taqdīr*) towards actuality (what actually occurs, i.e. the finite result or *tafṣīl*).[2] It is important to underline that it is not merely the *qā'im* who can be in concealment or non-manifest but also his *dā'īs*. This view, on a general scale, resembles the opinion that al-Qāḍī al-Nu'mān had expounded in his *al-Risāla al-Mudhhiba*: it was only with 'Abd Allāh al-Mahdī that the *dā'īs* became manifest during the era of unveiling (*dawr al-kashf*), whereby they have continued and will continue to carry out their mission until the end of this world upon the parousia of the final Resurrector.[3]

Al-Sijistānī seems to have modified his initial Qarmaṭī stances and espoused similar ideas, probably under the influence of al-Mu'izz's policy for the Fatimid *da'wa*: in the writings following the *Nuṣra*, it is the Fatimid caliphs who act as deputies (*khulafā'*) of the future messiah whilst being simultaneously Imams of a second heptad (the first ending with Muḥammad b. Ismā'īl).[4] According to this 'second round of seven', as Walker names it, al-Mahdī occupied the fourth position and al-Mu'izz the seventh (corresponding to the eleventh and fourteenth positions in the line of the early Ismaili Imams and the line of the Fatimid Imam-caliphs).[5] It appears that al-Sijistānī acknowledged particularly the strategic political role played by the fourth among these, whom he calls 'the one who conquers cities'.[6] This might have some significance when linked with the importance al-Nasafī had already assigned to the number four (associated with the prophet Moses), which will be examined later in this study.

Let us now look at the reference to the night of *qadr*. In the Ismaili view, the beginning of the cycle of the *qiyāma* is the advent of the

---

[2] In the *Iṣlāḥ*, al-Rāzī interprets the verses relative to the 'night of *qadr*' as referring to the *asās* (i.e. the *waṣī*) of the age who will guide his followers towards a reign of harmonisation until the advent of the final *qā'im*. See al-Rāzī, *Iṣlāḥ*, pp. 129–130.

[3] Al-Qāḍī al-Nu'mān, *al-Risāla al-mudhhiba*, pp. 66, 74, 79; Daftary, *The Ismā'īlīs*, pp. 164–165.

[4] Al-Sijistānī, *Kitāb Ithbāt al-nubuwwāt*, ed. 'Ārif Tāmir (Beirut, 1966), pp. 185, 187.

[5] Walker, *Intellectual Missionary*, p. 75.

[6] Such expression, Walker argues, can be found in al-Sijistānī's *Sullam al-najāt* as a way to refer to the Fatimid caliphs. See his 'Succession to Rule in the Shiite Caliphate', p. 243 note 22 and reference given there.

laylat al-qadr (Q 97). Exoterically and historically, the actual date for the night of *qadr* is not easily identifiable, although some Shi'i sources point to the 21st or 23rd of the month of Ramaḍān.[7] Esoterically, the night of *qadr* designates one of the *ḥudūd*s from the world of religion who inaugurates the last cycle.

Indeed, as explained by Amir-Moezzi, the Shi'i perception of the *laylat al-qadr* is intimately linked to the fundamental question of acknowledging, after the time of Muḥammad, the Imam as the highest spiritual and religious authority.[8] Many Shi'i sources recount that it is during this particular night that God decrees the future events that will be manifest during the year and which will descend on earth via His Command; the divine *amr* is then received by a man who, divinely chosen, is named the master of the command (*ṣāḥib/walī al-amr*),[9] and whose presence in this world represents a spiritual cosmic necessity.[10] In particular, the night of *qadr* refers not simply to the circumstances relative to the revelation of the Qur'an to Muḥammad, but also to the actual time when an Imam, via celestial intermediaries, is invested by God with his specific kind of *'ilm*.[11] Because such knowledge has been received by successive Imams from the dawn of creation and will continue to be received till the end of time, the reference to the *laylat al-qadr* conveys the idea of how the divine commandment

---

[7] One variant is mentioned by al-Kulaynī in his *al-Furū' min al-kāfī*, p. 159 note 9, in which is reported that according to the Imam Ja'far al-Ṣādiq, 'The night of the 19 [of the month of Ramaḍān] is the [night] of *taqdīr*, namely the estimation of God relative to the decrees for the coming year, the night of the 21 is that of *ibrām* (confirmation) and the night of the 23 that of *imḍā'* (execution).' Significantly, *taqdīr* appears to be prior to God's decision/decree of those events that will befall in the coming year (supposedly until the next *laylat al-qadr*).

[8] See M. A. Amir-Moezzi, '"La Nuit du *Qadr*" (Coran, sourate 97) dans le Shi'ism ancien', *MIDEO*, 31 (2016), p. 196.

[9] On this figure see more infra, p. 231 and note 5 at the same page.

[10] Amir-Moezzi, 'La Nuit du *Qadr*', p. 189 and references to Shi'i sources given therein.

[11] On the nature of this knowledge, see al-Ṣaffār al-Qummī, *Baṣā'ir al-darajāt fī 'ulūm āl Muḥammad*, ed. A. Zakīzādeh Ranānī (Qumm, 2012), p. 788, n 13; al-Majlisī, *Bīḥār al-anwār*, (Tehran, 1956–1972), vol. 25, p. 37, n. 4; al-Kulaynī, *al-Uṣūl min al-kāfī*, ed. J. Muṣṭafawī (Tehran, n.d.), vol. 1, p. 360 note 3. Sources are cited in Amir-Moezzi's 'La Nuit du *Qadr*', pp. 190–191 notes 28, 31, 32.

has been continuously perpetuated in actuality, thus also implicitly validating the incessant indispensability of the imamate.

In the context of the foregoing *faṣl*, the *laylat al-qadr* is said to signify the final *qāʾim*: this view apparently presents a slight shift in comparison to other perspectives for which the night of *qadr* does not identify the final Resurrector but, rather, his *bāb* or *ḥujja* who preceeds him.[12] Nonetheless, if this statement is read in connection with al-Sijistānī's early Qarmaṭī claims which were allegedly held in his *Nuṣra*, it becomes clear that, for Abū Yaʿqūb, the *laylat al-qadr* – in which there is a strong proximity between what is meant to occur and what actually occurs – indicates the Imam in *satr*, Muḥammad b. Ismāʿīl, as the *qāʾim* of his cycle who has temporal precedence – having already manifested himself as an Imam – but it also indicates the final *qāʾim* who will reappear at the end of time. Indeed, it is during this special night that the veil between potentiality and actuality is most diaphanous. The *laylat al-qadr* in a sense embraces what can potentially be and what already is, just as the final Resurrector (and his eschatological task) will be manifest, having already been actual – that is, present and active among his *daʿwa* in the person of the Imam in concealment.

This identification is also encoded in the link established between the night of *qadr* and the *kūnī-qadar* myth. Just as the female hypostasis of the creative imperative *kūnī* is accountable for the bringing into being of all existents, likewise the Imam, who in the general imamology of Ismaili Shiʿism corresponds to the feminine principle typified in the second intellect (the Soul), is the source of the spiritual birth of the initiates.[13] Just as in the myth, *qadar* is accountable for the determination of all existents, likewise the final *qāʾim al-qiyāʾma* will be responsible for their final destiny, dispensing reward or punishment.

---

[12] See for example: 'The *ḥujja* of the *qāʾim* comes before him in the world of religion and he is the night of *qadr*' (Nāṣir-i Khusraw, *Wajh-i dīn*, Discourse 33); 'The night of *qadar* is a symbol (*mathal*) of his *bāb* and *ḥujja* who is going to come before him. And thus, the *bāb* of the *qāʾim* is the lord of universal explanation (*ṣāḥib al-bayān al-kullī*) and the true unveiling (*khasf al-ḥaqīq*).' Al-Muʾayyad fiʾl-Dīn al-Shīrāzī, *al-Majālis al-Muʾayyadiyya*, ed. Ḥātim Ḥamīd al-Dīn (Oxford and Mumbai, 1975–2005), vol. 2, p. 612.

[13] Corbin, *Cyclical Time and Ismaili Gnosis*, p. 184. The person-archetype of the night of *qadr* is also identified with Fāṭima as the *ḥujja* of the Prophet's *waṣī* and the threshold of Mercy and Knowledge. See Corbin, *Temple and Contemplation*, p. 175.

Faṣl Seven

Secondly, the *qadar* signifies what the *nabī* (peace be upon him and his family) has brought, such as the *tanzīl* and the *sharīʿa*, the wise sayings (*ḥikam*) and the parables (*amthāl*) which, in their potentiality, are the sciences (*ʿulūm*) and the knowledge (*maʿārif*) which the souls need in order to achieve maturity (*bulūgh*) and actuality (*fiʿl*), by its [*qadar*'s] being in a form which encompasses all of these. Therefore, knowledge is not found in its exoteric aspect except through *ta'wīl*. The words of the author of the *Iṣlāḥ* in that regard steer the meaning to *qadar*.[1]

Analysis and interpretation: In *Faṣl* seven, al-Kirmānī repeats what he previously alluded to: the *qadar*, according to al-Rāzī, is in a *form* (i.e. the Imam) that encompasses the wisdom and knowledge contained in the revelation and in the *sharīʿa* and whose fullest meanings is only actualised through the Imam's *ta'wīl*.

---

[1]   Al-Kirmānī, *Riyāḍ* (HL), p. 128.

Faṣl Eight

Thirdly, the *qadar* signifies the world in all its parts which has within itself the potentiality to emerge into existence (*kawn*) and actuality (*fiʿl*) over the course (*mamarr*) of days, months, years; [it signifies] events (*aḥdāth*) and becomings (*akwān*) – whose existence comes from it by the perpetual movement (*bi'l-ḥaraka al-dā'ima*) of the moveable [things] (*mutaḥarrikāt*) over what is not moving – and whose existence is necessary (*ḍarūrī*) by [that movement] having been decreed (*muqaddara*) in it. Therefore, it is said: 'What God determines will come to pass.' Thus, the existence of what is determined (*muqaddara*) is due to the very necessity of its existence (*iḍṭirār wujūdihi*), and even if it takes a long time (*ṭālat al-mudda*), it is, as it were, an existent (*ka'l-kā'in*) in actuality. Therefore, God Almighty said: 'Indeed they see it [as] distant, but We see it [as] near' [Q 70:6–7]. Thus, whatsoever is in *taqdīr* (i.e. is under estimation) will come into existence and, when it comes into existence, it is *qaḍā'*, for the expression *qaḍā'* signifies that which was in potentiality and then came out into actuality. These are the meanings of *qaḍā'* and *qadar*.

If we reconsider the speech of the author of the *Iṣlāḥ* and his statement that 'the *qadar* precedes the *qaḍā'*', the only element of correctness in its meaning is in what the Prophet (peace be upon him and his family) has brought in terms of the revelation and law which precede the *qaḍā'*, which is the *ta'wīl* as he made and interpreted it, may God have mercy upon him. As for the statement of the author of the *Nuṣra* that 'the *qaḍā'* precedes the *qadar*', he was only correct with reference to the actual *nāṭiq* (peace be upon him), who is the *qaḍā'* which precedes the revelation and *sharīʿa*, which he brought, [this] being the *qadar*.[1]

---

[1]   Ibid., pp. 128–129.

Analysis and interpretation: Thirdly, the *qadar* signifies the world that apparently enters existence in the course of time but whose actuality has, in truth, been decreed from *aeternitate*. When in a state of potential disclosure, all existents and becomings might be associated with *taqdīr*, whilst their true actualisation is but the *qaḍāʾ*.

Besides this straightforward interpretation, I am tempted to suggest another view: *qadar* signifies the world whose true entrance into actuality (its 'awakening' to the reality of things) occurs according to what in human parameters is a temporal progression (the passage of days, months and years). However, entities in Nature are necessarily *actual* due to the perpetual movement of the moveable [things] (again, a reference to the spheres of the heavens, *aflāk*), which determines them in actual existence. What is not determined, however, is their awakening to the *ḥaqīqa* embedded in the potentiality of *taʾwīl*. Indeed, the world in all its parts is determined by dint of the very necessity of its existence so that what might appear to be a temporal delay in their coming-to-be is 'as it were [already] in existence (*kaʾl-kāʾin*)'. This is similar to the case of the third intellect's existence (namely, its first perfection) potentially 'becoming' actual: its coming-into-existence is, really, an instantaneous 'process', given that all entities have always been everlastingly *potentially actual* in the Intellect's oneness.[2] Nonetheless, just as the tenth intellect attains its second perfection by way of elevating itself to the rank of the third intellect – actualising its potentiality through acquisition of knowledge and action – likewise, human beings become truly existent by following the right teachers and their hermeneutical call, ascending to true knowledge.

Significantly, just as time can be perceived and measured in aggregates of days, months and years, likewise, in my opinion, al-Kirmānī understands the minor *qiyāma* – defined by Corbin as 'the metamorphosis of being'[3] – as an ever-occurring event which can be experienced through the teachings of temporal, 'transitional intervals', that is, the Imams. In particular, I believe that dwelling in al-Kirmānī's elaborations on the actuality of *qaḍāʾ* and *qadar*, and in his oft-repeated emphasis on the limits (*ḥudūd*) that are fulfilled and actualised by all

---

[2]   This is not different from what al-Sijistānī himself holds in *al-Risāla al-Bāhira* in relation to the element of 'permanence'.

[3]   Corbin, *Temple and Contemplation*, p. 154.

members of the *daʿwa*, rests the idea that any minor *qiyāma* is a type of 'ascending', from one level of consciousness to the next; an intellectual birth or awakening (*baʿth*), occurring at every moment or instant, in all religious followers practising the teaching of the rightful Imams, yet remaining imperceptible to the majority of believers. In what follows, I shall endeavour to elucidate these points.

Let us begin with the emphasis put (as in *Faṣl* Five) on the 'changes' that are necessitated by movements of movable entities, recalling what al-Kirmānī's predecessor, al-Sijistānī, thought of these.

In the twentieth Wellspring of his *Kitāb al-Yanābīʿ*, al-Sijistānī elucidates how the movements of the spheres occur in accordance with the extreme boundary (*ghāya*) and utmost degree (*nihāya*) that the Soul determines for them. Here is the idea that the Soul/*qadar* is responsible for imposing measures and limitations that cannot be transcended. However, what appears to be a form of compulsion (*jabr*) in the movements of the spheres is an agreement with the Soul's prior determination which, in turn, establishes such determination according to the benefits the Soul herself attains (*istifāda*) from her cause (*ʿilla*), the Intellect. Moreover, al-Sijistānī states that the spheres' movements (their unions, *ittiṣālāt*, and conjunctions, *iqtirānāt*) obtain what the Soul had chosen for them at the beginning (*awwal*[an]) of their manifestation, without the Soul having to intervene and change their status. In fact, the Antecedent (the Intellect) endows (*ifāḍa*) the Follower (the Soul) with a capacity (*maqdūra*) which liberates it from having to renew its deliberation (*ikhtiyār*) with regard to the organisation (*naẓm*) of the natural world. The idea that there might be forms of temporal determinations (*al-ikhtiyārāt al-zamāniyyāt*) occurring at a specific time (*waqt*) with regards to the movements of the spheres is anathema because this would imply a kind of deficiency (*nuqṣān*). Rather, the Follower determines only once, deriving its choice from a unique intellectual emanation (*istifāda wāḥida ʿaqliyya*) through which it arranges the world as a sublime order (*tarkīb*[an] *laṭīf*[an]). The Follower's single *ikhtiyār* corresponds to the constancy/resolution (*qarār*) of emanated benefits of the Antecedent (*fawāʾid al-sābiq*).[4] All of this

---

4   Al-Sijistānī, *Kitāb al-Yanābīʿ*, p. 110; tr. Walker, *The Wellsprings of Wisdom*, pp. 74–75. Some points need to be elaborated: (i) from the above passage it emerges that the Soul does not admit deficiency, whilst it is usually understood that for

mirrors the structural and functional ranks of the Ismaili imamate: in the same way as the Soul necessitates the movements of the celestial spheres and their bodies in accordance to the benefits received from the Intellect, likewise the *asās* necessitates – by appointing them – the 'changes', namely the Imams who will be the lords of the minor cycle in accordance to the succession that is designated by the *nāṭiq*. Just as the Antecedent releases the Follower from the need of having to intervene and modify its atemporal determination, likewise the Imam is dispensed from having to actually intervene – during periods of *satr* – directly on the decisions taken on his behalf by his deputies.

In addition, al-Kirmānī's reading in the eighth chapter of the *Riyāḍ* seems ironically to directly address some of the arguments al-Sijistānī will propound in the final chapter ('Discourse') of his *Kashf al-maḥjūb*. In this work, he endeavours to refute explicitly the doctrine of *tanāsukh* (or, at least, the idea of the transmigration of souls across species) and explains that Existing (*būdan*) is coupled with the Calling

---

al-Sijistānī Soul is not perfect; (ii) according to al-Sijistānī, the Soul acts in time and sets into existence all entities which are inferior to her. These beings include the individual souls that are parts of the Soul as they are from her and in her. Individual souls, including human souls, are therefore not merely traces of the Soul, as sustained by al-Rāzī, but parts of the Soul. Conversely, in the above passage, al-Sijistānī insists on the absolute timelessness of the Soul's determination in respect to the spheres' movements. This might suggest that the Soul's action is atemporal when it comes to celestial affairs whilst operating in time with respect to terrestrial issues. A somewhat clearer explanation for this is offered when al-Sijistānī analyses the nature of evil. He points out that whilst in the Antecedent there is no evil whatsoever and it is completely good both in its essence (*bi-dhātihi*) and in its intellegising (*bi-naẓarihi*), in its product, the Follower, one finds evil (*sharr*). This can be classified as evil only by ascription (*bi'l-iḍāfa*). This means that whilst the Follower is completely good in essence, it is not as good as the Antecedent in its action and it is therefore inferior to the Antecedent in its capacity (*dūnuhu bi'l-qudra*). If on the one hand, the Antecedent is able to produce in the Follower a capacity to derive benefits (*fawāʾid*) from itself at once – without the passing of time (*bi-lā zamān wa lā waqt*) – on the other hand, the Soul's activity is limited to the production of an imaginal movement (*al-ḥaraka al-wahmiyya*) in what requires the combination of matter and form to become manifest and attain benefits. It is from this angle that the Soul's action is deemed to be evil (or less perfect) if compared to the Intellect's contemplative activity (*ʿamal al-nafs sharr min naẓar al-ʿaql*). See al-Sijistānī, *Kitāb al-Yanābīʿ*, pp. 130–131; tr. Walker, *The Wellsprings of Wisdom*, pp. 85–86 (English translation slightly modified).

to Rise (*bar angīkhtan*) just as the Becoming (*kawn*) is coupled with the Awakening (*ba'th*) of the dead.[5] In a number of rather enigmatic passages, al-Sijistānī seems to suggest that from the Intellect (which is perpetually actual, hence living and therefore Existence itself), the procession (*inbi'āth*, which is the passive or reflexive verbal noun of *ba'th*) of the Soul reveals the latter as a Form arisen (namely, the same reading as the Calling to Rise, *bar angīkhtan*).[6] Likewise, from the Becoming (which can be read both as the passage from *potentia* into *actu* and as the 'change' entified in the person of any minor *qā'im*) comes the Awakening (both as the awakening of the dead and as an intellectual awakening). Now, al-Sijistānī seems to infer that the actualised Becoming which is nothing but 'creation (and re-creation)' cannot transcend certain limits/forms (probably the forms of all individuals as *qā'ims*).[7] This is so because, as he explains, 'the things that are "decreed" (*muqaddarisāt*) in Creation [...] will not depart from that formation (*khilqat*) under which they came into being-there, due to the pre-established "measuring" (*taqdīr*) of their Creator and

---

[5] Al-Sijistānī, *Kashf al-maḥjūb*, tr. Landolt, *Unveiling of the Hidden*, pp. 120–121.

[6] That is: the passage from potentiality to actuality which certain human souls undergo once they actualise their knowledge fully through a learning process from the lords of religion seems to anticipate the Final Rising of the ultimate Resurrector in 'a moving onward in the stages of Soul [...] so that Soul will have come down in perfect completeness'. Ibid., pp. 78, 98. It should be recalled that for al-Sijistānī, when the final *qā'im* attains his position (*manzilah*) – the one that God has ordered for him – then, will emerge a *form* that will be able to receive all the spiritual benefits (*al-fawā'id al-'aqliyya*) without redaction (*ta'līf*) or arrangment (*tartīb*); al-Sijistānī, *Kitāb al-Yanābī'*, p. 159; Walker, tr., *The Wellsprings of Wisdom*, p. 102. This reiterates the concept that, upon the final *qiyāma*, no spiritual mediation – be it the mediation of the Soul, the enunciator-prophet or the Imam – will be required for any human being. The *form* that will emerge is that of a new human being, a resurrected man, a human soul fully 'present to itself' (a *qā'im* in this sense) who is admitted to ultimate knowledge without limit or intermediation.

[7] 'Calling to rise (*bar angīkhtan*)' is said to mean 'making-to-be' or 'calling-to-existence' (*būdan kardan*)' (al-Sijistānī, *Kashf al-maḥjūb*, tr. Landolt, *Unveiling of the Hidden*, p. 120). This implies that the Soul is 'called-to-exist' from the Intellect, just as Nature is 'called-to-exist' by the Soul. In turn, in the realm of Nature, existents are perpetually 'called' and 're-called' to exist in a cycle of unending generation and corruption, guaranteeing the permanence (*baqā'*) in existence of the terrestrial world. See al-Sijistānī, ibid., pp. 120–121; De Smet, 'La transmigration des âmes', p. 95.

Existentiator.'[8] This idea reiterates both al-Sijistānī's belief in the fixed ranks of the *da'wa* members – which are established according to measured intellectual bestowals and mediated through the spiritual *ḥudūd* – and his idea, often misinterpreted, that the passage from potentiality into actuality (the sperm of the dog into the form of the dog in the example provided above) does not entail any crossing of the boundaries of any given form. Accordingly, the Awakening does not occasion any intellectual intersection (i.e. the ontological limit of each *ḥadd* is maintained through the poured gnoseological limits, which are well measured) nor any 'transmigration' of souls between 'species'.

Buried here is the idea that, most probably, *ba'th* cannot be considered as the definitive resurrection of human souls incarnated in recreated bodies but, rather, as a recurring phenomenon, linked to both time and matter since it happens within the individual soul whilst this is still in a body. It is in this sense that the Awakening is coupled with 'Existing' and 'Becoming', that is, coupled with the perpetual re-calling to life (i.e. recalling to a true existence/knowledge) both of souls that are still living (namely, 'present to themselves') and of souls that will be 'resurrected' and fully 'living' again[9] once they attain the whole truth upon the ultimate *qiyāma*.[10]

---

8   Al-Sijistānī, *Kashf al-maḥjūb*, tr. Landolt, *Unveiling of the Hidden*, p. 121 (translation very slightly modified).

9   Al-Sijistānī explains: 'To exist is to find again the life which has disappeared from the living person, just as being called to rise is to find again the life which has disappeared from the dead person'. Ibid.

10   Thus, *ba'th* is starkly different from *qiyāma* as the final resurrection which, according to Ismaili eschatology, will occur only once at the end of human history, and through which, with the advent of the final Resurrector and his unveiling of the totality of the *ḥaqā'iq* and the *bāṭin*, human souls' ultimate salvation (or damnation) will be realised. However, for al-Sijistānī, souls' ultimate destiny appears to be the consequence of the virtues or vices acquired by such souls subject to their perpetual summoning and resummoning, whilst waiting for the *qiyāma*. In fact, the notion of *ba'th*, as al-Sijistānī himself specifies in his *Kashf al-maḥjūb*, is based on the fundamental point of 'the reward *finding* [or *reaching*] (*yāftan*) "the humans of good" and the punishment *getting hold* (*rasīdan*) of "the humans of evil"'; ibid., p. 12 (English translation slightly modified). This seems to suggest that it is the conduct of *those* human souls (since not all souls are called to 'be resurrected'; see ibid., pp. 122–123) that undergo *ba'th* or 'call-to-existence' *in their bodies* (ibid.) that allows

Faithful to his plan of reconciling contrasting views among the *dāʿī*s, al-Kirmānī is willing to highlight that, despite clear incongruities and to a certain extent, both al-Rāzī and al-Sijistānī are correct in their signification of the *qaḍāʾ* and the *qadar*. More specifically, according to al-Kirmānī, al-Rāzī is accurate in his affirmation that the *qadar* (i.e. the Imam) precedes the *qaḍāʾ* which in the above excerpt is intended as *taʾwīl*. If al-Rāzī propounds such identifications, then he is right in asserting that the *qaḍāʾ* – as *taʾwīl* – follows the *qadar* – as the Imam – who carries out such esoteric hermeneutical interpretation. Al-Kirmānī states that the author of the *Nuṣra* would have been correct in giving precedence to the *qaḍāʾ* over the *qadar* had he identified the former with the *nāṭiq*, who is an actual existent. The *nāṭiq* is a *mutaqaddim* in the sense that he precedes what he himself has brought into existence in terms of the revelation and the *sharīʿa*, which are the *qadar*.[11]

What appears to emerge from the translated passage is al-Kirmānī's own idea that both *qadar* and *qaḍāʾ* are somehow related to actuality: *qadar* is a signifier for the world in its authentic existence (as an allusion of the 'awakened' *qāʾim*s who are present in the world) which has been made ineludibly actual through the necessary decreed movement of the celestial moveable [things]; the *qaḍāʾ* is a signifier for the objects of estimation/measuring (the Imams, namely the events – *aḥdāth* – and the qualitative changes – *istiḥālāt* – mentioned in *Faṣl* Five), which have themselves come to a true existence.

Briefly put, al-Kirmānī endeavours to correct al-Rāzī's and al-Sijistānī's tendency to imbue *qaḍāʾ* and *qadar* with a character of

---

them to be either 'humans of good' or 'humans of evil', earning them either reward or punishment. Thus, *baʿth*, both as a minor intellectual *qiyāma* and as the culmination and recompense (as either reward or punishment) of the actions and events in the life of an individual being, has to be taken as a spiritual kind of resurrection. Similarly, in *al-Risāla al-Bāhira*, al-Sijistānī portrays *baʿth* as a 'soul-related phenomenon', strictly linked to the 'psychic *changes*' that are experienced, in particular, by depraved souls. On these topics, see De Smet, 'La transmigration des âmes', particularly, pp. 95–103; see also Hirji, 'A Study of *al-Risālah al-bāhirah*', pp. 92, 207.

[11]   Al-Kirmānī himself identifies the revelation and the *sharīʿa* as 'creation' in *Faṣl* Twelve of the eighth chapter of the *Riyāḍ*. In that context, creation is acknowledged to be nothing but the actualised aspect of *qadar*.

potentiality. This was done, evidently, for a series of reasons: (i) from a cosmological/theological standpoint, in an attempt to discourage the association of these two terms with the *amr*, the *kalima* and the notion of the Antecedent with the aim of avoiding any deviance towards *shirk* and suggestions about the Imam's pre-eminence over the enunciator-prophet. (ii) More subtly, it was perhaps also the issue of potentiality and its dangerous interpretations in terms of Qarmaṭī and trasmigrationist undercurrents, emerging particularly from al-Sijistānī's assertions, that al-Kirmānī found threatening. Al-Kirmānī's reasoning seems to run as follows: if the *qadar* and the *qaḍāʾ* are as actual as both the events/changes (in the forms of the actual *qāʾim*s) and the world, it follows that all souls' destiny is initially built in the realm of Nature to be eventually sealed in the afterlife, when souls are exposed to the ultimate truth upon the *qiyāma*.

Although here al-Kirmānī does not dwell more on it, this stance is validated in his *Rāḥat al-ʿaql*, in which we read: 'the existence of the soul in the body is not for the body's sake but for the soul's essence (*dhātihā*) which becomes appropriate (*talīq*) for the Hereafter and whose fate is like the existence of the body deprived of the darkness and narrowness (*ḍayq*) of the viscera in which the body is initially created.' The capacity that the individual soul has of attaining divine benefits (*al-barakāt al-ilāhiyya*) and availing itself of all the sciences – through the deeds of the law (*bi aʿmāl al-sharīʿa*) with assiduity and diligence – together with the soul's predisposition (*tahyūʾ*) for the lights of *malakūt* (the world of mystery and sovereignty), is compared by al-Kirmānī to the development of the soul's body and its potentiality of growth (*namāʾ*). Just as the body that, still in the darkness of the viscera (*aḥshāʾ*), is destined (*maṣīr^an*) to develop outside it in the world of sensation (*ʿālam al-ḥiss*), which represents for it its advent (*wurūduhu*), likewise the parting (*mufāriqa*) of the soul from the body is destined to the Hereafter, which becomes for the soul its end (*nihāya*).[12]

A step towards the soul's perfection (and salvation) is offered by the occurrence of *baʿth*. The latter is described by al-Kirmānī as 'God's act

---

[12] See, al-Kirmānī, *Rāḥat al-ʿaql*, p. 508. Cf. al-Sijistānī's interpretation of 'the beginning' (*ibtidāʾ*), and 'the end' (*nihāya*) which is given in the 24th *faṣl* of al-Kirmānī's *Riyāḍ*.

(*fi'l Allāh*), operating – through the angels brought near (*al-malā'ik al-muqarribīn*) (i.e. the intellects) – in the 'naturally resurrected one (*al-mab'ūth al-ṭabī'ī*) as the latter's perfection (*kamāl[an]*)', with the aim of rendering any individual 'an emanated being (*al-mab'ūth*) through the second emanation (*inbi'āth al-thānī*)'.[13] Al-Kirmānī elucidates that the second emanation, which is said to be the greatest divine power corresponding to the *ta'yīd ilāhī*, acts upon the soul of the resurrected being (*al-mab'ūth*) who is *actual* (*al-kā'in*) in the world of Nature (*'ālam al-ṭabī'a*). This indicates that, in al-Kirmānī's opinion, *ba'th* occurs in this world so that the naturally resurrected individual might be disposed to be fully actualised – in other words, to become 'a perfected emanated being' as the result of a second emanation.[14] Implicitly, al-Kirmānī is suggesting that this kind of 'resurrection' is linked to souls that are still joined to their natural bodies.[15]

This position is also corroborated in a number of observations advanced in the *Rāḥat al-'aql*: after having defined the first creation (*al-khalq al-awwal*) or the first birth (*al-nash'a al-ūla*) as the generation of bodies from the same species,[16] al-Kirmānī quotes Q 31:28: 'And your creation (*khalqukum*) or your resurrection (*ba'thukum*) is in no wise but as an individual soul (*illā ka-nafs[in] wāḥidat[in]*)'. If *ba'th* is like the first creation, this suggests that *ba'th*, just as *al-khalq al-awwal*, has something to do with bodies within one species. Al-Kirmānī then adds: 'your resurrection is not in your souls – which is the second creation, attained through action – except as one soul […] as in the two examples [i.e. creation and resurrection in the Qur'anic verse] which are one thing (*wa lā ba'thukum fī anfusikum alladhī huwa al-khalq al-thānī alladhī yudarriku bi'l-fi'l illā ka-nafsin wāḥida […] wa mathalān ka-shay' wāḥid*).[17] This statement implies a number of things. Firstly, it suggests that *ba'th* relates to all souls as to *Soul*; it is the Soul, or Spirit of Holiness that, via her intellectual bestowals,

---

[13] Al-Kirmānī, *Rāḥat al-'aql*, p. 511.

[14] Ibid., pp. 511–512.

[15] De Smet, 'La transmigration des âmes', p. 104.

[16] Al-Kirmānī states: '"And you certainly know the first form of creation" [Q. 56:62] which is the creation of your bodies from the species/kind (*qabīl*) of your bodies.' Al-Kirmānī, *Rāḥat al-'aql*, p. 507.

[17] Ibid., p. 507.

allows such 'awakening' to occur in what are the Soul's 'traces'. Secondly, resurrection can be attained through action, namely through all the individuals' obeying to the *ḥudūd*, which also means obeying to the highest living dignitary, the *imām-qāʾim* of the time, al-Ḥakim. In addition, given that *baʿth* is defined as the other birth (*al-nashʾa al-ukhrā*), which is the creation of the spirits and their revivification through the Spirit of Holiness (*khalq al-arwāḥ wa iḥyāʾuhā bi-rūḥ al-quds*), it follows that *baʿth is* a *spiritual affair*, occurring for souls in bodies of the same species as these were one soul.[18] Finally, it can be inferred that as a minor *qiyāma*, *baʿth*, even though a soul-related event, is connected to creation (*khalq*) because it has effects and manifestations in the physical world (in the persons of the *imām-qāʾim*s as well as in all 'resurrected/awakened' individuals, *qāʾim*s). Ultimately, it can be argued that, in al-Kirmānī's view, *baʿth* is but a voluntary form of intellectual *qiyāma* which, despite being facilitated by the decreed providential succour of the Soul (rendering the resurrected soul a *naturally* resurrected soul), is in fact the fruit of individual souls' cognitive undertakings (intellectual *jihād*s) through which each soul 'dies' and returns to a fuller and deeper 'magnitude/presence' of itself.[19]

In *Faṣl* Nine, al-Kirmānī provides a more critical analysis of the two *dāʿī*s' positions. He rejects al-Sijistānī's traditional Neoplatonic triple-hypostasis cosmological schema and, by introducing hints of his own cosmogonic view of the ten intellects, speaks of the intellects' eschatological mission in attaining perfection as their way of fulfilling the divine decree.

---

[18]   Ibid. Further proofs for this kind of argument are provided by our author with reference to yet another Qurʾanic verse (Q 22:5). The arrangement of creation and resurrection is said to be the same: just as the creation of a human being occurs with the transformation of various elements through different degrees, such as dust, sperm, a clinging scab, etc. – i.e. as an individual informed completeness which 'journeys' within the boundary of its own species as an informed incompleteness – likewise, resurrection 'journeys' within the souls of one species as 'one soul'. Ibid.

[19]   In *Faṣl* Twenty-Three, al-Kirmānī speaks of the correction of natural dispositions as the greatest effort (*al-jihād al-akbar*).

Faṣl Nine

The author of the *Nuṣra* [al-Sijistānī] recounted a saying of the sages: 'God Almighty, by originating the Intellect finished [the creation of] the two worlds because he [the Intellect] is the totality of the forms of the two worlds.'[1]

We [al-Kirmānī] say: The intellect which is the totality of the forms of the two worlds is not the first originated intellect (*al-ʿaql al-awwal al-mubdaʿ*) nor is it the second intellect (*al-ʿaql al-thānī*) which is the first emanated being (*al-munbaʿith al-awwal*), but it is the intellect that ascends (*al-ʿaql al-murtaqī*) from the world of Nature (*min ʿālam al-ṭabīʿa*), through the acquisition (*biʾl-iktisāb*) of knowledge (*ʿilm^{an}*) and action (*ʿamal^{an}*), to the rank that is parallel to the first procession (*muwāzāt al-inbiʿāth al-awwal*). It proceeded through procession (*inbiʿāth*) whereby it [the above intellect] became a totality of the forms of the two worlds in all their multiplicity (*kathratihā*). Its essence (*dhāt*) was engraved (*tanaqasha*) with the forms of all the existents (*al-mawjūdāt kulluhā*), as is the state of the enunciator-prophets (*nuṭaqāʾ*), the guardians (*awṣiyāʾ*) and the Imams (*aʾimma*) (peace be upon

---

[1] Cf. Al-Kirmānī, *Riyāḍ* (Beirut, 1960), p. 220. De Smet links this to a difficult passage in the *Theology of Aristotle* (II, 32.10–14/§ 21, p. 67) and sees this as a paraphrase of the *Enneads* (IV. 4, 2). See De Smet, *La quiétude de l'intellect*, p. 185 note 189. In *Kashf al-maḥjūb*, al-Sijistānī describes the Intellect as a Perfect Form (*ṣūratī tamām*), a light poured forth upon creation, shining in everything, whose luminosity is in accordance with the measure (*miqdār*) of the substance of the thing receiving it. In this work, it is specified that 'it is by virtue of that "Form" that one can claim the Intellect to be the source for all beings to be (*būdanīhā*), and bring to evidence his issuing-forth by pointing to the fact that his light is shining in [all] things.' See al-Sijistānī, *Kashf al-maḥjūb*, tr. Landolt, *Unveiling of the Hidden*, pp. 96–97. The translation here has been slightly modified.

them). The first intellect is too sublime (*ajall*) to be multiplied by this, as his existence is an *ibdāʿī* existence (*al-wujūd al-ibdāʿī*) and the multiplicity of an *ibdāʿī* existence is according to the intellection of its essence (*bi-ḥasab mā ʿaqqala min dhātihi*) to be [both] a cause (*ʿilla*) and an effect (*maʿlūl*). His existence, with regard to what has become divinised in him, lying purely outside (*khārij*) him. As for the rest of the existents, namely the intellects (*al-ʿuqūl*), emanated (*al-munbaʿitha*) by the first emanation/procession (*inbiʿāth^{an} awwal^{an}*), their multiplicity is according to what they perceive of their own essences (*dhawāt*) and of [that] whose existence precedes them up to the first intellect. Their existence, despite that, with regard to what has become divinised in him [i.e. the Intellect], lies outside them (*khārij ʿanhā*). Thus, the multiplicity of the one that comes into existence (*fi'l-wujūd*) later (*muta'akhkhir*), is not like the multiplicity of the one who has preceded it in existence; its need for multiplicity in the intellection of the existents is an unavoidable necessity from which the first [intellect] can separate (*yanfakku*) himself in his entirity (*bi-tamāmiyatihi*). And if this is the case, it is clear that what is a totality of the forms of the two worlds is not the first intellect but rather [one of] the intellects which has emanated from the realm of Nature (*dār al-ṭabīʿa*) through a second emanation/procession (*inbiʿāth thānī*).

We say that with regard to the first intellect, he does not need to intelligise what is under him (*mā dūnahu*) or to conceptualise it, for his being encompasses in his essence eternality (*azal*), completeness (*tamāmiyya*), permanence (*baqā'*), unity (*waḥda*), resistence to qualitative change (*al-imtināʿ min al-istiḥāla*), not for the sake of what may come into existence from him, but because of what [already] exists from him. Since his existence is eternal, complete, permanent, unique and one, resistant to qualitative change not because of what may come into existence from him but because of his existence [from God] Almighty, he does not intelligise what is below him, for he has no need for that. In addition, we say for that whose existence is posterior (*al-mutaʾakhkhir*), namely the second emanation (*al-inbiʿāth al-thānī*), it is necessary to perceive (*yalzamahu ʿan yaʿqila*) that which precedes it in existence (*mā taqaddama ʿalayhi fi'l-wujūd*), in which way it becomes the totality of the forms (*majmaʿ li'l-ṣuwar*). This is because it acquires (*yaktasib*) the completeness (*tamāmiyya*), in which is its permanence, by its intellecting that whose existence precedes it. Since in its completeness it is in need of intellecting what precedes it in existence, such as the dignitaries (*ḥudūd*), who are appointed for the sake of the esoteric hermeneutical interpretative mission (*li'l-da'wa al-ta'wīliyya*) – which is the second worship – so that their ranks can be discerned, it is compulsory (*lazima*) for it to get to know them and intelligise them. And when it comes to know them and intelligises them, [on the one hand,] its essence becomes multiple (*takaththarat*) by virtue of the multiplicity of the intelligibles (*ma'qūlāt*), and on the other hand, it becomes one (*tawaḥḥadat*) by virtue of its own essence. Thus, it thereby resembles what has preceded it into existence. And our book the *Repose of the Intellect* (*Rāḥat al-'aql*) contains sufficient legal evidence and religious practices to satisfy the most thorough researcher. May God make us among those who seek His satisfaction in what is pleasant and unpleasant, and may we follow His close friends (peace be upon them) in what they have explained about the truth by His grace.[2]

Analysis and interpretation: According to al-Kirmānī, the first intellect is endowed with an *ibdā'ī* nature – since his origination occurs through the divine act of *ibdā'* – and because of this, the multiplicity that can be attributed to him is different from the multiplicity pertaining to the rest of the intellects which are of an *inbi'āthī* nature. The multiplicity of the *ibdā'ī* intellect is two-fold and consists of (i) intellection of himself and (ii) awareness that his existence is external to him, coming from God. Conversely, the multiplicity of the *inbi'āthī* intellects is three-fold, consisting of (i) intellection of themselves, (ii) intellection of what precedes them in their hierarchical order, and (iii) intellection of the first emanated intellect (i.e. the *ibdā'ī* intellect) from which their existence comes. The first intellect, despite being brought into existence by God, owes his permanence in existence to his own nature as an intellect who thinks of himself and has full knowledge of his character.[3] This is not different from what al-Sijistānī claimed about the Intellect who, by being eternal,

---

2   Al-Kirmānī, *Riyāḍ* (HL), pp. 129–131.

3   De Smet argues that al-Kirmānī appeals to the Neoplatonic concept of self-constitution as the way in which the Intellect self-generates. In a first instance, he enters existence thanks to the Principle in a fashion which our minds cannot comprehend; in a second instance, once in existence, the Intellect 'becomes' the cause

not perishable and complete, has full awareness of his essence. Where al-Kirmānī's thought diverges from al-Sijistānī's is with regard to the Intellect's object of thinking; in the opening statement of *Faṣl* Nine al-Sijistānī's position recalls al-Nasafī's understanding – discussed elsewhere in the *Riyāḍ*[4] – that the Intellect, by intelligising himself and the forms of the two worlds which God instantiates at once within him, encompasses such forms thus being simultaneously *in actu* and *in potentia*.[5] Al-Kirmānī is starkly in contrast with this idea and accuses al-Nasafī of having overlooked the difference occurring between the contemplation of the intellects in the sensible world with the kind of contemplation carried out by the Intellect, and of having addressed the Intellect with actuality as well as potentiality, a characteristic pertaining solely to the inferior beings.[6] According to al-Kirmāni, given the activity of self-contemplation that accounts for the Intellect's permanence in existence, the Intellect does not need to intellegise about the other intellects as he realises that his existence is the result of his permanence. The state of affairs is different for all other intellects: their *inbi'athī* nature makes them dependent on the first Intellect because,

---

of himself and, through his perpetual thinking of himself, keeps his self-generation going. De Smet, 'Le *Kitāb rāḥat al-'aql* de Ḥamīd al-Dīn al-Kirmānī et la cosmologie ismaélienne à l'époque fatimide', *Acta Orientalia Belgica*, 7 (1992), p. 89. On the notion of Intellect's self-generation, see Christian Rutten, 'La doctrine des deux actes dans la philosophie de Plotin', *Revue philosophique de la France et de l'Étranger*, 146 (1956), pp. 100–106; Stephen Gersh, *From Iamblichus to Eriugena: An Investigation of the Prehistory and Evolution of the Pseudo-Dionysian Tradition* (Leiden, 1978), pp. 48–54.

4   Al-Kirmānī, *Riyāḍ* (Beirut, 1960), p. 220.

5   Al-Nasafī's view was already developed in the *Plotiniana Arabica* (*Theologia Aristotelis*, II, 32.10–33.9/§ 21–27, p. 67. Cited in De Smet, *La quiétude de l'intellect*, p. 185) where it is explained that the Intellect takes on the forms of the known object (*taṣawwur al-'aql bi-ṣūrat al-ma'lūm*), this implying that whilst intelligising his own essence, the Intellect is in actuality, and that whilst intelligising the forms encompassed within him, the Intellect becomes such forms with his essence remaining merely potential. See *Theologia Aristotelis*, II, 32. 14–15/§ 22, p. 67, cited in De Smet, ibid. On this topic, see also Cristina d'Ancona, 'The Textual Tradition of the Graeco-Arabic Plotinus. The *Theology of Aristotle*, its "*ru'ūs al-masā'il*", and the Greek Model of the Arabic Version', in *The Letter Before the Spirit: The Importance of Text Editions for the Study of the Reception of Aristotle*, ed. Aafke M. I. van Oppenraay et al. (Leiden and Boston, 2012), pp. 37–71 esp. pp. 59–68. I am grateful to Prof. Hermann Landolt for pointing out these references.

6   Al-Kirmānī, *Riyāḍ* (Beirut, 1960), pp. 220–221.

in order to remain in existence, they are compelled to intelligise what precedes them in the chain of existence.[7]

In contrast to al-Sijistānī, in *Faṣl* Nine of chapter eight, al-Kirmānī seems to refer in particular to the third intellect as the totality of forms. Given its peculiar kind of multiplicity, the Intellect is disconnected from the other intellects, whose multiplicity is essentially necessary, and, due to this 'separateness', he is not 'fit' to be the totality of all the forms. The *majmuʿ li'l-ṣuwar* is instead to be identified with the intellect whose completeness, as the result of a second procession, as al-Kirmānī states, is in need of perceiving all that precedes it in existence; as a 'fallen' intellect that has been close to our world due to its hylomorphic nature, the third intellect is suitable to be the compendium of the forms of the two worlds. Implicitly, al-Kirmānī seems to point out that just like the Intellect, the enunciator-prophet cannot be identified with the most encompassing form of intellectual knowledge. This is rather the *qā'im bi'l-quwwa*, as the final Resurrector, which, as depicted in Table 1, corresponds to the raised intellect.[8]

In *Faṣl* Nine there also emerge two important points: (i) There is an unequivocal reference to posteriority that is experienced by 'the thing that comes into existence at a posterior stage (*al-muta'akhkhir fi'l-wujūd*)'. This testifies that our author believes, on the one hand, in the atemporality of the intellectual Pleroma, thus embracing the classical Ismaili idea that the origination of the world occurs via divine *ibdāʿ* in one swoop (*dafʿat^{an} wāḥidat^{an}*), and on the other hand, heralding Ṭayyibī cosmology in a form of 'diluted temporality' in which the tenth intellect (which, outside of time, is the third intelligence in the hierarchy), holding its demiurgic responsibility towards our world, actualises its own ascent, thus reaching its rank as the second emanated being.[9] Implicitly, al-Kirmānī is buttressing the idea that the final *qā'im*, with his redeeming function, has not yet manifested and will return at a later stage in human history. (ii) The perfection of the third intellect is not due to its own essence but it is rather

---

[7]   Just as the Ismaili believers need to hone their intellectual capabilities by knowing and serving the Imam of the time.

[8]   See above, p. 100.

[9]   Ibn al-Walīd, *al-Risāla al-Mufīda*, ed. and tr. Madelung and Mayer, *Avicenna's Allegory on the Soul*, p. 86.

an acquisition (*iktisāb*), and this means that perfection is attained by the third intellect by way of knowledge and action (for this intellect, the two are merged since knowledge of the preceding intellects corresponds to the action of acknowledging their teachings). However, whilst in a state of completeness, this intellect is still in need of what precedes it in order to be preserved in existence. Such preceding entities are, in the above excerpt, identified with the dignitaries (*ḥudūd*) who are appointed to carry out the *ta'wīl* of the Scriptures. Their hermeneutical mission (*al-daw'a al-ta'wīliyya*) corresponds to the second form of worship, namely worship through action. This might mean that the advent of the last Resurrector does not occur in a void but is prepared by the preceding work of his preceding representatives.

Interestingly, in his *Risāla* on *tawḥīd*, al-Kirmānī explains that the Ismaili religious dignitaries attain their mission by way of interpreting the Scripture through *ta'wīl* – for this is the way by which they can guide the human souls towards their perfection, thereby fulfilling their tasks. This, it is stressed, corresponds to the second worship (*al-'ibāda al-thānī*).[10] It is clearly detectable that just as the third intellect attains and preserves its completeness in the world of origination by knowledge and action, so does the *qā'im* in the world of religion, via his dignitaries, whose mission is fulfilled through comprehension and esoteric interpretation of the religious texts.

In particular, for the third intellect it is vital to acknowledge and intelligise the spiritual *ḥudūd* because, by doing this, its essence, despite being multiple due to the multiplicity of its objects of intellection, becomes truly itself: one. Therefore, the third intellect exercises its *tawḥīd* by being aware of (i) its rank (as it is preceded by other beings) and (ii) its nature as being characterised by the necessary multiplicity (of which it becomes aware by contemplating the multiple objects of its intellection). Similarly, the future *qā'im* will be fully aware of all his previous *ḥudūd*, including the *bāb/ḥujja* who will herald his dawn. This is subtly inferred in the passage that declares that the Intellect's existence and his divinisation are external to his essence

---

10   The second worship is the worship of action, namely rendering the human soul 'human' by also making it a macrocosm. See al-Kirmānī, *Risālat al-tawḥīd*, pp. 187–188.

(*wa inna wujūdahu ʿammā tāllahu fīhi mimmā huwa khārij*[un] *ʿinnahu faqaṭ*).[11] Such a view suggests that whilst the first intellect divests himself of any divine claim, the other intellects' more blemished way of intelligising might confer on the Intellect some degree of *ulūhiyya*, according to their flawed level of understanding. The final Resurrector, however, will be of a different nature (i.e. a purely spiritual one) from all preceding enunciator-prophets.[12]

---

[11] Al-Kirmānī, *Riyāḍ* (HL), pp. 129–130.

[12] In the same way, the final *sharīʿa* will be of a completely different nature from all the previous religious legislations.

Faṣl Ten

The author of the *Iṣlāḥ* said: 'Anyone who states that *qaḍāʾ* signifies the Antecedent and that *qadar* signifies the Follower is mistaken; this is because he [such an individual] has found that the religious authorities (*ʿulamāʾ*) had already called the Follower by the name *qadar*. This is its true (*bi'l-ḥaqīqa*) name because all existents (*aysiyyāt*) have proceeded (*inbiʿathat*) from the Antecedent in a decreed way (*muqaddarat[an]*).[1] For that procession was the essence (*dhāt*) of *qadar*, which is why the sages called it *qadar*. He found that they would say the word *qaḍāʾ* before *qadar*, hence [the expression] *qaḍāʾ wa-qadar*. As they [the religious authorities] could not arrive at a clear meaning for *qaḍāʾ* and *qadar*, they put *qaḍāʾ* first and *qadar* second, and one finds a mistake from this perspective. As we [al-Rāzī] have already stated, all existents have proceeded from the Antecedent in a decreed way. That procession was the essence of the *qadar* which is the totality of existents.[2] A corroboration for this can be found in the words of God: 'Verily, We have created all things through the *qadar* (*innā kulla shayʾin khalaqnāhu bi-qadar*)' [Q 54:49]. Just as all existents – which are the essence of

---

[1]   Excerpt is from al-Rāzī, *Iṣlāḥ*, p. 47. Here it is specified that the religious authorities have conferred the names of the Antecedent and Follower to, respectively, the *qaḍāʾ* and the *qadar* in a true sense (*ʿalā al-ḥaqīqa*) rather than in a metaphorical way.

[2]   Ibid., p. 48. The passage in the *Iṣlāḥ* continues: 'all of them (*kullihā*) that are decreed in it from the First (*al-awwal*) in potentiality (*bi'l-quwwa*). The *qaḍāʾ* falls under the *qadar* (*taḥt al-qadar*) and it is embedded (*muḥāṭ*) [in] the *qadar*. For the *qadar* is everything (*al-kull*). And the First cannot be called *qadar* or *qaḍāʾ*. Rather it is the *amr* from which proceeds the *qadar* which is God's creation (*huwa khalq Allāh*) [which is] a decreed [thing] (*muqaddar*). The decreed thing and the *qadar* are one existing [thing] (*huwa ays wāḥid*). Similarly, the product of origination (*mubdaʿ*) and the act of origination (*ibdāʿ*) that is the *amr* are one existing [thing]'. In this context, al-Rāzī seems to accentuate the precedence of *amr* (as the First) over the *qadar* (as creation).

qadar – proceed from the First, which is the *amr* in potentiality, in a decreed way, so [they] manifest themselves from the Second in actuality (*bi'l-fiʿl*) in matter (*hayūlā*) and form (*ṣūra*), and that actuality is the essence (*dhāt*) of the *qaḍāʾ*. It is possible that in *qadar* [there might be] an alteration (*taghyīr*) and a substitution (*tabdīl*), and it is the Book as God Almighty said: 'God destroys and establishes as He wills' [Q. 13:39].[3] *Qadar* is the essence of the Follower, as we have already stated, and *qaḍāʾ* is its act (*fiʿluhu*) because the Follower is the one that is decreed (*muqaddar*) by the Antecedent.'[4]

The gist of what he [al-Rāzī] said in this chapter is that *qadar* is the name of the Follower because all existents are emanated from the Antecedent in a decreed way as God Almighty has said 'Verily, We have created all things through the *qadar*' (*innā kulla shayʾⁱⁿ khalaqnāhu bi-qadarⁱⁿ*) and that *qaḍāʾ* is its act.[5]

---

[3]　The text of the *Iṣlāḥ* contains some subtle variations: 'All existents (*aysiyyāt*) proceed from the First, which is the *amr*, in potentiality (*bi'l-quwwa*) and [are] decreed [things] (*muqaddarātⁿ*). They are the essence of the *qadar* (*dhāt al-qadar*). Similarly, they manifest themselves from the Second, in actuality (*bi'l-fiʿl*) in matter (*hayūlā*) and form (*ṣūra*), and that actuality is the essence of the *qaḍāʾ* (*dhāt al-qaḍāʾ*). So it is possible in the *qadar* to [find] alteration (*taghyīr*) and substitution (*tabdīl*)'. It is the Book that 'God obliterates and confirms as He wishes' [Q 13:39]. The end of the preceding verse (Q 13:38) reads: 'For each time there is a Book prescribed.' This is a clear reference to the idea that God has commanded that in each historical time humankind must be provided with a holy book of guidance. Implicitly, this also refers to the fact that each prophetic era is characterised by a different revealed book which, just as the changes which can be found in the *qadar*, is replaceable and changeable (cf. al-Rāzī, *Aʿlām al-nubuwwa*. tr. Khalidi, *The Proofs of Prophecy*, pp. 81–82, featuring a discussion on the abrogable nature of the external aspects of the religious laws in their aspect as 'parables'). Interestingly, as early as Abū ʿĪsā al-Murshid's treatise, it is clarified that what pertains to *qadar* is changeable and destined to perish. In particular, it is stated in the treatise that what is subtle is either rewarded (*mathāb*) or inflicted with punishment (*muʿāqaba*) and remains permanent (*bāqa*), just as the First from which it is issued is not transitory (*zāʾil*). The Follower instead changes (*yataghayyiru*) from one state to another (*min ḥāl ilā ḥāl*) and what belongs to its limit moves towards annihilation (*fanāʾ*), change (*taghyīr*) and extinction (*zawāl*). See Stern, 'The Earliest Cosmological Doctrines', Arabic text, p. 9, English text, pp. 23–24.

[4]　The *Iṣlāḥ* reads: 'This is the Follower, who is the *qadar* from the Antecedent (*huwa al-qadar min al-sābiq*) when estimation (*taqdīr*) [is applied] to it'. Al-Rāzī, *Iṣlāḥ*, pp. 47–48.

[5]　Al-Kirmānī, *Riyāḍ* (HL), p. 131.

Analysis and interpretation: For al-Rāzī, the learned men's use of the expression *al-qaḍāʾ waʾl-qadar* is unsubstantiated; because in the Qurʾan the two words are separated, despite conveying a generic sense of predestination, the sages of earlier times dealt with the expression *al-qaḍāʾ waʾl-qadar* sketchily, being unable, or perhaps unwilling, to offer a significant explanation of their respective nature and positions. In *Faṣl* Ten, al-Kirmānī again cites al-Rāzī's idea that all existents have proceeded from the Antecedent in a decreed way (*muqaddarat[an]*) and adds some further information: (i) Al-Rāzī explicitly identifies the essence of the *qadar* with what *was* (*kāna*) the procession of all *aysiyyāt* (*fa-kāna dhalika al-inbiʿāth dhāt al-qadar*). It is important to note that he employs the verb *kāna*, which is usually translated into English with the third-person singular simple past tense indicative of the verb 'to be'. This means that according to al-Rāzī, such procession *was* the essence of the *qadar* which is the totality of existents (*huwa majmūʿ al-aysiyyāt*). This, in a sense, designates not only the processive character that develops, but also indicates that, at the stage of procession, existents are not yet manifested in actuality.[6] This point is clarified when al-Rāzī also states that (ii) all existents, which proceed from the First (as the Intellect/Antecedent), which is the *amr* in potentiality, become manifested matter and form only through the Second in actuality, that is, the first Follower/Imam, whose action is identifiable with the *qaḍāʾ* (i.e. the Imams' hermeneutical mission, *taʾwīl*).

Basically, al-Rāzī's arguments lead to the identification of the *qadar* with the (first) Follower because, in conformity with the Qurʾanic verse quoted above – 'Verily, We have created all things through the *qadar*' – the *qadar*, just as the Second, which is the Imam in matter and form, acts as an instrument by which the command (*amr*) is carried out.[7] Therefore, the *qadar* is truly the name and the essence of the Follower because: (i) it *follows* God's *amr* (as the Imam follows the enunciator-prophet), and (ii) it is the one which (as the Follower) is determined by what precedes it (the Antecedent), just as the Imam

---

[6] This point has already been hinted at in *Faṣl* Nine of the *Riyāḍ*, where al-Kirmānī has identified the third intellect as '*al-mutaʾakhkhir fīʾl-wujūd*'.

[7] It is worth noting that the instrumentality of *qadar* is only indirectly intimated by al-Rāzī. It is al-Sijistānī who explicitly denounces it in the analysis that follows. See al-Kirmānī, *Riyāḍ* (HL), pp. 132–133.

is determined (namely, appointed) by the *nāṭiq* who precedes him. Again, this position is further validated when it is suggested that whilst the *qadar* is susceptible to alteration and substitution (referring to the fact that, being in a state of potentiality in his unmanifested level, the Imam *in absconditus* is 'replaceable' by his deputies), *qadar*'s act, which is the essence of *qaḍā'*, is, according to what previous speculations have shown, immutable and fixed. Just as the first Follower is decreed by the Antecedent, likewise the (second) Follower is decreed, namely made unchallengeable as a *ta'wīl* which is carried out by the Imam's representatives (i.e. the Imam's *ḥujja*s and *dā'ī*s such as al-Rāzī himself!).

> The author of the *Nuṣra* said: 'The evidence for what he [al-Rāzī] has stated about the *qaḍā'* and the *qadar* is from the words of God "Verily, We created all things by the *qadar*"; but he [al-Rāzī] was wrong in his *ta'wīl* of this verse for its *ta'wīl* is as we are about to explain and interpret. So we [al-Sijistānī] say: the meaning of "*innā*" [in the above verse] by which is intended "pure haecceity" (*al-inniyya al-maḥḍa*) is [what is] not adulterated (*lā yushūbuhā*) by any attribute (*ṣifa*) or non-attribute (*lā ṣifa*).[8] By "*kulla shay'in*" is intended the Intellect (*'aql*) that is all things; by "*khalaqnāhu*" is intended the forms of the two worlds between them; by "*bi-qadar*" is intended the Follower upon which the *amr* dwells (*istiqarra*), and the totality of forms (*jamī' al-ṣuwar*), both spiritual (*rūḥānī*) and corporeal (*jismānī*) between them [which] becomes manifest in the present world (*shāhid*). [Such totality] is [i.e. signifies] the Pen (*qalam*) and the Tablet (*lawḥ*), and the act of Writing down (*kitāba*) and the Writer (*kātib*). The *kātib* corresponds (*bi-izā'a*) to "*innā*" and it is the pure haecceity, the Pen corresponds to the Intellect who is the pen

---

8   Al-Sijistānī declares that the pure identity that is attributable to the Originator who is above 'Himself' (*huwa*) and 'not-Himself' (*lā huwa*) is simply the existentiality of the Antecedent (*aysiyyat al-sābiq*) whose existence (*mawjūd*) is given from the existentiality of the act of origination (*aysiyyat al-ibdā'*). More specifically, the Originator's identity stands for the Antecedent's awareness (*ma'rifa*), through its own existentiality (*bi-aysiyyatihi*), that its own identity (*huwiyya*) is that of a being that has been originated (*al-mubda'*). See al-Sijistānī, *Kitāb al-Yanābī'*, p. 71; tr. Walker, *The Wellsprings of Wisdom*, p. 49. This concept is parallel to al-Kirmānī's understanding of *tawḥīd* as the Intellect's action of divesting himself and the rest of creation of any claim of self-origination and divinity.

of pens, "*khalaqnāhu*" corresponds to the letters which appear on the Tablet, and "*bi-qadar*" corresponds to the Tablet which is the recipient (*qābil*) of the totality of the forms of the letters. In the same way as the totality of all the corporeal and spiritual things, simple and complex, fall under these morphemes (*al-ḥurūf al-manṭiqiyya*), which appear from the Writer through the Pen upon the Tablet, the totality of higher and the lower forms is manifested by God Almighty through the intermediary of the Intellect and the Soul. And nothing escapes them, and nothing escapes from the graphemes (*al-ḥurūf al-murattaba*) that appear from the Writer through the Pen upon the Tablet.' This is what has been said by the author of the *Nuṣra* in the counter-argument (*naqḍ*).[9]

Analysis and interpretation: Firstly, al-Sijistānī provides an elucidation for al-Rāzī's identification of the *qadar* with the Follower as the one who *follows* [i.e. comes after] the divine *amr*. In the above passage, al-Sijistānī stresses that '*bi-qadar*' means 'through the Follower' upon which the command dwells (*istiqarra*), as this is exactly what his fellow *dāʿī* al-Rāzī had inferred.

Secondly, al-Sijistānī concludes that hidden in the forms of the letters there is a deeper meaning; these letters in their totality mirror the forms (corporeal/spiritual, simple/complex) that – encompassed in the first intellect – manifest all things through the intermediacy of the Intellect and the Soul. Nothing escapes from them – an allusion to God's knowledge of particulars, examined in the first section of this volume – in the same way no letter escapes from the act of the Writer (God) when He writes upon the Tablet by means of the Pen. The *qadar* corresponds to the Tablet and, presumably, the *qaḍā'* should be identified with the Pen used by the *kātib*. From this it can be deduced that, according to al-Sijistānī, the *qadar* (i) as the Follower, receives the forms coming from the Antecedent and that, (ii) as the Tablet, it is the

---

[9]   Al-Kirmānī, *Riyāḍ* (HL), pp. 132–133. The mention of both morphemes and graphemes is not accidental. Al-Sijistānī assigns special significance to the correspondence between letters, their numerical value, spiritual entities and earthly elements. See particularly his *Kitāb al-Yanābīʿ*, pp. 62–75; tr. Walker, *The Wellsprings of Wisdom*, pp. 45–53.

recipient (*qābil*) of all the forms of the letters written by the *kātib* upon it, and it is the recipient of God's *amr*.[10]

Al-Kirmānī goes on to clarify that the arguments used both by al-Sijistānī and al-Rāzī are not sufficient to validate their discourses:

> We [al-Kirmānī] say: what [has been quoted by] the two other authors in this chapter is untenable, both in [al-Rāzī's] correction (*iṣlāḥ*) and in [al-Sijistānī's] counterargument (*naqd*). And this is because the author of the *Iṣlāḥ* makes the *qadar* to be necessarily the name of the Follower, offering as proof the words of God 'Verily, We created all things by the *qadar*.' However, what emerges from his own discourse on *al-qaḍā' wa'l-qadar* is that it is not possible to call *qadar* the Follower.
>
> The author of the *Nuṣra* contradicted what is said by the author of the *Iṣlāḥ* in his interpretation of the verse, and that [argument] is off balance and inapplicable to the issue (*lā bi-muṭābiq li'l-amr*). This is because he [al-Sijistānī] said in his interpretation: '[In] the word of God Almighty by "*innā*" is intended the "pure haecceity" (*al-inniyya al-maḥḍa*) which is not adulterated (*lā yushūbuhā*) by any attribute (*ṣifa*) or non-attribute (*lā ṣifa*).'
>
> [Al-Kirmānī's argument]: the expression '*innā*' signifies *al-jadd* [and] from its authority the Prophet (peace be upon him and his family) and the Imams of his offspring (peace be upon them) emerge. It is communication (*ikhbār*) about oneself ('*an nafsihi*) and the meaning in it returns to the Prophet (peace upon him and his family) through taking his place in the world; [it is] not 'haecceity'. How could *innā* have been understood to signify pure haecceity when between this [pure haecceity] and that [all things] there are intermediaries (*wasā'iṭ*)? Certainly not! For it signifies the closest intermediary (*al-wāsiṭa al-qarība*) to the Prophet (peace be upon him and his family), in pouring forth (*ifāḍa*) him, i.e. the Prophet, for he is the one who carries out (*al-mu'addī*) [his task, i.e. as the enunciator-prophet] through it.[11]

10　It should be noted that in this context al-Sijistānī is merely saying that *qadar* is the Follower only with respect to the *amr*, but nothing is said of its rank with respect to the *qaḍā'*.

11　Al-Kirmānī, *Riyāḍ* (HL), pp. 133–134.

Analysis and interpretation: Al-Kirmānī identifies the inaccuracies of his predecessors: firstly, al-Rāzī's 'correction' identifies the *qadar* with the essence of the Follower but, in truth, the proof that he adduces for his statement (the Qur'anic verse 'Verily, We have created all things through the *qadar*') and previous discussions on the issue have made it clear that it is implausible to call *qadar* the Follower-*qua*-Follower. Secondly, contrary to al-Sijistānī's interpretation of *innā* as a reference to the ultimate divine identity which is unsullied by any attribute or lack of non-attributes, al-Kirmānī signifies this as *al-jadd*.

In order to comprehend what al-Kirmānī is referring to when he mentions this term, it might be helpful to observe firstly what al-Rāzī and al-Sijistānī understand of this entity. Like his Ismaili peers, al-Rāzī differentiates between the spiritual ranks (*al-ḥudūd al-rūḥāniyya*) and their corporeal counterparts (*al-ḥudūd al-jismāniyya*). To the first group belong what corresponds to the Neoplatonic Universal Intellect, the Universal Soul together with the three spiritual faculties of *al-jadd*, *al-fatḥ* and *al-khayāl*, which are bestowed upon the divinely inspired leaders. These are respectively linked to three archangels, Gabriel, Michael and Serafiel.[12] These entities are named by al-Rāzī in the *Iṣlāḥ* in his interpretation of the Prophet's night journey, where he attempts to explain the relationship between the Prophet and the celestial ranks.

---

[12] The early mention of these three entities seems to have occurred in the no longer extant *Sīrat al-Nāṣir li-Dīn Allāh Aḥmad ibn al-Hādī* by ʿAbd Allāh b. ʿUmar al-Hamdānī which survives in extracts in Abū al-Jamr Musallam b. Muḥmmad b. al-Jaʿfar al-Laḥijī's *Kitāb Akhbār al-Zaydiyya biʾl-Yaman*. On the meaning of these names, see al-Sijistānī's chapter on *al-jadd, al-fatḥ* and *al-khayāl* in his *Kitāb al-Iftikhār*, pp. 116–122; *idem*, 'Risālat Tuḥfat al-mustajībīn', pp. 145–155; see also the description of the spiritual ranks in Jaʿfar b. Manṣūr al-Yaman, *Sarāʾir wa-asrār al-nuṭaqāʾ*, ed. Muṣṭafā Ghālib (Beirut, 1984), pp. 18–26; Corbin, *Étude préliminaire*, pp. 91–112; Halm, *Kosmologie*, p. 72; Nomoto, *Early Ismāʿīlī Thought on Prophecy*, p. 187; Daniel De Smet, 'La function noétique de la triade *al-jadd, al-fatḥ* et *al-khayāl*. Les fondements de la connaissance prophétique dans l'ismaélisme', in *Differenz und Dynamik im Islam/Difference and Dynamism in Islam: Festschrift für Heinz Halm zum 70 Geburtstag/Festschrift for Hanz Halm on his 70th Birthday*, ed. Hinrich Biesterfeldt and Verena Klemm (Würzburg, 2012), pp. 319–336; Antonella Straface, 'The Representation of *al-Jadd, al-Fatḥ* and *al-Khayāl* in the Ismaili Literature: Some Examples and Further Remarks', in *L'ésotérisme shi'ite/Shi'i Esotericism*, ed. Amir-Moezzi et al. pp. 423–440.

Significantly, al-Rāzī states that the ascent of a prophet to the rank of enunciation (*martabat al-nuṭq*) is not suddenly granted but it is, rather, acquired through a process.[13] This is explained as a change in the status of the prophet, which undergoes an elevation (i.e. an earthly resurrection?) from his conjunction with the Follower to his conjunction with the Antecedent. Al-Rāzī claims that any enunciator-prophet-to-be comes into conjunction with *al-jadd* (Fortune-Majesty) of the Antecedent through *al-khayāl* (Vision-Imagination) of the Follower, until he rises up to the rank (*ḥadd*) of enunciation.[14] This explanation remains quite obscure and al-Rāzī himself endeavours to expound it by commenting on Q 17:1: 'Glory to (God) Who did take His Servant for a journey by night from the Sacred Mosque to the Furthest Mosque.'[15] With reference to the Prophet's journey, al-Rāzī offers an elucidation of the nature of *al-jadd* and states: 'He [the Prophet] rides al-Burāq from the Sacred Mosque to the Furthest Mosque, and this means that he has entered into conjunction with *al-jadd* and, due to the light that *al-jadd* springs upon him (*mā baraqa lahu*), [he has entered into conjunction] with *al-khayāl* of the Follower. Moreover, he has performed the *mi'rāj* and he is elevated to Heaven, which means that *al-jadd* makes him enter into conjunction with the Antecedent, as was established in the dignity of the enunciation.'[16] Al-Rāzī identifies al-Burāq (the steed ridden by the Prophet) with *al-jadd*, thus highlighting the abridging function which the latter

---

[13] The idea of the gradual development of the prophetic faculty in relation to the encounter with angelic beings is discussed also by al-Qāḍī al-Nu'mān in his *Kitāb Asās al-ta'wīl*, ed. 'Ārif Tāmir (Beirut, 1960), pp. 190–192. Just as for other prophets, so Muḥammad's prophetic ascent implies that his soul is being purified by being in contact with the higher souls (*al-arwāḥ al-'ulwiyya*) (ibid., pp. 108–109). Particularly significant is that, as in the case of Abraham's reception of revelation, the transmission of divine *ta'yīd* is believed to occur through the members of the religious realm which, according to al-Qāḍī al-Nu'mān, include – as for al-Sijistānī – the higher celestial as well as the lower, earthly ranks. Ibid., pp. 109–113, 338–339.

[14] Al-Rāzī, *Iṣlāḥ*, p. 120.

[15] On the interpretations of Muḥammad's night journey and the *mi'rāj*, see Amir-Moezzi, ed., *Le voyage initiatique en Terre d'Islam*.

[16] Al-Rāzī, *Iṣlāḥ*, p. 120 cited in De Smet, 'La function noétique de la triade', pp. 330–331 (my translation from the French).

exercises for the Prophet.[17] More specifically, he indicates that *al-jadd* allows the Prophet to enter into conjunction with both the Follower and the Antecedent, thus realising a spiritual awakening.

In another passage from the *Iṣlāḥ*, Abū Ḥātim emphasises that the rank of *al-jadd* is 'limited' in relation to the two Roots (*aṣlān*). Al-Rāzī underlines that once Abraham attained the rank of the enunciator-prophet, he became informed about significant issues such as the degree of *al-jadd* as well as the level occupied by the latter and by the Soul, 'whose limit is given by the Antecedent and by the Antecedent whose limit is given by the Word'.[18] This stress on 'limits' is proffered in order to underscore that no enunciator-prophet is admitted to communicate directly with the divinity. Clearly, al-Rāzī's concern is to keep God at a safe distance from the earthly domain whilst also ensuring the pre-eminence of prophecy.[19] However, hidden beneath this stance is probably also the rejection that the cycle of Muḥammad was to coincide with the cycle of the last *qāʾim*, during which believers are meant to receive benefits directly from all the five spiritual *ḥudūd*.[20]

These ideas are reiterated in another section of the *Iṣlāḥ*, where al-Rāzī recounts the dialogue between God and Moses on Mount Sinai (Q 7:143).[21] The Qurʾanic story, according to al-Rāzī, refers to the fact

---

[17] On further interpretations of the Prophet's *isrāʾ*/*miʿrāj*, see B. Schirieke et al., 'Miʿrādj', *EI2*, vol. 7, pp. 97–105; Gerard Böwering, 'Miʿrāj', *The Encyclopedia of Religion* (New York, 1987), vol. 9, pp. 552–556; Amir-Moezzi, ed., *Le Voyage initiatique en terre dʾ Islam* and references given therein.

[18] Al-Rāzī, *Iṣlāḥ*, pp. 184–185, cited in De Smet, 'La function noétique de la triade', p. 331.

[19] In the *Iṣlāḥ*, al-Rāzī propounds that prophecy comes from the Antecedent; from it emanate the providential bestowals (*mawādd*) via *al-Jārī* (the one who flows) to *al-jadd*. From the latter, the *nāṭiq* receives the *mawādd*, thus becoming a *muʾayyad*. If, on the one hand, this hierarchy of hypostases maintaines God's transcendence, on the other hand, it also links Him to the Prophet. See al-Rāzī, *Iṣlāḥ*, pp. 120–121; Nomoto, *Early Ismāʿīlī Thought on Prophecy*, p. 223; Hollenberg, *Beyond the Qurʾān*, p. 80.

[20] Shafique N. Virani, 'The Days of Creation in the Thought of Nasir-i Khusraw', in *Nasir Khusraw: Yesterday, Today, Tomorrow*, ed. Sarfaroz Niyozov and Ramazon Nazariev (Khujand, 2004), p. 80.

[21] Al-Rāzī, *Iṣlāḥ*, pp. 185–186.

that Moses, who is admitted to the vision of *al-jadd* (which al-Rāzī identifies with the Mount), still yearns to attain a direct visualisation of one of the highier dignitaries (i.e. the Follower or the Antecedent) and is struck down. The story teaches of the impossibility for even a *nāṭiq*-to-be to go beyond his assigned limit, that is, the highest cognitive degree that is given to him by *al-jadd*.[22]

The exact nature of *al-fatḥ* and *al-khayāl* are not clearly identified by al-Rāzī; to the best of my knowledge, *al-fatḥ* is not even mentioned in his works, whilst references to *al-khayāl* are made to suggest that a *nāṭiq*, having reached the status of the enunciator-prophet, is a spiritually supported being (*muʾayyad*) thanks to what is granted to him from the two Roots (*aṣlān*) through both *al-jadd* and *al-khayāl*.[23] Significantly, *al-jadd* and *al-khayāl* are also mentioned with reference to other members of the corporeal dignitaries (*al-ḥudūd al-jismāniyya*) other than the *nāṭiq*. Among the *muʾayyadūn* or 'the spiritually supported ones', one finds the *asās* (foundation) or *waṣī* (executor), who is responsible for the esoteric teaching of religion, and the Imam or *mutimm* (completer) who is in charge of maintaining peace and order after the first two figures have passed away.[24] Thus, al-Rāzī appears to maintain that all five earthly *ḥudūd* are the recipients of *taʾyīd*. This idea was to be shared by Nāṣir-i Khusraw for whom *nāṭiq*, *asās*, Imam, *bāb* and *ḥujja* were all recipients of spiritual inspiration. The latter, however, is denied to all minor ranks, that is, the *dāʿī*, the greater and lesser *maʾdhūns* (the licentiates) and the *mustajibs* (the initiates), who are merely recipents of *taʾwīl*.[25]

Al-Rāzī declares that the instruction (*tarbiyya*) of all the enunciator-prophets and those who are subordinate to them, such as the foundations and the completers, proceeds from the Antecedent and the Follower through the mediation of *al-jadd* – concerning what proceeds by the Antecedent, and through the mediation of *al-khayāl* – concerning what proceeds by the Follower.[26]

---

[22]   On this topic see more infra, pp. 229–230 (esp. note 3 at page 229), 232.

[23]   Al-Rāzī, *Iṣlāḥ*, p. 185.

[24]   Nomoto, *Early Ismāʿīlī Thought on Prophecy*, pp. 186–188.

[25]   Virani, 'The Days of Creation in the Thought of Nasir-i Khusraw', in *Nasir Khusraw*, ed. Niyozov and Nazariev, pp. 76–77, and references given in note 23, p. 82.

[26]   Al-Rāzī, *Iṣlāḥ*, pp. 185–186.

Further information about the nature and role of these faculties is provided by al-Sijistānī. Like his fellow *dāʿī*, referring to the ten dignitaries of the world of normative order (*ʿālam al-waḍʿ*), al-Sijistānī distinguishes between five spiritual and five corporeal *ḥudūd*: the five spiritual dignitaries are the two Roots followed by *al-jadd*, *al-fatḥ* and *al-khayāl*. As already mentioned, the corporeal dignitaries are identified with the enunciator-prophet, the foundation, the completer (*mutimm*), the lieutenant (*lāḥiq*) and the wing.[27] However, in contrast to al-Rāzī, it seems that for al-Sijistānī the spiritual *ḥudūd* of *al-jadd*, *al-fatḥ* and *al-khayāl* function as causes (*asbāb*) meant to 'perfect' exclusively the rank of the enunciator-prophet since, he states, it is through these causes that the *nāṭiq* apprehends the treasures of the celestial sciences (*khazāʾin al-ʿulūm al-malakūtiyya*).[28] In addition, al-Sijistānī provides a more detailed picture of *al-jadd* and its role:

It is fortune (*bakht*) … it makes the pure soul (*al-nafs al-zakiyya*) become a lord (*rabb*) of the people of his age … it is his vehicle (*markab*) into the divine realm (*malakūt*) … it helps him in the redaction of his revelation (*taʾlīf tanzīlihi*) as a clear instruction of spoken and written words (*talqīnan mubāyinan ʿan al-aṣwāt waʾl-ḥurūf*).[29]

In the above excerpt, one can note that *al-jadd* is said to act on the 'pure soul' (*al-nafs al-zakiyya*); the appellative of *al-nafs al-zakiyya* was attributed to Muḥammad b. ʿAbd Allāh (d. 145/762–763), the ʿAlid rebel who during Jaʿfar al-Ṣādiq's imamate, together with his full brother Ibrāhīm, led the revolt against the ʿAbbāsid caliph al-Manṣūr

---

[27] Al-Sijistānī, *Kitāb al-Maqālīd*, iqlīd 27.

[28] Al-Sijistānī, *Kitāb Ithbāt al-nubuwwāt*, p. 128, cited in De Smet, 'La function noétique de la triade', p. 330.

[29] Al-Sijistānī, *Kitāb al-Iftikhār*, pp. 117–118. The translation, slightly modified, is from Nomoto, *Early Ismāʿīlī Thought on Prophecy*, p. 221. In similar parlance, in his *Risālat Tuḥfat al-mustajībīn*, al-Sijistānī describes *al-jadd* as 'Fortune (*bakht*), a noble power (*quwwa sharīfa*) whose closeness (*mujāwara*) to the one who possesses it makes him feel affection (*maḥabba*) for the spiritual world, see it with his own eyes and talk about it'. Translation is from Straface, 'The Representation of *al-Jadd*, *al-Fatḥ* and *al-Khayāl* in the Ismaili Literature', in *L'ésotérisme shiʿite/Shiʿi Esotericism*, ed. Amir-Moezzi et al., p. 437. It is significant that *al-jadd* is here acknowledged as a power that enables whoever owns it to see the spiritual world with his/her own eyes, this being exactly what Moses requests in Q 7:143.

at Medina in 145/762–763. His father, the *shaykh* of the Ḥusaynids, ʿAbd Allāh (d. 149/766) had designated him, since his birth, for the role of the awaited Mahdī, a belief likely encouraged by a tradition circulating in Shiʿi milieux wherein the final Resurrector would arise from the *ahl al-bayt*, bearing the same name as the Prophet himself.[30] Probably following such beliefs, in the *Kitāb al-Iftikhār* al-Sijistānī mentions the figure of *al-nafs al-zakiyya* in relation to the Messianic task of the last Resurrector. In particular, the pure soul is placed in a different category from the rest of creation, as he is considered pivotal in the process of retribution.[31] In the same work, after having explained the nature of the *qiyāma* as a purely spiritual state,[32] al-Sijistānī states that the *qiyāma* is realised 'from the manifestation of a pure soul (*nafs zakiyya*) within whom come to light (*yatajallā*) the traces (*āthār*) of the luminous world which bestows upon him the power to reward souls.'[33] Similarly, in *al-Risāla al-Bāhira*, the *nafs zakiyya* – here identified with the cosmic figure of the Form of Man (*ṣūrat al-insāniyya*) (i.e. the soul-*qua*-soul) – is mainly linked to the concept of resurrection, due to the *nafs zakiyya*'s ability to understand fully the notion of retribution.[34]

From these portrayals it can be deduced that, according to al-Sijistānī, if on the one hand, the pure soul can be identified with the final Resurrector with whose manifestation the cycle of the Resurrection begins, on the other hand, he might also signify the soul of any individual within whom the *qiyāma* is realised and the significance of reward is fully grasped. It is according to the last perspective that *al-jadd* is made accountable for allowing a pure soul, such as that of the enunciator-prophet, to become the lord of the people of his age. This temporal reference is significant when it is linked with both the Prophet's night journey – epitomising Muḥammad's reaching the ultimate

---

[30] Daftary, *The Ismāʿīlīs*, pp. 71–75; Moojan Momen, *An Introduction to Shiʿi Islam: The History and Doctrines of Twelver Shiʿism* (New Haven and London, 1985), pp. 50–52.

[31] Al-Sijistānī, *Kitāb al-Iftikhār*, p. 186.

[32] Ibid., pp. 182–184.

[33] Ibid., p. 186. See also reference in De Smet, 'La transmigration des âmes', p. 98.

[34] Hirji, 'A Study of *al-Risālah al-bāhirah*', pp. 86–87, 182–198.

stage of intellectual awakening[35] – and with the *nāṭiq*'s task of compiling a revelation which, according to al-Sijistānī's doctrine, is destined to become redundant with the advent of the ultimate Resurrector.

Conversely, it could be claimed that for al-Rāzī the potential meaning of the revelation, which is hidden in the exoteric aspect of the scripture – the above-mentioned 'speech and written words' to which

---

[35] Overall, in the above passage surfaces the idea, already expressed by al-Rāzī, that *al-jadd* acts as an instrument leading the soul of the enunciator-prophet towards the celestial dominion. The same concept is advanced in the *Risālat al-mawāzin*, attributed to al-Sijistānī. This work proposes once again the common identity of *al-jadd* and *al-burāq*; moreover, in this text it is expressely stated that *al-jadd* functions 'as a mount (*markūb*) for our enunciator-prophet in his cycle'. As such, it operates as an 'vehicular' instrument which 'carries' the enunciator-prophet through various degrees of knowledge until he is capable of writing down his law (*sharīʿatahu*), reciting (*qaraʾa*) his revelation (*tanzīlahu*), establishing his foundation and having the possibility of designating an intermediary capable of producing an exegesis (*taʾwīl*) of his *sharīʿa*. In addition, one finds also more detailed descriptions of the nature of *al-fatḥ* and *al-khayāl*. The former is identified with a holy power (*quwwa qudsiyya*) which belongs to the foundation of each enunciator-prophet. *Al-khayāl* is a power that returns to the completers within the cycles of the enunciators through *al-jadd* and *al-fatḥ* (see the whole passage in Arabic in *Kitāb al-Iftikhār*, ed. Poonawala, pp. 328–329; the French translation can be found in De Smet, 'La function noétique de la triade', p. 332).

Straface has highlighted that, again in *Risālat al-mawāzin*, the three spiritual faculties' influence on the religious dignitaries is explained through the symbolism of numbers and letters: 'And the word *jadd* (is composed) of two letters [j d] since the cause of this power is the two principles [*aṣlān*, i.e. *kūnī-qadar*] and according to the *ḥisāb al-jummal* it corresponds to number seven [j=4 and d=3] and this means that *al-jadd* transmits (*muwaṣṣil*) to the [enunciator-prophets], their "Provisions" (*ḥuẓūẓ*) from the seven sublime letters [i.e. k w n y q d r]. And *al-fatḥ* is a holy power, belonging to the fundament of every [enunciator-prophet] calling for *al-jadd* that will bring after it [*viz. al-jadd*] what was inspired in himself [*viz.* the fundament] of it [*viz.* power]. And the (word) *fatḥ* is formed by three letters [f t ḥ] so as to provide evidence that *al-fatḥ* was generated by the two principles and *al-jadd* that is above it. And *al-khayāl* is a power that acts towards those who complete the cycles, as it it is part of the aforementioned two powers, namely, *al-jadd* and *al-fatḥ*, likewise the imamate is the authority generated from the two fundaments [i.e. *nāṭiq* and *asās*].' See Straface, 'The Representation of *al-Jadd*, *al-Fatḥ* and *al-Khayāl* in the Ismaili Literature', in *L'ésotérisme shiʿite/Shiʿi Esotericism*, ed. Amir-Moezzi et al., pp. 438–439 (English translation slightly modified.)

al-Sijistānī also refers and which are uttered by the enunciator-prophet through *al-jadd* – reaches its ultimate completeness through the *ta'wīl* of the *asās/waṣī* who is endowed with the faculties of *al-fatḥ* and *al-khayāl*.

Let us move onto the references in the tenth *faṣl* of the *Riyāḍ*: al-Kirmānī openly criticises al-Sijistānī's suggestion that *innā* signifies the pure haecceity (*al-inniyya al-maḥḍa*) which is unblemished by any attribute or any non-attribute. In al-Kirmānī's view, however, the expression *innā* indicates *al-jadd*, whose power allows the evolution of the prophet-to-be into a *nāṭiq* who is thus enabled to fulfill his decreed mission in this world. When our author states, with reference to *al-jadd*, '*huwa ikhbār 'an nafsihi*', he identifies '*ikhbār*' with that specific form of communication that is the prophetic message, effused from the Antecedent and conveyed through the Prophet's soul.[36] Al-Kirmānī seems also to be referring to the idea expressed by al-Rāzī according to which *al-jadd* represents a liminal gnoseological entity, as any direct approach to the Intellect and the Soul remains hindered.

---

[36] Cf. Al-Qāḍī al-Nuʿmān's understanding of *waḥy* as an intimate conversation (*mushāfaha*) of the lower souls with the superior souls. See Feki, *Les idées religieuses*, p. 230.

Faṣl Eleven

And when He says: '*kulla shay'in*', he [al-Sijistānī] means the Intellect which is all things. But in this context '*kulla shay'in*' is not the Intellect. We [al-Kirmānī] have already explained that the multiplicity of the first intellect is not like the multiplicity of that whose existence is by his [the first intellect's] existence. Rather, '*kulla shay'in*' is what the community needs in terms of the two [forms] of worship (*'ibādatayn*) which encompass all the sciences (*'ulūm*), exoterically by action (*bi'l-'amal*) and esoterically by conceptualisation (*bi'l-taṣawwur*), and which is what leads to salvation from punishment (*'adhāb*) by the Lord of the two worlds.[1]

Analysis and interpretation: According to al-Kirmānī, al-Sijistānī is also incorrect when he comes to state that *kulla shay'in*, from the same Qur'anic verse 54:49 cited in *Faṣl* Ten, signifies the Intellect. This is because, as already explained, the Intellect's multiplicity is of a different kind and cannot be correlated to the multiplicity of the corporeal world. Rather, the expression *kulla shay'in* signifies the two forms of worship, namely knowledge (here, expressed as conceptualisation) and action, which the community needs in order to attain salvation in the hereafter.

Interestingly, al-Kirmānī specifies that potential punishment for those who do not commit to the double form of worship is carried out by the *rabb al-'ālamayn*. At this stage, one might be led to think that this lord is the Qur'anic God. However, by probing deeper into the analysis of the *Riyāḍ*, such identification is no longer convincing. I have had occasion to note, and it will also be shown in the following passages, that throughout chapter eight various 'lords' are mentioned. So for instance, in *Faṣl* Sixteen, the *tafsīr* of the term *rabb* from

---

[1] Al-Kirmānī, *Riyāḍ* (HL), p. 134.

Q 3:191, 'Our Lord, You did not create this aimlessly', seems possibly to refer to the Intellect rather than God. Pointing towards this idea is al-Kirmānī himself, who clarifies that the object of the phrase, 'this', is a plain reference to creation rather than to the first originated being. Implicitly, the subject of the same phrase, 'you' is probably the first *'aql*. Indeed, just a few lines above, in the same *faṣl*, al-Kirmānī stresses that divine creation is carried out by the superior beings. Similarly, in *Faṣl* Twenty, Moses' 'lord', quoted from Q 7:143, is identified with the Follower that instructs Moses on the need to abide in his appointed status before attaining the degree of a *nāṭiq*. From these examples, it can be deduced that a hierarchical system of *rubūbiyya* is in place: the enunciator-prophet Muḥammad identifies his *lord* in the Antecedent, namely the Intellect, who is also the *qadar* as the Prophet himself seems to have explained and whose quote is reported in *Faṣl* Sixteen, *bāb* eight of the *Riyāḍ*: 'I return to what [the Antecedent] has given to me through *al-jadd* as a whole, towards the *qadar*.' Moses, on the other hand, not yet a *nāṭiq* at the time of the Mount Sinai episode, mistakenly thinks he can attain a direct vision of his lord which, in truth, is nothing but a lower dignitary in accordance with the foregoing explanantion.[2] In a sense, just as the Intellect – by his abnegation, that is, his denying divinity for himself – 'becomes the Veil, the horizon or limit (*ḥadd*) by which the Divine shines through and appears to the following Intelligence' – so that each intellect ascribes the Divine to the next *ḥadd* which precedes it and which is the Veil through which the Divine appears to it[3] – likewise, each terrestrial *ḥadd* identifies its lord in conformity with its own intellectual/gnoseological limits, which are decreed for it by its proximate bestower of spiritual benefits.

---

[2]   Cf. the story of Abraham's discovery and ascent towards monotheism as recounted in Qur'an 6: 75–79. On the interpretation of such an episode, see Hermann Landolt, 'Ghazālī und *Religionswissenschaft*', *Asiatische Studien*, 45, 1 (1991), pp. 31ff.

[3]   Corbin, *Cyclical Time and Ismaili Gnosis*, p. 177.

<h1 align="center">Faṣl Twelve</h1>

And when He says: '*khalaqnāhu*', He does not mean what was attributed to it [by al-Sijistānī] because '*khalaqnāhu*' means 'we have decreed it (*qadarnāhu*)',[1] namely, 'we have made it (*jaʿalnāhu*)' in the shape (*ṣīgha*) of the *tanzīl* and the *sharīʿa*, a fashioning/shape [which has] in its potentiality all things from the sciences (*ʿulūm*) and the religious actions (*al-aʿmāl al-dīniyya*) which the community (*umma*) needs in order to set aside the travails of the soul in this world and the hereafter.

It is as if he [the Prophet], peace be upon him and his family, had said about God's words, 'Verily, we have created everything' from the command of the two [forms] of worship, as knowledge (*ʿilm^{an}*) and action (*ʿamal^{an}*), which the community needs in both its religious [aspect] and in its earthly [dimension], which we have decreed (*qadarnāhu*) according to what we have brought in the *tanzīl* and the *sharīʿa* in a measured way (*taqdīr^{an}*); that is, '*jaʿalnāhu*', we have made it in its potentiality (*quwwatihā*) so that it may emerge through *taʾwīl* to a deserving individual (*mustaḥiqq*).[2]

Analysis and interpretation: Again, al-Kirmānī is not satisfied with al-Sijistānī's interpretation. There are at least two points that need to be highlighted: Firstly, al-Kirmānī makes it clear that the expression *khalaqnāhu* in this context is to be used as a synonym for *qadarnāhu*, meaning that God has decreed 'it' (i.e. the 'everything/knowledge+action' cited in the Qurʾanic verse used by al-Rāzī), and He has made it (with reference to 'We have made it', *jaʿalnāhu*) in the fashioning/shape of the wording of the revelation and the *sharīʿa*. This is a significant

---

[1]   In this context, 'it' is a reference to 'everything' namely, the entified '*amr*/Intellect' through which God carries out His creation.

[2]   Al-Kirmānī, *Riyāḍ* (HL), p. 134.

199

statement as al-Kirmānī confidently reveals thereby that creation itself has been produced in the shape (*ṣīgha*) of the revelation and the law.[3] The latter are not simply part of creation but, rather, they signify creation itself and contain potentially in themselves all forms of knowledge and actions necessary for individual souls to avoid grief and unhappiness in this world and the next.

Al-Kirmānī further claims that the Prophet would have said that God's words, 'Verily, We have created everything', are a reference to a creation that takes place *through* the *amr*/Intellect, namely an imposition that makes mandatory the two forms of worship (knowledge and action), which the community needs for its own welfare in this as well as the other world, and which have been decreed according to 'measured' *tanzīl* and *sharīʿa*. This means that the two forms of worship are *commandments* to which obedience is required as these have been decreed in the light of what is contained in the revelation and the *sharīʿa*. God, in fact, has made the actual revelation and the law (including due obedience to the two forms of worship) also as a potential revelation and a potential law whose true actualisation occurs through their esoteric hermeneutical interpretation carried out by a *mustaḥiqq*. Underpinning these comments is al-Kirmānī's belief in (i) human freedom (i.e. the choice between obedience and disobedience), (ii) the necessity of the imamate (and all the ranks of its hierarchy) in general, and (iii) the necessity of *taʾwīl* in particular.[4]

---

[3]   Perhaps the choice of this word (*ṣīgha*) is not accidental, as it might be an allusion to al-Sijistānī's idea of the mental form of the cloth and its embedded potential character, which has been discussed in *Faṣl* One.

[4]   Cf. al-Kirmānī, *al-Maṣābīḥ fī ithbāt al-imāma*, Arabic text, pp. 28–32, English text, pp. 63–67.

Faṣl Thirteen

The author of the *Iṣlāḥ* said 'that the *qaḍā'* is the act (*fiʿl*) of the Follower', and this is correct (*aṣāb*) from the perspective that what proceeds into actuality within the world of Nature comes through its [the Follower's] influx (*bi-fayḍihi*), and through this it becomes complete and, from the same perpective, it attains perfection (*tamāmiyya*). Hence, the *qaḍā'* signifies the *nāṭiq* by dint of having exited [from potentiality] into actuality and of having attained completeness (*kamāl*) through its [the Follower's] influx and its spiritual assistance (*taʾyīdihi*).[1]

Analysis and interpretation: Al-Kirmānī propounds the idea that the second perfection of souls in the world of Nature is actualised once these receive their influx from the Follower. It is reasonable to believe that al-Kirmānī is here referring to the concept of the perpetual influx (*fayḍ*) which, differing from procession (*inbiʿāth*), is not accountable for the creation of further entities but it is providentially responsible for sustaining all beings in existence and for helping them to attain their second perfection.[2]

As I have briefly mentioned, any human soul in this world is believed by al-Kirmānī to 'be resurrected' by way of a second emanation which is identified with *taʾyīd* itself. It can be tentatively argued that latent again

---

[1]   Al-Kirmānī, *Riyāḍ* (HL), p. 134.

[2]   It has been already adduced that in al-Kirmānī's cosmology all the intellects except the first that is originated by *ibdāʿ*, are the products of a procession. Al-Kirmānī rejects emanation as the primordial process of existentiation from God, being an emanationist solution incompatible with the absolute transcendence of the divine. Emanation, in fact, entails a kind of homogeneity, resemblance and association of God with the emanated existents. See Hunzai, 'The Concept of *Tawḥīd*', pp. 157–158. On al-Kirmānī's arguments against divine emanation, see his *Rāḥat al-ʿaql*, in particular pp. 171–175.

here is the idea for which *ba'th* is a resurrection occurring in souls which are still attached to their bodies: ultimate actualisation, that is, second perfection, is attainable only at the stage of the *qiyāma* when the souls that have been purified and 'resurrected' due to the influx coming from the *rūḥ al-quds* are already prepared to be perfectly completed.[3] Thus, al-Rāzī's definition of *qaḍāʾ* as 'the act of the Follower' is indeed correct as far as it is established that the 'actualisation of human souls' in this world occurs through the influx bestowed from the Soul/Follower/*qadar*, which is materialised as the *qaḍāʾ* or as the Imam's *taʾwīl*. It is interesting to note that this influx operates at the level of Nature (i.e. the level of souls within bodies), this being in accordance with the idea previously noted that the world of the Soul/world of Holiness participates in providence.[4]

As far as the *qaḍāʾ* is concerned, al-Kirmānī holds, al-Rāzī's identification with the act of the (first) Follower/*qadar* is correct if one reads this from a purely cosmological angle which, nonetheless, must be slightly different from al-Rāzī's interpretation. That is, if we operate a shift and we do not speak of 'relative' Followers but rather identify the Follower-*qua*-Follower – namely, the *tālī* that follows the Intellect/Antecedent/Command – with the Soul, then it is correct to state that any entity in the world of Nature is actual (i.e. perfect and complete) thanks to the influx that is emanated upon them by the Follower-*qua*-Follower. The same discourse is valid for the *nāṭiq*: if the *qaḍāʾ* can be identified with the act of the Soul/Follower-*qua*-Follower, then it can be propounded that *qaḍāʾ* brings out the enunciator-prophet from a state of potentiality to that of actuality, this ultimately meaning that the *nāṭiq* attains completeness through the Soul's *taʾyīd*.

The foregoing term features in the Qur'an and refers to a special kind of support or spiritual aid that God bestows on believers striving against enemies.[5] It is often linked to the term spirit (*rūḥ*) as in *rūḥ al-quds*, which is sometimes taken to signify the source of revelation and it is for this reason identified with the Archangel Gabriel.[6] In the Ismaili context, and in some passages of the *Riyāḍ*, *taʾyīd* defines the transmission of a specific knowledge that flows from the spiritual world connecting

---

[3]　　Cf. De Smet, 'La transmigration des âmes', pp. 104–105.

[4]　　See *supra*, pp. 77, 173–174.

[5]　　See, for example, Q 3:13; 8:26, 62; 9:40; 58:22.

[6]　　On this topic, see Ebstein, *Mysticism and Philosophy in al-Andalus*, p. 36.

it to the corporeal realm and to its representatives in the persons of the prophets and the Imams.[7] It is through *ta'yīd* that the Imams become both the depositaries of the divine knowledge that is revealed in the *sharī'a*[8] and the individuals who are capable of carrying out its esoteric interpretation.[9] Significantly, in Ismaili writers such as al-Sijistānī and al-Kirmānī, as previously mentioned, *ta'yīd* does not flow down directly from God but rather from the Pleroma of the intellects and reaches the prophets, the Imams and the corporeal *ḥudūd* of the *da'wa* via the intermediacy of other spiritual entities (*al-jadd*, etc.).[10]

---

[7] On *ta'yīd* in Ismaili literature, see Ikhwān al-Ṣafā', *Rasā'il*, vol. II, p. 127; Ikhwān al-Ṣafā', *al-Risāla al-Jāmi'a*, vol. II, p. 36; al-Ḥāmidī, *Kanz al-walad*, pp. 104–105, 269. On al-Kirmānī's views on *ta'yīd*, see also his *Rāḥat al-'aql*, pp. 190, 517, 585.

[8] Al-Sijistānī states that what is revealed to the inspired person becomes a legal source (*nāmūs^{an} aṣliyy^{an}*) whose use (*isti'māl*) is incumbent for the duration of his cycle (*dawrihi*); see al-Sijistānī, *Kitāb al-Yanābī'*, pp. 172–173, tr. Walker, *The Wellsprings of Wisdom*, p. 111. This suggests that, according to al-Sijistānī, the religious law as a legal source produced by a prophet/inspired person preserves its necessary validity within the limits of one prophetic era. Hence, the prophets of all eras cannot set aside the use of the *sharī'a* – with the exception of the first and the last prophets who are not meant to bring forth laws but, rather, spiritual truths.

[9] On the term *ta'yīd* and its link with the concept of *imdād* (aid, assistance, sustentation, increasing, succouring, reinforcing), see Ebstein, *Mysticism and Philosphy in al-Andalus*, pp. 65–67. In relation to al-Sijistānī's thought, Hirji defines *ta'yīd* as 'the divine gift of fortitude and the capacity to accept divine teaching and knowledge'. See Hirji, 'A Study of *al-Risālah al-bāhirah*', under '*ta'yīd*' in index, p. 233. See also Corbin, *Trilogie ismaélienne* (Tehran and Paris, 1961), p. 19 note 23.

[10] Al-Sijistānī, *Kitāb al-Yanābī'*, pp. 62–63, tr. Walker, *The Wellsprings of Wisdom*, pp. 45, 119–120. Al-Sijistānī identifies the Antecedent/Intellect, the Follower/Soul, the enunciator-prophet and the foundation as the sources of special functions: the Antecedent provides spiritual assistance (*ta'yīd*); the Follower is responsible for corporeal composition (*tarkīb*); the enunciator-prophet provides compilation (*tā'līf*); and the foundation interpretation (*ta'wīl*). Al-Kirmānī specifies that the *nāṭiq* and the Imam receive their knowledge from the intellects via *ta'yīd* which, like the circular motion of the spheres, is perpetual. This is why the enunciator-prophets and the founders are constantly *in actu* (i.e. their intellects, as the Agent Intellect of the Aristotleian tradition, are always in actuality without necessitating a passage from potentiality into actuality as in the case of other human beings) and are acknowledged as *al-mu'ayyadūn min al-samā'*. Al-Kirmānī, *Rāḥat al-'aql*, pp. 190, 326, 405, 474, 488, 501; De Smet, *La quiétude de l'intellect*, p. 366; Walker, *Early Philosophical Shiism*, pp. 117–118, 127.

Faṣl Fourteen

In his [al-Rāzī's] statement: 'All existents (*aysiyyāt*) have proceeded (*inba'athat*) from the Antecedent in a decreed way
(*muqaddarat^{an}*)', there is a contradiction (*tanāquḍ*). This is
because the Follower is an *ays* and it is an emanated being
(*munba'ith*) from the Antecedent, and it is not through a decree
(*laysa bi-muqaddar*). What is meant by his [al-Rāzī's] words is
that this is the emanated being, from which came the corporeal
world and which has been decreed in order for things to become
existent as we have discussed with regard to the *qadar*, not the
Follower.[1]

Analysis and interpretation: Al-Kirmānī reiterates that to claim that
all existents are the result of a direct procession from the Antecedent
and that such procession occurred in a decreed way is a contradiction
in terms. This statement proposes that the Antecedent cannot be identified with the decreeing *amr*, as al-Rāzī wished to infer. Al-Kirmānī
underlines that the Follower-*qua*-Follower indicated by al-Rāzī (i.e.
the Soul) is in truth an existing entity (*ays*) (*qā'im bi'l-fi'l* as in Table 1),
and this might suggest its being actual (perfect, present and actually
operative as the *imām-qā'im*) at the very instant its procession (i.e.
appointment) occurs through the Antecedent (the Intellect/*nāṭiq*),
without the 'delay' that characterises the procession of the third intellect (i.e. the final Resurrector as *qā'im bi'l-quwwa*). Because the Follower proceeds from the Antecedent through *inbi'āth* rather than
ibdā' – the latter presupposing a direct divine volitional intervention
– it goes without saying that it has not been directly decreed. Indeed,
the nomination of the Imams is the unequivocal responsibility of the
enunciator-prophet. What remains quite incomprehensible is why the

---

[1]   Al-Kirmānī, *Riyāḍ* (HL), p. 135.

third intellect which, like the Follower, proceeds via *inbiʿāth*, can be said to have been decreed, unlike the *tālī*. The possible explanation for this lies in what our author covertly argues, that is, that it makes sense to speak of predestination with reference to a form of procession such as the 'delay' that the tenth intellect undergoes as it is raised to the level of the third intellect. Congruently, the advent of the final Resurrector must be understood as an event situated at a level other than that of temporality. Implicitly, it would not seem right to consider the Imam of the time as the manifestation of the final *qāʾim*. This argument, al-Kirmānī reminds his reader, has already been discussed with regard to the *qadar*.

Faṣl Fifteen

And the words of the author of the *Nuṣra*: 'Concerning his [al-Rāzī's] interpretation of *"khalaqnāhu"*, he means thereby the forms of the two worlds [and what is] between them, and by *"bi-qadar"* he means the Follower upon whom the *amr* dwells, and the totality of the spiritual and corporeal forms which have become manifest between them.' [However] the affair in the existence of things, be they corporeal or incorporeal, is not as he mentioned it in a wrong manner (*bi-fasād*) as we [al-Kirmānī] have pointed out [with regard to] the basis upon which he constructed his argument. Had his interpretation on the arrangement (*tartīb*) of the existence of the existents from the start not fallen beyond the scope of this book, we would have treated it [here] and we would not have had to refer to our [other] treatises and books.[1]

Analysis and interpretation: In this passage, al-Sijistānī's arguments against al-Rāzī are once again criticised by al-Kirmānī. Abū Yaʿqūb's interpretation of the *amr* does not correspond to al-Kirmānī's idea and the argument had already been explained in the tenth *faṣl*.

---

[1] Al-Kirmānī, *Riyāḍ* (HL), p. 135.

Faṣl Sixteen

The author of the *Iṣlāḥ* said: 'As for the *ta'wīl* regarding what the Prophet of God (peace be upon him and his family) said: "I flee (*afirru*) from the *qaḍā'* of God towards His *qadar*",[1] he [the Prophet] intended to flee from the subtle (*laṭīf*) spiritual assistance (*ta'yīd*) of the Antecedent towards the explanation (*bayān*) of the Follower; in the same way as the flight of a man from fire is a proof of *ta'yīd* and [the flight] towards water is a proof of *bayān*.[2] Indeed he [the Prophet] wanted to flee from the thing

---

[1] In Ibn Bābūya's *Risālat al-I'tiqādāt al-imāmiyya* we read: 'It is related that once upon a time the Prince of Believers, on whom be peace, avoided a slanting wall and went to the other side. He was asked: "O Prince of Believers, do you flee from the *qaḍā'* of God?" He replied: "I flee from the *qaḍā'* of God towards His *qadar*". For references, see Fyzee's translation, *A Shiite Creed*, p. 37. I have avoided translating *qaḍā'* as destiny and *qadar* as decree, as indicated in Fyzee's edition, in order to be as faithful as possible to the meanings assigned to these terms by the three Ismaili *dāʿī*s.

[2] This explanation is rather obscure; some light can be shed if we examine how al-Rāzī's argument is articulated further in the *Iṣlāḥ*. Al-Rāzī holds that: 'He [al-Nasafī] intended [to say] flee from a thing which has already been made hot and separated (*fuṣṣila*) [...] towards something which does not separate (*lam yufaṣṣal*)'. This is what was said first, and it is not without mistake. This is because if you link the *qaḍā'* to the Antecedent and the *qadar* to the Follower, then you say that [the Prophet] fled from a thing which was already [...] separated towards something that does not separate, and that what is separated comes before that which does not separate. And in saying [this] you [say] that the *qaḍā'* signifies the First and that the *qadar* signifies the Second, by all means, and that the *tafṣīl* is before the *taqdīr'* (see al-Rāzī, *Iṣlāḥ*, pp. 50–51). Al-Sijistānī, following al-Nasafī, also speaks of fire as something resembling the Antecedent. They are both invisible and, moreover, as is explained, the *sābiq* warms up (*yusakhkhinu*) – that is, ignites – the Soul in order to actualise her passage from the boundary of potentiality to the boundary of actuality (*min ḥadd al-quwwa ilā ḥadd al-fiʿl*). Both al-Nasafī and al-Sijistānī's ideas suggest references to the separated community (the dissident Qarmaṭī splinter-group?) and the identification of

209

that had been made certain (*ḥutima*) and decreed (*quḍiya*), but this does not [mean] being propelled (*dafʿu*) towards the *qadar* which is [something that] has not been decreed (*lam yuqḍā*).'

This is what he [al-Rāzī] said, but this is unsystematic (*ghayr muntaẓam*). For the Prophet (peace be upon him and his family) fled from the *qaḍāʾ* of God towards His *qadar* for a cause (*ʿilla*), and that cause was the leaning wall (*al-ḥāʾiṭ al-māʾil*) about whose collapse (*suqūṭ*) he was warned (*ḥudhdhir*). As he hurried (*fa-asraʿ al-mashy*) [past it] he [the Prophet] said: 'I flee from the *qaḍāʾ* of God towards His *qadar*', and he intended to provide them [the members of his community] with a parable (*mathal*ᵃⁿ). The leaning wall is a structure (*bināʾ*) which already inclines to fall; it signifies one of the limits (*ḥudūd*),³ which is at the point of cracking (*nakth*)⁴ and splitting (*nifāq*)⁵ and which inclines towards sinfulness (*fisq*) and away from obedience (*ṭāʿa*). This is because if it [the wall/*ḥadd*] breaks, it falls outside its station (*manzila*), as God Almighty has said: 'And they found therein a wall about to

---

the *qaḍāʾ*/*tafṣīl* (the mental tailoring in the analogy examined in the first *faṣl*) with the Imam in *satr* and the *qadar*/*taqdīr* (the mental decision in the same analogy) with the returning Resurrector. This is proven particularly when they speak of the Antecedent as fire, which as a subtle, invisible element, is like the Imam in *satr* who, despite being *in potentia*/*in absconditus*, will nonetheless actualise the passage, returning as the last *qāʾim* (the Follower). It is due to the Follower's influence (*athar*), al-Sijistānī also declares, that 'some individuals return rewarded (*mathāb*ᵃⁿ) whilst others return punished (*muʿāqab*ᵃⁿ)', thus strengthening the Follower's link with the figure of the Mahdī. Conversely, it is the enunciator-prophet who, according to al-Sijistānī, is the one who resembles water: from the *nāṭiq* flows the holy law pertaining to a specific prophetic era which, with its temporal character, differs from other normative codes just as the waves differ from each other. And just as the clash of waves can be potentially destructive, so at the degree of enunciation, the waves of dissension (*ikhtilāf*) can arise. See al-Sijistānī, *Kitāb al-Yanābīʿ*, pp. 65–66, tr. Walker, *The Wellsprings of Wisdom*, pp. 46–47.

³ Here, literally, the expression *ḥadd min al-ḥudūd* can also mean 'one among the religious dignitaries'.

⁴ Significantly, *nakth* might also be translated as 'breach', 'violation' (of a contract/agreement). Here there is a reference to breaching the commands of the religious law and a possible reference to breaching the Prophet's will in appointing his successor.

⁵ *Nifāq* also means hypocrisy, which might be an indication for the subsequent explanation regarding the potential corruption leading to the splitting of the community of believers.

collapse, so he restored it' [Q 18:77].[6] This means that one among the *ḥudūd* became aware of the imminent splitting and infringement and set [this individual] upright again so that he became stable and did not fall [out of his assigned station]. Likewise [can be said of] the leaning wall past which the Prophet (peace be upon him and his family) hurried, for he had realised it was on the very point [lit. 'the limit of the limits', *ḥadd min ḥudūd*] of breaking and falling so that it was clear that he should walk past it faster. This is because the slow pace in walking (*al-ta'annī fi'l-mashy*) is a proof for explanation (*bayān*) and demonstration (*burhān*), [whilst] the fast pace (*al-surʿa fi'l-mashy*) signifies what is manifest (*ẓāhir*) [the law]. And he [the Prophet] (peace be upon him) addressed what [the community] was on the point of breaking with advice and a warning on the exoteric/manifest [meaning] without explication on the esoteric/hidden [meaning]. For *qadar* signifies what is manifest as we [al-Rāzī] have explained, whilst the *qaḍā'* signifies what is hidden (*bāṭin*).[7] His [the Prophet's] (peace be upon him and his family) flight from the *qaḍā'* of God towards His *qadar* was a warning against the leaning wall's falling,[8] not a warning for himself for he was not fleeing from the nobility with which God Almighty had enobled him in terms of the rank to which God had elevated him, for he was not averse to their abundance.

The author of the *Nuṣra* said: 'The interpretation in the *ta'wīl* regarding "I flee from the *qaḍā'* of God towards His *qadar*", is not as the author of the *Iṣlāḥ* has imagined it to be (*tawahhamahu*), namely, a flight from the Follower towards the degree of the Antecedent, because the prophets (peace be upon them) according to his claim always seek elevation, seeking the sublime and not the base (*sufl*); we would say of that, with the help of God Almighty

---

[6] Our author creates a binary between the leaning wall and the religious dignitary. Just as the leaning wall is on the verge of breaking and crumbling apart, thus falling out of its upright position, similarly one of the *ḥudūd* inclines towards sinfulness and disobedience, thus falling out of his assigned status.

[7] If the *qadar* is said to signify what is manifest, it cannot correspond to the Imam in concealment but, rather to the Imam's deputy, who, according to al-Rāzī, is not to be necessarily identified with a Fatimid Imam-caliph. As *qaḍā'* is the *ta'wīl*, it must logically correspond to what is *bāṭin*.

[8] Al-Kirmānī, *Riyāḍ* (HL), pp. 136–137. Cf. al-Rāzī, *Iṣlāḥ*, pp. 53–56. This can be interpreted as the Prophet's appealing to the prescriptions of the *sharīʿa* as a unifying means against the disintegrating community (i.e. the leaning wall).

and His blessing, that the meaning in that [expression] is three-fold (*thalātha maʿānī*), and each one of these [three meanings] corroborates that the *qaḍāʾ* signifies the Antecedent and that the *qadar* signifies the Follower. The greatest and most precise [of these meanings] is that he [the Prophet] (peace be upon him) in fleeing from the *qaḍāʾ* of God towards His *qadar* [means] that from the Antecedent [there] is the instituting of *taʾyīd*, and from the Follower [there is] the composition (*tarkīb*); from the *nāṭiq* [there] is redaction (*taʾlīf*) of the *sharīʿa*, [and] from the Foundation (*asās*) [there] is the *taʾwīl* of the totality [of these things]. The *taʾwīl* which comes last is similar to *taʾyīd*, and the *taʾlīf* is similar to *tarkīb*. The *nāṭiq* (peace be upon him) according to his [the Prophet's] statement is similar in his redaction (*taʾlīf*) of laws to the Follower in the composition (*tarkīb*) of the world, but he [the *nāṭiq*] is not similar to the Antecedent.[9] He [the Prophet] fled 'from the *qaḍāʾ* of God' – which is the Antecedent, which bears no resemblance from the perspective that is the instituting of *taʾyīd* – 'towards his *qadar*', which is the Follower, to which he compares himself.[10]

And the second meaning is his [the Prophet's] informing his community that he benefits from the First (*yastafīd min al-awwal*) through the intermediary of the Second (*bi-wāsiṭat al-thānī*) and that all that he wished to comprehend of it from the First by the intermediary of the Second, returns to it.[11] It is as if he [the Prophet] had said 'In everything I wish to comprehend,

---

9   Cf. al-Sijistānī, *Kitāb al-Yanābīʿ*, pp. 62–64, tr. Walker, *The Wellsprings of Wisdom*, p. 45.

10   These extracts can be interpreted bearing in mind what al-Sijistānī has already elucidated in the first *faṣl* in terms of the mental form/shape linked with the *qaḍāʾ*: because the composition of the law is likened to the composition of the world of Nature – in which souls are parts of the Soul, thus pre-existing the latter – it follows that the *sharīʿa*, as a yet unwritten code, pre-exists, as a form, in the mind of the *nāṭiq* prior to the latter's act of redaction (*taʾlīf*) of the law. Similarly, the Soul pre-exists, as the form of the Intellect, prior to her particularisation in this world. Consequently, according to al-Sijistānī, the enunciator-prophet bears no resemblance to the Antecedent/Intellect but is rather more closely associable with the Follower/Soul.

11   This could be a reference to the Prophet's comprehension of the essence of the First as purely unadulterated Oneness. Given that God remains unfathomable, all that the Prophet wishes to know, and is meant to know, of the Intellect is the latter's non-divinity, namely the Intellect's *tawḥīd*.

I return to that which is the cause (*sabab*) between me and the Intellect, which is the Second.' And this is the second meaning.

The third meaning, which is the most noble [of the three], has been mentioned by the bearer of the Book (peace be upon him) and this is his flight from the strength of light (*nūr*) of the Antecedent's spiritual assistance (*ta'yīd al-sābiq*), towards the spiritual assistance of the Follower (*ta'yīd al-tālī*), just as *al-jadd* with all its spiritual potentiality was not strong enough to bear it [the intensity of the light] (*lam yaqwa ʿalā iḥtimāl dhālika*) to the point that its identity (*huwiyyatuhu*) almost faded away (*tatalāsha*). This is what he [al-Rāzī] said of the story of Moses (peace be upon him)'. This is what they both [al-Rāzī and al-Sijistānī] stated.

But we [al-Kirmānī] say: With regard to the author of the *Iṣlāḥ*, his interpretation of the verse is in conformity with the issue of the meaning of *qaḍā'* and *qadar*, and this is sound. And when he said that the *nabī* (peace be upon him) has prophesised a prophecy about the hidden things (*mughaybāt*) among existentiated beings (*akwān*) and events (*aḥdāth*), and about what is in people's conscience (*ḍamā'ir*), using what God had designated for him (*khaṣṣahu bihi*) in terms of inspiration (*waḥy*), he intended to explain (*yubayyin*) how things became open to him [the Prophet] of what had been bequeathed (*yulqā*) to him through *al-jadd*. And he said: 'I return.' This is [like] his saying 'I flee', which I [al-Kirmānī] designate by *al-jadd* with regard to the *ḥudūd* of God Almighty to be the totality (*jumla*) of what is on the verge of coming into existence (*yakād yakūn*) such as events and existentiated beings which are the *qaḍā'* of God. [The latter] exits into actuality resolutely (*ḥatm^{an}*) towards the *qadar* of God which is the creation (*khalq*) of God Almighty from the horizons (*āfāq*) and the souls (*anfus*) and their functional movements (*ḥarakāt al-dālla*), as He has decreed them to be. This has become clear to me in what was discussed in the chapter on inspiration. For this reason, God Almighty said: 'We will show them Our signs in the horizons (*āfāq*) and within their souls until it becomes clear to them that it is the truth' [Q 41:53], and He said: 'Who [...] give thought to the creation of the heavens and the earth, [saying], "Our Lord, You did not create this aimlessly"' [Q 3:191]. This means that 'You did not create this aimlessly' does not point to what has preceded its existence or what has followed its existence among the existentiated beings, but it points to itself and addresses itself. It is as if he [the Prophet] had said: 'I return to what is cast upon me through *al-jadd* as a totality (*jumla*), towards the *qadar*, so that by its similitude and its conceptualisation (*taṣawwuruhu*), it will become visible and clear to me.' Hence his statement, 'I flee from the *qaḍā'* of God towards His *qadar*.' This is the sort of revelation and the book *Raḥat al-ʿaql* includes an explanation for this.[12]

Analysis and interpretation: This *faṣl* opens with al-Kirmānī examining al-Rāzī's position which, he states, is unsystematic. This criticism is almost certainly due to the fact that al-Kirmānī does not quote al-Rāzī's relevant passage from the *Iṣlāḥ* in its entirety and he might have been led to overlook certain details. The text in the *Iṣlāḥ* reads as follows:

> And the Prophet of God (peace be upon him and his family), said: 'I flee from the *qaḍā'* of God towards His *qadar*.' For the *qaḍā'* is two *qaḍā's* (*qaḍā'ān*): the *qaḍā'* of evil (*qaḍā'al-sū'*) and the *qaḍā'* of goodness (*qaḍā'al-ḥusn*). And following this he said to the people: 'We seek refuge through God from the *qaḍā'* of evil.' And the *qadar* here [in the prophetic saying] signifies the limit of the enunciator-prophet (*ḥadd al-nāṭiq*) (peace be upon him) and [signifies] what is bestowed upon him by the two Roots (*al-aṣlayn*) and [signifies that] he [the enunciator-prophet] composed (*allafa*) through it [i.e. through the *qadar*] a decreed (*muqaddarat*^{an}) and manifested (*ẓāhir*^{an}) law (*sharīʿa*), and [signifies] explanation (*bayān*) and demonstration (*burhān*).[13] This is because his composition is decreed (*muqaddar*^{an}) and does not [admit of] division (*mufaṣṣal*^{an}). And the *qaḍā'* of goodness signifies the limit of the foundation (*ḥadd al-asās*) and what is bestowed upon him by the two Roots. And [it signifies] the realisation of the mission (*daʿwa*) through explanation and demonstration. This is because there is division with regard to the *ẓāhir* [i.e. the exoteric aspect of the law], the latter having been decreed by the enunciator-prophet but not its division. The *qaḍā'* of goodness signifies the *asās* as we have explained. For it is the

---

[12]   Al-Kirmānī, *Riyāḍ* (HL), pp. 136–139.

[13]   This *qaḍā'* is linked to evil probably because the religious law which the enunciator-prophet established is limited (to a prophetic cycle) and its determination excludes possible contrasting views relative to its interpretation.

explication that leads the people of agreement (*ahl al-wifāq*) to their accord [...], towards goodness which is Paradise (*janna*) and the reward of those who do good (*thawāb al-muḥsinīn*); this is what they said in the *tafsīr* of His [God's] words: 'He shall have a good reward' [Q 18:88], and the good reward is Paradise. As for the *qaḍāʾ* of evil, this signifies the adversary (*ḍidd*). For he knows the detailed explanation (*al-bayān al-mufaṣṣal*) which is the *qaḍāʾ* [of evil]. He [the adversary] transgresses (*nakatha*) and leads to an evil state. And whoever is bestowed with it becomes tired, and evil is [bestowed] upon [this individual] and his followers. And these are led towards evil which is the Fire (*nār*). And the punishment of the transgressing evildoers (*al-nākithīn al-mustiʾīn*) is as they said in the *tafsīr* of His [God's] words: 'In the long run evil in the extreme will be the end of those who do evil' [Q 30:10]. They said 'evil' (*sūʾ*) which is Fire. And the Prophet of God (peace be upon him and his family), in passing the leaning wall, hurried up (lit. his gait became faster) and said: 'I flee from the *qaḍāʾ* of God towards His *qadar*'.[14]

An analysis of al-Rāzī's text leads to a series of reflections. Al-Rāzī distinguishes between two types of *qaḍāʾ*: the *qaḍāʾ* of evil and that of goodness. Of the first not much is said except that (i) it is from it that the Prophet seeks refuge in God, and (ii) that it signifies a detailed explanation (*al-bayān al-mufaṣṣal*) which might be provided, by an antagonist (*ḍidd*), to the exoteric aspect of the religious law which is revealed by the enunciator-prophet. This supposition might be validated by the fact that, as specified in the passage, there might be divisions with regard to the *ẓāhirī* facet of the law, because it is exclusively the composition of the *sharīʿa* that has been decreed (*muqaddar*^{an}) to the exclusion of its potentially conflicting explanations which might be carried out by a hypothetical adversary.

Al-Rāzī steers his discourse on the nature of *qadar* – featuring in the quoted prophetic saying – which, besides being responsible for the above composition, signifies also the *limit* of the enunciator-prophet (*ḥadd al-nāṭiq*). Now, such a limit is to be understood as: (i) the limit of the *nāṭiq* (i.e. the *nāṭiq* being the 'limit' of each major cycle) whose

---

[14] Al-Rāzī, *Iṣlāḥ*, pp. 53–56. From this point, the text of the *Iṣlāḥ* reads as the quotation that is reported in the *Riyāḍ*.

task is to compile a law and reveal only its exoteric meaning, and (ii) the highest level of explanation (*bayān*) and demonstration (*burhān*) of the law which is bestowed by the two Roots. This means that even though the enunciator-prophet establishes the decreed exoteric facet of the law, such a decree does not extend to the law's explication and its demonstration. These, in fact, belong to the dominion of the *qaḍāʾ* of goodness; the latter is said to signify the limit of the foundation (*ḥadd al-asās*) (i.e. the *asās* being the liminal 'interval' within the minor cycles) and what is bestowed upon him by the two Roots as well as being a signifier for the actualisation (*aqām*) of the mission (*daʿwa*) which is fulfilled through explanation and demonstration (of the law). So, whilst the *nāṭiq* decrees the manifest aspect of the law, the *asās* provides an esoteric elucidation for it and this constitutes his ultimate task/limit, which is established by what is granted upon the *asās* by the Intellect/Antecedent and the Soul/Follower. Embedded in the passage is the idea that just as the enunciator-prophet comes before the foundation, so does the *qadar* with respect to the *qaḍāʾ*.

Moreover, al-Rāzī suggests that the Prophet's saying 'I flee from the *qaḍāʾ* of God towards His *qadar*', must be contextualised with reference to the episode of the leaning wall (Q 18:77), which is employed by the Prophet as a warning for his community. More specifically, just as the individual mentioned in the Qurʾanic verse (commonly identified with Khiḍr) became aware of the imminent crumbling of an unspecified wall and restored it to its upright position,[15] likewise the Prophet became aware that his leaning wall was on the verge of being compromised. The Prophet's leaning wall, which is here identified with the *qaḍāʾ*, in the light of the foregoing, is very possibly a reference to the community and its future fragmentation because of the contrasting interpretations of the law (probably also a reference to the discordant ideas among members of the community with regard to the establishment of the Prophet's successor and the identification of the *qāʾim*).[16] Even more prominently, all the above might be a suggestion for the association of *qaḍāʾ* with, on the one hand, the leaning wall and, on the other, the second Follower.

---

[15] See Q 18: 65–82.

[16] The splitting of the *umma* after the Prophet's passing is a topic discussed in detail in *Faṣl* Twenty-three.

In uttering his saying, al-Rāzī reiterates, the Prophet was aware that the leaning wall had within itself the potential to crumble and fall, meaning that the *qaḍā'* – as the hidden (*bāṭin*) aspect of the law – has within its 'architecture' limitations (which need to be complemented by the exoteric/manifest aspect of the law) corresponding to the limits that the leaning wall preserves in its slanting structure (*bināʾ*). It is probable that this understanding might have served to highlight the usefulness of the *ẓāhirī* facets of the *sharīʿa* – linked to the administrative maintenance of this world and to the religious dimension of the superogatory acts – and their cohesive force with regard to the *ummaʾs* unity. In addition, the limitations of the *qaḍāʾ/bāṭin/*leaning wall match the limited, circumscribed power of the *bayān* bestowed by the Follower upon the Prophet.

Another point of interest is the emphasis laid on the rapidity of the Prophet's gait which, covert in the Prophet's saying, enables him to put a distance between himself and the crumbling wall. The modification in the Prophet's pace (another reference to the so-often-mentioned change = Imam?) becomes for al-Rāzī a further proof that the *qaḍāʾ* is the signifier of the *taʾwīl* and that, consequently, the *qadar* is the signifier of the Imam who delivers such *taʾwīl*. Indeed, the slowness of gait (*al-taʾannī fiʾl-mashy*) is a proof of the explanation (*bayān*) of the law, which is the responsibility of the *asās* just as the *bayān* is the responsibility of the Follower.

It should be noted that the emphasis is placed on the pace of the gait as well as on the act of walking itself. The pace is a reference to time, whilst the act of walking alludes to a form of motion – probably an indication of the passage from the *bayān* transmitted to the Prophet by the Follower to the *taʾyīd* transmitted by the Antecedent. According to al-Rāzī, motion (*ḥaraka*) and quiescence (*sukūn*) are inherent in the very nature of both the Intellect and the Soul.[17]

Furthermore, the slow pace should be linked with al-Kirmānī's idea of the third intellect and the nature of its actions. It should be recalled that, for al-Kirmānī, the third intellect is by its very nature potential, despite being issued as a procession from the perfect preceding intellects. Its nature, as well as its action, acquire perfection through an acquisition that occurs in what 'resembles' the passage of time, in other words the

---

[17]   Al-Kirmānī, *Riyāḍ* (Beirut, 1960), Chapters 2 and 6.

slow pace.[18] Conversely, because the first originated being and the act of origination are identical (*ays wāḥid*),[19] and since there is no time before the origination, time and the origination are one and the same thing in actuality and therefore no elapsing of time can ever be attributed to the Antecedent. The speed of the pace could hint at the fact that no delay or pause can ever be ascribed to the Antecedent, as the Intellect, in its constituting the act of extra-temporal origination, *ibdāʿ*.[20]

In contrast to the slowness of gait/second Follower/*qaḍāʾ*/*bāṭin* (*taʾwīl*), al-Rāzī speaks of the Prophet's haste (*isrāʿ*) in walking past the wall as something that is manifest and, a few lines further on, he specifies that the *qadar* is what is *ẓāhir*. We already know from his previous identification of the *qadar* with the essence of the Follower-which-follows-the-*amr* that *qadar*, in truth, corresponds to the Antecedent (with respect to the *qaḍāʾ*), so we find here a complete picture of equivalences: the fast pace of walking/Antecedent (or first Follower)/ *qadar*/*ẓāhir*.

The very fact that the Prophet flees from God's *qaḍāʾ* towards His *qadar* might also refer to the opportunity humans have to flee from the idea of an unjust divine determinism towards a fairer concept of human free will. More particularly, al-Rāzī's exegesis of the Prophet's saying might allude to the possibility all humans have of attaining a correct understanding of their role in the universe as well as the scope of the divine law which they can either obey or disobey. Besides the hidden meaning of revelation (*qaḍāʾ*/*bāṭin*), humans can aspire to correct their imperfect nature by becoming aware that there is a dimension of manoeuvrability in which their actions can be carried out. This is the realm of the *sharīʿa* which, like the *qadar*, pertains to those

---

18   Al-Kirmānī has already highlighted that the third intellect is tardy in its procession. See above, *Faṣl* Eight. Again, correspondences might be drawn between the third intellect/slow pace and the final Resurrector who, according to al-Kirmānī, is still awaited, causing disappointment and confusion for many Ismaili followers convinced that the era of Islam had come to an end with al-Ḥākim.

19   Al-Rāzī, *Iṣlāḥ*, pp. 36–37.

20   The timelessness of *ibdāʿ* is poetically depicted by Nāṣir-i Khusraw: 'Never ascribe to Him any act, if you have intellect other than the *ibdāʿ* of the originated being (*mubdaʿ*) whose [act] is like the twinkling of an eye or less (*ka-lamḥ al-ʿayn aw adnā*)' [Q 16:77]. Nāṣir-i Khusraw, *Dīwān-i Ashʿār*, ed. N. A. Taqawī (Tehran, 1335 AH), p. 27, cited and translated by Hunzai, 'The Concept of *Tawḥīd*', p. 81.

things which can undergo and, as shown by Q 18:77, have undergone changes (as in the case of Muḥammad b. Ismāʿīl having been represented by many deputies), also in light of the various *taʾwīl* that might be produced by the Imams.

According to the above passage from the *Iṣlāḥ*, it is through the explication of the law (namely, through the *bayān* of the *bāṭinī* nature of the law which pertains to the *taʾwīl/qaḍāʾ*) that people can come to an agreement with respect to the ultimate significance of the revelation (obtainable by complementing the *ẓāhir* and *bāṭin* of the *sharīʿa*) and attain Paradise. This is a clear indication of the necessity to identify the right Foundation: the leaning wall/divided community is described as being on the very point of falling out of its/their station (the right path to salvation); therefore, human intervention is necessary in order for the wall's/community's position to be fixed and rectified against any misleading interpretation of any illegitimate guide who could potentially direct the abiding community towards erroneous beliefs. This intervention is the action of 'one among the dignitaries' – including a *dāʿī* such as al-Rāzī himself – whose contribution towards the explication of the truth would make it incumbent for humans' intellective faculty to spring into action, thus spurring obedience to the law's truthful precepts.

As mentioned earlier, the changeable nature of *qadar* was the object of discussion in some previous *faṣls*. It is in this regard that al-Kirmānī may have accused al-Rāzī of being un-systematic. Al-Rāzī had previously emphasised that the *qadar* is decreed (*muqaddar*) and this would lead one to think that it is immutable. And indeed, this is the case, but only regarding the exoteric aspect of the law, which, within the boundary of any given prophetic era, has to remain unchangeable as it differentiates what is commendable from what is reprehensible. However, humans still enjoy the freedom of choosing either obedience or disobedience. And obviously, they are encouraged to choose obedience once they attain a more complete understanding of the *sharīʿa* thanks to the explanation of its esoteric dimension offered by the Imam. Another perspective would be to read al-Rāzī's statement as a reference to the decreed appointment of the Imam (specifically, Muḥammad b. Ismāʿīl) and the un-decreed appointment of his representatives whilst the Imam is in *satr*. This could, again, be a veiled denial of the legitimacy of the Fatimid caliphs' claims to the imamate.

Al-Rāzī also touches upon the issue that religious knowledge – necessary to attain the state of the enunciator-prophet – is transmitted from God to the earthly ranks through the help of *al-jadd* and other spiritual intermediaries. The reference is, in this context, to the light of *ta'yīd* bestowed upon dignitaries such as the *nāṭiq*, the *asās* and the *imām*s of the age.[21] The individual with *ta'yīd* (*mu'ayyad*) is granted the capacity to perceive the realities of the unseen (*ḥaqā'iq min 'ulūm al-ghayb*), thus becoming able to guide people and establish a basic law (*nāmūs aṣlī*).[22] Significantly, the foregoing passage, as well as the other passages that will follow, reiterates that *ta'yīd* is attained by individual souls through the intermediacy of the Follower, thus implying that the cycle of the *qiyāma* has not yet begun.

As for al-Sijistānī, al-Kirmānī lists in the sixteenth *faṣl* all the specific tasks that Abū Yaʿqūb assigns to the celestial as well as the terrestrial dignitaries: from the Antecedent occurs the instituting of spiritual assistance (*ta'yīd*); from the follower, composition (*tarkīb*); from the *nāṭiq*, legislation of the *sharīʿa*, whilst the Foundations carry out the hermeneutical esoteric interpretation of the totality of these things. In particular, al-Sijistānī is reported to have declared that, implicit in the Prophet's saying, is the similarity of the *nāṭiq*'s *ta'līf*, namely the redaction of the law, to the Follower's *tarkīb*, namely the composition of the forms of the world of Nature, and it is to one of these forms that the Prophet compares himself (a reference to the Form of Man?). Specifically, al-Sijistānī explains that in carrying out *ta'līf*, the *nāṭiq* can be compared to the Follower performing the *tarkīb* of this world. This comparison is made possible because the enunciator-prophet, in redacting a religious legislation, is rendering temporal and specific the spiritual assistance (*ta'yīd*) which has a universal/atemporal character. He is basically putting into written form a revelation, where the act of writing something down usually denotes a temporal action. Likewise, the Follower (the Soul), in composing the corporeal beings of this world, is joining matter and form, thus generating them as specific and temporal compounds, that is, the natural,

---

[21] Al-Sijistānī, *Kitāb Ithbāt al-nubuwwāt*, p. 190, 192; *idem*, 'al-Risāla al-Bāhira', pp. 37–50.
[22] Nomoto, *Early Ismāʿīlī Thought on Prophecy*, p. 192.

corporeal entities.[23] Al-Sijistānī hastens to specify that the *nāṭiq*, however, is not comparable to the Antecedent precisely because, from the perspective of the instituting of *ta'yīd*, the enunciator-prophet is bound to the limitedness of the *ta'līf* of the *sharī'a* which, although in Muḥammad's era is as complete as a normative code might be, is still fixed in time and space, and directed to a specific culture. This means that whilst the *nāṭiq* operates in time, as does his *ta'līf*, the perfect completeness of the Antecedent makes its *ta'yīd* eternally unchangeable.[24]

Referring to the second meaning of the above-mentioned prophetic saying, al-Sijistānī reiterates that the knowledge that pertains to the First reaches the Prophet (in his status as a *nāṭiq*) through the Second. Even more specifically, al-Sijistānī contends that the Prophet would have identified the second entity (i.e. the Soul or second intellect) as the cause (*sabab*) placed between himself and the first intellect. The third meaning of the expression uttered by Muḥammad identifies the Prophet's flight from the *qaḍā'* to the *qadar* as the flight from the unendurable intensity proceeding from light of the *ta'yīd* by the Antecedent towards the manageable *ta'yīd* of the Follower. This understanding shows again the idea of the impossibility for *al-jadd* to bear a direct vision of the Antecedent, an episode that is recounted in the story of Moses as set out by al-Rāzī.

Al-Kirmānī believes that al-Rāzī is correct regarding the meanings he applies to *qaḍā'* and *qadar*. He reinforces the previously mentioned idea that *al-jadd* is the liminal entity, a kind of gnoseological threshold, towards which the enunciator-prophet-to-be can turn. In commenting on the flight of the Prophet from the *qaḍā'* towards the *qadar* as discussed by al-Rāzī, al-Kirmānī states that it is a flight from a manifested actuality towards a 'creation' that has resulted from movable and mutable beings. The generated beings and events/changes are identified with the *qaḍā'* because the latter is what exists in actuality

---

[23] Cf. al-Sijistānī, *Kitāb al-Yanābī'*, p. 110, tr. Walker, *The Wellsprings of Wisdom*, p. 72 in which the Soul is said to carry out, through the souls of the world, different kinds of organising, formation and inventing of pure arts. See also Hirji, 'A Study of *al-Risālah al-bāhirah*', p. 184.

[24] Cf. Walker's comments in *The Wellsprings of Wisdom*, pp. 119–120. On al-Sijistānī's idea on the legislations' necessary changes, see his *Kashf al-maḥjūb*, tr. Landolt, *Unveiling of the Hidden*, p. 116.

(for al-Kirmānī, the changes are all the *qāʾim*s, namely all human beings that are undergoing a spiritual resurrection by following the Imams' teachings and who are in actuality in their bodies).[25] The *qadar*, on the other hand, is acknowledged to be a creation (*khalq*) from God (probably either the World mentioned in *Faṣl* Eight which has reached perfection, or the 'perfected emanated being' who is for al-Kirmānī the result of a second emanation) which operates through superior beings – the celestial entities belonging to the higher dimension – and their movements which have been decreed directly by God Himself, just as God directly appoints all of His *nuṭaqāʾ*.[26] It is most likely with reference to the *qāʾim*s and the resurrected human beings that al-Kirmānī quotes Q 41:53.

From this, al-Kirmānī, espousing al-Rāzī's thought, deduces that the *qaḍāʾ* is not decreed because the *qaḍāʾ* signifies the possible perfected human souls, since the *qaḍāʾ*, as already specified in the fourteenth *faṣl*, is *laysa bi-muqaddar* (not through a decree).[27] The *qadar*, conversely, has been decreed just, as the raised intellect whose acquired perfection through knowledge and action – decreed by the ordered movements of the celestial beings – has predestined it to become the third of the ten intellects.

---

[25] Al-Rāzī had identified it with the actualisation of the mission of the foundation.

[26] Cf. the argument above on p. 175.

[27] See *supra*, p. 205.

Faṣl Seventeen

With regard to the author of the *Nuṣra* and the method of answering he pursued, regarding the proof to submit to the author of the *Iṣlāḥ*, he did not write anything that invalidates (*lam yuwarrid shay*^{an} *yanquḍu*) what the author of the *Iṣlāḥ* built his argument upon, and his explanation, except for the meanings which he adduced for it according to his [al-Sijistānī's] interpretation mentioning that each one [of these meanings] confirms that *qaḍāʾ* signifies the Antecedent and that the *qadar* signifies the Follower.

It is not because the *nāṭiq* in his composition of the *sharīʿa* is like the Follower, as he [al-Sijistānī] adduced, nor is it because in everything that he wants to make comprehensible [he] returns to the Follower, for he has established, [that] it was incumbent upon him [al-Rāzī] to confirm that *qaḍāʾ* signifies the Antecedent and *qadar* signifies the Follower; there is no correspondence (*munāsiba*) between *qaḍāʾ*, *qadar* and the meanings that he has explained. For if the meaning of *qaḍāʾ* and *qadar* were applicable (*muṭābiq*^{an}) to the First and the Second, or corresponding to them in any way, he should have called them *qaḍāʾ* and *qadar* from that perspective. As for *qaḍāʾ*, its meaning has been established by the Speech [of God]. And similarly for *qadar*. Hence, they do not deserve to be called the First and the Second for they are free (lit. innocent, *barīʾān*) from what these two meanings impute. For if anyone says that of them, it is like calling honey, whose nature is sweetness, an aloe, whose nature is bitterness.[1]

Analysis and interpretation: For al-Kirmānī, generally speaking, the author of the *Nuṣra* does not aim to demolish the arguments of the author of the *Iṣlāḥ* in their entirety. Al-Sijistānī, in fact, only contradicts

---

[1]　Al-Kirmānī, *Riyāḍ* (HL), pp. 139–140.

what was stated by his fellow *dāʿī* in terms of the meanings he applies to the *qaḍāʾ* and the *qadar*. However, starting with this section and in the following two, al-Kirmānī's gentle approach wanes as he advances a series of arguments aimed at demolishing al-Sijistānī's attempts to provide further proofs for the identification of the *qaḍāʾ* with the Antecedent and the *qadar* with the Follower. In the above passage, al-Kirmānī propounds that al-Sijistānī makes the mistake of not explaining the real meanings of *qaḍāʾ* and *qadar*. These do not bear any correspondence with the 'First' and 'Second' but nonetheless al-Sijistānī simply signifies them as just, respectively, the First and the Second. This, al-Kirmānī comments, is not a real explanation as it is devoid of any sound connotation. It is probable that the implied temporal succession that characterises the First as first and the Second as second bears no coherence vis-à-vis al-Sijistānī's disguised indentifications of the *qaḍāʾ* with the *qāʾim* in concealment and the *qadar* with the final Resurrector. These, al-Sijistānī has intimated in previous arguments, both have a potential nature and therefore defy any temporality, which is generally associated with actualised entities. That al-Kirmānī found al-Sijistānī's method incongruous is underlined by the simile on the honey and the aloe.

Faṣl Eighteen

As for the analogy, in the second meaning, between the *nāṭiq* and the Follower, it is not in conformity with what the rule (*qānūn*) of the guiding mission (*al-daʿwa al-hādiyya*) [states]. For the *nāṭiq* is present (*qiyām*) in the corporeal world and, in the world of religion, he occupies the position (*maqām*) of the Antecedent whereas the position of the Follower in the world of origination (*ʿālam al-ibdāʿ*) belongs to the *waṣī*. This is because the *nāṭiq* and the foundation (*asās*) are two symbols (*mithlān*) [respectively] for the Antecedent and the Follower, and symbols for the sun and the moon.[1]

Analysis and interpretation: Al-Kirmānī continues his criticism of al-Sijistānī. Referring to what al-Rāzī stipulates in his *Iṣlāḥ*, al-Kirmānī declares that if the *qaḍāʾ* corresponds to the Antecedent and the *qadar* to the Follower, this leads to the incongruity that the *nāṭiq* corresponds to the *tālī* although he is responsible for bringing about the *sharīʿa*. It is therefore erroneous to make such an association, for it is against the rules of the rightly guided religion. The *nāṭiq* should rather be seen as a symbol of the Antecedent, whilst the foundation as a symbol of the Follower. As previously mentioned, Ivanow has argued that the erroneous reversal of the official *qānūn* might have been due to the persisting tendency, in some Shiʿi milieux, to acknowledge the rank and role of the Imam as being above those of the Prophet, and the esoteric doctrine as being above the exotericism of the *sharīʿa*. The implication would have meant that the esoteric interpretation

---

[1] Al-Kirmānī, *Riyāḍ* (HL), p. 140. The translation here has been slightly modified from De Cillis, 'A Preliminary Study on the Significance of *Qaḍāʾ* and *Qadar*', pp. 362–363.

provided by the Imam superseded the prescribed forms of worship indicated in the letter of the *sharīʿa* brought about by the *nāṭiq*.[2] Just as the moon succeeds the sun, so in the major cycle, the *nāṭiq* is represented by the sun and the *asās* by the moon.[3]

---

[2]   Ivanow, 'An Early Controversy', p. 109.
[3]   Nāṣir-i Khusraw, *Wajh-i dīn*, p. 195.

Faṣl Nineteen

As for the third meaning, he [al-Sijistānī] wrote adducing from it that the flight of the *nāṭiq* was from the intensity of the light of the *ta'yīd* of the Antecedent towards the *ta'yīd* of the Follower, but this is unsubstantiatable (*manāf li'l-wājib*). The *ta'wīl* in the state of *al-jadd* which he uses as his evidence needs deeper investigation and greater thought, and we will return to this. On the whole, what the author of the *Iṣlāḥ* said on the matter in the chapter is sounder (*aqwā*).[1]

Analysis and interpretation: Al-Kirmānī's comments are upfront in this *faṣl*: al-Sijistānī's argument, that in the prophetic saying mentioned earlier the flight of the Prophet is a flight from the intensity of the the *ta'yīd* of the Antecedent towards the *ta'yīd* of the Follower, is unsustainable.

---

[1]   Al-Kirmānī, *Riyāḍ* (HL), p. 140.

Faṣl Twenty

The author of the *Iṣlāḥ* spoke regarding the interpretation of a verse from the story of Moses (peace be upon him): "'Oh my Lord, show (Thyself) to me that I may look upon Thee.' God said: "By no means can thou see Me; but look upon the Mount'" [Q 7:143].[1] This request for God to unveil Himself to him [Moses] was above (*fawqa*) what was destined for him (*quddira*) from the limit (*ḥadd*) of the Antecedent. In saying to him [Moses], 'By no means can Thou see Me; but look upon the Mount', it was made clear that he could not attain that, and he was ordered (*umira*) to restrict (*bi'l-iqtiṣār*) [himself] to what proceeds towards him through *al-jadd*, and it was made clear to him [Moses] that his request was not within the capability of *al-jadd* or of any other subtle thing like him. So how could he attain it?[2] Did He not say: "'If it abides in its place, then shalt thou see Me.' When his Lord manifested His glory to the Mount, He made it as dust. And Moses fell down in a swoon' [Q 7:143]? Then he [Moses] knew he had made a mistake in requesting the unattainable (*mā lā yanāluhu*) and he humbled himself to his Lord: 'When he recovered his senses he said: "Glory be to Thee! To Thee I am repentant"' [Q 7:143]. That is what he [al-Rāzī] said.[3]

---

[1] The impossibility for any human being to gaze upon God can be found also in Exodus (33:18–20): 'And he [Moses] said, I beseech thee, shew me thy glory. ... And he said, Thou canst not see my face: for there shall no man see me, and live' (King James Version).

[2] Al-Kirmānī, *Riyāḍ* (HL), p. 141.

[3] Cf. al-Rāzī, *Iṣlāḥ*, pp. 52–53. Al-Rāzī holds that the story of Moses recounted in the Qur'an exemplifies the need not to transgress one own's limits and not to long for something whose appointed time has not yet come. These topics are inferred when al-Rāzī speaks negatively of the burning desire some souls have in attempting to gain more and more divine blessings so as to attain to a higher spiritual status. This attitude,

The author of the *Nuṣra* said that: '"Oh my Lord! Show (Thyself) to me, that I may look upon Thee" means that you do not have the endurance (*taṭīq*) and the forbearance (*taṣbīr*) to that degree (*murattaba*), "but look upon the Mount" and this is *al-jadd* with its proximity to Me. "If it [the Mount/*al-jadd*] abides in its place, then shalt thou see Me" means if it abides in its degree which I granted to it, and if it can bear what is outside what I have allotted (*iṭṭalaʿtu*) for it, then you will also be able to bear that. But *al-jadd* could not bear it when [the Antecedent] manifested itself to it, and [*al-jadd*'s] identity was on the verge of fading away.' And this is what he [al-Sijistānī] said.[4]

We [al-Kirmānī] say: With regard to the interpretation of the verse according to what the two authors have said, they set Moses (peace be upon him) in the position of the prophets of the highest rank, those who can communicate with the highest dignitaries (*al-ḥudūd al-ʿulwiyya*), and they have set him apart from the totality of the *ʿulamāʾ*, and counted him in the party of the ignorant (*zumrat al-juhalāʾ*) because of his requesting what he did not know to be above his limits. But what of him and how did the matter develop?

The *taʾwīl* of the verse is not as the two of them have expounded. This is because Moses (peace be upon him) did not have a conversation (*mukhāṭaba*) with the highest dignitaries [i.e. the Intellect/Antecedent and the Soul/Follower] but with the lower *ḥudūd* (*al-ḥudūd al-sufliyya*) because he had not yet reached the degree of *nāṭiq*-ship (*darajat al-nuṭq*), and [because] he had asked the

---

he claims, is to be condemned as but another form of greed. Even the Qurʾan warns against this kind of attitude and does so with direct references to Muḥammad. The Prophet, al-Rāzī explains, 'was told: "Move not thy tongue concerning it [the Qurʾan] to make haste therewith" [Q 75:16] and then He said: "But when We have promulgated it, follow thou its recital" [Q 75:18]. So he [the Prophet] was commanded to wait (to take time, *yatāʾannā*) until it [the Qurʾan] had reached him, without hastening its revelation. And God said in another verse: "Be not in haste with the Qurʾan before its revelation to thee is completed but say My Lord advance me in knowledge" [Q 20:114]' (al-Rāzī, *Iṣlāḥ*, pp. 50–53). The question of hastening towards something is also intimated in the Prophetic saying 'I flee from the *qaḍāʾ* of God towards His *qadar*', whose interpretation has been already discussed.

4　　Al-Sijistānī infers that Moses requested something that would have superseded the limits imposed upon his rank and for this reason he was not able to endure the experience that befell him.

author/possessor of the command (*ṣāḥib al-amr*)[5] for something whose time had not yet arrived (*mā lam yakun qad ān waqtu-hu*).[6] This is because it was a time of interval (*zaman fatrat*[in]), during which the people of the truth were undergoing tribulation, disguise and concealment from [their] opponents and those who would do them harm. Moses (peace be upon him) saw from himself a power (*quwwa*) and he estimated (*qaddara*) that it was possible at that time, through it, that he had been ordered (*umira*) to remove an ordeal from the people of the truth and [attain] vengeance over the enemies of God, and that [he had been ordered to replace] the policy of the community (*siyāsat al-umma*) with the policy of the truth (*siyāsat al-ḥaqq*), as the *asās* (peace be upon him) had decreed. [This] until he realised that the power within himself was what had been decreed [for him], so he repented as he acknowledged that he had been mistaken; the sun returned to him and threw light upon what we have explained in our epistles (*rasā'il*) by way of *ta'wīl*. And Moses (peace be upon him) asked the author/possessor of the command, who was Shuʿayb, when he came across him, about who was his Lord. This [occurred] after he [Shuʿayb] explained to him [Moses] what His [God's] command was, and that he [Moses] would find the power and the capacity within himself to carry out the policy; and he [Shuʿayb] said to him [Moses]: "My Lord, show (Thyself) to me, that I may look upon Thee." This means, order me and I shall prepare (*udabbiru*) this order and remove the affliction [of

---

[5]   The title 'ṣāḥib al-amr', often rendered also as 'the Lord of the Cause', indicates an enigmatic dignitary in Ismaili literature. Such nomenclature is in some instances employed to refer to the hidden, expected Imam. However, in the specific context of this study, both al-Kirmānī and al-Rāzī confer this title to the prophet Shuʿayb. Specifically, according to al-Rāzī, Shuʿayb served as the missionary leader of the twelve adjuncts (*lawāḥiq*), acting as the Imam's deputies during the Imam's *fatra*. On the other hand, al-Kirmānī describes Shuʿayb as a prophet (he is said to own the staffs of preceding prophets, i.e. the exoteric facets of the preceding religious laws) and as the knower of esoteric readings, namely as the person who instructs Moses on the hidden significance of Q 7:143.

[6]   Interestingly, in the Ikhwān al-Ṣafā's *Rasā'il*, Epistle 3 (*On Astronomia*), the whisper of Iblīs suggests that the voice Moses is hearing is not God's utterance: 'These words that you hear are perhaps not the words of God', to which Moses replies with the statement reported in Q 7:153. See Ikhwān al-Ṣafā', *Rasā'il*, vol. I, p. 143, ed. and tr. F. Jamil Ragep and Taro Mimura, *On Astronomia* (London and Oxford, 2015), p. 71.

the *umma*]. He [Shu'ayb] said: '[God] said: "By no means can thou see Me."' This means, you will not see Me do any of that, and I shall not give you any command at this time. Indeed, there is a time and a season for everything,[7] but this time is not the time for taking them, namely the [members of the] community (*umma*), away from pursuing their whims (*ittibā' ahwā'*), and it is not the time to respond to [other] matters, [and making them follow] a regulated policy (*qawānīn al-siyāsa*) for what we say to you will not be accomplished [now].

In telling him [Moses] of his mistake, when he requested [to see] the most sublime face,[8] Shu'ayb (peace be upon him) wanted to teach him that he had asked for something out of reach that would not be completed at that time, [but subsequently] at the hands of someone with power (*quwwa*) and support (*najad*) and preparedness (*'udda*) and organisation (*'idda*) [like Moses came to have].[9] How could that be? From his [Moses'] perspective, he

---

[7] Cf. Ecclesiastes 3:1: 'To everything there is a season, and a time to every purpose under the heaven (לַכֹּל זְמָן; וְעֵת לְכָל-חֵפֶץ, תַּחַת הַשָּׁמָיִם)' (King James Version). It is worth recalling that al-Kirmānī was well acquainted with the Hebrew text of the Old Testament, the Syriac version of the New Testament and the post-Biblical Jewish writings. See Daftary, 'Hamid al-Din al-Kirmani', in *The Internet Encyclopedia of Philosophy*, ed. James Fieser at http://www.utm.edu/research/iep/k/kirmani.htm, 2003. An electronic version appears on the website of The Institute of Ismaili Studies at https://iis.ac.uk/encyclopaedia-articles/hamid-al-din-al-kirmani, last accessed on 24 May 2018. See also Paul Kraus, 'Hebräische und syrische Zitate in ismā'īlitischen Schriften', *Der Islam*, 19 (1931), pp. 243–263; Daniel De Smet and Jan M. F. Van Reeth, 'Les citations bibliques dans l'œuvre du dā'ī ismaélien Ḥamīd al-Dīn al-Kirmānī', in *Law, Christianity and Modernism in Islamic society*, ed. Urbain Vermeulen and Jan M. F. Van Reeth (Leuven 1998), pp. 147–160.

[8] It should be remembered that, according to al-Sijistānī, the face of God is a reference to the Intellect. Thus, Moses' request is to be admitted to a direct contact with the ultimate knowledgeable limit, the first originated being. It has already been noted that a direct approach to the highest spiritual *ḥudūd* is contemplated only upon Resurrection. In denying that Moses entertained a direct conversation with the highest celestial ranks, al-Kirmānī once again emphasises that the time of the final *qiyāma* had not yet arrived during the era of Islam.

[9] In this context, Shu'ayb's attitude recalls Khiḍr's replies to Moses in Q 18: 'Verily, thou wilt not be able to have patience with me.' (Q 18:67); 'Did I not tell thee that thou canst have no patience with me?' (Q 18:72 and again at Q 18:75); and 'This is the parting between me and thee: now will I tell thee the interpretation of [those things] over which thou wast unable to hold patience.' (Q 18:78). On the identification

was very high ranked in the *da'wa*, a great wordly leader, and he had support, and money and men [at his disposal] and sovereignty.[10] He [Shu'ayb] said to Moses (peace be upon him): 'You have discovered that this thing will not be accomplished at this time for it is very difficult, and do not consider that I have forbidden anything to you out of meanness or that I have delayed you reaching your station (*ithār li-ta'khīrak 'an manzilatik*).' 'But look upon the Mount' means this man who has the wordly power and the capacity and the preparedness; 'if it abides in its place, then shalt thou see Me' means that if he stayed steady (*thabita*) on what He had ordered him [to do and not to do], He would have enabled (*imkana*) him with the power and assistance that he had to expound the rulings of the policy of the truth and complete it; 'Then shalt thou see Me' [means then shalt thou see me] doing what you asked and I shall make you an executor (*wasī*) in the matter; 'When his Lord manifested His glory to the Mount' means He ordered him [Moses] to establish a beacon of truth (*manār al-ḥaqq*); 'He made it as dust' means the command unto the people (*qawm*) was too difficult (*ḍāqa*), and they did not accept it and they broke away from the community, and so [Moses] was greatly troubled and perturbed, and the leaders planned to [make Moses' community] set out against him at noon.[11] Moses (peace be upon him) knew that what he [Shu'ayb] thought he would be able to accomplish at the time was impossible and that the author/possessor of the command, who was his lord, knew more of the matter than he did. He bestirred himself from his confusion about that [situation] through that warning sign [the leadership's plotting against him] and he said: 'Glory be to Thee! To Thee I am

---

of Khiḍr with Shu'ayb, see Brannon M. Wheeler, *Moses in the Quran and Islamic Exegesis* (London and New York, 2002), pp. 58–60. On the relationship between Khiḍr and Moses, see Roberto Tottoli, *Biblical Prophets in the Qur'ān and Muslim Literature* (Richmond, 2002), p. 34.

[10] This is a reference to the Qur'anic account that Moses was adopted by Pharaoh and his wife and brought up as their own son, a prince.

[11] This is a reference to Q 28:20. After having undergone a violent encounter with a corrupt Egyptian in the land of Pharaoh, Moses receives from a man who had befriended him a warning to flee, as rumours of his actions had reached men in power who were plotting to have him slaughtered. The story referred to in the Qur'an sees Moses reaching the land of Madyan where he is introduced to the old prophet Shu'ayb by his daughters, one of whom, Zipporah, was to become Moses' wife.

repentant.' He retracted his words and regretted (*nadam*) [having said them] and he found forbearance [to do] what the author/possessor of the command had commanded until the end of that period in which he [the author/possessor of the command] had engaged him. And when that time came, His [God's] word proved to be correct: 'then shalt thou see Me' [meaning] I shall hand over (*usallimu*) the matter to you [and you] will do as you wish. This is the *ta'wīl* of the verse and not as he [al-Sijistānī] wrote it down and promoted it, for that is inapplicable (*lā yuṭābaq*).[12]

Analysis and interpretation: As mentioned previously, according to Q 7:143, on Mount Sinai Moses implored God to show Himself. God ordered Moses to look towards the mountain so that he might see Him. Struck down, Moses fell unconscious. Once back to his senses, he acknowledged his arrogance in trying to see God and repented. Moses' falling into unconsciousness and his successive awakening might be compared, purely speculatively, to al-Sijistānī's idea of the Soul's obligatory plunge into oblivion (*nisyān*) – epitomising the Soul's incarnation in the physical world – prior to the recollection of her spiritual origin and rank below the Intellect.

The theory of Soul's descent into particular souls, which was allegedly upheld in the *Nuṣra*, is a topos found in Plotinus' *Enneads*. When explaining how life spreads within the cosmos as well as in individuals, Plotinus states that the Soul, overflowing into the motionless mass of the world, expands and closely penetrates it, enlightening it like the sun's rays illuminate and gild a dark cloud. By descending into the world, the Soul drags the latter out of its inertia, gifting it with movement, life and immortality.[13] The Soul's power manifests by embracing and governing the world according to her will, and by the way the Soul vivifies at once all parts of the world's immense body, remaining whole and indivisible, like the unity of the Intellect that has engendered the Soul.[14]

Al-Sijistānī borrows from Plotinus' view but modifies it: in his *Kitāb al-Maqālīd* (*iqlīd* 49), al-Sijistānī infers that the Soul rises up to the Intellect in order to receive benefits from him in two stages, and it is exactly by virtue of these motions that the Soul's expansion of her

---

[12] Al-Kirmānī, *Riyāḍ* (HL), pp. 141–144.

[13] Plotinus, *Enneads*, V. 1.5.

[14] Ibid.

individual parts occurs in Nature, with this spurring a passage from potentiality into actuality. Because of those two stages, duration (*daymūma*) is said to pertain to the Soul perpetually. Similarly, in his *Kashf al-maḥjūb*, al-Sijistānī explains that between the Intellect and the Soul there are two powers, love (*maḥabba*) and domination (*ghalaba*): through love, the Intellect gives benefits to the Soul; through domination, the Soul receives benefits from the Intellect.[15] Again in the *Kitāb al-Yanābī'*, al-Sijistānī, hinting at the Soul's incapacity to attain her perfection and rank with respect to the Intellect by herself, adduces that the Soul is in need of the 'intellectual benefits' (*fawā'id 'aqliyya*) which partial souls (*juz'iyyāt*) acquire (*iktisabat*) in this world through the intermediacy of sensible things (*maḥsūsāt*).[16]

What emerges from all these arguments is that the Soul needs to particularise herself in individual souls, with the latter, in turn, relying for their subsistence on the forms of the sensible things. Only the benefits that the Soul attains from the sensible realm allow her to receive the benefits from the Intellect. The corollary of such an understanding is that individual souls pre-exist within the Soul whose fall into Nature merely actualises the individualisation of all *juz'iyyāt*. Al-Sijistānī, by speaking of the Soul's attempt to ascend to her second rank, heralds what is further elaborated in the decadic Ṭayyibī doctrine with regard to the third intellect. For al-Sijistānī, the Soul's upward journey occurs after her 'fall/incarnation' in the lowest levels of the vegetative and animal souls. Inherent in this Platonic redemptive journey is the necessity for some human souls to be embodied in the Ismaili religious dignitaries – just as in the Ṭayyibī myth – as this offered, as Mayer words it, 'an ultimate archetype for the dynamics of the earthly *da'wa*'.[17]

It is not difficult to guess why such standpoints were condemned by al-Kirmānī for their implications of metempsychosis. Souls,

---

[15] Tr. Landolt, *Unveiling of the Hidden*, p. 98. For discussions on the Empedoclean sources of this doctrine, see De Smet, *Empedocles Arabus Une lecture néoplatonicienne tardive* (Brussels, 1998), pp. 121–128.

[16] Al-Sijistānī, *Kitāb al-Yanābī'*, p. 165, tr. Walker, *The Wellsprings of Wisdom*, p. 105; Daniel De Smet, 'La doctrine avicennienne des deux faces de l'âme et ses racines ismaéliennes', p. 82.

[17] Ibn al-Walīd, *al-Risāla al-Mufīda*, tr. Madelung and Mayer, *Avicenna's Allegory on the Soul*, p. 82; see also the analysis by De Smet in 'La doctrine avicennienne', pp. 83–84.

al-Kirmānī explains, are absolutely deprived of knowledge before their association with bodies; even if it can be admitted that souls have descended into bodies aiming to acquire such knowledge in order to attain their perfection, it cannot be said that the Soul needs their intermediacy for herself because she already has a sufficient degree of perfection.[18] Al-Kirmānī's theory of 'double worship' and his frequent allusions to the soteriological function of learning is a testimony to his rejection of al-Sijistānī's Platonic-inspired *anamnêsis*: particular souls do not pre-exist before entering bodies, and their active cognitive ascension begins in conjunction with the sensory perceptions attained through the *jism*.[19]

Al-Rāzī's rendering of Moses' story corroborates not only his but also al-Kirmānī's understanding of particular souls being merely traces of Soul; as opposed to some contemporary radical Jewish views, which believed in a quasi-divinised Moses and in the eternal validity of the Mosaic legislation,[20] al-Rāzī redimensions the uniqueness of Moses' experience and mandate by inferring that, as per the Qur'anic verse, Moses' knowledge/intellectivity is inseparable from his bodily perceptiveness which, being bound to sensorial data, hinders a direct vision of the spiritual dignitaries.[21] Moses attains knowledge/understanding only in the forms of benefits bestowed by the Roots through the branches (*furū'*) (such as *al-jadd*) which, according to al-Kirmānī, can be approached through their corresponding terrestrial *ḥudūd* such as Shu'ayb.

Al-Rāzī employs Q 7:143 to explain the gradual formation of prophethood through the encounter with celestial beings. We have mentioned that, in his *Iṣlāḥ*, he examines how the development of the prophetic faculty and the attainment of *nāṭiq*-ship occur through

---

[18] De Smet, 'La doctrine avicennienne', pp. 84–85) referring to al-Kirmānī, *Riyāḍ* (Beirut, 1960), pp. 87–99, 132.

[19] On Plotinus' denial of the existence of memory in souls within the intelligible world, see d'Ancona, 'The Textual Tradition of the Graeco-Arabic Plotinus', pp. 59–60.

[20] Alfred L. Ivry, 'Ismāʿili Theology and Maimonides' Philosophy', in *The Jews of Medieval Islam: Community, Society and Identity*, ed. Daniel Frank (London, 1995), pp. 288–290.

[21] Also mirrored in the emphasis al-Rāzī laid on the seventh rather than the fourth *nāṭiq* as held by al-Nasafī, see below.

the bestowal by the Intellect and the Soul of those spiritual faculties (*al-jadd*, *al-fatḥ* and *al-khayāl*) upon the highest dignitaries of the earthly hierarchy (i.e. the *nāṭiq*, the *asās* and the *imām*). The passage we find in the *Riyāḍ* testifies that al-Kirmānī was well informed about the discussions that al-Rāzī and al-Sijistānī, among others, were holding on this topic.[22] In the *Iṣlāḥ*, al-Rāzī argues that it is impossible even for prophets to attain a direct vision of the Intellect and the Soul without intermediates. The Qurʾanic verse cited above is, in a sense, employed to validate this idea: it is advanced that 'the Lord' referred to is but the Follower who instructs Moses as well as other dignitaries who are placed below the rank of the *nāṭiq*. The *tālī* is considered to be entrusted (*mutawallī*) with the task of granting spiritual faculties upon the dignitaries, whilst the Antecedent does so through intermediaries (*wāsiṭāt*) such as *al-jadd* and *al-khayāl*.[23] What seems to be at stake is the idea, previously mentioned, that only in the cycle of the final *qiyāma* will humans be admitted to a direct contact with all the highest spiritual dignitaries.

In the *Riyāḍ*, al-Kirmānī alludes to the same concept. The foregoing passage suggests that the capacity to attain a direct vision of one of the higher beings (the Follower) is 'above what is destined for him [Moses] from the rank of the Antecedent'. Unsurprisingly, al-Kirmānī claims that the interpretation of the Qurʾanic verse that both al-Rāzī and al-Sijistānī provide is not correct. Contrary to what the two thinkers propose, Moses did not hold a conversation with any of the highest celestial dignitaries (such as the Antecedent and the Follower) but with one of the lower *ḥudūd*. Moses then turns his call towards an initially unidentified 'author/possessor of the command' (*ṣāḥib al-amr*), demanding something whose time had not yet come. Initially convinced that the powers with which he had been endowed would have made him able to rescue his languishing community, Moses soon realises his wrong estimation and atones. It is at this point that al-Kirmānī sets aside vagueness and identifies the *ṣāḥib al-amr* with

---

[22]   This was an oft-discussed issue over which many Ismaili thinkers pondered. It can already be found in Jaʿfar b. Manṣūr al-Yaman's *Kitāb al-Kashf*. For references see Feki, *Les idées religieuses et philosophiques de l'Ismaélisme fatimide*, pp. 223–227.

[23]   Al-Rāzī, *Iṣlāḥ*, pp. 185–186.

the prophet Shu'ayb,[24] who enlightens Moses on the real significance of the command contained in the Qur'anic verse.[25]

Moses' wish to see the divine face should not be interpreted literally as the appeal for a visual divine epiphany but, rather, as Moses' yearning to obey the divine instruction and liberate his community from false beliefs. However, Shu'ayb emphasises that despite Moses' power and preparedness, the time had not yet come for the divine command to be ordered and for Moses' mission to be accomplished. The Arabic words generally referring to time (*waqt* and *zamān*) are mentioned in this passage six times in order to convey the sense of

---

[24] According to al-Rāzī, Shu'ayb was a *mustawda'* (trustee) at the time of the disappearance of the *mutimm* of that time. Shu'ayb's title is shared by Lot who is also indicated in al-Rāzī's *Iṣlāḥ* as the *ṣāḥib al-wadā'i'* or as the 'completer of the *dawr*' (al-Rāzī, *Iṣlāḥ*, pp. 211–224). Such a nomenclature, Ivanow has highlighted, had been adopted because the *mutimm*'s followers had become irremediably corrupt, committing all sorts of sins. Such trustees (*mustawda'īn*) were employed in similar grave circumstances and were the people to whom the true religious ideas were handed over until the advent of the 'fully accomplished' Apostle of God. See Ivanow, 'An Early Controversy', pp. 120–121.

[25] Shu'ayb is mentioned eleven times in the Qur'an, particularly in *sūra*s that highlight God's mercy and patience contrasted by human ingratitude and love of falsehood and vanity. Shu'ayb plays the role of a warner for his people, the Biblical Midianites, who, despite his attempts to lead them to the right path of God, reproached him and continued to devote themselves to fraud and mischief, thus finding themselves tragically punished (Q 7:85–95; 11:84–95; 26:176–191; 29:36–37). It is for this reason, Tottoli has observed, that Shu'ayb's story, as well as the Qur'anic episodes on two other prophets, Hūd and Ṣāliḥ, are relative to the so-called accounts of punishment (see Tottoli, *Biblical Prophets*, pp. 45–50). Just as in Shu'ayb's case, in Q 11:96 Moses is mentioned as having been sent by God as a redeeming figure for the unbelievers and as an authority against Pharaoh. Again, the Qur'anic chapter emphasises the human ingratitude manifest in Pharaoh's arrogance and in his act of misleading his people, thus condemning them to sin and penance. Later Qur'anic commentators identify Shu'ayb with the unnamed old father-in-law of Moses, the Old Testament Jethro, who lived in Madyan, as mentioned in Q 28:23, 28:25, 28:26. In Exodus, an episode (18:13–23) describes Moses' father-in-law giving Moses advice on the institution of a ranked system of justice prescribing the delegation of jurisdiction for minor legal issues and disputes to men delegated by Moses whilst leaving the weightiest questions for Moses himself to deal with. On Qur'anic references to Shu'ayb, see Brannon M. Wheeler, *Prophets in the Quran: An Introduction to the Quran and Muslim Exegesis* (London and New York, 2002), pp. 146–156; on the much-debated identification of Shu'ayb with Jethro, see *idem*, *Moses in the Quran and Islamic Exegesis*, pp. 56–58.

a divine determinism for which events will take place only when their decreed moment is meant to occur. Particular attention should be paid to the expression *zamān al-fatr*: in early Ismaili literature, it generally refers to the idea that, in each prophetic cycle, an interval (*fatra*) occurs between the presence of the seventh Imam and the advent of the *nāṭiq* who would inaugurate the new era, during which time the seventh Imam is represented by his deputies.[26] In particular, in the *Iṣlāḥ*, al-Rāzī holds that the time preceding Moses' *nāṭiq*-ship was such an interregnum, during which the community of believers was made vulnerable under the misguidance of an illegitimate *daʿwa*'s leader. Until the return of the absent Imam, al-Rāzī propounds, one of twelve adjuncts (*lawāḥiq*) was to act as the Imam's chief and deputy. During this *fatra*, Shuʿayb[27] served as the missionary leader of the twelve deputies.[28]

In the context of the passage from the *Riyāḍ*, the expression reveals much of how Fatimid *dāʿī*s such as al-Rāzī and al-Kirmānī interpreted Ismaili hierohistory, conditioned by the new 'doctrinal trends' that were undergoing development in their times. Probably shocked by the shameful episode of the 'Persian Mahdī,'[29] al-Rāzī – who like al-Kirmānī sets out to correct the antinomian tendencies in al-Nasafī's *Maḥṣūl* – denounces not only the illicitness of some aspects

---

[26] Daftary, *The Ismāʿīlīs*, pp. 226–227. Closely linked to Fatimid Ismailism, the Ṭayyibī tradition maintained that, in their hierohistory, the Islamic era was to be divided into cycles of concealment (*satr*) and manifestation (*kashf* or *ẓuhūr*) during which the Imams were either hidden or manifest. The first period of *satr* concluded with the appearance of ʿAbd Allāh al-Mahdī. This time was followed by a period of *ẓuhūr* which lasted until the concealment of the 21st Ṭayyibī Imam, al-Ṭayyib. On this topic, see Daftary, ibid., pp. 238–239. On the use of these concepts in Nizārī Ismailism, see *idem*, pp. 380–381; Ibn al-Walīd, *al-Risāla al-Mufīda*, tr. Madelung and Mayer's *Avicenna's Allegory on the Soul*, pp. 78–79.

[27] Shuʿayb's role defines the difference between the appointed Imam (*mustaqarr*) and an Imam who is merely a depositary or curator (*mustawadaʿ*), performing the functions of the true Imam whilst the latter is in concealment during particularly dangerous times. On this difference, see Corbin, *Temple and Contemplation*, p. 167.

[28] Apparently, al-Nasafī too held that in the absence of the Imam, twelve lieutenants would have led the community. This would have occurred until the return of Muḥammad b. Ismāʿīl.

[29] See W. Madelung, *Religious Trends in Early Islamic Iran* (Albany, NY, 1988), pp. 96–102; *idem*, 'Ḳarmaṭī', *EI2*, vol. 4, pp. 661–662.

of the Qarmaṭī propaganda but also the illegitimacy of an unidentified
'leader of the *da'wa*' claiming the imamate for himself.[30] This could be
a reference to a Fatimid caliph,[31] probably al-Mu'izz, given the correspondence between Moses as the fouth *nāṭiq* and al-Mu'izz as the fourth
Fatimid Imam.[32] When al-Rāzī, in his *ta'wīl* of the Qur'anic verse 7:143
suggests that Moses had requested the unattainable (*mā lā yanāluhu*),
he is probably denouncing al-Mu'izz's claim to the imamate. Just like in
the days of Moses, the Imam of the time was in a state of concealment,
whilst Moses – as the next *nāṭiq* – was en route towards the attainment
of his full *nāṭiq*-ship, likewise, at the time of al-Mu'izz, the legitimate
Imam (Muḥammad b. Ismā'il) was hidden whilst being, in al-Rāzī's
opinion, erroneously represented by the Fatimid caliph. Al-Kirmānī,
on his part, focused on legitimising the succession of all Fatimid Imams
(down to al-Ḥākim), uses the reference to *zamān al-fatr* to counter-
argue al-Rāzī's position and implement the rightfulness of al-Mu'izz (as
an Imam-caliph) and the lawfulness of his successor's appointment.[33]

As well as time, al-Kirmānī emphasises again the value of obedience: if Moses, like al-Mu'izz and all other Fatimid Imam-caliphs,
stands resolute in his appointed station without breaching the limits
that have been assigned to him, he will be made capable of carrying
out his mission by way of expounding, according to what he himself
will be entrusted with ('I shall make you a *walī* in the matter'), the
rulings of the policy of the truth.

Interestingly, in his *Kitāb Asās al-ta'wīl*, al-Qāḍī al-Nu'mān details
Shu'ayb's gradual training of Moses into prophethood and creates a
correspondence with the individual believer's initiatory ascent, which
is achieved by the attainment of knowledge through divine *ta'yīd*,

---

[30]	Al-Rāzī, *Iṣlāḥ*, p. 312; Nomoto, *Early Ismā'īlī Thought on Prophecy*, p. 345.

[31]	Hollenberg argues that al-Rāzī did not recognise the Fatimid Imam in North
Africa as one of the Imam's deputies. He rather viewed himself in such a role. Hollen-
berg, *Beyond the Qur'ān*, p. 23 note 80 and p. 112. Hollenberg refers also to Crone and
Treadwell, 'A New Text on Ismailism', pp. 37–67.

[32]	Madelung, 'Das Imamat', pp. 100–102.

[33]	This obviously served also to validate the legitimacy of al-Ḥākim. Fatimid mis-
sionaries, endeavouring to justify al-Mu'izz's unusual choice of successor, often found in
the *ta'wīl* of prophets from previous cycles – such as the Moses-Joshua succession – apt
parallelisms for al-Mu'izz's decision. See Hollenberg, *Beyond the Qur'ān*, pp. 112–113.

conveyed upon the followers of the *daʿwa*. In the above work, al-Qāḍī al-Nuʿmān specifies that Moses attained to the degree of *ḥujja* by fulfilling Shuʿayb's request of selecting headmen (*nuqabāʾ*) and making them righteous and knowledgeable, thereby becoming worthy of God's spiritual assistance. After attaining the exoteric facet of the request, Moses actualises his call, thus progressing from the rank of *naqīb* to that of *ḥujjat al-qārib*.[34] In the *Iṣlāḥ*, al-Rāzī too mentions Shuʿayb on several occasions.[35] Particularly in the last chapter of the *Correction*, Shuʿayb is denied the status of the sixth *mutimm* from the progeny of Isḥāq, which was apparently conferred to him in al-Nasafī's *Maḥṣūl*.[36]

What attracts our attention is Shuʿayb's attitude towards the laws compiled by the preceding enunciator-prophets, as this issue is linked to the discussion that al-Rāzī levelled against al-Nasafī's understanding of the rank of the fourth *nāṭiq*, Moses. Allegedly, according to al-Nasafī, Moses completed the manifestation of the Word (*ẓuhūr al-kalima*) through his 'rank of four-ness' (*ḥadd al-arbaʿiyya*) which he shared with the sun, in the cosmology of that time considered to be the fourth planet.[37] Al-Rāzī follows on the idea of the perfection

---

[34] Al-Qāḍī al-Nuʿmān, *Kitāb Asās al-taʾwīl*, p. 190.

[35] See in particular al-Rāzī, *Iṣlāḥ*, p. 205. Here, there are hints of the controversial topic of whether Adam had not brought a system of law. Al-Rāzī rejects this idea (*Iṣlāḥ*, p. 135), thus contrasting with al-Sijistānī's belief that, of the seven enunciator-prophets in the Ismaili hierohistory, only five were law-giving prophets: Noah, Abraham, Moses, Jesus and Muḥammad. Just as Adam had not prescribed religious rites or reformatory tasks, similarly, according to al-Sijistānī, upon his manifestation, the final *qāʾim* will not issue any new prophetic law. To al-Sijistānī's position, al-Kirmānī replies that Adam could not have implemented commands or prohibitions if not through a divine revelation, so that the establishment of a divine law was for Adam not only incumbent, but strictly necessitated by revelation itself. Similarly, according to al-Kirmānī, for the final Resurrector the instituting of a law will be obligatory for the wellbeing of all humankind. See al-Kirmānī, *Riyāḍ* (Beirut, 1960), pp. 176–212; De Smet, 'Adam, premier prophète et législateur? La doctrine chiite des *ulū al-ʿazm* et la controverse sur la pérennité de la *šarīʿa*, in *Le shīʿisme imāmite quarante ans après. Hommage à Etan Kohlberg*. ed. Mohammad A. Amir-Moezzi, Meir M. Bar-Asher and Simon Hopkins (Turnhout, 2009), pp. 187–202; Halm, *Kosmologie*, p. 102; Poonawala's Introduction, pp. 42–43.

[36] Al-Rāzī, *Iṣlāḥ*, pp. 211–224.

[37] Ibid., pp. 199–200. See also Ivanow, 'An Early Controversy', p. 118; Madelung, 'Das Imamat', p. 128 note 128; Cf. Nomoto's Introduction, p. 17, particularly note 73.

associated with the number four but addresses it to the seventh *nāṭiq*, that is, the last *qāʾim* (as Muḥammad b. Ismāʿil?).[38] The latter is truly the fourth *nāṭiq* because he emerges as a 'fourth one' (*rābiʿ*) following the manifestation of three preceding pairs of *nuṭaqāʾ*:[39]

> The first of the *nuṭaqāʾ*, who is the first to bring a *sharīʿa* and completes it and realises it by way of commandments and prohibitions, is the first of the masters of the laws (*aṣḥāb al-sharāʾiʿ*). This enunciator-prophet does not participate in the esoteric interpretation of the law. This is carried out by one amongst the *ḥudūd* who comes after him until the manifestation of the second *nāṭiq*. When the second *nāṭiq* appears, he abrogates (*nasakha*) the law of the first enunciator-prophet and brings a new *sharīʿa*; he does not only carry out the abrogation, but he legislates a new law. He is the first master of resolution (*awwal ṣāḥib al-ʿazāʾim*) and his resolution is called a resolution with regard to the abrogation of the law which comes before him [...] Successively, one amongst the *ḥudūd* who comes after him [i.e. the second *nāṭiq*] [interprets the law esoterically] until the time when the third enunciator-prophet manifests himself. With him the first [of the first three] *nuṭaqāʾ* are manifest. Because of his completion of the laws, [the degree of] 'first-ness' (*al-awwaliyya*) belongs to him. Just as to the first of the *nuṭaqāʾ* belongs 'the primacy in enunciation' (*al-awwaliyya bi'l-nuṭq*), so to the second [of the first three *nuṭaqāʾ*] pertains 'the primacy in abrogation and resolution' (*al-awwaliyya bi'l-naskh wa'l-ʿazīma*). The first is the first of the *nuṭaqāʾ*, the second is the first *walī* of resolution and the third is the first of completion. After these three [*nuṭaqāʾ*] who are the first [three *nuṭaqāʾ*], there are other three who are 'the other [last] ones' (*al-ākhirūn*). The *Sunna* of God which is given with

---

Nomoto has pointed out that the perfection of the number four was held by theories of natural philosophy contemporary to al-Nasafī, which found evidence of such perfection in the realm of nature. (On al-Nasafī's numerological speculations, see Madelung, 'Kawn al-ʿālam', pp. 26–28.) Conversely, one finds al-Sijistānī holding that six is the perfect number: it finds correspondence, *inter alia*, in the six days of creation, their signifying powers (motion, rest, prime matter, form, place and time) and the six parts of the human body. See al-Sijistānī, *Kitāb al-Yanābīʿ*, pp. 153–155, tr. Walker, *The Wellsprings of Wisdom*, pp. 98–99.

38   Al-Rāzī, *Iṣlāḥ*, pp. 203–205.
39   Ibid., pp. 211–212.

> the first [three *nuṭaqā'*] becomes a parable (*mathalᵃⁿ*) for 'the
> last ones' as in the words of God Almighty: 'And We made them
> people of the past and a parable for later ages' [Q 43:56]. And
> through those three who are the first [*nuṭaqā'*], the laws are com-
> pleted. When the fourth *nāṭiq* appears, he reiterates the *sharī'a*
> of the first one [i.e. the first *nāṭiq*] (*karrara sharī'a al-awwal*),
> enforces that [preceding] regulation (*rasm*) and corroborates it
> (*akkadahu*) by supplementing its regulation. He does not bring
> a new law (*bi-sharī'a jadīda*), rather, applies (*a'āda*) regulations
> (*rusūm*) [to the law of] the first of the *nuṭaqā'* and renews it
> (*jaddadaha*).[40]

Thus, the first *nāṭiq* among the *ākhirūn* (namely, the second set of
three enunciator-prophets) who is actually the forth *nāṭiq* (Moses)
does not bring a new law but renews the law brought by the first
enunciator-prophet. The second *nāṭiq* among the 'last ones' renews the
law of the second enunciator-prophet, just as the third *nāṭiq* renews
the law of the sixth of the *nuṭaqā'*. This means that the seventh and last
nāṭiq does not renew any law: he is the last *qā'im* whose mission is to
seal the three [pairs of] laws (*al-sharā'i' al-thalāth*).

In order to emphasise the singularity of the seventh enunciator-
prophet and the specificity of his role, in another counterargument to
al-Nasafī, al-Rāzī evaluates the kind of relationship occurring among
the letters forming the paired words *kūnī-qadar* and stresses the special meaning accorded to the seventh letter, *rā'*.[41]

> The seventh letter (*al-ḥarf al-sābi'*) is the repository for the master
> of unveiling (*ṣāḥib al-kashf*) and it is single (*mutafarrid*) for its
> blessing (*bi'l-faḍīla*) with regard to the letters which precede it, in
> the same way as the master of unveiling is single for his excellence
> and he is made particular (*khuṣṣ*) [...] with regard to his similars.
> In truth, we say that Shu'ayb with whom were the staffs (*'indahu
> 'iṣīy*) of the enunciator-prophets [who preceded him], gave
> (*dafa'a*) to Moses the staff of Adam, this meaning that his letter
> is separated from the letter which is [commonly] paired to it.[42]

---

40   Ibid., pp. 203–204.

41   Ibid., pp. 204–208.

42   Ibid., p. 205. Shu'ayb is said to possess the staffs of preceding prophets, which
is probably an allusion to his having inherited the exoteric facets of the preceding

[With regard to] the matter of the pairing of some letters with some other letters it is not as stated in his [al-Nasafī's] book [the *Maḥsūl*]. The pairing [of the letters forming the words *kūnī-qadar*] is [according to al-Nasafī]: the *kāf* is with *wāw*, the *nūn* with the *yā'* [i.e. the letters forming the word *kūnī*], and the *qāf* with the *dāl*; the *rā'* stays single and there is no pairing to it.[43] And this is a proof for the seven days during which God created His creation (*khalaqa Allāh... fīhā al-khalq*). Then the seventh, which is the [letter] *rā'*, is the proof for the seventh day in which there was no creation (*lā khalq fīhā*). There is a mistake [occurring] in that chapter (*bāb*) [in *al-Maḥsūl*]. However, what this pairing proves has another aspect to it. According to the pairing [exhibited] in that chapter, it is the pairing of the first three letters [i.e. the three letters belonging to the first group of letters, *k ū n*] with the second three letters [i.e. the three letters belonging to the second group of letters – *q d r*] whilst the fourth letter is not paired [...]. And some of them are the product of a procession (*munbaʿith*) from some [of the letters], just as the Second is separated from the First and proceeds from it. The *qāf* which is from the second [set of] three letters proceeds from the *kāf*, it

---

religious laws (see the Qur'anic verse in which God addresses Moses and makes him observe that, beside the outer form of his staff, there exist also its inner, living aspect – the moving serpent. Q 7:107; 20: 17–20). Shuʿayb, in the extract above, passes onto Moses Adam's staff, thus suggesting that, contrary to what al-Sijistānī believed, in al-Rāzī's opinion, Adam did bring forth a *sharīʿa*. Al-Rāzī concurs, however, with al-Nasafī's idea that Adam could not be classified among the *ulu'l-azm* prophets in that he did not abolish the law of any preceding *nuṭaqā'* (Daftary, *The Ismāʿīlīs*, p. 226). Noticeably, Shuʿayb is mentioned after al-Rāzī has spoken of the seventh letter and the latter's association to the 'master of unveiling'. It is not clear whether Shuʿayb himself should be identified with the 'master of the unveiling'; however, it is noteworthy that in the *Riyāḍ* he is dubbed as the *ṣāḥib al-wadāʾiʿ* and also as the 'the possessor of the command' (*ṣāḥib al-amr*). The latter epithet is repeated by al-Rāzī a few lines below (see his *Iṣlāḥ*, p. 208). Interestingly, Moses' obtaining of the staff – which in Qur'anic exegesis is often linked with the concepts of immortality and fertility as in Q 28:21–28 – is closely associated with Moses' marriage to Shuʿayb's daughter, Zipporah, their offspring, and Shuʿayb's acknowledgment of Moses' prophetic nature. See Muḥammad b. Jarīr al-Ṭabarī, *Jāmiʿ al-bayān fī tafsīr al-Qurʾān* (Beirut, n.d.), on Q 28:27–28, and Maḥmūd b. ʿUmar b. Muḥammad al-Zamakhsharī, *al-Kashshāf ʿan haqāʾiq ghawāmiḍ al-tanzīl wa ʿuyūn al-aqāwīl fī wujūh al-taʾwīl* (Beirut, 1315/1995), on Q 28:27–28. For further references, see Wheeler, *Moses in the Quran and Islamic Exegesis*, pp. 60–63.

43   The last three letters (*qāf, dāl, rā'*) are the ones forming the word *qadar*.

Table 3. The Coupling of the Letters kūnī-qadar according to al-Rāzī

أَرْبَعَةٌ	ثَلَاثَةٌ	إِثْنَيْنِ	وَاحِدٌ	الأَوَّلُ
ى	ن	و	كـ	

	سَبْعَةٌ	سِتَّةٌ	خَمْسَةٌ	ألثَّانِي
	ر	د	قَ	

is separated (*mushtaqq*) from it and coupled with it; the *yā'* [in *kūnī*] is single. It is the fourth letter from the first [set of] three letters. The first [three letters] are separated through it from the second [set of letters] by virtue of its excellence. It is the seventh of the letters, of all of them [i.e. the *rā'*], [that] is the repository of the seventh [*nāṭiq*], the master of the unveiling. There is not for this letter any partner (*zawj*) from the second [set of] letters, and because of [this] second [set of letters] he is the master of composition (*ṣāḥib al-tarkīb*), and because of the seventh cycle (*al-dawr al-sābiʿ*) it [the seventh letter] actualises its master. There is no composition in it, rather it is the cycle of expansion (*dawr al-basīṭ*). The coupling of the letters follows this example:

This is the pairing of the higher letters [but] is not as it is recounted in that book [*Maḥṣūl*]. There is a mistake in that perspective. This is because the pairing of the letters makes it incumbent for each of the letters of the second [set of] letters to be paired with each of the letters from the first [set of letters] and this is because they proceed from them just as the second proceeds from the first and it is paired with it as we have mentioned. As for these [set of] three letters, they proceed from the [first set of] three letters and some of them are paired with some of them. Similarly, the laws of the *nuṭaqā'* become three through the splitting (*niṣf*) of the second [group of the *nuṭaqā'* from the first group], and they are separated from the laws of the [other] three enunciator-prophets through the splitting from the first [three *nuṭaqā'*]; they are paired with them and separated from them. As for the fourth letter, it is fourth and it is the medium (*wāsiṭa*) between them: three [letters] before it and three [letters] after it. In addition, it is their seventh [letter] (*sābiʿuhā*), to all of them (*kulluhā*), because it is the repository (*muddakhar*) for the master of the seventh cycle and it is not paired with anything. Likewise, [as for] the master of the seventh cycle, who is the fourth of the masters of the laws after reiteration (*takrīr*) and after the [three] pairs of laws,[44] there is no law with him that is paired to any of the laws, and he is the master of the seventh cycle.[45]

---

[44] The master of the seventh cycle corresponds to the fourth of the *nuṭaqāʾ*, who has carried out the clarification of the Scriptures brought forth by the first three enunciator-prophets. There is no law or letter corresponding to him.

[45] Al-Rāzī, *Iṣlāḥ*, pp. 205–206. The text continues: 'Just as the seventh letter is single through its position with regard to corresponding letters, in the same way the master of the seventh cycle is single because of his position of the unveiling (*kashf*) with regard to the [potential] corresponding masters of the cycles. [...] The seventh cycle corresponds to the cycle of expansion, and just as it becomes the repository for the master of the seventh cycle which is ultimate and different from the [preceding] cycles, likewise [the seventh letter] establishes [a different role] in the remaining letters of the alphabet, and it is called letter of interjection (*ḥarf al-nidāʾ*) and letter of ascription (*ḥarf al-nisba*). [...] And there is to the third [enunciator-prophet] a degree of completeness (*tamām*) without perfection (*kamāl*); and to the sixth (enunciator-prophet) there is a degree of completeness and perfection together [...] This is because to him pertains the perfection of the two blessings, through action (*ʿamal*) without knowledge (*ʿilm*) and because the laws, which are works, are perfected through him. And the actualised mission (*al-daʿwa al-qāʾima*) is after him [the sixth enunciator-prophet] until it is completed and perfected [by] the seventh [enunciator-prophet], for to him pertains the degree of perfection (*kamāl*), of action (*ʿamal*) and of knowledge (*ʿilm*); he reaches the degree of four-ness (*martabat al-arbaʿiyya*) and of seven-ness (*martabat al-sabʿiyya*) and with him the cycles are completed' (see ibid. pp. 206–208). It should be noted that even the last enunciator-prophet, Muḥammad, is said to be perfect only in knowledge. Is there here a suggestion that ultimate perfection is attainable only upon the *qiyāma*? This would explain why only the last Resurrector will be perfect in both knowledge and action.

Faṣl Twenty-one

The author of the *Nuṣra* said: 'Regarding his [al-Rāzī's] argument in his statement, "It is He who had created everything according to measure (*wa khalaqa kulla shay*^{in} *fa-qaddarahu taqdīr*^{an})" [Q 25:2]', in saying that, he [al-Sijistānī] clarified the proofs for which *qadar* is a symbol (*mathal*) for the Follower and that the *qaḍāʾ*, which is creation (*khalq*), signifies the Antecedent; therefore in His statement, "it is He who had created everything", by "He" he means the Antecedent; this is because the Intellect is all things and all things are the Intellect (*al-ʿaql huwa al-ashyāʾ kulluhā wa al-ashyāʾ kulluhā hiya al-ʿaql*).'

We [al-Kirmānī] say: In the previous discussion about the *qadar* and the *qaḍāʾ*, what has become evident is that it is impossible to say that the *qaḍāʾ* and the *qadar* signify the Antecedent and the Follower, for what is meant by God's words: 'It is He who had created everything according to measure', is not what the author of the *Nuṣra* arrived at. For we have shown his wrongness (*fasād*) and it can neither be said of the Antecedent nor of the Follower that they can be called *qaḍāʾ* and *qadar*. Rather, the meaning of His words, 'it is He who had created everything according to measure', is that He [God] gave (*jaʿala*) all things, regarding religious matters and the benefits (*maṣāliḥ*), an exoteric and esoteric sense in the potentiality of the revelation and the *sharīʿa*; and '*fa-qaddarahu taqdīr*^{an}' signifies what for Him is the source (*ʿayn*) of the revelation and the *sharīʿa* from their contents (*iḥtiwāʾihumā*) in terms of all the sciences with regard to religious matters and the benefits and these [sciences], which are in potentiality in them both [i.e. the revelation and the *sharīʿa*], and the *taʾwīl* extracts it from them.[1]

---

[1] Al-Kirmānī, *Riyāḍ* (HL), pp. 144–145.

Analysis and interpretation: According to al-Sijistānī, al-Rāzī's interpretation of the *qadar* as the Follower should have led him to identify the *qaḍāʾ* as the Antecedent. Because al-Rāzī has described the *qaḍāʾ* as the act of *qadar*, it is reasonable to say that the *qaḍāʾ* is creation (*khalq*). Thus, the 'He' in Q 25:2 – 'It is He who had created everything according to measure' – must necessarily be identified with the Antecedent which, for al-Sijistānī, is the *amr/kalima* manifested through and with the Intellect. This is because the Intellect is all things and all things are the Intellect.

At this stage, al-Kirmānī remarks that it is an aberration to imbue the *qaḍāʾ* and the *qadar* with meanings such as the Antecedent or the Follower, with which they do not bear any relation. More simply put, he declares that the foregoing *āya* (Q 25:2) reminds the human being that God has provided all matters regarding religious issues and the welfare of the community with both an exoteric and an esoteric meaning, which are meant to be extracted from the revelation and the *sharīʿa*. Needless to say, such a hermeneutical task pertains to spiritually guided individuals such as Moses, who in their appointed time are able to explain the scripture and the law within the limits (so often stressed!) of their ongoing *nāṭiq*-ship, which has been decreed to deal with 'incomplete' revelations in need of that completeness which is brought to the *tanzīl* by the *taʾwīl*.

Faṣl Twenty-two

With regard to his [al-Sijistānī's] saying 'the Intellect is all things and that all things are the Intellect', it is a premise that is not sound (*lā taṣiḥḥ*). [This is] because the corporeal world in its totality is not an intellect, it is a thing, and the best meaning that can be given to it is 'the Intellect is all things, and all things are the Intellect'. Indeed, the Intellect who is the essence of the command of God Almighty (*dhāt amr Allāh*), is a cause (*'illa*) of the existence of all corporeal and non-corporeal things, and the existence of all things depends on the Intellect and this is what he [al-Sijistānī] intended.[1]

Analysis and interpretation: Al-Sijistānī's description of the Intellect as 'all things' is deemed unsound because the corporeal world cannot be classified as an intellect. To each entity, spiritual or corporeal, pertains a rank which cannot be superseded. The intellect precedes and encompasses all things but not vice versa. It is probably true, al-Kirmānī admits, that the expression 'the Intellect is all things and that all things are the Intellect' is the best to convey the idea that the Intellect is, in truth, the essence of God's *amr*, which is the cause of existence for corporeal and non-corporeal things. So, in a sense, al-Kirmānī is once again refuting al-Sijistānī's idea that the Intellect might embrace all the forms of the two worlds. It is quite significant that the Intellect is identified with the essence of the command of God (*dhāt amr Allāh*) rather than with the command itself so as to clarify that there are facets of the Intellect that transcend the *amr* itself. For the Intellect is the command but also simultaneously the recipient of the command, the subject and object of its thought, the act of origination and the

---

[1] Ibid., p. 145.

originated being acted upon, the cause and the effect of himself as well as the principle of all existents. Similarly, it is implicitly clarified that it is the Intellect who acts as the cause for all existents rather than the *amr*, as suggested by al-Sijistānī.

Faṣl Twenty-three

The author of the *Nuṣra* said: 'God authorised (*rakhkhaṣa*) the prophets in interpreting the meaning of the laws (*sharā'i'*) and the abandonment (*tark*) of their use (*isti'māl*) in His words: "On those who believe and do deeds of righteousness, there is no blame for what they ate [in the past], if they guard themselves from evil, and believe, and do deeds of righteousness – [or] again, guard themselves from evil and believe – [or] again, guard themselves from evil and do good. For God loveth those who do good"' [Q 5:93].[1]

We [al-Kirmānī] say: The verse does not contain either exoterically or esoterically any mention of authorisation for the prophets (peace be upon them) to abandon the use of the *sharī'as*. I do not know how he [al-Sijistānī] could arrive at saying that without having probed it [the matter] properly. The *tafsīr* for this verse and its *ta'wīl* are contrary to his conclusion. For God Almighty knew that souls do not reach happiness and do not attain the degree of perfection and do not exit from the rank of potentiality to that of actuality except by action and knowledge (*illā bi'l-'amal wa'l-'ilm*). The Almighty tasked (*kallafa*) the entirety of humankind to perform (actualise, *iqāma*) the two forms of worship (*'ibādatayn*), knowledge and action, so that thereby they could attain the two [forms of] happiness (*sa'ādatayn*) in the two realms. As souls cannot attain perfection and happiness except through the two [forms of] worship, should any soul abandon either of the two [forms

---

[1] In his *Kitāb al-Yanābī'*, al-Sijistānī claims that once the *qā'im* has attained the position (*manzila*) set up for him by God, there will surface a form capable of receiving the intellectual benefits (*al-fawā'id al-'aqliyya*) directly without (*balā*) these having to be redacted (through *ta'līf*) or having to be arranged (through *tartīb*). This obviously implies that the final *qā'im* will not preach any new *sharī'a*. See al-Sijistānī, *Kitāb al-Yanābī'*, p. 159, tr. Walker, *The Wellsprings of Wisdom*, p. 102.

of] worship, perfection would be out of reach (*nīl*) for that soul.[2] Someone who performs the two [forms of] worship, as legislated (*qunnina*) and exemplified (*muththila*) as long as [this person] is alive, either continues [performing] them until the time when he is transported into Paradise, or stops [performing] both or either of them, and finds himself in Hell, unless God forgives him. We have already explained in our books and in the foregoing discussion that souls are only raised through action and the correction of [natural] dispositions (*iṣlāḥ al-akhlāq*) – which is the greater effort (*al-jihād al-akbar*) as the Prophet of God (peace be upon him and his family) said, and [we have already explained] – and that [the souls'] acquisition (*iktisāb*) of blessings (*faḍā'il*) [comes] through spiritual exercise (*riyāḍa*) and the knowledge (*'ilm*) of that whose existence has preceded them [the souls] according to what has been made incumbent by the regulations (*qawānīn*) of the hermeneutical mission (*al-da'wa al-ta'wīliyya*).[3]

As the state of the souls in worship is such, how could God authorise the souls, or the *nuṭaqā'* or the *ḥudūd* beneath them, to abandon (*tark*) action (*'amal*) and the righteousness (*ṣalāḥ*) of the perfect soul [coming] from them? For this would bring about insufficiency.[4] By no means![5] Indeed, the verse has a *ta'wīl* which is other than his [al-Sijistānī's] interpretation. For in it [there] is a specificity (*khuṣūṣiyya*) [addressed to] those who perform the mission (*da'wa*) of calling [people] to the *tawḥīd* of God Almighty and the knowledge of His *ḥudūd* on the part of the Imams (peace be upon them). And this is because the *nāṭiq* (peace be upon

---

[2]   The two kinds of happiness are the eternal happiness (*sa'āda*) and the earthly happiness as intellectual *eudaemonia*. Here there is clear criticism towards those thinkers (including philosophers such as al-Fārābī), according to whom happiness could be attained through purely philosophical/intellectual speculation. Ultimate *sa'āda*, for our author, cannot prescind the combination of knowledge and action.

[3]   Cf. al-Kirmānī, *al-Maṣābīḥ fī ithbāt al-imāma*, Arabic text, pp. 24–25, English text, pp. 59–61.

[4]   The translation has been slightly modified from De Cillis, 'A Preliminary Study on the Significance of *Qaḍā'* and *Qadar*', pp. 365–366.

[5]   Al-Kirmānī refers here to the celestial blessings which, together with the influx descending from the Pleroma of the intellects, constitute the spiritual assistance that grants the souls of prophets and Imams with perpetuity in action and knowledge. See al-Kirmānī, *Rāḥat al-'aql*, pp. 209, 239, 273, 314, 324, 377–378, 384.

him) knew that his community would be fractious after him and that each group would set itself apart with its own *madhhab* established through their [each group's] deficient opinions and intellectual [speculations] (*bi-ārā'ihā wa 'uqūliha al-nāqiṣa*) and by their choice of (*ikhtiyārihum*) rightly guided Imams (the prayers of God upon them); 'And he for whom God hath not appointed light, for him there is no light' [Q 24:40]. For the *dā'īs* have had to endure every form of hardship from the fractious community (*al-umma al-mukhtalifa*) in their causing them harm having to disprove their *madhhab*, and their allegiance to the pure (*al-ṭāhirīn*) Imams (peace be upon them). He [God] authorised the *dā'īs* who perform the mission to have insight (*naẓar*) into the sciences that are not from their belief (*laysat min i'tiqādihum*), according to conditions (*sharā'iṭ*) that He has explained, as a tool (*'udda*) against their controversies (*munāẓirātihim*).

And He said: 'On those who believe and do deeds of righteousness there is no blame for what they ate, if they guard themselves from evil, and believe, and do deeds of righteousness', that is, not upon the performers of the *da'wa* of the *tawḥīd* of God who have knowledge of His *ḥudūd* from the perspective of the Imams (peace be upon them); 'those who believe' [means] people who complied (*al-mustajībīn*) in holding God's rope (*ḥabl*),[6] and preserved their loyalty against uncertainties (*shukūk*) and obscurities (*shubhāt*) in the religion of God, and who are brought to a degree of perfection (*kamāl*) and maturity (*balāgh*); there is no 'blame' (*junāḥ*), that is, restricting (*taḍyīq*); 'for what they ate', meaning what they read of the sciences which are not their belief, [and] it becomes for them like a weapon (*silāḥ*) to fight their opponents in the affirmation of the truth; 'if they guard

---

[6] This might be a reference to Q 3:103: 'and hold fast, all together, by the rope (*bi-ḥabl*) that God (stretches out for you), and be not divided among yourselves'. In the context of Ismaili symbolic cosmology, al-Qāḍī al-Nu'mān identifies Muḥam-mad's followers as the 'rope of God', thus, Elizabeth Alexandrin explains, establishing a continuous chain linking together individual practitioners to the Imams, the *asās* and the Prophet himself. Al-Qāḍī al-Nu'mān's aim was to clarify the superiority of the Prophet whilst stressing 'the necessity of obedience to the lower ranks of reli-gion in terms of individual practice'. See Elizabeth R. Alexandrin, 'Prophetic Ascent and Initiatory Ascent in Qāḍī al-Nu'mān's *Asās al-ta'wīl*', in *The Prophet's Ascension: Cross-Cultural Encounters with the Islamic* Mi'rāj *Tales*, ed. Christiane Gruber and Frederick Colby (Bloomington and Indianapolis, 2010), p. 163.

themselves from evil, and believe, and do deeds of righteousness', this is a condition (*shart*) so long as they follow the straight path in obedience to God Almighty and in following His Prophet (peace be upon him and his family), and have faith in His *ḥudūd* and perform the two [forms of] worship jointly, as he [the Prophet] brought these forth to them.

'If they guard themselves from evil and believe', this is the second condition, meaning they obeyed the Prophet in his legateeship (*waṣiya*) and [obeyed] the divinely appointed *qā'im*, and carried out the mission for him exoterically and esoterically.

'If they guard themselves from evil and do good', this is the third condition, meaning they obeyed the Imam inasmuch as God appointed him (*yuqīmuhu*) and gave him deputyship of the command (*yuwallīhi al-amr*), and they excelled in their mission towards the *tawḥīd* of God Almighty through His imamate. In doing that and fulfilling these conditions, no harm (*lā bā's*) came to them by their insight into those *madhhab*s and sciences that [were done] for the people and their study of them; and [this was] not a restriction (*lā ḍaīq*) on their beliefs for this was an aid (*ma'ūna*) for them [in] what they needed in order to resist enemies and those who wanted the defamation (*ṭa'n*) of the *ḥudūd*.

This is the *ta'wīl* of the verse and it does not contain any authorisation (*tarkhīṣ*) to abandon (*tark*) the use of the law (*isti'māl al-sharī'a*), for it is an authorisation to [have] insight into the sciences according to the afore-mentioned conditions. The sum-total of the discourse is that any *ta'wīl* that leads to permitting (*taḥlīl*) what God Almighty has forbidden, or to forbidding (*taḥrīm*) what God Almighty has permitted, or to changing (*taghyīr*) the ranks (*marātib*) of the dignitaries of the religion of God Almighty, or to blemishing (*ghamīza*) the *sharī'a* and the rituals of the monotheistic community, calling for the abandonment of any action through it [the *sharī'a*] and [calling for] the attainment of happiness through bending (*bi'l-'ukūf*) it [i.e. the *sharī'a*'s meaning], is a false (*fāsid*) *ta'wīl*. And our pure Imams (the blessings of God upon all of them), are innocent before God Almighty for his [al-Sijistānī's] interpretation and for all the *ta'wīl*s that are contrary to what the Prophet (peace be upon him and his family) arrived at.[7]

---

7 Al-Kirmānī, *Riyāḍ* (HL), pp. 145–148.

Analysis and interpretation: Al-Kirmānī cannot but disapprove of al-Sijistānī's idea that God has allowed some of His prophets to abandon the use of a given *sharīʿa*. It should be borne in mind that this was one aspect of al-Sijistānī's thought that his critics perceived as antinomianism. As is well known, al-Sijistānī lived an active life as an Ismaili *dāʿī* during the first half of the 4th/10th century, a time that saw the rise of the Būyid *amīr*s. During his lifetime, the Būyids, of Daylamite origin, initially of Zaydī persuasion later turned Twelvers, were one among the numerous Shiʿi dynasties that controlled wide territories of the Muslim world (the Fatimids of North Africa and Egypt, the Ḥamdānids of Syria and the Qarmaṭīs of Baḥrayn).[8] Whilst for the Qarmaṭīs, Muḥammad b. Ismāʿīl had already appeared as the *imām-qāʾim* and will return as the final *qāʾim*, thus justifying the abolition of the law's exoteric aspect, according to al-Sijistānī, who only in the more mature phase of his career and certainly after authoring the *Nuṣra* was persuaded to rebuke the Qarmaṭīs' teaching and embrace al-Muʿizz's Fatimid Ismailism, the *ẓāhir* of the *sharīʿa* was to be considered as mandatory as its *bāṭin*, so that observations of religious duties during the era of Islam could not be lifted. However, in his view, suspension of the religious law might well happen in the future at the end of human history when pure intellectuality will prevail upon binding obligations.[9]

Such ideas, despite having been curbed by al-Sijistānī, were still unacceptable for the Fatimid missionary al-Kirmānī; the belief that the last *qāʾim* would rescind from the law was defective, for no spiritual knowledge could be based on anything different from the prophetic laws and their injunctions for worship. The abrogation of the religious law hinted at by al-Sijistānī is absolute nonsense, al-Kirmānī states emphatically in the above passage of the *Riyāḍ*, and goes on to elucidate

---

[8]   Poonawala's Introduction, pp. 47–48; Tilman Nagel, 'Būyids', *EIr*, vol. IV, pp. 578–586.

[9]   According to Madelung, al-Sijistānī held that whilst the intellectual (*ʿaqlī*) laws will remain, the conventional (*waḍʿī*) laws will be abrogated in stages, thus leaving the final Resurrector with no laws to abrogate. Madelung, 'Das Imamat', p. 108; Hollenberg, *Beyond the Qurʾān*, p. 137 note, 81. On this topic, see also De Smet, 'Loi rationnelle et loi impose. Les deux aspects de la *šarīʿa* dans le chiisme ismaélien des Xᵉ et XIᵉ siècles', *Mélanges de l'Université Saint-Joseph*, 61 (2008), pp. 515–544.

why. Firstly, it is acknowledged that God Himself is aware of the fact that individual souls can only exit from the boundaries of potentiality and imperfection through knowledge and action. God, therefore, has imposed upon and assigned to the whole of humankind the task of performing the two forms of worship. This is not a capricious imposition but, rather, an act of providence which demands humans to fulfil an obligation for their own good: the attainment of happiness in this and the next life. Secondly, it is highlighted that action and the striving to correct natural dispositions can be carried out once the soul becomes conscious of what to do. This knowledge is exactly what has been made incumbent upon men by the laws legislated by the enunciator-prophets and which are explained by the directive hermeneutical mission of the *da'wa*.[10] Action and righteousness depend on compliance with the laws and it is consequently absurd to believe that the *sharī'a* can be dispensed with.[11] Thirdly, al-Kirmānī clarifies that the Qur'anic verse al-Sijistānī quotes bears a very specific explanation which is other than the one offered by his fellow *dā'ī*. Such specificity is directed towards every single missionary of the Ismaili cause, who, in his own rank, is entrusted with a precise assignment aimed at validating God's *tawḥīd* and the knowledge of His *ḥudūd*.

Following the Prophet's death, the community split and established different schools of law following diverse opinions. Because of this situation, Ismaili missionaries had to endure many difficulties in order to prove the veracity of their mission. However, they were able to carry it out because they were blessed with special insights into doctrinal positions different from their own. This capacity, al-Kirmānī explains, which functioned as a tool (*'udda*) and a weapon (*silāḥ*) against false beliefs, is granted to 'those who believe and do deeds of righteousness',

---

[10]   On God's commanding humankind to perform the two forms of worship, see *Faṣl* Twelve.

[11]   In his *Risāla al-waḍī'a*, Walker has observed, al-Kirmānī lists all the ritual obligations of an Ismaili Muslim – not dissimilar to the summary provided by al-Qāḍī al-Nu'mān in his *Da'ā'im al-Islām*. See Walker, 'The Ismaili *Da'wa* in the Reign of the Fatimid Caliph al-Ḥākim', p. 179 note 134. The doctrine regarding the abolition of all religious laws upon the advent of the Resurrector during the final cycle was propounded by al-Sijistānī in a number of works but, according to what al-Kirmānī reports, it was particularly emphasised in the *Nuṣra*. See al-Kirmānī, *Riyāḍ* (Beirut, 1960), pp. 198 and 201.

namely those who comply (*al-mustjībūn*) with the divine commands, keeping themselves steady before uncertainties and ignorance. Those are the men who, according to the above verse, can 'guard themselves from evil' on condition that they: (i) stay on the path of obedience, (ii) follow the Prophet's teaching, (iii) have faith in God's *ḥudūd* and (iv) perform the two forms of worship (knowledge and action). Their condition is the first in a series of degrees listed in the Qur'anic verse used by al-Sijistānī. To the first condition, a further clause is added for a second rank of individuals, that is, 'those who guard themselves from evil and *believe*'. True belief (and, by extension, belief in the true religion) entails: (i) obedience to the Prophet and his legatee-ship, (ii) obedience to the divinely appointed *qā'im* and (iii) carrying out the hermeneutical mission both exoterically and esoterically.

On the third level of people identified as 'those who guard themselves from evil and *do good*', a third condition is imposed comprising: (i) obedience to the divinely appointed Imam, (ii) recognition of the Imam as the deputy of God's command and (iii) the fulfilling of the mission via the imamate, which takes place by testifying to God's *tawḥīd*.

Clearly, any individual belonging to these groups is called, firstly, to obey, secondly, to know and, thirdly, to act. According to al-Kirmānī's reasoning, these degrees of requirements are made obligatory so that the Ismaili mission might be fulfilled by way of promoting knowledge in the divinely appointed dignitaries and, above all, by way of professing divine *tawḥīd*. The latter, as has already been mentioned, signifies for al-Kirmānī not only the *ibdāʿ* of the *wāḥid* (i.e. the first Intellect) by God, but also the act of divesting the Intellect (as well as all other existents) of divinity by the true *mu'min*.[12] Buried here is again al-Kirmānī's intent to discredit any claim to al-Ḥākim's divinity and validate the crucial tasks carried out by the Imam's teaching hierarchy. It is merely the latter that the last *qā'im* will abolish, whilst restoring the religious law in its uttermost authentic form.

---

[12] On the identification of *ibdāʿ* and *waḥda*, *mubdaʿ* and *wāḥid*, see al-Kirmānī, *Rāḥat al-ʿaql*, pp. 176–180. Hunzai has explained that al-Kirmānī uses *tawḥīd* in the sense of a circular function in which the act of God (*ibdāʿ* of the Intellect) makes up half the circle of *tawḥīd*, whilst the act of the *mu'min* (divesting the Intellect of divinity), makes up the other half. See Hunzai, 'The Concept of *Tawḥīd*', p. 168.

Paradoxically then, the central Islamic dogma, *tawḥīd*, seems to point out that for the person who guards himself/herself from evil, believes and does good, is made mandatory: (i) *to obey* the guiding instructions of the revelation and the legislated impositions of the *sharīʿa* in both their exoteric and esoteric significances;[13] (ii) *to know* the non-divinity of all existents up to the Intellect and to acknowledge all existents' imperfection and their dependence on the teachings of the divinely appointed *ḥudūd* (both in the corporeal and non-corporeal realms); and (iii) *to act* in order to acquire what is conveyed in the hermeneutical potentialities of the revelation and the *sharīʿa* as interpreted by divinely appointed guides.

---

[13] This is not merely an indication that the religious law cannot be made 'redundant', but it also hints at the precedence of the Prophet who brings about the *sharīʿa* over the Imam/*asās* who carries out *taʾwīl*.

Faṣl Twenty-four

The author of the *Nuṣra* said: '[The] *qaḍā'* is the beginning (*ibtidā'*), *taqdīr* is the middle (*wasaṭ*), and *tamām* is the end (*nihāya*), because *taqdīr* can only be through a *qaḍā'*.' Then he said: 'should the *qaḍā'* be the end, it would be not appropriate for it to be called a *qaḍā'*, for the *qaḍā'* comes before all things and things come after the *qaḍā'*. The *qaḍā'* is for something whilst completeness is not for something, [but] it is for what is [itself] complete'.

We [al-Kirmānī] say: that in the foregoing discussion there is the answer to [the issue of] *qaḍā'* and *qadar*, in its exhaustiveness fulfilling the discourse and its [various] *ta'wīl*s [to the extent that] no one could impute to us any thing that we did not intend to say.[1]

Analysis and interpretation: In the last *faṣl* of *bāb* eight, al-Kirmānī reports al-Sijistānī's conclusion that the *qaḍā'* is the beginning because it corresponds to the Antecedent who comes before all things and through whose estimation/measuring (*taqdīr*) completeness is achieved. Implicitly, following the *qaḍā'* (which has already been said to correspond to the *tafṣīl*, i.e. the mental tailoring in the analogy examined in the first *faṣl*), is the *taqdīr*, which acts as a middle term before the *tamām/nihāya*. Whilst the *qaḍā'* (like the Imam in concealment) acts for a thing (i.e. the salvation of the believers), completeness (*tamām*) is not the completing of a thing but completeness itself (like the complete final Resurrector). This means that the *qaḍā'* acts on things whilst completeness is the effect itself, namely the *following* result or the end of the efficient action carried out through the *qaḍā'*. Moreover, if *qaḍā'* is equated to the Antecedent/Intellect, then

---

[1] Al-Kirmānī, *Riyāḍ* (HL), pp. 148–149.

it is obviously not the end but the point of return for every existent. *Tamām*, on the other hand, as completeness, equals the perfection of knowledge and action that pertains to the last Resurrector, marking the end of all prophetic cycles and of human history.[2]

Al-Kirmānī concludes this chapter by recalling that his arguments have been analysed thoroughly and that he has systematically substantiated his positions.

---

[2] Cook's rendering of the term *amr*, featuring in messianic and apocalyptic Shiʿi *ḥadīths*, as 'the End' is particularly fitting in this case. For the same word he provides also further translations such as 'period' or 'dispensation'. See David Cook, *Studies in Muslim Apocalyptic* (Princeton, 2002), pp. 195, 199, 232–233.

Conclusion

Throughout this study, it has become evident that with regard to the issue of the divine decree, al-Kirmānī's main agenda was to clarify the nature of the *qaḍāʾ* and the *qadar* as *manifestations* (i.e. actualised *forms*) belonging to the world of nature and the world of religion rather than the world of the intellects. These are not merely distant Qurʾanic notions but *actual* signifiers of the world in its aspect as (i) the members of the Ismaili *daʿwa*, particularly the enunciator-prophet and the Imam, and as (ii) the latter's tasks that are accomplished in their bringing forth, respectively, the *tanzīl* and *sharīʿa*, and their *taʾwīl*.

In the cosmological system expounded by al-Kirmānī, the first three intellects' creative functions, it has been observed, are said to operate at the level of forms: thus, the first intellect produces the forms of the *qaḍāʾ* and the *qadar*, the second intellect allots them, according to the providential mission assigned to the world of the Soul, and the third intellect, tasked with the *tarkīb* of things, endows the *qaḍāʾ* and the *qadar* with their material substrata, thus rendering them actual, entified existents as the pairs *nāṭiq/Imam, tanzīl+sharīʿa/taʾwīl*. It is in this sense that, contrary to al-Sijistānī's and al-Nasafī's idea in which the Intellect could be associated with both actuality and potentiality – through the Intellect's capacity of intelligising all forms encompassed within his essence – al-Kirmānī, in order to preserve the absolute perfection and intrinsic unity of the first intellect, makes exclusively the third intellect the compendium of all forms. Despite being named 'the one who is delayed' in attaining its second perfection when compared to the first two intellects' instantaneousness, the third *ʿaql*'s multiplicity – which is the result of its diverse objects of contemplation – preserves, like the two intellects preceding it, its actuality just like its corresponding terrestrial compositions.

This investigation has shown how the terms *qaḍāʾ* and *qadar* offer themselves to parallel interpretations; thus, according to al-Sijistānī, the first two intellects of the Pleroma – which are also indicated by the terms Antecedent and Follower – correspond to the Imam as the *qāʾim* in potentiality in his double aspect as (i) the current Imam who, despite being in concealment, is yet virtually actual through the undertakings carried out by his devoted representatives of the *daʿwa*, and (ii) the same Imam who will return as the absolute, final Resurrector. Against such views is al-Kirmānī's idea of the Fatimid notion of the *imām-qāʾim*, with specific reference to the Fatimid Imam of his time – al-Ḥākim – whose divine nature is refuted and whose cycle does not bring to an end the *dawr* of Islam. Conversely, because al-Rāzī speaks of the *qaḍāʾ* and the *qadar* as two followers that are preceded by the *sābiq/al-ʿaql al-awwal/amr*, he indirectly identifies them with the Imam in concealment and with *taʾwīl*. So, in a way, by avoiding any connection with the first and the second intellect, al-Rāzī's idea comes closer to al-Kirmānī's standpoint.

The 'meritocratic enactment of *tawḥīd*', which underscores the intellectual hierarchy and which makes the devotional efforts of all believing practitioners 'salvific', truly underpins al-Kirmānī's idea of what predestination entails. In a sense, it explains why emphasis on the permanent actuality of the decree and destiny had important theoretical and doctrinal implications. Firstly, such an idea infers the necessity of the imamate and the absolute indispensability, at all times in human history, of appointed guides such as the *nāṭiq* and the *imām*; secondly, it points out the mandatory quality of the religious law and its hermeneutical esoteric interpretation; and, thirdly, it also serves as an instrument against certain undercurrents of antinomianistic and transmigrationist implications. Needless to say, from al-Kirmānī's Fatimid perspective, this meant that just as the Imam of his time, al-Ḥākim – as the current, present or actual *qāʾim* – was enforcing the law so as to deter any deviance from the Ismaili Fatimid 'canon', so the future *qāʾim* will implement an unparalleled form of *sharīʿa*, leading humankind to the most complete form of knowledge and, despite the law's binding force, to ultimate intellectual freedom.

In Part One of this study, I analysed how al-Kirmānī evaluates the agency of human actions. He links it with the notion of the recompense and clarifies that the latter is the form of a divine principle (Providence/Justice) which makes humans aware of the distinction occurring between good and evil, reward and punishment. All the indications that draw these distinctions are specified in the *sharīʿa* which, consequently, renders all individuals morally responsible for obedience or disobedience to its edicts and its guidelines, which are further explained by divinely appointed teachers. Humans can acquire the capacity to pursue the path of compliance and the understanding of such guides' teachings by actualising the passage from their potential to their actual intellect, that is, from their first to their second perfection, from their biological birth to their spiritual rebirth, thus becoming true *qāʾim*s. Luckily, help is at hand: the intellectual Pleroma, with the support of the celestial bodies, endows human beings not only with a body – an instrument that is necessary in the initial cognitive process in performing superogatory and devotional acts – but above all, endows them with a soul that must be trained and become fit to recognise and receive celestial benefits. By actualising their spiritual make-up, human souls become more and more truthful to their nature as 'vestiges' of the Universal Soul, thus prompting the latter's providential bestowals. Individual souls retain and augment their 'soulness' through a purposeful surrender to the celestial benefits which are brought and 'entified' in creation in the guise of the members of the *daʿwa* and their soteriological 'tools'.

In Part Two, we witnessed al-Kirmānī's criticism of al-Rāzī's and al-Sijistānī's attempts to identify the *qaḍāʾ* and the *qadar* with the cosmological figures of the Antecedent and the Follower. On several occasions, he clarifies that these endeavours are metaphysically and logically redundant because, just like the *sābiq* and the *tālī*, neither the *qaḍāʾ* nor the *qadar* can be associated with temporality, nor with a temporal passage from potentiality into actuality. It is admissible, as mentioned above, to acknowledge some correctness in al-Rāzī's merely logical sequence which identifies both the *qadar* and the *qaḍāʾ* as two Followers with regard to the *amr* and the *qadar* itself, respectively. And, in turn, it is possible to discern some degree of accuracy also in al-Sijistānī's confirmation of *qadar*'s nature as being the Follower apropos the *amr* but not with regard to the *qaḍāʾ*. Nevertheless, even these stances, which not only infer the precedence of the *amr/ kalima* to the first originated being, but also lead to mistaken identifications of the *qāʾim*s, had to be re-evaluated. To prove his point, al-Kirmānī ventures into strenuous associations, subtly elaborating what his colleagues' idea of 'potentiality' really entails.

Thus, in the three meanings addressed to both the *qaḍāʾ* and the *qadar* – recounted in *Faṣl*s Three to Eight – al-Kirmānī's understated focus is on reassessing the meaning of *biʾl-quwwa* as *kaʾl-kāʾin*: the actual commands and prohibitions that are manifested in any prophetic cycle by clear religious laws are 'potential' only with regard to their esoteric interpretations, which may vary despite being continuously present and being carried out by the Imams. The significations of the *qaḍāʾ* and the *qadar* as, correspondingly, (i) the events and qualitative changes actualised by moveable and quiescent things and, (ii) the world of Nature determined in actuality by means of its very existence, highlight exactly this argument. The foregoing meant that just as the Fatimid Imams are actually perfected and alive (recall the importance of *ḥayāt* in the discussion on the Intellect and the meaning of *baʿth* as an intellectual coming-back-to-life), likewise, the world (with its members) *is* purely by dint of its own existence becoming, however, truly *existent* through its receptiveness to *taʾyīd* (namely, upon receiving and accepting a lawful religious guidance). It is probably in the line of such reasoning that al-Kirmānī maintains an accommodating approach towards his fellow *dāʿī*s' speculative flaws when, as reported in *Faṣl* Eight, they identify the *qadar* as the actual creation of the revelation and the divine law, whilst signifying the *qaḍāʾ* as the act of *qadar*, namely as the esoteric hermeneutical interpretation of the divine *khalq*, serving the survival of all humankind in general, and the 'resurrection' of the believing community in particular.

The lengthy discussion about Moses' not yet accomplished *nāṭiq*-ship, whose full attainment is said to depend on his obedience to the explanatory injunctions and spiritual benefits conveyed by the lower celestial faculty *al-jadd*, requires the latter's intermediacy to be conveyed through an actualised member of the *ʿālam al-dīn*, Shuʿayb. It is he who, according to al-Kirmānī, echoing Khiḍr's endeavours, which are illustrated in the Qurʾān, instructs Moses on his appointed time and assignment, thus highlighting the import of a divinely measured allotment. Shuʿayb, as the archetype of the *ṣāḥib al-amr*, acting during the *zamān al-fatr*, testifies – whilst denouncing al-Rāzī's contention of al-Muʿizz's claim as the Imams *khalīfa* – Moses' nature as an *asās* prior to his transition onto a full *nāṭiq*-ship.

The emphasis placed on individual limits – as both ontological/metaphysical ranks and gnoseological/temporal thresholds – resonating in al-Kirmānī's idea of the intellects' enactment of *tawḥīd* as a realisation of their own non-divinity (hinting at the non-divinity of al-Ḥakīm himself), is also propounded by al-Rāzī in the *Iṣlāḥ*, both in his reassessment of Moses' degree of four-ness (*martabat al-arbaʿiyya*), and in his acknowledging the *qadar* as the *ḥadd al-nāṭiq* and the *qaḍāʾ* as the *ḥadd al-asās*.[1]

Fulfilling his role as one of the greatest *dāʿis* of the Fatimid time and harmonising the views of al-Rāzī and al-Sijistānī on an issue with such numerous doctrinal repercussions meant the need for al-Kirmānī to provide a clear-cut Ismaili – and specifically Fatimid – response against distorted ideas on messianism, accusations of illegitimate imamism, divine incarnationism and antinomianism. But it also meant encouraging individual practitioners to experience a whilst-on-earth-spiritual 'resurrection' – epitomised in the Prophet's *isrāʾ* – by becoming *qāʾim*s themselves. This is to be achieved by following, whilst acknowledging their specificity, the spiritual trainings offered by the diverse members of the *daʿwa*. For them, knowledge of the law's inner meaning does not make the *sharīʿa* redundant, but rather, understanding of the *bāṭin* accentuates the crucial role of actions, enacting soul's 'elevation'.

Ultimately, in his political and doctrinal agenda, what really counted for al-Kirmānī was to underscore the essential, inescapable nature of *tawḥīd* whose authentic and deepest sense unfurls in the recognition of all existents' non-divinity (including that of the Imam of the time!), obedience to the religious law, and the actualisation/acquisition of the potentialities that are inherent in every trait of God's creation.

---

[1] Interestingly, arguing on the authorship of actions, Nāṣir-i Khusraw was later to quote the Scripture text: 'These are the limits ordained by God, so do not transgress them' (Q 2:229). With such a quote, Nāṣir-i Khusraw intended to clarify that in Qurʾanic expressions such as 'we did such' or 'we created such' or 'we said such', the 'we' does not signify God Himself or His haecceity – as al-Sijistānī propounded – but either two spiritual ranks (i.e. the Intellect and the Soul) or two physical ranks (i.e. the *nāṭiq* and the *asās*). See Nāṣir-i Khusraw, *Gushāyish wa rahāyish*, English text p. 107, Persian text p. 70.

Bibliography

Abrahamov, Binyamin. ''Abd al-Jabbār's Theory of Divine Assistance', *Jerusalem Studies in Arabic and Islam*, 16 (1993), pp. 41–58.

Acar, Rahim. 'Reconsidering Avicenna's Position on God's Knowledge of Particulars', in *Interpreting Avicenna: Science and Philosophy in Medieval Islam*, ed. John McGinnis and David C. Reisman. London, 2004, pp. 142–156.

Adamson, Peter. *The Arabic Plotinus: A Philosophical Study of the 'Theology of Aristotle'*. London, 2002.

—— 'On Knowledge of Particulars', *Proceedings of the Aristotelian Society*, 105 (2005), pp. 273–294.

Alexandrin, Elizabeth R. 'Prophetic Ascent and Initiatory Ascent in Qāḍī al-Nuʿmān's *Asās al-taʾwīl*', in *The Prophet's Ascension: Cross-Cultural Encounters with the Islamic Miʿrāj Tales*, ed. Christiane Gruber and Frederick Colby. Bloomington and Indianapolis, 2010, pp. 157–171.

—— *Walāyah in the Fāṭimid Ismāʿīlī Tradition*. Albany, NY, 2017.

Aminrazavi, Mehdi. 'Ḥamīd al-Dīn al-Kirmānī', in *An Anthology of Philosophy in Persia, vol. II: Ismaili Thought in the Classical Age*, ed. Seyyed Hossein Nasr and Mehdi Aminrazavi. London, 2008, pp. 179–207.

Amir-Moezzi, Mohammad Ali. *The Divine Guide in Early Shiʿism: The Sources of Esotericism in Islam*, tr. David Streight. Albany, NY, 1994.

—— ed. *Le voyage initiatique en Terre d'Islam: Ascensions célestes et itinéraires spirituels*. Leuven and Paris, 1996.

—— *The Spirituality of Shiʿi Islam: Beliefs and Practices*, tr. Hafiz Karmali. London, 2011.

—— '"La Nuit du *Qadr*" (Coran, sourate 97) dans le Shiʿism ancien', *Mélanges de l'Institut dominicain d'études orientales*, 31 (2016), pp. 181–203.

Anawati, Georges C., and Louis Gardet. *Introduction à la théologie musulmane*. Paris, 1970.

Arabic Plotinus. *'Risāla fiʾl-ʿilm al-ilāhī'*, in *Plotinus apud Arabes*, ed. Abdu Rahman Badawī. Cairo, 1955.

Archer, George. *A Place Between Two Places: The Qurʾānic Barzakh*. Piscataway, NJ, 2017.

Aristotle. *De Anima*, tr. Hugh Lawsont-Tancred as *De Anima (On the Soul)*. London, 1987.

Armstrong, Arthur H. 'Emanation in Plotinus', *Mind*, 46 (1937), pp. 61–66.

—— *The Architecture of the Intelligible Universe in the Philosophy of Plotinus.* Cambridge, 1940, repr. 2013.

—— *The Cambridge History of Later Greek and Early Medieval Philosophy.* Cambridge, 1980.

Asatryan, Mushegh. *Controversies in Formative Shiʿi Islam: The Ghulat Muslims and Their Beliefs.* London, 2017.

al-Ashʿarī, Abū al-Ḥasan. *Kitāb al-Lumaʿ*, tr. Richard J. McCarthy as *The Theology of al-Ashʿarī: The Arabic texts of al-Ashʿarī's Kitāb al-Lumaʿ and Risālat Istiḥsān al-khawḍ fī ʿilm al-kalām*. Beirut, 1953.

Avicenna, *see* Ibn Sīnā.

Baffioni, Carmela. 'Contrariety and Similarity in God according to al-Farabi and al-Kirmani: A Comparison', in *Classical Arabic Philosophy: Sources and Reception*, ed. Peter Adamson. London-Turin, 2007, pp. 1–20.

—— 'Ibdaʿ', Divine Imperative and Prophecy in the *Rasāʾil Ikhwān al-Ṣafāʾ*', in *Fortresses of the Intellect: Ismaili and other Islamic Studies in Honour of Farhad Daftary*, ed. Omar Ali-de-Unzaga. London-New York, 2011, pp. 213–226.

Belo, Catarina. *Chance and Determinism in Avicenna and Averroes*. Leiden and Boston, 2007.

Betts, Robert Brenton. *The Druze*. New Haven, CT, 1988.

al-Bīrūnī, *Kitāb fī Taḥqīq mā li'l-Hind*. Delhi, 1958.

Böwering, Gerard. 'Miʿrāj', *The Encyclopedia of Religion*. New York, 1987, vol. 9, pp. 552–556.

Bréhier, Émile. *The Philosophy of Plotinus*, tr. Joseph Thomas. Chicago, 1958.

Bryer, David R. W. 'The Origins of the Druze Religion', *Der Islam*, 52 (1975), pp. 47–83 and 239–262; 53 (1976), pp. 5–27.

Calderini, Simonetta. '"*Ālam al-dīn*" in Ismāʿīlīsm: World of Obedience or World of Immobility?', *BSOAS*, 56 (1993), pp. 459–469.

Carra de Vaux, B. 'Barzakh', *EI2*, vol. 1, pp. 1071–1072.

Chittick, William C. *The Self-Disclosure of God: Principles of Ibn al-ʿArabi's Cosmology*. Albany, NY, 1988.

Chlup, Radek. *Proclus: An Introduction*. Cambridge, 2012.

Cook, David. *Studies in Muslim Apocalyptic*. Princeton, 2002.

Corbin, Henry. *Étude préliminaire pour 'Le livre réunissant les duex sagesses' (Kitāb-e Jāmiʿ al-Ḥikmatayn) de Nāṣir-e Khosraw*. Tehran and Paris, 1953.

—— ed. and tr. *Trilogie ismaélienne*. Tehran and Paris, 1961.

—— *Cyclical Time and Ismaili Gnosis*, tr. Ralph Manheim and James W. Morris. London, 1983.

—— *Temple and Contemplation*, tr. Philip Sherrard and Liadain Sherrard. London and New York, 1986.

Crone, Patricia, and Luke Treadwell. 'A New Text on Ismailism at the Samanid Court', in *Texts, Documents and Artefacts: Ismaili Studies in Honour of D. S. Richards*, ed. Chase F. Robinson. Leiden and Boston, 2003, pp. 37–67.

d'Ancona, Cristina. 'The Textual Tradition of the Graeco-Arabic Plotinus: The *Theology of Aristotle*, its *"ru'ūs al-masā'il"*, and the Greek Model of the Arabic Version', in *The Letter before the Spirit: The Importance of Text Editions for the Study of the Reception of Aristotle*, ed. Aafke M. I. van Oppenraay and Resianne Fontaine. Leiden and Boston, 2012, pp. 37–71.

Daftary, Farhad. 'Ḥamīd-al-Dīn Kermānī', *EIr*, vol. XI, pp. 639–641.

—— 'Hamid al-Din al-Kirmani', *The Internet Encyclopedia of Philosophy*, ed. James Fieser, at http://www.utm.edu/research/iep/k/kirmani.htm, 2003.

—— *Ismaili Literature: A Bibliography of Sources and Studies*. London, 2004.

—— *The Ismāʿīlīs: Their History and Doctrines*. Second Edition, Cambridge, 2007.

——, and Faquir Muhammad Hunzai. 'Free Will in Ismaʿili Shiʿism', *EIr*, vol. X, pp. 202–205.

Damascius. *Traité des premiers principes*, ed. and tr. Leendert G. Westerink and Joseph Combès, 3 vols. Paris, 1986–1991.

Davidson, Herbert Alan. *Alfarabi, Avicenna & Averroes on Intellect*. New York and Oxford, 1992.

De Cillis, Maria. 'Avicenna on Matter, Matter's Disobedience and Evil: Reconciling Metaphysical Stances and Qur'anic Perspectives', *Transcendent Philosophy*, 12 (2011), pp. 147–168.

—— *Free Will and Predestination in Islamic Thought: Theoretical Compromises in the Works of Avicenna, al-Ghazālī and Ibn ʿArabī*. London and New York, 2014.

—— 'A Preliminary Study on the Significance of *Qaḍā'* and *Qadar* in the Eighth Chapter of al-Kirmānī's *Kitāb al-Riyāḍ*', in *L'ésotérisme shiʿite: ses racines et ses prolongements/Shiʿi Esotericism: Its Roots and Developments*, ed. Mohammad A. Amir-Moezzi, Maria De Cillis, Daniel De Smet and Orkhan Mir-Kasimov. Turnhout, 2016, pp. 345–367.

De Smet, Daniel. 'Le *Kitāb rāḥat al-ʿaql* de Ḥamīd al-Dīn al-Kirmānī et la cosmologie ismaélienne à l'époque fatimide', *Acta Orientalia Belgica*, 7 (1992), pp. 81–91.

—— '*Mīzān al-diyāna* ou l'equilibre entre science et religion dans la pensée ismaélienne', *Acta Orientalia Belgica*, 8 (1993), pp. 247–254.

—— *La quiétude de l'intellect: Néoplatonisme et gnose dans l'oeuvre de Ḥamîd al-Dîn al-Kirmânî (X^e/XIe s)*. Leuven, 1995.

—— *Empedocles Arabus Une lecture néoplatonicienne tardive*. Brussels, 1998.

—— '"Perfectio prima'– 'perfectio secunda', ou les vicissitudes d'une notion", *Recherches de Théologie et Philosophie Mediévales*, 66/2 (1999), pp. 254–288.

—— 'La doctrine avicennienne des deux faces de l'âme et ses racines ismaéliennes', *Studia Islamica*, 93 (2001).

—— *Les Epîtres sacrées des druzes, Rasā'il al-ḥikma: Introduction, édition critique et traduction annotée des traités attribués à Ḥamza b. ʿAlī et Ismāʿīl at-Tamīmī*. 2 vols. Leuven, 2007.

—— 'Loi rationnelle et loi impose: Les deux aspects de la *šarī'a* dans le chiisme ismaélien des Xe et XIe siècles', *Mélanges de l'Université Saint-Joseph,* 61 (2008), pp. 515–544.

—— 'Al-Fārābī's Influence on Ḥamīd al-Dīn al-Kirmānī's Theory of Intellect and Soul', in *In the Age of al-Fārābī: Arabic Philosophy in the Fourth/Tenth Century,* ed. Peter Adamson. London, 2008, pp. 131–150.

—— 'Adam, premier prophète et législateur ? La doctrine chiite des *ulū al-'azm* et la controverse sur la pérennité de la *šarī'a',* in *Le shī'isme imāmite quarante ans après. Hommage à Etan Kohlberg,* ed. Mohammad A. Amir-Moezzi, Meir M. Bar-Asher and Simon Hopkins. Turnhout, 2009, pp. 187–202.

—— 'La function noétique de la triade *al-jadd, al-fatḥ* et *al-khayāl.* Les fondements de la connaissance prophétique dans l'ismaélisme', in *Differenz und Dynamik im Islam/Difference and Dynamism in Islam: Festschrift für Heinz Halm zum 70 Geburtstag/Festschrift for Hanz Halm on his 70th Birthday,* ed. Hinrich Biesterfeldt and Verena Klemm. Würzburg, 2012, pp. 319–336.

—— 'L'âme humaine: une 'partie' ou une 'empreinte' de l'Âme universelle', in *La Philosophie Ismaélienne: un ésotérisme chiite entre néoplatonisme et gnose.* Paris, 2012, pp. 113–125.

—— *La Philosophie Ismaélienne: un ésotérisme chiite entre néoplatonisme et gnose.* Paris, 2012.

—— 'La transmigration des âmes. Une notion problématique dans l'ismaélism d'époque fatimide', in *Unity in Diversity: Mysticism, Messianism and the Construction of Religious Authority in Islam,* ed. Orkhan Mir-Kasimov. Leiden and Boston, 2014, pp. 77–110.

—— '"Le Mystère des Mystères est inaccessible à l'engagement du cœur et à la perception de l'intellect': Néoplatonisme et (anti)mysticisme dans la pensée ismaélienne", in *Mystique at philosophie dans les trois mon-othéismes,* ed. Danielle Cohen-Levinas, Géraldine Roux and Meryem Sebti. Paris, 2015, pp. 67–87.

—— 'al-Kirmānī, Ḥamīd al-Dīn', *EI3,* vol. 1, pp. 131–135.

De Smet, Daniel, and Jan M. F. Van Reeth. 'Les citations bibliques dans l'œuvre du dā'ī ismaélien Ḥamīd al-Dīn al-Kirmānī', in *Law, Christianity and Modernism in Islamic Society,* ed. Urbain Vermeulen and Jan M. F. Van Reeth. Leuven, 1998, pp. 147–160.

Deck, John N. *Nature, Contemplation and the One: A Study in the Philosophy of Plotinus.* Toronto, 1967.

Ebstein, Michael. *Mysticism and Philosphy in al-Andalus: Ibn Masarra, Ibn al-'Arabī and the Ismā'īlī Tradition.* Leiden and Boston, 2014.

——, and Sara Sviri. 'The So-called *Risālat al-ḥurūf* (*Epistle on Letters*) ascribed to Sahl al-Tustarī and Letter Mysticism in al-Andalus', *Journal Asiatique,* 299, 1 (2011), pp. 213–270.

Elmore, Gerald T. *Islamic Sainthood in the Fullness of Time: Ibn al-ʿArabī's Book of the Fabulous Gryphon*. Leiden, Boston and Cologne, 1999.

Fakhry, Majid. 'Some Paradoxical Implications of the Muʿtazilite View of Free Will', *Muslim World*, 43 (1953), pp. 95–109.

—— 'The Muʿtazilite view of Man', in *Recherches d'islamologie: recueil d'articles offert à G. Anawati et L. Gardet par leurs collègues et amis*. Leuven, 1977, pp. 107–121.

al-Fārābī, Abū Naṣr. *Mabādiʾ ārāʾ ahl al-madīna al-fāḍila*. Beirut, 1982; ed. and tr. with commentary, Richard Walzer as *Al-Farabi on the Perfect State*. Oxford, 1995.

Feki, Habib. *Les idées religieuses et philosophiques de l'ismaélisme fatimide*. Tunis, 1978.

Firro, Kais M. *A History of the Druzes*. Leiden, 1992.

Frank, Richard M. 'The Structure of Created Causality according to al-Ashʿarī: An Analysis of the *Kitāb al-Lumaʿ*', *Studia Islamica*, 25 (1966), pp. 13–75.

—— *The Metaphysics of Created Being according to Abūʾl-Hudhayl al-Allāf*. Istanbul, 1966.

—— 'The Divine Attributes according to the Teachings of Abūʾl-Hudhayl al-Allāf', *Le Muséon, Revue des Études Orientales*, 82 (1969), pp. 451–506.

—— 'Several Fundamental Assumptions of the Baṣra School of the Muʿtazila', *Studia Islamica*, 33 (1971), pp. 5–18.

—— '*Kalām* and Philosophy, a Perspective from One Problem', in *Islamic Philosophical Theology*, ed. Parviz Morewedge. Albany, NY, 1979, pp. 71–95.

—— 'The Autonomy of the Human Agent in the Teaching of ʿAbd al-Jabbār', *Le Musèon, Revue des Études Orientales*, 95 (1983), pp. 323–355.

—— 'Bodies and Atoms: the Ashʿarite Analysis', in *Islamic Theology and Philosophy*, ed. Michael E. Marmura. Albany, NY, 1984, pp. 39–53.

—— *Early Islamic Theology: The Muʿtazilites and al-Ashʿari. Texts and Studies on the Development and History of Kalam*, vol. II. London and New York, 2007.

—— *Classical Islamic Theology: The Ashʿarites. Texts and Studies on the Development and History of Kalam*, vol. III. London and New York, 2007.

Gardet, Louis. *Dieu et la destinèe de l'homme*. Paris, 1967.

—— 'Quelques reflexions sur un problème de théologie et de philosophie musulmanes: toute-puissance divine et liberté humaine', *Revue de l'Occident musulman et de la Méditerranée*, 13–14 (1973), pp. 381–394.

—— 'Al-Ḳaḍāʾ waʾl-ḳadar', *EI2*, vol. 4, pp. 365–367.

Gersh, Stephen. *From Iamblichus to Eriugena: An Investigation of the Prehistory and Evolution of the Pseudo-Dionysian Tradition*. Leiden, 1978.

—— *Being Different: More Neoplatonism after Derrida. Ancient Mediterranean and Medieval Texts and Contexts*. Studies in Platonism, Neoplatonism, and the Platonic Tradition, 16. Leiden and Boston, 2014.

—— ed. *Interpreting Proclus: From Antiquity to the Renaissance*. Cambridge, 2014.

al-Ghazālī, Abū Ḥāmid. *Iḥyā' 'ulūm al-dīn*. 4 vols. Beirut, ca. 1980.

—— *Al-Maqṣad al-asnā fī sharḥ ma'ānī asmā' Allāh al-ḥusnā*, ed. Fadlou Shedadi. Beirut, 1986, repr. Beirut, 1982; tr. David B. Burrel and Nazih Daher as *The Ninety-nine Beautiful Names of God*. Cambridge, 1992.

—— *Tahāfut al-falāsifa*, tr. Michael E. Marmura as *The Incoherence of the Philosophers*. Provo, UT, 1997.

Gimaret, Daniel. 'Un problème de théologie musulmane: Dieu veut-il les actes mauvais? Thèses et arguments', *Studia Islamica*, 40 (1974), pp. 5–73, and 41 (1975), pp. 63–92.

—— 'Théories de l'acte humain dans l'école Hanbalite', *Bulletin des Études Orientales*, 29 (1977), pp. 157–178.

—— *Théories de l'acte humain en théologie musulmane*. Paris, 1980.

—— *Les noms divins en Islam: exégése lexicographique et théologique*. Paris, 1988.

—— '*Tanāsukh*', *EI2*, vol. 10, pp. 181–183.

Goichon, Amelie Marie. *La Distinction de l'Essence et de l'Existence d'après Ibn Sīnā (Avicenne)*. Paris, 1937.

Gutas, Dimitri. *Avicenna and the Aristotelian Tradition*. Leiden and New York, 1988.

Haji, Hamid. *A Distinguished Dā'ī under the Shade of the Fatimids: Ḥamīd al-Dīn al-Kirmānī and His Epistles*. London, 1998.

Halm, Heinz. *Kosmologie und heilslehre der frühen Ismā'īlīya: Eine studie zur Islamischen gnosis*. Wiesbaden, 1978.

—— 'Methoden und Formen der frühesten ismailitischen da'wa', in *Studien zur geschichte und Kultur des Vorderen Orients. Festschrift für B. Spuler zum siebzigsten Geburtstag*, ed. Hans R. Römer and Alberecht Noth. Leiden, 1981, pp. 123–136.

—— 'The Cosmology of the pre-Fatimid Ismā'īliyya', in *Medaieval Isma'ili History and Thought*, ed. Farhad Daftary. Cambridge, 1996, pp. 75–84.

—— *The Fatimids and their Traditions of Learning*. London, 1997.

Ḥamdani, Abbas. 'Evolution of the Organizational Structure of the Fāṭimī Da'wah', *Arabian Studies*, 3 (1976), pp. 85–114.

al-Ḥamdānī, Ḥusayn F. 'Some Unknown Ismā'īlī Authors and their Works', *JRAS* (1933), pp. 359–378.

——. *Al-Ṣulayḥiyyūn wa'l-ḥaraka al-Fāṭimiyya fī'l-Yaman*. Cairo, 1955.

al-Ḥamīdī, Ibrāhīm b. al-Ḥusayn. *Kitāb Kanz al-walad*, ed. Muṣṭafā Ghālib. Wiesbaden, 1971; repr. Beirut, 1979.

Helmig, Christoph, and Carlos Steel. 'Proclus', *The Stanford Encyclopedia of Philosophy* (2015), ed. Edward N. Zalta, at http://plato.stanford.edu/archives/sum2015/entries/proclus/.

al-Hindī, ʿAlī al-Muttaqī. *Kanz al-ʿummāl fī sunan al-aqwāl waʾl afʿāl.* Beirut, 1971.

Hirji, Boustan. ʾA Study of *al-Risālah al-bāhirah*ʾ, PhD thesis, McGill University. Montreal, 1994.

Hodgson, Marshall G. S. ʾAl-Darazī and Ḥamza in the Origin of the Druze Religionʾ, *JAOS*, 82 (1962), pp. 5–20.

—— ʾal-Darazīʾ, *EI2*, vol. 2, pp. 136–137.

—— ʾDurūzʾ, *EI2*, vol. 2, pp. 631–634.

—— ʾGhulātʾ, *EI2*, vol. 2, pp. 1119–1121.

Hollenberg, David. *Beyond the Qurʾān: Early Ismāʿīlī Taʾwīl and the Secrets of the Prophets.* New York, 2016.

Hunzai, Faquir Muhammad. ʾThe Concept of *Tawḥīd* in the Thought of Ḥamīd al-Dīn al-Kirmānīʾ, PhD thesis, McGill University. Montreal, 1986.

Ibn ʿArabī, Muḥyi al-Dīn Muḥammad b. ʿAlī. *Al-Futūḥāt al-Makkiyya.* Cairo, 1329/1911, repr. Beirut, 1968; partial trans. Michel Chodkiewicz as *Les illuminations de la Mecque: textes choisis.* Paris, 1988.

—— *Fuṣūṣ al-ḥikam*, ed. and tr. R. W. J. Austin as *The Bezels of Wisdom.* London, 1980.

Ibn Bābūya, al-Shaykh al-Ṣadūq. *Risālat al-Iʿtiqādāt al-imāmiyyah.* Tehran, 1370/1992, tr. Asaf A. A. Fyzee as *A Shīʿite Creed.* Oxford, 1942.

—— *Kitāb al-Tawḥīd*, tr. A. Adam as *The Book of Divine Unity.* Birmingham, 2014.

Ibn Fūrak, b. Muḥammad b. al-Ḥasan. *Mujarrad maqālāt al-shaykh Abī al-Ḥasan al-Ashʿarī: Exposé de la doctrine dʾal-Ašʿarī*, ed. Daniel Gimaret. Beirut, 1987.

Ibn Sīnā, Abū ʿAlī al-Ḥusayn b. ʿAbd Allāh (Avicenna). *Al-Ishārāt waʾl-tanbīhāt*, ed. J. Forget. Leiden, 1892.

—— *Kitāb al-Najāt*, ed. Ṣabrī al-Kurdī. Cairo, 1938.

—— *al-Risāla al-Aḍḥawīya fiʾl-maʿād*, tr. Francesca Lucchetta as *Avicenna, Epistola sulla Vita Futura: Testo Arabo, Traduzione, Introduzione e Note.* Padova, 1969.

—— *Kitāb al-Hidāya li-Ibn Sīnā*, ed. Muḥammad ʿAbduh. Cairo, 1974.

—— *Risālat fiʾl-qaḍāʾ*, tr. Y. Michot in *Lettre au Vizier Abū Saʿad.* Beirut, 2000, pp. 103–107.

—— *Kitāb al-Shifāʾ: al-ilāhiyyāt*, tr. Michael E. Marmura as *The Metaphysics of the Healing.* Provo, UT, 2005.

Ibn al-Walīd, ʿAlī b. Muḥammad. *Tāj al-ʿaqāʾid wa maʿdin al-fawāʾid*, tr. Wladimir Ivanow as *A Creed of the Fatimids.* Bombay, 1936.

—— *al-Risāla al-Mufīda*, ed. and tr. Wilferd Madelung and Toby Mayer as *Avicennaʾs Allegory on the Soul: An Ismaili Interpretation.* London, 2016.

Ikhwān al-Ṣafāʾ. *Jāmiʿat al-jāmiʿa*, ed. ʿĀrif Tāmir. Beirut, 1970.

—— *Rasāʾil Ikhwān al-Ṣafāʾ wa khullān al-wafāʾ*, ed. Buṭrus Bustānī. 4 vols. Beirut, 1957.

—— Epistle 3, ed. and tr F. Jamil Ragep and Taro Minura as *On Astronomia: An Arabic Critical Edition and English Translation of Epistle 3*. London and Oxford, 2015.

Inge, William Ralph. *The Philosophy of Plotinus*. London and New York, 1948, repr. London, 1954.

Ivanow, Wladimir. 'An Early Controversy in Ismailism', in *Studies in Early Persian Ismailism*. Bombay, 1955, pp. 116–122.

—— *Ismaili Tradition Concerning the Rise of the Fatimids*. London, etc., 1942.

—— *Ismaili Literature: A Bibliographical Survey*. Tehran, 1963.

Ivry, Alfred L. 'Ismāʿili Theology and Maimonides' Philosophy', in *The Jews of Medieval Islam: Community, Society and Identity*, ed. Daniel Frank. London, 1995, pp. 271–300.

Jannsens, Jules. 'Creation and Emanation in Ibn Sīnā', *Documenti e Studi sulla Tradizione Filosofica Medievale*, 8 (1997), pp. 455–477.

Janos, Damien. *Method, Structure and Development in al-Fārābī's Cosmology*. Leiden and Boston, 2012.

Jolivet, Jean. 'La repartition des causes chez Aristote et Avicenne: le sens d'un déplacement', in *Lectionum Varietates: Hommage à Paul Vignaux (1904–1987)*, ed. Jean Jolivet, Zénob Kaluza and Alain de Libera. Paris, 1991, pp. 49–65.

al-Jurjānī, ʿAbd al-Qahir. *Kitāb al-Taʿrīfāt*. ed. Flügel. Leipzig, 1845; French trans. Maurice Gloton as *Le Livre des Définitions*. Tehran, 1994, repr. Beirut, 2006.

Ḥasan-i Maḥmūd-i Kātib. *Haft bāb*, ed. and tr. S. Jalal Badakhchani as *Spiritual Resurrection in Shiʿi Islam: An Early Ismaili Treatise on the Doctrine of Qiyāmat*. London, 2017.

al-Khwārizmī, Muḥammad b. Mūsā. *Mafātiḥ al-ʿulūm*, ed. G. Van Vloten. Tehran, 1968.

al-Kirmānī, Ḥamīd al-Dīn Aḥmad b. ʿAbd Allāh. *Al-Risāla al-Wāʿiẓa*, ed. M. Kāmil Ḥusayn, *Bulletin of the Faculty of Arts, Fouad I University*, 14, Part 1 (1952), pp. 1–29; ed. Muṣṭafā Ghālib in *Majmūʿat rasāʾil al-Kirmānī*. Beirut, 1969, pp. 113–133.

—— *Rāḥat al-ʿaql*, ed. M. Kāmil Ḥusayn and M. Muṣṭafā Ḥilmī. Cairo, 1953; ed. Muṣṭafā Ghālib. Beirut, 1967.

—— *Kitāb al-Riyāḍ*, ed. ʿĀrif Tāmir. Beirut, 1960. Extracts from Chapter 8 refer to the Arabic text in the yet unpublished edition by Faquir M. Hunzai and Hermann Landolt, indicated in the text as *Riyāḍ* (HL).

—— *Al-Risāla al-Muḍīʿa fī al-amr waʾl-āmir waʾl-maʾmūr*, ed. Muṣṭafā Ghālib in *Majmūʿa rasāʾil al-Kirmānī*. Beirut, 1969, pp. 49–53.

—— *al-Risāla al-Kāfiya*, ed. Muṣṭafā Ghālib in *Majmūʿa rasāʾil al-Kirmānī*. Beirut, 1969, pp. 148–182.

—— *Risālat al-Rawḍa*, ed. Muṣṭafā Ghālib in *Majmūʿa rasāʾil al-Kirmānī*. Beirut, 1969, pp. 81–91.

—— *Risālat Mabāsim al-bishārāt biʾl-imān al-Ḥākim bi-Amr Allāh*, ed. Muṣṭafā Ghālib in *Majmūʿat rasāʾil al-Kirmānī*. Beirut, 1969, pp. 113–133.

—— *al-Risāla al-Durriyya fī maʿnā al-tawḥīd waʾl-muwaḥḥid waʾl-muwaḥḥad*, ed. Muṣṭafā Ghālib in *Majmūʿa rasāʾil al-Kirmānī*. Beirut, 1969, pp. 19–26; tr. Faquir M. Hunzai, ʿal-Risālat al-durriyahʾ, in *An Anthology of Philosophy in Persia, vol. II: Ismaili Thought in the Classical Age*, ed. Seyyed Hossein Nasr and Mehdi Aminrazavi. London, 2008, pp. 200–207.

—— *al-Maṣābīḥ fī ithbāt al-imāma*, ed. Muṣṭafā Ghālib. Beirut, 1969; ed. and tr. Paul E. Walker as *Master of the Age: An Islamic Treatise on the Necessity of the Imamate*. London and New York, 2007.

—— *Tanbīh al-hādī wa-al-mustahdī*, MS 1230, The Zahid Ali Collection, Ismaili Special Collections Unit at The Institute of Ismaili Studies, London.

Kraus, Paul. ʿHebräische und syrische Zitate in ismāʿilitischen Schriftenʾ, *Der Islam*, 19 (1931), pp. 243–263.

al-Kulaynī, Muḥammad b. Yaʿqūb. *Al-Uṣūl min al-kāfī*, ed. ʿAlī A. Ghaffārī. 2 vols. Tehran, 1375/1955; repr. Beirut, 1405/1985; ed. J. Muṣṭafawī. Tehran, n.d.

Landolt, Hermann. ʿGhazālī und *Religionswissenschaft*ʾ, *Asiatische Studien*, 45:1 (1991), pp. 19–72.

—— ʿIsmāʿīlī and Ṣūfī Attitudes to Transmigrationʾ, in *International Congress of Human Sciences in Asia and North Africa. Proceedings of ICHSANA*, vol. I, ed. Y. Tatsuro. Tokyo, 1984, pp. 293–294 (abstract of paper).

—— ʿWalāyahʾ, in *The Encyclopedia of Religion*, ed. Mircea Eliade. London and New York, 1987, vol. 15, pp. 316–323.

Lane, Edward W. *Arabic-English Lexicon*. London, 1863.

Lewisohn, Leonard. ʿFrom the "Moses of Reason" to the "Khidr of the Resurrection": The Oxymoronic Transcendent in Shahrastānīʾs *Majlis-i maktūb-i…dar Khwārazm*ʾ, in *Fortresses of the Intellect: Ismaili and Other Islamic Studies in Honour of Farhad Daftary*, ed. Omar Ali-de-Unzaga. London, 2011, pp. 403–429.

McDermott, Martin J. *The Theology of al-Shaikh al-Mufīd*. Beirut, 1978.

Macdonald, Duncan B. ʿThe Development of the Idea of Spirit in Islamʾ, *Acta Orientalia*, 9 (1931), pp. 307–351.

Madelung, Wilferd. ʿImamism and Muʿtazilite Theologyʾ, in *Le Shīʿisme imamate*, ed. Toufic Fahd. Paris, 1970, pp. 13–29.

—— ʿAspects of Ismaili Theology: The Prophetic Chain and the God beyond Beingʾ, in *Ismāʿīlī Contributions to Islamic Culture*, ed. Seyyed Hossein Nasr. Tehran, 1977, pp. 53–65.

—— *Religious Trends in Early Islamic Iran.* Albany, NY, 1988.

—— 'Abū Ya'qūb al-Sijistānī and Metempsychosis', in *Iranica Varia: Papers in Honor of Professor Ehsan Yarshater,* ed. D. Amin, M. Kasheff and A. Sh. Shahbazi. Leiden, 1990, pp. 131–143.

—— 'Das Imamat in der frühen ismailitischen Lehre', *Der Islam,* 37 (2009), pp. 43–135.

—— '*Kawn al-'ālam:* The Cosmogony of the Ismā'īlī *dā'ī* Muḥammad b. Aḥmad al-Nasafī', in *Ismaili and Fatimid Studies in Honor of Paul E. Walker,* ed. Bruce D. Craig. Chicago, 2010, pp. 23–31.

—— 'The Late Mu'tazila and Determinsism: the Philosophers' Trap', in *Yādnāma in Memoria di Alessandro Bausani, Volume 1, Islamistica,* ed. Biancamaria Scarcia Amoretti and Lucia Rostagno. Rome, 1991, pp. 245–257.

—— '*Badā*'', *EIr,* vol. III, pp. 354–355.

—— 'Ḥamza b. 'Alī', *EI2,* vol. 5, p. 154.

—— 'Ḳarmaṭī', *EI2,* vol. 4, pp. 661–662.

——, and Paul E. Walker. 'The *Kitāb al-Rusūm wa'l-izdiwāj wa'l-tartīb* Attributed to 'Abdān (d. 286/899): Edition of the Arabic Text and Translation', in *Fortresses of the Intellect: Ismaili and Other Islamic Studies in Honour of Farhad Daftary,* ed. Omar Ali-de-Unzaga. London, 2011, pp. 103–165.

al-Majlisī, Muḥammad Bāqir. *Biḥār al-anwār al-jāmi'a li durar akhbār al-a'imma al-aṭhār.* Tehran, 1956–1972; Beirut, 1983.

Marmura, Michael E. 'Some Aspects of Avicenna's Theory of God's Knowledge of Particulars', *JAOS,* 82 (1962), pp. 299–312.

—— 'Avicenna on Causal Priority', in *Islamic Philosophy and Mysticism,* ed. Parviz Morewedge. New York, 1981, pp. 65–83.

—— 'Divine Omniscience and Future Contingents in Alfarabi and Avicenna', in *Divine Omniscience and Omnipotence in Medieval Philosophy: Islamic, Jewish and Christian Perspectives,* ed. Tamar Rudavsky. Dordrecht, 1985, pp. 81–94.

Mir-Kasimov, Orkhan. *Words of Power: Ḥurūfī Teachings between Shi'ism and Sufism in Medieval Islam.* London and New York, 2015.

—— ed., *Unity in Diversity: Mysticism, Messianism and the Construction of Religious Authority in Islam.* Leiden and Boston, 2014.

al-Mufid, al-Shaykh. *Taṣḥīḥu'l-i' tiqādāt.* Tabriz, 1371/1951.

Momen, Moojan. *An Introduction to Shi'i Islam: The History and Doctrines of Twelver Shi'ism.* New Haven and London, 1985.

al-Mu'ayyad fi'l-Dīn al-Shīrāzī, Abū Naṣr Hibad Allāh. *Al-Majālis al-Mu'ayyadiyya,* ed. Ḥātim Ḥamīd al-Dīn. 3 vols. Oxford and Mumbai, 1975–2005.

Murata, Sachico. *The Tao of Islam: A Sourcebook on Gender Relationships in Islamic Thought.* Albany, NY, 1992.

Nagel, Tilman. 'Būyids', *EIr*, vol. IV, pp. 578–586.

Nakamura, Kojiro. 'Imam Ghazālī's Cosmology Reconsidered with Special Reference to the Concept of "*Jabarut*"', *Studia Islamica*, 80 (1994), pp. 29–46.

Nanji, Azim. 'Ismaili Philosophy', in *History of Islamic Philosophy*, ed. Oliver Leaman and Seyyed Hossein Nasr, vol. I. London, 2008, pp. 144–154.

Nāṣir-i Khusraw. *Zād al-musāfirīn*, ed. M. Badhl Raḥmān. Berlin, 1923.

—— *Diwān-i ashʿar*, ed. N. A. Taqawī et al. Tehran, 1304–1307/1925–1928.

—— *Khwān al-ikhwān*. ed. Yaḥyā al-Khashshāb. Cairo, 1359/1940.

—— *Jāmiʿ al-ḥikmatayn*, ed. Henry Corbin and M. Muʿīn. Tehran and Paris, 1953. French trans. Isabelle de Gastines as *Le livre réunissant les deux sagesses*. Paris, 1990; English trans. Eric Ormsby as *Between Reason and Revelation: Twin Wisdoms Reconciled*. London, 2012.

—— *Wajh-i dīn*, ed. Gholam-Reza Aavani. Tehran, 1977.

—— *Gushāyish wa rahāyish*, ed. and tr. Faquir Muhammad Hunzai as *Knowledge and Liberation: A Treatise on Philosophical Theology*. London and New York, 1998.

Nasr, Seyyed Hossein. *An Introduction to Islamic Cosmological Doctrines*. Cambridge, MA, 1964.

Netton, Ian Richard. *Allāh Transcendent: Studies in the Structure and Semiotics of Islamic Philosophy, Theology and Cosmology*. London and New York, 1989.

Nomoto, Shin. 'Early Ismāʿīlī Thought on Prophecy according to the *Kitāb al-Iṣlāḥ* by Abū Ḥātim al-Rāzī', PhD thesis, McGill University. Montreal, 1999.

al-Nuʿmān, al-Qāḍī Abū Ḥanīfa b. Muḥammad. *Daʿāʾm al-Islām*, ed. Asaf A. A. Fyzee. Cairo, 1951–1960 ; tr. Fyzee, and rev. Ismail K. Poonawala as *The Pillars of Islam*. 2 vols. New Delhi, 2002–2004.

—— *al-Risāla al-Mudhhiba*, in *Khams rasāʾil Ismāʿīliyya*, ed. ʿĀrif Tāmir. Salamiyya, Syria, 1956, pp. 27–88.

—— *Kitāb Asās al-taʾwīl*. ed. ʿĀrif Tāmir. Beirut, 1960.

Peterson, Daniel C. 'Cosmogony in the *Rāḥat al-ʿaql* of Ḥamīd al-Dīn al-Kirmānī', PhD thesis, Los Angeles, 1990.

—— 'Al-Kirmānī on the Divine *Tawḥīd*', in *Proceedings of the Third European Conference of Iranian Studies, II: Mediaeval and Modern Persian Studies*, ed. Charles Melville. Wiesbaden, 1999, pp. 179–194.

—— 'Repose of the Intellect', in *An Anthology of Philosophy in Persia, vol. II: Ismaili Thought in the Classical Age*, ed. Seyyed Hossein Nasr and Mehdi Aminrazavi. London, 2008, pp. 181–199.

Plotinus. *Enneads*, tr. A. H. Armstrong. Cambridge, MA, 1966–1988.

Poonawala, Ismail K. 'An Early Doctrinal Controversy in the Iranian School of Ismaili Thought and its Implications', *Journal of Persianate Studies*, 5 (2012), pp. 17–34.

—— *Biobibliography of Ismāʿīlī Literature*. Malibu, CA, 1977.

Proclus. *The Elements of Theology*, tr. E. R. Dodds. Oxford, 1963.

—— *Theologia platonica*, ed. H. D. Saffrey and L. G. Westerink. 6 vols. Paris, 1968–1987.

al-Qummī, al-Ṣaffār. *Baṣāʾir al-darajāt fī ʿulūm al-Muhammad*, ed. A. Zakīzādeh Ranānī. Qumm, 2012.

Rahman, Fazlur. *Avicenna's Psychology: An English Translation of Kitāb al-Najāt, Book II, Chapter VI, with Historico Philosophical Notes and Textual Improvements on the Cairo Edition*. Oxford, 1952.

al-Rāzī, Abū Bakr Muḥammad b. Zakariyā. *Rasāʾil Falsafiyya*. Cairo, 1939.

al-Rāzī, Abū Ḥātim Aḥmad b. Ḥamdān. *Kitāb al-Iṣlāḥ*, ed. Hasan Mīnūchehr and Mehdī Moḥaghegh. Tehran, 2004.

—— *Aʿlām al-nubuwwa*, ed. and tr. Tarif Khalidi as *The Proofs of Prophecy*. Provo, UT, 2011.

Reisman, David Colum. 'Al-Fārābī and the Philosophical Curriculum', in *The Cambridge Companion to Arabic Philosophy*, ed. Peter Adamson and Richard C. Taylor. Cambridge, 2005, pp. 52–71.

Rutten, Christian. 'La doctrine des deux actes dans la philosophie de Plotin', *Revue philosophique de la France et de l'Étranger*, 146 (1956), pp. 100–106.

Schirieke, B., et al. 'Miʿrādj', *EI2*, vol. 7, pp. 97–105.

al-Shahrastānī, Muḥammad b. ʿAbd al-Karīm. *Mafātīḥ al-asrār wa maṣābīḥ al-abrār*, tr. Toby Mayer as *Keys to the Arcana: Shahrastānī's Esoteric Commentary to the Qurʾān. A Translation of the Commentary on Sūrat al-Fātiḥa*. London, 2009.

al-Sijistānī, Abū Yaʿqūb Isḥāq b. Aḥmad. 'Tuḥfat al-mustajībīn', in *Khams Rasāʾil Ismāʿīliyya*, ed. ʿĀrif Tāmir. Salamiyya, 1956, pp. 145–156.

—— *Kitāb al-Yanābīʿ*, ed. Muṣṭafā Ghālib. Beirut, 1965; tr. Paul E. Walker as *The Wellsprings of Wisdom: A Study of Abu Yaʿqub al-Sijistani's Kitāb al-yanābīʿ*. Salt Lake City, 1994.

—— *Kitāb Ithbāt al-nubuwwāt*, ed. ʿĀrif Tāmir. Beirut, 1966.

—— *Kashf al-Maḥjūb*; French trans. Henry Corbin as *Le dévoilement des choses cachées*. Lagrasse, 1988; partial English trans. Hermann Landolt as *Unveiling of the Hidden*, in *An Anthology of Philosophy in Persia, vol. II: Ismaili Thought in the Classical Age*, ed. Seyyed Hossein Nasr and Mehdi Aminrazavi. London, 2008, pp. 74–129.

——. 'al-Risāla al-Bāhira', ed. Boustan Hirji in *Taḥqīqāt-i Islāmī*, 7 (1992), pp. 21–62.

—— *Kitāb al-Iftikhār*, ed. Ismail K. Poonawala. Beirut, 2000.

—— *Kitāb al-Maqālīd al-malakūtiyya*, ed. I. K. Poonawala. Tunis, 2011.

Steel, Carlos, ed. *Proclus: Commentaire sur le Parménide de Platon. Traduction de Guillaume de Moerbeke. Tome II: Livres V à VII et Notes marginales de Nicolas de Cues*. Leuven, 1985.

Stern, Samuel M. 'The Earliest Cosmological Doctrines of Ismāʿīlism', in *Studies in Early Ismāʿīlism*. Jerusalem and Leiden, 1983, pp. 3–29.

Straface, Antonella. 'The Representation of *al-Jadd*, *al-Fatḥ* and *al-Khayāl* in Ismaili Literature: Some Examples and Further Remarks', in *L'ésotérisme shiʿite: ses racines et ses prolongements/Shiʿi Esotericism: Its Roots and Developments*, ed. Mohammad A. Amir-Moezzi, Maria De Cillis, Daniel De Smet and Orkhan Mir-Kasimov. Turnhout, 2016, pp. 423–440.

al-Ṭabarī, Muḥammad b. Jarīr. *Jāmiʿ al-bayān fī tafsīr al-Qur'ān*. Beirut, n.d.

Takeshita, Masataka. *Ibn ʿArabi's Theory of the Perfect Man and its place in the History of Islamic Thought*. Tokyo, 1987.

Tottoli, Roberto. *Biblical Prophets in the Qur'ān and Muslim Literature*. Richmond, 2002.

al-Ṭūsī, Naṣīr al-Dīn. *Sayr wa-sulūk*, ed. and tr. S. Jalal Badakhchani as *Contemplation and Action: The Spiritual Autobiography of a Muslim Scholar*. London, 1998.

—— *Rawḍa-yi taslīm*, ed. and tr. S. Jalal Badakhchani as *Paradise of Submission: A Medieval Treatise on Ismaili Thought*. London, 2005.

van Ess, Josef. 'Bio-bibliographische Notizien zur islamichen Theologie. I. Zur Chronologie der Weke des Ḥamīdaddīn al-Kirmānī', *Die Welt des Orients*, 9 (1978), pp. 255–261.

Virani, N. Shafique. 'The Days of Creation in the Thought of Nasir-i Khusraw', in *Nasir Khusraw: Yesterday, Today, Tomorrow*, ed. Sarfaroz Niyozov and Ramazon Nazariev. Khujand, 2004, pp. 74–83.

Walker, Paul E. 'An Ismāʿīlī Answer to the Problem of Worshipping the Unknowable, Neoplatonic God', *AJAS*, 2 (1972), pp. 12–22.

—— 'The Ismaili Vocabulary of Creation', *Studia Islamica*, 40 (1974), pp. 75–95.

—— 'Cosmic Hierarchies in Early Ismaili Thought', *Muslim World*, 66 (1976), pp. 14–28.

—— 'Eternal Cosmos and the Womb of History: Time in Early Ismaili Thought', *IJMES*, 3 (1978), pp. 355–366.

—— 'The Doctrine of Metempsychosis in Islam', in *Islamic Studies Presented to Charles J. Adams*, ed. Wael B. Hallaqq and Donald P. Little. Leiden, 1991, pp. 219–238.

—— 'The Universal Soul and the Particular Soul in Ismāʿīlī Neoplatonism', in *Neoplatonism and Islamic Thought*, ed. Parviz Morewedge. New York, 1992, pp. 149–166.

—— 'The Ismaili *Daʿwa* in the Reign of the Fatimid Caliph al-Ḥākim', *JARCE*, 30 (1993), pp. 161–182.

—— *Early Philosophical Shiism: The Ismaili Neoplatonism of Abū Yaʿqūb al-Sijistānī*. Cambridge, 1993.

—— 'Abū Tammām and his *Kitāb al-Shajara*: A New Ismaili Treatise from Tenth-century Khurasan', *JAOS*, 114 (1994), pp. 343–352.

—— 'Succession to Rule in the Shiite Caliphate', *JARCE*, 32 (1995), pp. 239–264.

—— *Abū Yaʿqūb al-Sijistānī: Intellectual Missionary*. London and New York, 1996.

—— *Ḥamīd al-Dīn al-Kirmānī: Ismaili Thought in the Age of al-Ḥākim*. London and New York, 1999.

—— 'The Role of the Imam-Caliph as Depicted in Official Treatises and Documents Issued by the Fatimids', in *The Study of Shiʿi Islam: History, Theology and Law*, ed. Farhad Daftary and Gurdofarid Miskinzoda. London and New York, 2013, pp. 411–432.

Wensinck, Arent J. *The Muslim Creed*. Cambridge, 1932.

Wheeler, Brannon M. *Moses in the Quran and Islamic Exegesis*. London and New York, 2002.

—— *Prophets in the Quran: An Introduction to the Quran and Muslim Exegesis*. London and New York, 2002.

Wright, William. *A Grammar of the Arabic Language*, 3rd ed. Cambridge, 1981.

al-Yaman, Jaʿfar b. Manṣūr. *Sarāʾir wa-asrār al-nuṭaqāʾ*, ed. Muṣṭafā Ghālib. Beirut, 1984.

al-Zamakhsharī, Maḥmūd b. ʿUmar b. Muḥammad. *al-Kashshāf ʿan haqāʾiq ghawāmiḍ al-tanzīl wa ʿuyūn al-aqāwīl fī wujūh al-taʾwīl*. Beirut, 1315/1995.

Index

Page numbers in **bold** refer to tables; 'n' after a page number indicates the footnote number.